susan, linda, nina & cokie

Also by Lisa Napoli

*Radio Shangri-La: What I Discovered on My Accidental Journey
to the Happiest Kingdom on Earth*

*Ray & Joan: The Man Who Made the McDonald's Fortune
and the Woman Who Gave It All Away*

Up All Night: Ted Turner, CNN, and the Birth of 24-Hour News

susan, linda, nina & cokie

The Extraordinary Story of the Founding Mothers of NPR

LISA NAPOLI

ABRAMS PRESS, NEW YORK

Library of Congress Control Number: 2020944990

ISBN: 978-1-4197-5040-3
eISBN: 978-1-64700-107-0

Printed and bound in the United States
10 9 8 7 6 5 4 3

Abrams books are available at special discounts when purchased
in quantity for premiums and promotions as well as fundraising
or educational use. Special editions can also be created to
specification. For details, contact specialsales@abramsbooks.com
or the address below.

Abrams Press® is a registered trademark of Harry N. Abrams, Inc.

ABRAMS The Art of Books
195 Broadway, New York, NY 10007
abramsbooks.com

For Bill Siemering,
the founding father I'm fortunate to call a friend

For all who work behind the scenes, without public acclaim,
in newsrooms everywhere

and

For my mother, Jane, who told me how it used to be
and worked so hard for my experience to be different.

Many women may be fine in everyday conversation, but put them in front of a microphone—and a camera as well—and something happens to them. They become affected, overdramatic, high-pitched. Some turn sexy and sultry. Others get patronizing and pseudocharming. Not that they all put on an act. But with a man you seldom have this problem.

—NBC network radio executive, 1964

Interviewer: How do you feel when you meet younger women in journalism who haven't any idea how rough things used to be in the "bad old days"?

Nina Totenberg: Murder comes to mind.

History looks very different when seen through the eyes of women.

—Cokie Roberts

Contents

AUTHOR'S NOTE   xi

PROLOGUE: Living Legend   I

CHAPTER ONE: Susan   II

CHAPTER TWO: ". . . and sex"   26

CHAPTER THREE: "The airwaves belong to all the people"   37

CHAPTER FOUR: Linda   48

CHAPTER FIVE: Purposes   66

CHAPTER SIX: Nina   75

CHAPTER SEVEN: *Ms.*   90

CHAPTER EIGHT: Scoop   IOI

CHAPTER NINE: Cokie   II3

CHAPTER TEN: "Not even slightly a feminist"   144

CHAPTER ELEVEN: Woman, Ascendant   151

CHAPTER TWELVE: Transition   161

CHAPTER THIRTEEN: Frank   178

CHAPTER FOURTEEN: *Star Wars*   197

CHAPTER FIFTEEN: The Drive to Survive   218

EPILOGUE: Hollywood Walk of Fame   245

CONTENTS

ACKNOWLEDGMENTS   279
TIMELINE   283
NOTES   287
METHODOLOGY AND BIBLIOGRAPHY   323
INDEX   329

Author's Note

As I write this in October 2020, our world is in a perilous state, even beyond the deadly pandemic that has us in its grip.

For decades, we've ignored dire warnings about our environmental destruction—note that Earth Day was launched back in 1970 to call urgent attention to our dwindling resources. Similarly, society has dismissed or minimized the issue of what today we call "diversity and inclusion."

To serve those whose needs were woefully underrepresented by commercial broadcasting, National Public Radio was chartered, coincidentally, also in 1970. Later that decade, a task force concluded after an eighteen-month review that, on the air and behind the scenes in public radio and television, minorities remained "nonentities" who were "still drinking from segregated water fountains."* A detailed report called for immediate change.

---

* "A Formula for Change: The Report of the Task Force on Minorities in Public Broadcasting, 1978," https://files.eric.ed.gov/fulltext/ED172269.pdf. The task force was chaired by Dr. Gloria L. Anderson, whose appointment to the Corporation for Public Broadcasting by President Nixon in 1972 made her the first Black woman to serve on that board.

Today, at the network level at least, there has been a slight increase in the number of employees of color and other marginalized groups. But, on the national and local levels, public radio (indeed, all of the fourth estate, as news media are called) faces a vocal reckoning from a new generation: Address this shameful inequity once and for all.

From its beginnings, public radio did, in one arena, a slightly better job of addressing the needs of a constituency that, at the time, also was rarely given a voice: women.* This is the story of how that happened, quite by accident—and how a man almost did the place in.

—Lisa Napoli, Downtown Los Angeles, October 2020

---

* A 2019 study showed that women comprised 57 percent of NPR's staff.

PROLOGUE
Living Legend

On August 18, 2019, Mary Martha Corinne Morrison Claiborne Boggs Roberts, age seventy-five, did what she'd done for thousands of Sundays. She left her beloved home on Bradley Boulevard in Bethesda, Maryland—the magical, *Gone with the Wind*–style property she'd begged her parents to buy nearly seventy years before, where she slept each night in the antique cherrywood rope bed that had been in her family for generations—and made her way to the studios of ABC News in Washington, DC.

Her manicured nails polished fire-engine red and her short hair neatly styled to perfection, the woman—nicknamed "Cokie" as a child due to her brother's inability to pronounce "Corinne"—had learned to enjoy that pampering necessity of television, a turn in the makeup chair. Cosmetic flourishes, like chopping off her long, straight "gym teacher" hair into a more glamorous do when she transitioned from radio to TV, were part of the job. Celebrity came with many perks—like a better table at a restaurant and gratis wine from starstruck flight attendants, if they hadn't already upgraded her to first class. It also meant being on display on a run to the grocery store.

Glamour wasn't what attracted the audience to Cokie. The adulation was sparked by the fact that she seemed like a woman in your book club, someone you ran into at the local farmers' market who remembered your husband's recent surgery, or your daughter's recital—a PTA mom consumed with her own family, canning tomatoes from her garden, rushing to church on Sunday morning.

Except that Cokie rushed to church after appearing on national television, where it was her job to break down inside-the-Beltway shenanigans for a rapt audience of millions as if she were dissecting a football game with the guys at the local bar. Except that Cokie knew the inner workings of Washington so intimately that she tutored newly elected lawmakers in its history and protocol. Cokie, unlike anyone else you knew, was on a first-name basis with the power elite. She happened to be one of them herself.

Yes, Cokie might have *looked* like a prettier version of your average neighbor, but there was no one else like her on earth.

This August Sunday, she joined what the producers called a "power roundtable" of commentators on the long-standing program she once cohosted, *This Week*. She was emeritus now. Back in 1988, the show had boldly added a skirt, hers, to the boys' club cast of characters flanking the original host, David Brinkley, the wry raconteur from her parents' generation, whose career arc spanned the evolution of broadcast news. A North Carolinian by birth, Brinkley first made a name for himself in radio, when World War II instructed Americans in the value of what was then the ascendant medium.

Back then, Washington was infinitely simpler; the burgeoning city was so relaxed, went the stories, that a motorist on Pennsylvania Avenue could drive right up to the portico at the White House and turn around. Media, then, were infinitely simpler, too; covering the White House was a part-time beat. When one of the first studio cameras was wheeled into the newsroom, Brinkley and his colleagues demanded to know, "What in the hell are we supposed to do with *that*?" As broadcasters struggled to redefine news with pictures, Brinkley morphed and changed and rose to stardom in TV, too—one of a handful of the medium's plentiful lot of patrician white men so elevated. As homogenous as their makeup was their belief system: "None of us had any ax to grind; none of us had any political ambitions. Our only real purpose in life, and in work, was to tell people what we knew to be true."

By the time Brinkley jumped from NBC to ABC to launch his weekly inside-the-Beltway analysis show in 1981, cable news and satellites and videotape were accelerating and changing news yet again. And at the exact same time, after years of legislation and lawsuits and activism and sheer determination, women—long marginalized into dead-end jobs as secretaries, researchers, and weather girls, acceptable waystations en route to their supposed true and primary purpose in life, marriage and motherhood—were finally beginning to emerge from the shadows, propelled to the meatier assignments they'd been longing to tackle.

Looking to acknowledge the underrepresentation of half the population, producers of the Brinkley show invited a variety of female pundits on the air for live screen tests. Cokie, who'd been generating a buzz around town for her work as a congressional reporter on National Public Radio and her contributions on its television cousin, PBS, was among them.

Hers was one in the quartet of voices that listeners around the country could hear report the news every day. Colleagues Susan Stamberg, Linda Wertheimer, and Nina Totenberg had each come before her at NPR. They'd joined the network at its marginal and bedraggled beginnings and put it on the map. Together, these four had done more than make careers for themselves in public radio at a time when female newscasters were unicorns. They'd changed journalism, the public's perception of women, and, while they were at it, women's perceptions of themselves.

Some women in the 1970s marched for equality, or sat on the sidelines angrily lamenting the lack of it. Susan, Linda, Nina, and Cokie had, through a combination of will, timing, and talent, used their distinctive perches to elevate the status of their sex in a different way—working a hundred times harder than men while wielding microphones, as Susan described them, as "magic wands waved against silence."

Male reporters would query lawmakers about defense spending. Women, once they were allowed, posed questions that had previously gone unasked about different essential matters, such as health care and schools and equality. What was a policy's impact, they demanded to know, on the family, on the elders, on the *children?*

Though NPR has risen over the last half of the twentieth century to its stature as an almighty soundtrack of the American media landscape, hardly anyone remembers its years of struggle to find an audience in a medium called "hidden" or, worse, "bedridden." Fewer still recall that the place had once come within moments of shutting down. Proud and aware of their influence in creating this cultural and journalistic force, Susan had taken to calling them NPR's "founding mothers."

It was Cokie who had zoomed to a rarefied, enduring stratosphere of fame. As soon as the network television people witnessed her in action during that live audition, she'd been granted admission to the typically stag lot of Brinkley regulars. ABC wanted her so badly, in fact, that they cut an unusual deal so she could also keep the radio job she loved. She was that good a "get" that they agreed to share.

"Cokie knows more about Congress than any single member knows, and ten times more about it than I ever did," effused the usually understated legendary dean of broadcasting, Brinkley. "She looks nice, she talks well, what more do you want?" He confessed that he couldn't take credit for the discovery. Fellow reporter and inveterate wag Sam Donaldson had noticed her in action on the Hill and just knew Cokie could work as "one of the boys."

Audience reaction affirmed the choice. She was the total package of smarts, connections, and nonchalant beauty that TV programmers had only dreamt of finding. No one had seen or heard anyone like her before. So distinctive was her voice—that hint of a drawl overlaid with a bit of crackle—that a mere photograph of her could conjure the sound.

Men approached her on the street and told her they appreciated her common sense. Women admired her gumption: "We love the way you don't let them interrupt you and that you hand it right back to them."

"I get the feeling," Cokie said, "that the country is full of women who've never gotten a word in edgewise when men talk about politics." It was. Just as women hadn't gotten a word in, for so long, on TV.

But this had never been the case in Cokie's household. Though Brinkley and Donaldson and so many other inhabitants of the clubby, insider DC press corps inhaled politics like oxygen, she herself had been feeding on it since she was in the womb. Her parents were as close to royalty as it got in America. Her blustery father was the mighty Democratic congressman from Louisiana Hale Boggs, first elected when he was just twenty-six years old. A natural orator who understood the power of the media, he'd trek through snow and sleet, it was said, just to appear on *Meet the Press*. Cokie's magnolia mother, Lindy, to the manor born, won election to the seat her husband had held for decades after his untimely demise, making the unlikely transition from perfect political spouse to revered political operative, fighting for racial and gender equality while maintaining her reputation as the most genuinely sweet woman to roam Capitol Hill.

The family dinner table, where Cokie sat elbow to elbow with power brokers from her earliest memory, had imbued her with an innate and reverent understanding of politics and politicians—and how to behave fearlessly around them, to speak her mind, while maintaining social graces, of course.

"If you interrupt too much and are too aggressive and ready to get in there, you come across as a bitchy, shrill witch," Cokie said. "And if you don't talk enough and are polite and wait, then you come across as a wallflower with nothing to say." Formula for a media superstar: One part proper, one part ferocious, equal parts sage. One hundred percent Cokie.

* * *

This summer Sunday in 2019, wearing a smart green jacket plucked out of what her husband called the "drive-in"–size closets that housed her TV-ready wardrobe of discount dresses, Cokie couldn't mask what became instantly apparent as the on-air light illuminated on the studio camera. Host Martha Raddatz—one of a legion of fellow journalists who counted Cokie as a role model, mentor, and hero—introduced her "power roundtable" of guests. The fact that Raddatz was solo host, and that she herself was still on the air well into her sixties, was a testament to at least a tiny bit of progress, for some. Cokie herself hadn't reached what a reporter called "critical mass in cathode-ray consciousness" until her late forties, an age when women on TV (the very few who'd gotten there in the first place) routinely got dumped. That was not long after a lawsuit filed by onetime Kansas City anchorwoman Christine Craft, who lost her job because she was assessed to be, at age thirty-eight, "too old, too ugly, and not deferential to men."

Despite the cosmetics and her put-together look, Cokie—beautiful Cokie, ubiquitous omni-media superstar Cokie—appeared gravely ill. Her almond-shaped eyes and her cheeks were sunken, her styled hair clearly thinned. It was impossible to overlook her skeletal frame. Something was very wrong.

But this was neither the time nor the place to notice. Raddatz powered ahead with a discussion on the man who dominated so much of the media mind share of the last years, Donald Trump. "The president is banking on a strong economy propelling him to reelection," Raddatz said, directing her comments first toward the elder stateswoman whom she so admired. "But it's not really a do-or-die, and 'you have no choice whether to vote for me or not.'"

Cokie didn't miss a beat, answering the nonquestion effortlessly, with the confidence and candor that was her trademark. "The president has had a great economy working for him," she said, her voice labored and raspier than was typical. She sounded as if she were gasping for air. A fiercely devout Catholic, she wore a gold cross that shone brightly behind her jade green necklace like an amulet. "That's what's kept his approval ratings up, though they don't go much beyond his base. When they do, it's when the economy is thriving. And he's scared, and he should be scared, because if the economy tanks, he really doesn't have anything else to fall back on."

In that peculiar way that an audience feels ownership of the people they see on television, viewers immediately took to the internet to express alarm. "Oh my goodness, has Cokie's cancer returned?" a viewer who went by the handle dwood37 wrote on the *This Week* website. "I hope not. I love Cokie Roberts on here and on NPR."

Her devoted fans remembered that Cokie had successfully battled breast cancer back in 2002. That was just around the time she'd announced she was leaving the cohosting duties she'd inherited when Brinkley retired. Then, she'd segued full time into writing books about women, particularly the overlooked "founding mothers" of our nation—the wives and mothers who'd supported the famous men who'd garnered all the glory in the history books. Sure, Cokie and her friends had encountered discrimination and restricted rights on their way up, but once she recognized the full scope of the conditions earlier generations had endured, she began to believe that modern women, herself included, were "sissies."

Writing about the struggles and contributions of these overlooked Americans, using her fame to draw attention to their stories, had been, in her mind, her greatest achievement. These books landed her on the bestseller lists and amped up an already robust demand for her high-priced services as a speaker. For her wide-ranging influence and contributions, they also earned her a commendation in 2008 from the Library of Congress as one of the nation's "living legends," along with fellow honorees civil rights activist Julian Bond, race car driver Mario Andretti, jazz great Herbie Hancock, and author David McCullough.

Fame and acclaim were no armor against illness. For the last three years, only her family and closest friends knew her secret: that the cancer had returned.

It was a cruel repetition of the Boggs family history. Cokie's beloved older sister, Barbara, the mayor of Princeton, New Jersey, had died of the disease in 1990, at the ridiculously young age of fifty-one. The cancer to which Barbara had lost her left eye years earlier, and which she had battled back with grace and humor, had cruelly, she quipped, "grown up and decided to take a field trip."

While facing death inspired her to revel in the "exquisiteness of life," Barbara coped with the inevitable anger and depression by writing poetry. One poem, titled "Cokie in the Hospital," celebrated the watchful care she received from her "private duty sister," who slept in the chair beside her as she received an experimental chemotherapy drug. In the devastating moments after Barbara slipped away, Cokie crawled into her bed to keep her company and sang.

* * *

Facing her own cancer, Cokie herself had equally refused to allow the illness to define her. She might feel wretched, but she wasn't going to lie in bed waiting to die. After six months of chemotherapy and six weeks of radiation, ever accompanied by a friend or family member, she was always at work the next day. Wracked with discomfort, she'd pray it away with a thought for others who were suffering, say her novenas to Saint Jude, and soldier on.

Prayer sustained her. She'd pray as she walked to get the newspaper from the driveway, and she'd pray as thanks for the abundant blessings she'd been given: her adoring husband, with whom she'd had an enduring relationship; two beautiful children, who'd given her six precious grandchildren. Her religious training taught her to cling to hope, for to despair was to despair of God's goodness. Her belief in this was unwavering (yet, she told an eminent nun, she was well aware that many considered believers like her to be "a little bit simpleminded").

Though she felt that heaven wasn't a place as much as "being in the presence of God," she hoped there was something after this life, "where you feel complete, where you do check in with people you've missed—friends and family." In the afterlife, perhaps she'd encounter—and get to interview—estimable women like Elizabeth Seton, the patron saint of Catholic schools in the United States; Frances Cabrini, patron saint of immigrants; or Rose Philippine Duchesne, a missionary of the Sacred Heart who'd brought to the United States the schools in which Cokie had been educated.

Just as her sister had when her cancer made its unwelcome recurrence, Cokie, too, continued working, from early morning to late at night—in her case, on a new book about the suffrage movement. She did this while continuing to juggle her busy schedule of public and media appearances. Linda Wertheimer marveled on one visit at how her friend couldn't sit still in the kitchen, despite the pain.

The outpouring of concern after her turn on *This Week* forced Cokie to issue a statement. She appreciated the kindness, she told her fans, and explained: "Over the summer, I have had some health issues which required treatment that caused weight loss. I am doing fine. I . . . expect to be, as I have been, working away in the days and months to come, covering what promises to be a fascinating election." In fact, she added, she planned on attending a debate among the Democratic presidential candidates in Houston in just a few weeks.

* * *

The hopeful plan was not to be. After the Sunday show, she managed to pop into the Shrine of the Most Blessed Sacrament, and the following Saturday, despite the fact that she could hardly eat, she insisted on keeping the weekly Saturday dinner date (at the Pines of Rome, in Bethesda) that she'd had with Linda and Nina and their husbands for years.

Her fierce blend of optimism and stubborn denial notwithstanding, Cokie could fight no more. Even in her last hours of consciousness at the National Institutes of Health hospital, she ministered to the people assigned to care for her—dispatching her husband to their kitchen to fetch a recipe for crawfish corn bread for one nurse and playfully pestering another to share pictures of her children. The valet parking attendants asked with concern after "Miss Cokie." Decades before, when they'd first met as teenagers and were in the early flush of love, Steve had learned that to live with Cokie was to share her.

By Monday night, as Cokie was beginning to slip away, Nina arrived to say goodbye. She wasn't sure her friend could hear her, but still, she whispered that "I'd see her on the other side, at that big broadcasting studio somewhere, and that I knew she would be a star."

The next day, she was gone.

It was fitting that Cokie should expire on September 17, said Nina—the date the founders signed the final draft of the Constitution. Cokie had always seen her work as a journalist as a calling to carry out the values of the document she held sacred.

But just as so many citizens forgot the struggles that had led to the formation of the United States, and didn't know the stories of the women who'd helped shape it, most people did not remember—if they ever knew—the struggles Cokie and the other founding mothers had faced as women at the start of their careers, at the dawn of public radio. These women had been such an indelible part of the media landscape for so long that hardly anyone could remember a time before them.

On the afternoon of her death, in the NPR newsroom—the same place that had amplified each of their resounding voices—tearful colleagues, even those who didn't know Cokie personally, paused for a poignant tribute. In honor of this woman whose words rang so strong and true and touched so many, they observed a moment of silence.

CHAPTER ONE

Susan

Once upon a time in the last century, before television lumbered like Godzilla into the nation's living rooms and bigfooted the once-dazzling medium that had come before it into second-class oblivion, Sue Levitt found herself worshipping at the altar of her family's Emerson Bakelite Radio. The Levitt home's set, perched in the kitchen and encased in the distinctive, clunky revolutionary plastic, was the color of ivory. Out of it spouted oracular pearls, entertainment and news and wisdom that Sue would consume intently, with devotion. Those voices, she believed, spoke directly to her.

On Saturdays, she and millions of other Americans eagerly tuned in for the week's installment of the dramatic series *Grand Central Station*, which was vivified by the day's top actors and dazzling sound effects. To signal the start of the show, an organ would play, an engine would rev *choo-chooooo*, a bleating horn would sound, and an announcer would intone the introduction Sue had memorized word for word:

> As the bullet seeks its target, shining rails in every part of our great country are aimed at Grrrrand Centrrrral Staaation, part of the nation's greatest city . . . crossroads of a million private lives, a gigantic stage on which are played a thousand dramas, daily.

In that "palace of make-believe," as one of the show's writers called the majestic train depot, lingered runaways, love lost and found, chance encounters, and despair leading to a life of crime. Wherever they were headed, every single soul who stepped into that fabled, majestic train terminal on New York City's Forty-Second Street was possessed of a backstory.

On the Upper West Side of Manhattan in the 1940s, Sue Levitt lived only several dozen blocks north and to the west of the real, live Grand Central. But the radio allowed her to witness life's rich pageant without stepping out of her nightgown. To be sure, there were myriad other diversions to stoke her dreams and imagination. The New York Public Library branch on West 100th Street dispensed books she'd lug home by the sackful and voraciously devour, graduating from the kids' section to the adult in search of "dreams and romance and lessons in life." The double features at the Loews movie theater up on West 107th Street provided hours of escapism at a clip. Her father, Robert, trotted her around to the city's magnificent museums, a perk of inhabiting the great island that was the centerpiece of glorious New York City. Her mother, Anne, sang her the first song she ever learned, "Alice Blue Gown," a tune from another transporting cultural wonder nearby, Broadway.

But it was radio that was considered, as Sue called it, the "glamour medium" of the day—a little box that beckoned you "to stretch out" and jump inside, "just as the voice inside put itself into you." With the volume up and your eyes closed, you could instantly inhabit another universe. Still, Sue preferred to listen with her eyes open, often with a box of paint or crayons and a sketch pad at hand. When Sue was sick, her mother would move the radio into her bedroom, fluff her pillows, and sit with her, and together they'd devour the soap operas.

Sue would gaze out the window and fire escape at the once-grand Victorian Gothic redbrick building across the avenue, home to the Association for the Relief of Respectable Aged and Indigent Females, and do what she loved to do: daydream. Why, she wondered, misreading the word *indigent* for *indignant*, were the woman *angry*?

Burglars scurried up that fire escape several times, motivating her family to relocate eight blocks south, where they rented an apartment on the ninth floor of 12 West Ninety-Sixth Street, a prewar building replete with a bench in front of the elevator where residents could take a load off as they waited for the operator to clank open the metal gate and ferry them home to their floor.

Her father frequently found himself between jobs as a salesman of everything from real estate to phonographs to trinkets to booze, but he possessed, Sue said, a fabulous sense of humor, a larger-than-life personality: "performer, joke-teller, schmoozer, narrator." He was also an unbridled romantic. Once, he gifted her mother a massive pale purple amethyst ring, sending only child Sue, age five, into shrieks of envy. She was accustomed to the presents being for *her*.

As the daughter of a tailor-turned-designer, Anne dressed impeccably, always with gloves, no matter the season. To help the family out, she made the long trek from the Upper West Side into the borough of Brooklyn to work for the city as a bookkeeper. There, she labored so hard that her colleagues asked her to please slow down. She couldn't help herself. Giving her all was in her nature. From her mother, Sue inherited this, as well as her infectious, raucous laugh. Their life was hardly fancy, but still, Sue felt cloaked in a warm veil of "kindness, attention and affection."

Each Sunday, they'd head up to Washington Heights to visit family. Both Anne's and Bob's parents hailed from Vilnius, the capital of Lithuania, one grandfather a carpenter, the other a tailor who designed ladies' apparel. Though both Sue's parents had been raised Jewish, they weren't themselves devout. They even deigned to place a Christmas tree in their home, adorned with blue lights, an action that gave the elders pause. It took Sue's friend Ruth, the daughter of German refugees, to introduce her to the Jewish tradition of lighting candles on Friday nights. She'd never seen anything like this lovely ritual.

Her admiration of Shabbat didn't inspire her to become observant herself. When her parents sent her for religious study to Temple Rodeph Shalom, one of the oldest synagogues in New York, she was informed in the middle of the semester that it was time to learn a dance. Sue's insolent retort—"I didn't come here for rumba lessons"—landed her in the principal's office. Her mother allowed her to drop out. There were so many other ways to while away the hours.

By the time the new sensation of television arrived in the Levitt home in the early 1950s, Sue was tiptoeing into womanhood, and the world was rapidly changing, especially in her immediate surroundings. Once, this neighborhood had been considered the countryside, named Bloemendaal, "Valley of the Flowers," by Dutch settlers long ago. Tobacco farms and fields of green had gradually been replaced by tenements and immigrants from Germany and Ireland—and later, from Puerto Rico and the Dominican Republic. The once-splendiferous Central Park, sculpted in the middle of the last century from an old neighborhood populated by Black people and immigrants, had deteriorated into disrepair.

The demolition of the Ninth Avenue elevated train had uncluttered the skies above the treetops, leaving behind a graveyard of station entrances. Over a swath of several miles, stretches of slums were being torn down, clearing the way for a massive housing project to the north and, to the south, an arts complex to be known as Lincoln Center.

And Sue herself was morphing in ways she never could have imagined.

The invitation to enroll as a visual arts student at Music and Art, one of the city's most competitive public high schools (created by Mayor Fiorello La Guardia in 1936, and not to be confused, proud pupils were careful to point out, with the less academically rigorous *vocational* school named the High School of Performing Arts), set her life on course.*
Though she wished for a voice like that of jazz great Sarah Vaughan, Sue found her artistic proclivities emerge during all those hours spent at the kitchen table drawing and daydreaming and listening to another of her favorite radio shows, *Let's Pretend*.

Each day, she'd trundle up to Hamilton Heights, to 135th Street and Convent Avenue, then climb the several hundred steep steps to the Gothic Revival "castle on the hill" that housed the school, her own ivory tower, replete with gargoyles. There, she'd slip into a rarefied world where mundane teenage concerns shifted behind a higher mission—the Arts—as part of the class of '55.

---

* The two schools merged in 1984.

In rebellion against her mother's proper attire, Sue, who "always had a weight issue and was rarely groomed," took to wearing counterculture denim. Her peers, she observed, seemed to fall into four groups: "the Rocks," the Bohemians, the typical American teenagers, and the intellectuals—the school's elites, who possessed "unerring good taste in sound and color." As unique as her classmates might have been, they were all ultimately cut from the same cloth, said Sue. "If we'd gone to some suburban high school in Des Moines, we would have been the weird ones, the fat girl who liked poetry, or the nerdy guy who was gifted at music. But we were all like that. And here was a school that was out to protect, nurture and burnish us."

The school paper, the *Overtone*, provided a sanctuary within the sanctuary. Sue served as Features editor, the logical next step after the "Cheery Chatter" column she'd written for the middle school paper about "whatever." (She later said her style employed "lots of ellipses.") When classmate Peter Yarrow (later a celebrated third of the folk trio Peter, Paul and Mary) submitted an essay on French kissing, editor Sue turned it down as inappropriate. It was at the paper where she collided with the Sports and Special Events editor, Ed Kleban, so chosen for that position because he lived a stone's throw from Yankee Stadium, up in the Bronx. Hands down, the red-haired Ed was the most interesting man she'd ever met; he served as her emissary to a sophisticated world she yearned to make her own. A musician, he'd spirit her down to Birdland to listen to the vogue music of the day, jazz from Count Basie, John Coltrane, Dave Brubeck, and Miles Davis—so different from the showtunes and classical music with which she'd been raised. They'd sit rapt until the very last note. Seated at her family's Steck baby grand, he'd entertain their friends, stoking Sue's dream of one day presiding over a salon. (Until then, keeping her girlfriends up during sleepovers by chatting late into the night would have to suffice.)

Ed didn't just play music, as so many of their schoolmates did; he wrote it, too. Sue was equally impressed by his masterful use of the written word. He was the first person she knew who subscribed to that weekly bible of the effete, the *New Yorker*, and actually read it. All the kids were dazzled by writer J. D. Salinger and his angst-riddled gut punch of a novel *The Catcher in the Rye*. Ed would call Sue in the middle of the night and read to her across the phone line while they each, on their respective ends, dragged on cigarette after cigarette, pockmarking their voices with "little prickers." (Ed would go on to a dazzling career on Broadway, winning a Tony Award and the Pulitzer Prize for his lyrics for *A Chorus Line*.)

Sue's fellow students, along with the teachers, stoked her ambition; by now she knew for certain that an ordinary life, the life of a book-keeper or salesman, would not do. For the quote below her yearbook photo, she chose this from Walt Whitman: "There is that in me. I do not know what it is, but I know it is in me." The quote she wished to use—"whistling to keep from being afraid"—had already been taken by another student. That sentiment summed up her resolve to conquer the world, no matter what.

* * *

Had she attended the area high school for which her neighborhood had been zoned, Sue might not have even bothered with college. Higher education had been a luxury her parents themselves couldn't afford. Her first stab at it involved making her way across the East River to city-run Queens College, a fine free, public commuter institution attended by thousands of other students looking to bootstrap themselves into a dif-ferent echelon than their families.

So proud of his daughter was Bob Levitt that he offered support unthinkable for a man of his generation: to wash and dry the dishes every night so she could devote her utmost attention to her studies. In truth, her parents' pride in her educational quest was offset a bit by their intimidation. As the innate confidence they'd lovingly nurtured in their beloved daughter blossomed further, and as her spirit became enriched with the gift of knowledge, Sue drifted off to unfamiliar intel-lectual terrain, able to hold her own in rigorous debates on a wide vari-ety of subjects.

Winning a state scholarship made it possible for her to transfer to the elite private school for women, Barnard College, just a neighborhood north from her home, as life-changing a switch as her decision to attend a special high school had been. Barnard was named after the former president of Columbia University, a forward-thinking fellow who'd pushed for girls to enter higher education. The school had been the first in New York to offer degrees to women. Incoming students from twenty-one states and six nations who joined the class of 1959 were told that great things were expected of them—after they married and began families, of course.

The "veritable crazy quilt of contradictions" faced by young women in the 1950s was the life's work of noted sociologist Dr. Mirra Komarovsky, one of Sue's professors, who'd written the book *Women in the Modern World: Their Education and Their Dilemmas*. On the one hand, said Dr. Komarovsky, women were encouraged to seek education and become more independent; on the other, they were criticized for their ambitions. Komarovsky espoused a revolutionary sort of feminism: choice. "The girl who wishes to marry and have five children should be permitted to do so," she wrote, "and likewise it should be made possible for those who wish to combine marriage and careers to achieve that." And, she continued, it was essential to consider the impact of women's changing place in society on the men, who now had to adjust to a "cooperative" rather than a "dominant" position.

In a paper about the book, Sue described a boy she knew who struggled to choose between a traditionally dependent, feminine girl and a more modern, independent girl with strong opinions of her own. This created, she observed, not just a war *between* the sexes, but a war *within* them.

A shining example of someone who "had it all" stood at the helm of Barnard: Millicent Carey McIntosh, who'd earned a PhD from Johns Hopkins with a thesis on fourteenth-century English mystery dramas and who was raising five children (albeit with assistance from a governess, a cook, and two other helpers). McIntosh was, in fact, the first married woman to serve as president of one of the elite Seven Sisters colleges, an accomplishment so unusual that *Newsweek* magazine had featured her on its cover in 1951. As educators of women struggled to figure out whether they should "turn out homemakers or Who's Who-ers, or both," the magazine lauded McIntosh for her personal achievement in combining motherhood and career. For her part, "Mrs. Mac" believed women were better mothers if they didn't "sell their souls into bondage" and devote every moment to their children. A woman who applied discipline and worked hard could achieve anything.

Well, almost. Barnard dean Margaret Pickel was of the mind that women possessed "less physical strength, a lower fatigue point and a less stable nervous system," and were also encumbered by "marriage mortality," the "conscious or unconscious" absorption in the distractions that kept them from dedicating their entire being to their careers.

The dizzying array of expectations and possibilities didn't distract Sue. While she worked as an assistant to the Columbia University library archivist, served in student government, contributed to the college newspaper, and organized guest lectures and lunches for the Sociology Club, she reveled in the "ecstasies of intellectual discovery." She pored over texts like T. S. Eliot's *The Waste Land* and James Joyce's *A Portrait of the Artist as a Young Man,* and became "totally absorbed in symbols and implications and subtleties" of poetry and prose. She spent hours memorizing, in Middle English, the first page of *The Canterbury Tales* and perfecting another language, music, as she learned to sing every note of Dave Brubeck's nine-minute piano solo on "Balcony Rock," from his album *Jazz Goes to College.* And as she pondered her future place in the world, she was well aware that the opportunities she had had not been available to her mother.

Still, tradition loomed large. In June 1959, as she graduated with degrees in sociology and English, she was just one of five of her classmates to receive her diploma whose left hand was not adorned with an engagement ring. She also graduated from "Sue" to "Susan."

* * *

Along with her blue-chip education, Susan possessed an essential skill: the ability to type ninety-nine words a minute. This landed her a summer job as secretary at the two-year-old celebrity magazine *16*, launched by a onetime literary agent who'd switched to publishing after being busted for swindling his clients.

At *16*, Susan's editor, Gloria Stavers, entrusted her recent college graduate employee with the enormously important task of choosing the winner of the "I Miss Elvis Contest," an event inspired when the swaggering pop heartthrob had been shipped off for a stint in the army. As someone wired to revere jazz over pop, Susan was the perfect impartial judge. She sifted through bags and bags of letters submitted by desperate women fretting over Elvis's temporary absence from the public eye. Two letters stood out—one from a sixty-year-old grandmother and the other purportedly written by a three-year-old who claimed she needed a role model. (Susan winked admiringly at this precocious child's penmanship.)

At summer's end, she headed north to Massachusetts to enroll at Brandeis University, where she'd received a scholarship for further study in English. She recognized pretty quickly that this was not for her. After three months, she dropped out and landed a fifty-five-dollar-a-week job as an editorial assistant (a fancy word for "secretary") at *Dædalus*, a four-year-old Cambridge-based literary publication produced by the American Academy of Arts and Sciences. Named for the ancient Greek inventor, scientist, and "unriddler of riddles," the journal had a mission to "lift each of us above his cell in the labyrinth of learning in order that he may see the entire structure as if from above, where each separate part loses its comfortable separateness."

In her off hours, Susan volunteered with teenagers and became involved with advocacy for the improvement of Boston's public schools. And in the meantime, she met a handsome young man named Louis Stamberg. She hadn't quite been looking for a nice Jewish boy, but she'd always had the feeling that when she did fall in love, that's exactly who she'd choose.

The son of a prominent lawyer in Allentown, Pennsylvania, Lou had earned his undergraduate degree at Columbia and was now himself studying law at Harvard. Ever the curious soul, Susan tagged along with her beloved new man to some of his classes, to understand why contracts and international law caused him to suffer so intensely. He persisted, graduated, and decamped to Washington in search of a job, a crucial next step so that he and Susan could marry. For their wedding at the Carleton House hotel in New York City on the evening of April 14, 1962, Rabbi Steven Schaffer had been imported from the Stamberg family synagogue in Allentown. Afterward, off to Europe jetted "Sue-Lou," as their close friends called them, on a trip Susan had meticulously budgeted and planned.

Ultimately, her husband landed work at the newly created U.S. Agency for International Development, part of President Kennedy's commitment to a "decade of development" in foreign nations. As a new bride in the nation's capital, Susan applied the same dogged meticulousness to her job search as she had to her honeymoon, sketching out a wish list of potential employers, from publishers and trade associations to magazines and television stations. In her hand she held a glowing recommendation from her bosses at *Dædalus*, who described her as friendly, bright, and understanding, with "great taste" and a sense of responsibility that, in an emergency, was downright heroic.

To Susan the job seeker, her former employers offered bolstering words of wisdom: to look at herself not as a mere applicant but as a "national resource" whom "anyone would be glad to take on." While that might have been true, finding someone to take on a woman to perform anything other than administrative work—"women's work"—was an elusive challenge. This proved to be so even in the face of a formidable female elder, *Dædalus* contributor Mrs. Helen Hill Miller, who held a PhD in political science from the University of Chicago. So unusual was it for a woman to have achieved that level of education that, upon Miller's appointment to St. John's College in 1940, the headline in the local newspaper read, "Mrs. Miller, Mother of Two Small Children, to Teach Economics." That a mother would maintain a demanding career was unimaginable. In addition to her work as an educator, Miller had juggled a long career as an author, photographer, and correspondent for *Newsweek* and *The Economist*. Perhaps even more unusual than all those accomplishments was her unorthodox outlook on family finances, formulated when she'd first married. Watching men commute to their jobs while their wives stayed at home managing the house and "primping and gossiping," Mrs. Hill concluded that she despised the "slave mentality" of marriage. She insisted on splitting household expenses with her husband right down the middle—a remarkable request at a time when married women possessed no financial rights, much less much capacity to earn. Men, once they became husbands, were legally obliged in most states to support their wives financially.

This estimable elder offered Susan a paltry assignment: to fetch her mail at home and office while she was away for the summer. It wasn't exactly the kind of stimulation Susan was angling for, but it came with a perk. In that spring of 1962, she'd bring along Lou to sit with her in the garden behind Mrs. Miller's house, savoring the experience of an authentic DC backyard.

When her employer returned, Susan told her that the pleasure of using the garden had been ample pay. Mrs. Miller not only insisted on writing a check, but went one step further: She made a call to Gilbert Harrison, the editor and owner of *The New Republic*, a magazine to which she was a contributor. It turned out he was looking for a secretary. Susan landed the job. Each day at the office, as she typed and proofread letters and longed to be sprung to a headier challenge, she thought of Mrs. Miller and her "perseverance and curiosity" behind the typewriter.

For the next nine months, Susan performed the "exacting and very responsible job" required of an administrative assistant, receiving a crash course in Washington all the while and experiencing the thrill of seeing in print the book review headlines that she'd been allowed to write as a nod to her intellect. The thrill stopped there. She was "bored silly."

In search of weightier employment, she consulted her personal list of contacts, scanning the entries she'd collected in her short time on earth, and made some calls. A friend from up in Boston, a vivacious woman named Diana Michaelis, had moved to Washington. Michaelis, a dozen years Susan's senior, had herself managed to bust out of the secretarial grind, landing work as a producer on *Prospects of Mankind*, a public television talk show about important issues that featured former First Lady Eleanor Roosevelt as host.* Michaelis was one of those people who knew everyone and whose door was always open; her backyard pool in Georgetown was a popular hive of activity and connection. And she had a tip for her friend.

American University in DC had recently launched an educational radio station, WAMU-FM 88.5. The station management was seeking a producer for a new public affairs program. This show would be the linchpin of a modest experiment called the Educational Radio Network. Thanks to underwriting from the Ford Foundation, five noncommercial stations in the Northeast would be interconnected, allowing the show to air simultaneously, a pricey undertaking otherwise unaffordable to noncommercial broadcasters. Though student volunteers would take on the majority of the jobs at WAMU, this assignment required a full-time paid worker, the station's first.

"What does a producer do?" Susan asked her friend.

"It's someone who doesn't take no for an answer," was Michaelis's response.

"That," said Susan, "I can do."

After the ecstatic discovery of radio earlier in the century, no one had imagined that this invention might ever amount to anything more than a practical bit of magic to, at best, extend the reach of schools or churches to which the first radio stations were licensed. But as wily, opportunistic entrepreneurs recognized radio's tremendous potential and began wielding its power to entertain and communicate, the medium began to grow willy-nilly. Before long, Radio became, as

---

* In one episode of particular interest, Eleanor discusses the status of women with President Kennedy, https://americanarchive.org/catalog/cpb-aacip-15-98z8wt6q.

Secretary of Commerce Herbert Hoover lamented, "drowned in advertising chatter."

The nation's airwaves weren't exclusively filled with news and entertainment interrupted by ads for soap, oil, and soup. Hundreds of stations like WAMU, served as independent islands in an otherwise commercial stream. For noncommercial use, the government had cordoned off the left-hand side of the FM band of the radio dial. Programming there typically consisted of an eclectic and unpredictable smorgasbord of lectures, theatrical productions, concerts, conversations on local issues, and book and poetry readings. With few exceptions, though, these stations were hardly more than glorified playthings for their institutions, airing paltry programs, erratic schedules, and, given their tiny signals, limited potential reach. Another equally vexing matter was whether anyone could tune those signals in, for the majority of radios hadn't even been built with the capacity to receive them.

Though World War II firmly established radio's stranglehold on the American brain, the newer and more dazzling medium of television arrived after war's end to burst that bubble, leapfrogging its way to center stage in the nation's living rooms as the dominant in-home entertainment force, and taking with it radio's biggest stars. Soon, the entire medium, not just the educational stations, became a broadcasting backwater—a bit of music, a bit of news, some talk—its use limited, for the most part, to the car.

In 1962, about the only place in broadcasting where a woman, particularly a woman without an iota of experience, could walk in the door and land an editorial position was at a start-up, noncommercial station like WAMU. Women were risky hires, even those who were already married; babies were an inevitable next step to distract from workplace focus and ambition—plus, it would never do to have a woman in a supervisory position to a man. But this start-up station was so new and precarious, the pay so low, and the new program so untested that convention and chauvinism didn't, couldn't, prevail.

When Susan first entered the modest studios for a tour, the lack of resources didn't register. She'd never been in a station before and had never considered working in the medium; at Barnard, she'd gone out of her way to avoid the King's College station in the dark basement attached to Columbia, across the street. After all, "there were all those boys who certainly didn't want us around." The vision now before her, of this "enormous array of buttons and switches and cords and cables, with strange words on them: VU meter, filter, on-off," was at once dazzling and terrifying, and it captivated her bright imagination, as did the sense of excitement in the air.

For the next four months, she'd check in every week to see if a job had materialized, in the meantime becoming hooked on WAMU as a listener. The fright of the Cuban Missile Crisis diverted the attention of the broadcasters. Then, one Wednesday, her call finally yielded fruit. Would she come in on Friday? Of course.

In short order, Susan anointed the show she was to produce with a lofty title: *Viewpoint: Washington*. The use of a colon had helped her when she'd deployed it in her college papers, she quipped, so, why not "keep it up! Put a colon in the title of this first broadcast you're doing, and it will do well!" And well it did.

"The franticness and excitement never stopped" as she learned the tricks of the control room and how to operate the board. She became accustomed to lugging unwieldy audio recorders and editing the tape she'd collected with surgical precision. She loved being paid to deploy her brain and her love of learning and language in ways she had never imagined.

The fact that the job paid less than her secretarial magazine work, she and Lou agreed, was a worthy sacrifice. She was engaged with the world, enthralled by this license to explore the community around her—tracking down guests, formulating topics. No longer was she just subserviently typing all day, hoping to write a headline.

On the day the weather girl called in sick, another seed was planted for Susan. As rare as it was for a woman to have waltzed into the role of producer, rarer still was it for a woman to appear on the air, except in a sideline role, or in the discussion of womanly matters. Typically, this low-grade meteorologist gathered her information the way mere mortals did: by picking up the phone and dialing the number WE6–1212 for the latest automated, city-provided forecast. Susan was so flummoxed by the prospect of appearing on the host's side of the producer's glass in the studio that she forgot to make that call. When it came time for her to speak, she floundered and flopped around, inventing the temperature, barometer, and wind pressure. She couldn't even gaze out a window for guidance—the only one in the studio was covered with curtains and so high up that it was impossible to peel them away.

"It's ninety-two degrees," she announced on the air. Never mind that it was February. When it came time to repeat the number, as was the format, her nerves prevailed, and in her invented world, the temperature had plummeted; now she reported that it was sixty-two degrees. She'd learned an important lesson: Never go before an open microphone without being prepared.

She'd also learned something else. Speaking into the microphone was even more compelling than working behind the scenes. A flitter of a fantasy formed: Maybe one day she'd get into a cab, state her destination, and the driver would recognize her voice.

CHAPTER TWO
". . . and sex"

Then came August 28, 1963, a historic day that underlined for Susan the power and potential of this medium in which she'd landed.

Since his election three years earlier, President John F. Kennedy had been working to pass a sweeping civil rights bill that would finally squelch the racial indignity and inequality that prevailed a hundred years after Lincoln's Emancipation Proclamation put an end to the scourge of slavery. In these modern times, job ads remained segregated by both race and gender, and unemployment among Black Americans clocked in at twice what it was for the nation's white citizens. Activists recognized that the only way left to tip the balance was with a mighty show of force, and they descended on the nation's capital city to demand equality.

The civil rights activist Asa Philip Randolph was tired of empty promises. The president of the Brotherhood of Sleeping Car Porters, the only Black labor union in the American Federation of Labor, Randolph remembered the pain he felt after World War I. After serving in the segregated army for lesser pay than whites, Black military members had been promised that they'd return to a more equal society. Instead, they encountered deadly mob violence and an intensified struggle to survive.

At the dawn of World War II, Randolph had pushed the rapidly expanding defense industries to give much-needed jobs to Black workers. He informed President Roosevelt of his plans to convene a hundred thousand people on the National Mall on July 1, 1941. The president did not welcome a march—"someone might get killed"—and where would all those visitors sleep and eat in a segregated city? But neither did the president wish to be forced to issue an order mandating whom defense contractors must hire. The potential gathering was scuttled when Roosevelt signed Executive Order 8802, which created the Fair Employment Commission. The order prohibited discrimination in defense hiring, but it was toothless: Employers who violated it would not be punished.

Now, twenty-two years later, pushed to the limit after the bloody conflagrations at spring protests around the South, unrest capped by the assassination of the activist Medgar Evers, Randolph and other leaders of the civil rights movement informed President Kennedy of their intention to stage a massive demonstration.

Different president, similar fears. "We want success in Congress, not just a big show at the Capitol," declared Kennedy, who explained that violence might lead the already skittish members of Congress disinclined to vote for the legislation to kill it. White supremacists and neo-Nazis had announced their intention to counter-demonstrate, intensifying the concern.

The civil rights leaders responded, unwavering, "Mr. President, the Black masses are restless and we are going to march on Washington."

To announce details of their upcoming protest, the activists called a news conference at the National Press Club, a central location where newsmakers routinely met with reporters. Eight years prior, in 1955, the club had voted to admit its first Black member, Louis Lautier, representative of both the *Atlanta Daily World* and the National Negro Publishers Association. Women, however, were still prohibited from joining or even entering the club. They'd formed their own, the Women's National Press Club, in 1919 (just as women were pushing to get the vote), the idea being to combat what its founding president said was a "conspiracy of men to keep women off the newspaper."

A tiny crack in the blockade had come when it was decided that credentialed female press would be permitted to observe key speeches by newsmakers from the balcony of the male-only Press Club's auditorium—as long as they were escorted on their way in and out. This upstairs area was jammed with the newsreels' unwieldy cameras and scorching lights, which made it both unbearably hot for the women and impossible for them to hear all that was being said. Even if they could have from their perch, they were not permitted to ask questions.

Having to look down at "the male members and their guests scarfing up a four-course lunch on the ballroom floor," said one lady journalist, only amped up the humiliation.

There'd been only one visitor to the club for whom this segregation had been unacceptable. In 1959, Soviet leader Nikita Khrushchev insisted that female reporters be allowed to attend his speech as equals. A onetime exception had therefore been granted.

Now, as the city prepared for the March on Washington for Jobs and Freedom, women appealed to the civil rights leaders to hold their press conference at a nonsegregated location so they might attend. "Surely you who are fighting for a cause with such high purposes would not be party to such discrimination," their entreaty read. If anyone should treat them fairly, it should be these activists.

When the march organizers refused to budge, female reporters restated their dismay—especially after one of them lost her assignment to cover the march because she couldn't attend the press conference. "We find it hard to imagine that this group would not recognize and fight discrimination wherever it exists."

Another pre-march briefing, held by the Washington Police, was open to all reporters. Susan Stamberg attended this on behalf of her station. The Educational Radio Network planned to transmit a marathon fifteen hours of coverage of the big day; some of it would also be fed out to the Canadian Broadcasting Company and, through its New York affiliate, overseas. None of the other sixteen hundred wire, TV, radio, and print reporters specially credentialed for this event, in addition to the usual DC press corps of twelve hundred, planned anything like this blanket coverage—not even the mighty commercial networks, which had only recently expanded their nightly newscasts from fifteen minutes to a half hour. CBS personnel would fan out over the District with twenty cameras and two "mobile flash" units, cutting in and out of afternoon programming. But only the "skinny" alliance of educational radio stations, with its tiny audience, would stay on from morning until hours after the march's end, allowing anyone who tuned in to hear every single minute of the proceedings.

A press conference rookie, Susan didn't quite know how to conduct herself at the police briefing. She'd gaze over at other reporters to see what they were doing and then make notes as they did. To her, this kind of pack encounter seemed more like public relations than "news." News should be original, shouldn't it? Not merely copying down or recording what some official or bureaucrat has said.

As new to the city as she was to the news business, Susan fumbled when it was time to phone into the station to explain the police briefing live on the air to host George Geesey. He gently helped her navigate her newbie confusion over which was the Washington Monument and which one honored Lincoln.

Come the big day, and given the worries that a conflagration might ignite amid the throngs, Susan and the lone other woman working on the production, up at the educational affiliate WGBH, in Boston, were assigned to stay safely put in the control rooms of their respective stations. They worked the phones to line up commentators and analysts and alerted the host in the field with cues. The march was simply considered too risky for lady personnel.

As protestors converged on the city by car, bus, rail, and on foot (one arrived on roller-skates), the crowd swelling to an unprecedented quarter of a million people, it was clear that peace would prevail—a stunning display of solidarity to announce that segregation's time had gone and that the laws, once and for all, must change. "Pass the bill," the crowd chanted, their voices united, reverberating in support of the Civil Rights Act. "Pass the bill."

The Educational Radio Network's live-from-the-scene broadcast transported listeners to the capital city, allowing them to hear the impassioned speeches being delivered there, the comments from the crowd and supportive Hollywood celebrities, and the musical performances. The rousing climax of it all was Dr. Martin Luther King Jr.'s spectacular, impassioned oratory, in which he declared his dream for equality. Hearing him speak, particularly at length, was a rare treat reserved for those lucky enough to witness him in person, since the network broadcasts typically had space only for sound bites.

Safely sequestered back at the studio in the upper reaches of Northwest Washington, Susan soaked up the energy as it crackled over the radio, excited at playing a tiny part both in the history of the civil rights movement and in the show of force for this burgeoning network employing her, which she found to be a technological marvel. As it had since she was a child, radio imbued her with the fantastic illusion that she was right smack in the center of the universe. She longed to actually inhabit it herself.

* * *

Despite the mighty show of strength, it took the shocking and tragic assassination of President Kennedy that fall to goad lawmakers to consensus. There had been enough talk about civil rights for too many years now, declared the newly installed president, Lyndon Johnson, in his first address to the nation, as he implored lawmakers to see that

> no memorial oration or eulogy could more eloquently honor President Kennedy's memory than the earliest possible passage of the civil rights bill for which he fought so long. . . . It is time now to write the next chapter, and to write it in the books of law.

That February, as the House Judiciary Committee began its deliberations, the bill now known as the 1964 Civil Rights Act would take a new and more expansive turn at the instigation of an unlikely actor. After four days of debate, the segregationist congressman Howard Smith of Virginia—on record as believing that "the colored races" were not equal in intelligence to whites—made a shocking political play. To the list of protected classes outlined in the legislation's section on equal employment (race, religion, national origin), he proposed the addition of another "minority": women. A letter from a female constituent had inspired him to make this recommendation, he said; she sought help regarding the "gross inequity of gender imbalance" that had led to a "proliferation of spinsters."

Smith had an ulterior motive. He knew that, for his fellow segregationist lawmakers, the only thing worse than granting equal rights to Black Americans was granting equal rights to women. Surely, he reasoned behind the scenes, his inclusion of "and sex" in the bill would tank its prospects.

Rep. Emanuel Celler of New York took Smith literally. First, he explained, women weren't a minority in *his* household; his fifty-year marriage had succeeded because of two words: "Yes, dear." Then he argued that adding "and sex" to the bill was "illogical, ill-timed, ill-placed and improper." Imagine the societal upheaval if total equality for Black people *and* women were adopted at the same time. He ticked off other issues that legislated equality would raise:

> Would male citizens be justified in insisting that women share with them the burdens of compulsory military service? What would become of traditional family relationships? What about alimony? Who would have the obligation of supporting whom? Would fathers rank equally with mothers in the right of custody to children? What would become of the crimes of rape and statutory rape? . . . Would the many State and local provisions regulating working conditions and hours of employment for women be struck down? . . . The list of foreseeable consequences . . . is unlimited.

All these well-worn arguments had been holding back the advancement of women since the founding of the nation—even once suffrage was mercifully attained.

In an instant, a crucial and long-awaited discussion about race detoured to one of sex that riled the fourteen female members of Congress. To Smith's claim that women were a minority, Rep. Frances Bolton of Ohio offered a ready retort. Women, she corrected, were the *majority*, totaling 90,991,681 of the citizenry, versus the nation's

88,331,494 men. And while women were well accustomed to being clas-sified as "miscellaneous," she jabbed that it was clear they were hardier than men. "Even your bones harden long before ours do," she contin-ued. "We live longer; we have more endurance."

As the male-dominated chamber erupted in mocking snickers, a disgusted Rep. Martha Wright Griffiths of Michigan rose to speak. After hours and days of deliberations, she said, the decorum had been somber and reserved, until the word *woman* had been introduced. "Mr. Chairman, I presume that if there had been any necessity to have pointed out that women were a second-class sex," she intoned, silencing her colleagues, "the laughter would have proved it."

Since her election to Congress in 1954, Griffiths had established herself as a crusader for the rights of women and the poor, considered by the men around her as a "bulldog with the jaws of a tiger." She wasn't going to squander her position. Her mother had taken in boarders dur-ing the Great Depression to make sure her only daughter, born in 1912, could attend college; she didn't want the girl to ever be dependent on a man. Martha's father fully supported the effort; he believed girls were smarter. (It wasn't lost on him, either, that his daughter was a superior marksman to his son.)

At the University of Missouri, fellow student Hicks Griffiths couldn't help his attraction to the smartest girl in the class. He declined his admission to Harvard Law School because women weren't allowed there, and after marrying Martha (without wedding rings, because they were so poor), he headed with her to the University of Michigan Law School, where they became the first husband-and-wife duo to graduate. Hired in equal positions as counsel to a trade association, they encoun-tered wage discrimination: Because he was the "man of the house," his salary was thousands of dollars higher. After they'd set up a legal practice together, he'd pushed Martha to seek office.

Once stationed in DC, Martha railed against the "laws of the Middle Ages" that allowed employers to deny jobs to women with school-age children and to fire women who deigned to get married; she also pushed for reforms to help single women, widows, and the poor. Of an executive who insisted that stewardesses hired by his airline be young, attractive, and unattached, she'd responded, "What are you running, an airline or a whorehouse?"

Every year since she'd set foot inside the Capitol, Griffiths had introduced the Equal Rights Amendment, continuing a push to have it passed that dated back to 1923. The amendment was crucial because, she said, you couldn't depend on the Supreme Court ("just nine old idiots") or lawmakers to enact women's rights. "Men make the laws which govern women's lives," she said. "Like a slave and a master, the master could pass the best legislation on earth in behalf of the slave, but it's still viewed through his eyes. What's the slave's idea of the best legislation?"

Before Representative Smith beat her to it, Martha had planned to propose that gender be included as a protected class in the Civil Rights bill—but for a very different reason. Should the Act pass without the inclusion of the words "and sex," the law would, in essence, divide American labor into three groups: white men, with their abundant rights; Black men and women, who would now be considered equal; and white women, who, as an unprotected class, would have no rights at all. She explained this pointedly to her colleagues: "your wives, your sisters, your mothers and your daughters. . . . A vote against this amendment today by a white man is a vote against his wife, or his widow, or his daughter, or his sister."

Rep. Katharine St. George of New York echoed her colleague's argument. "We are entitled to this little crumb of equality," she said, adding that eighteen states still denied basic equality to women, such as the right to serve on juries. "The addition of that little, terrifying word 's-e-x' will not hurt this legislation in any way. In fact, it will improve it. It will make it comprehensive. It will make it logical. It will make it right.*

* Not every female lawmaker was on board with the inclusion of the words "and sex." Rep. Edith Green of Oregon rose to say that while she, too, was tired of discrimination against women, she was most concerned now about the plight of Black Americans. "For every discrimination I have suffered," she said, "I firmly believe the Negro woman has suffered ten times that amount of discrimination. . . . I suppose this may go down in history as 'women's afternoon,' but the women of the House, I feel sure, recognize that you men will be the ones who finally make the decision." Still, she said, discrimination against Black Americans was far worse than it was toward women.

As the bill won passage in the House—with the words "and sex" included—the voice of an unseen woman echoed through the chamber. "We made it!" she shouted. "We are human!" After enduring weeks of filibusters in the Senate, the bill finally came up for a vote. A dramatic "aye" was cast by California senator Clair Engle, who, dying of a brain tumor and unable to speak, was wheeled onto the floor and motioned to his eye three times.

A triumphant President Johnson wasted no time in signing the bill, which established voting rights; the abolition of "separate but equal" public facilities, including in housing and education; and the creation of an Equal Employment Opportunity Commission. In a ceremony broadcast on radio and television, he first congratulated his fellow Americans for having achieved "a turning point in history." This act, he said,

> is a challenge to all of us . . . to eliminate the last vestiges of injustice in our beloved country. So tonight I urge . . . every American to join in this effort to bring justice and hope to all our people. . . . Let us close the springs of racial poison. Let us pray for wise and understanding hearts. Let us lay aside irrelevant differences and make our nation whole.

Then, he proceeded to pick up one pen after another, using each one to mark a tiny bit of his signature on the historic document. As a throng of well-wishers surrounded him—among them, Dr. Martin Luther King Jr. himself—Johnson passed out a hundred pens as souvenirs of the historic day.*

The next day, all across America, Black citizens joyously tested their new freedoms by descending on restaurants where they had, until now, been denied service. The other protections guaranteed them, and women, would be harder won.

---

* You can watch the historic signing here https://www.c-span.org/video/?300956-1 /civil-rights-act-50th-anniversary.

* * *

As equality for all became the law of the land, if not yet the practice, Susan, having successfully escaped the pink-collar dead-end to which so many of her peers were relegated, flourished. When the foundation backing the Educational Radio Network pulled its support to redirect the funds to educational television, WAMU kept its first paid employee around anyway. For a time, she even took on the role of station manager, overseeing coverage of the National Teach-in on Vietnam, which was transmitted to 130 educational stations around the nation in March 1965. A few months later, she got her chance to report from the center of another major news event, a peace rally that flooded the capital with twenty thousand protestors demanding an end to the war. As it had for the March on Washington, the station provided the only continuous coverage.

What WAMU lacked in budget, it made up for in experimental spirit. For a while, Susan hosted a jazz show called *Sue's Blues*, during which she played a rickety old piano. After briefly producing a daily magazine show called *Kaleidoscope*, she stepped in as its host when the male host moved on. There were no objections. The stakes were so low at this off-the-radar educational station, allowing a woman on the air in a key role wasn't an issue.

As host, Susan found her love of the written word colliding fully with the magic of the spoken; she could offer the audience a chorus of different voices, bits and bobs of commentary, reviews, interviews, conversations, music, books, and theater—or, as she said in the introduction, fragments of reality, "a weeknightly gaze at the bummer called life." It was "the magazine you read with your ear."

She loved being able to sit in a room and have a conversation "designed to be overheard." The "artificiality and technicality" of the studio could be off-putting, she allowed; there was nothing natural about sitting across from a complete stranger, surrounded by equipment and that foam acoustic soundproofing that resembled egg cartons, wearing a headset and glancing at a clock while a microphone, linked to transmission gear, lofted the voices into the sky and out to the cars and kitchens of total strangers. And yet, when such a conversation was crafted expertly, she thrilled to this socially permissible form of eavesdropping. Radio was like a "wonderful novel"—or, better yet, like that salon she'd been dreaming of hosting since high school.

While the absence of the visual was precisely what made the medium such a rich stimulant for the mind, she took care to apply fresh lipstick before each show. This was a preparatory trick she borrowed from that writer she'd long admired, J. D. Salinger, whose invented characters the Glass family dutifully polished their shoes before appearing on their fictitious radio broadcast, *It's a Wise Child*. The cosmetic allowed her to be the "best and warmest and most attractive person" possible for her audience—no matter how tiny that audience might be.

CHAPTER THREE

"The airwaves belong to all the people"

An exciting twist was about to take Susan away from this job she loved, though, and into a grand adventure. Through his work with the U.S. Agency for International Development, Lou accepted a posting in New Delhi, India. The couple arrived in February 1966, and every moment of every day that followed, Susan delighted in the strange, vivid universe into which she'd been dropped. Their two-bedroom apartment in a brick house was attached to a huge garden, with a part-time gardener to tend it. The property also came with a full-time cook, a sweeper, and a laundry man. To the mix, they eventually added a dachshund puppy they named "Hotspur Swadeshi," after the freedom movement spurred by Gandhi. Each morning, a crow served as alarm clock, and a lizard lived under the fridge. Susan relished her role as memsahib, the "wife of sahib," her man.

She'd promised her WAMU colleagues that she'd make use of the diplomatic pouch available to her to send back tape each month, an audio "letter" she signed off with a unique "soc out," as the radio byline was called: "This is Susan Stamberg in New Delhi. Namaste."

With the power of her Uher recorder and her reporter's gaze, she was a foreign correspondent now, collecting sound from places unlike any she'd visited before—such as a leper colony. Along with her open-reel tapes, she'd send along detailed instructions on how to edit her stories, reminding her colleagues to share the finished product with the other educational radio stations. When an exhibition titled *Two Decades of American Painting* arrived from New York's Museum of Modern Art, she showed up to the opening with her microphone to find how the Indians would react to Andy Warhol's *Campbell's Soup Cans*. They wandered "through the halls, squinting, shuffling like a boxer, closing in then backing away," trying to make sense of this proto-pop art.

She searched for other assignments, too, offering her services to the Canadian Broadcasting Company and ultimately finding scraps of work with Voice of America, where she wrote scripts and filed taped news bits.

She toured All India Radio and TV, admiring the abundant studios and excellent equipment that provided service to dozens of stations around the country and that housed a special orchestra comprised of sitar and tabla players who performed live studio concerts. Just as it didn't back home, television news in this exotic land didn't impress her, though she was surprised to see that, unlike in America, Indians routinely seated women as emcees and newsreaders.

Sometimes, she'd play a game where she'd close her eyes and spin herself around, fluttering her lids open in search of the familiar: Not one vision in her line of sight resembled anything she'd ever seen before; even the ring of the telephone sounded different (not to mention the fact that the person on the other end was usually speaking Hindi, which she was doing her best to learn). The romance of the monsoons, until the roads got blocked by landslides and the mugginess led to temperatures hotter than she'd ever endured; the clouds, the flying roaches, the mangoes; and the people, the people, the people—all of it was unimaginable to a girl of modest means for whom a trip each summer to camp up in Connecticut had once constituted a grand, faraway adventure. Now she could boast of having visited Calcutta one Christmas and Kabul on another; of sipping sherry in Kashmir; gazing at the Taj Mahal by moonlight; witnessing Tibetan monks and goat sacrifices and her first sighting of royalty in Nepal. As they packed the car with the necessary ten gallons of water to drink on road trips, she observed that the roadside convenience of Howard Johnson's hadn't made its way to "Inja" yet. The restaurant chain's hot dogs with mustard and relish were the only thing she really missed—besides her radio station.

Despite the stirring wonders of India, Susan's Voice of America work eventually became tedious and repetitive—all those short, clipped stories—so she didn't mind dropping that in exchange for a plum job as assistant to the "memsahib" of the ambassador, Mrs. Chester Bowles, a kind of "latter-day Eleanor Roosevelt." Mostly, it was secretarial work again, but with a distinctly Indian twist: Susan never knew when the Maharajah of Jaipur might appear on her doorstep adorned with the most magnificent pearls and a turban of purple silk.

Ultimately, the "marvelous, warm and mystifying busy-ness" of each day did not compensate for the otherworldly and itinerant nature of the Foreign Service, which proved not to SueLou's liking. They could have opted for another turn of duty, or transferred to another country, but instead, after a little over two years abroad, they made the choice to return to Washington.

Before they arrived, Susan was thrilled to receive a letter from WAMU's general manager, who told her she'd be welcomed back, even if just part time. She had no idea what home would feel like—she knew she'd never be the same again after this experience—but she couldn't wait to get there.

* * *

As their plane prepared to land in Washington in April 1968, the Stambergs could spot the "smoke from angry fires" that rose in the aftermath of Martin Luther King Jr.'s assassination: riots, National Guardsmen, a curfew. While she and Lou had been immersed in a faraway, otherworldly culture, swirling social changes had continued unabated on their native soil: second-wave feminism, the escalating conflict in Vietnam, the starry promise of the space race, the psychedelic wildness of hippies, and the sexual revolution.

Amid this backdrop, President Johnson launched his movement for a "great society," in which he declared there would be "abundance and liberty for all." His "war on poverty" involved sweeping social programs intended to feed and educate every child, beautification projects to improve the nation's roads and neighborhoods, health care for the poor and elderly, as well as a boost to the arts—including a government-financed alternative to commercial television designed to spark a cultural revolution. "We should insist that the public interest," he said, "be served by the public airwaves."*

Intellectuals had come to believe, over the last two decades, that commercial media had not only *not* lived up to its potential, but, indeed, had run amok and was destroying the essence of society. Television, enthroned as the centerpiece of 90 percent of all homes and switched on for more hours each day than most children spent in school, now exercised a powerful, almost frightening, control over the American psyche. The chairman of the Federal Communications Commission, Newton Minow, stood before a gathering of the nation's broadcasters and accused them of squandering the great resource of the airwaves with which they'd been entrusted. Sit down in front of your own broadcasts, he advised them, and watch until station sign-off:

I can assure you that what you will observe is a vast wasteland . . . a procession of game shows, formula comedies about totally unbelievable families, blood and thunder, mayhem, violence, sadism, murder, western bad men, western good men, private eyes, gangsters, more violence, and cartoons. And endlessly, commercials—many screaming, cajoling, and offending. And most of all, boredom. True, you'll see a few things you will enjoy. But they will be very, very few . . .

Is there one person in this room who claims that broadcasting can't do better?

President Johnson believed he could help broadcasters "do better" by investing and recasting the fallow utility of noncommercial broadcasting. Of the 130 television stations licensed to universities around the nation, a handful were robust local operations, like those in Pittsburgh, St. Louis, and San Francisco. One, in Indiana, even attempted

---

* In 1943, the Johnsons had purchased a commercial radio and TV station in Austin, Texas, with money Lady Bird inherited from her grandmother.

beaming taped school lessons to classrooms across six states using an innovative technique called Stratovision. For the most part, though, educational TV was an "undernourished and sickly enterprise" in a "deplorable" condition. With scant resources and unable to adequately link together, there was no way the public stations could ever provide a viable alternative to their commercial brethren, much less hope to elevate the sorts of messages being pumped into America's homes each day. "Educational" when used to describe a form of broadcasting should not be a synonym for "boring." A more robust public media system was sure to stimulate the creation of more quality news and information programs from the commercial networks. Johnson now pledged to rescue and transform this slice of the wasteland with the 1967 Public Television Act.*

Critics quaked with fear. Instead of envisioning a paragon of broadcasting excellence, as had been created overseas in the not-for-profit British Broadcasting Service, funded with taxes on radios and televisions, they instead imagined a Hitleresque, government-controlled propaganda machine. The president made it clear: Politics would be kept entirely out of public broadcasting's programming decisions, as well as its funding. Stations would be locally, not centrally, controlled and licensed to universities and school districts responsible to local boards and governance—and insulated from the federal government.

Missing from this legislation and discussions about this proposed system was any explicit mention of the more than three hundred stations in the broadcasting backwater of educational radio. The typical budget for one of them hovered at around ten thousand dollars a year. Ardent believers in the power of this rough diamond were few but fierce. With adequate investment, they believed that they, too, could

---

* Skepticism about the need for such connectedness came from Henry David Thoreau, who in 1844 said that when he heard about Mr. Morse's telegraph, he made this sour comment about the race for faster communication: "Perchance," he warned, "the first news which will leak through into the broad, flapping American ear will be that Princess Adelaide has the whooping cough."

offer intelligent programming to a wider audience. They pointed to their successes, such as their interconnected coverage of the 1963 March on Washington for Jobs and Freedom and that show Susan had first been hired to produce, *Viewpoint: Washington*. Together the stations united to lobby for inclusion in the president's bill, commissioning a report on radio's virtues titled "The Hidden Medium," which they distributed around the Capitol, demanding to know: Why not use the more inclusive word *broadcasting* in the title of the act and not just the word *television?**

Fortunately for the radio minions, a Washington bureaucrat sympathetic to the cause found himself in charge of drafting the legislation. Just as the words "and sex" had been slipped into the Civil Rights Bill, so, too, the words "and radio" were tacked into what had now been renamed the 1967 Public Broadcasting Act. Various notions about how to finance this grand idea—levying a tax on the sale of televisions and radios, or by taxing commercial broadcasters—were shot down. Ultimately, Congress (and the American people) would foot the bill. How the nation's geographically diverse lot of stations would resolve their varying needs and interests—the avant-garde of New York's theater scene versus the need of educators in Mississippi concerned with reducing illiteracy—was anyone's guess. CBS and the Carnegie Corporation each ponied up a million dollars in what the *New York Times* declared a "measure of immense potential significance."

The U.S. Marine Symphony Orchestra serenaded the crowd gathered in the East Room of the White House on November 7, 1967, as President Johnson signed the law that promised to usher in a whole new era in broadcasting—a "great movement" for the next century, a vast network for knowledge that demonstrated that "our Nation wants more than just material wealth; our Nation wants more than a 'chicken in every pot.' We in America have an appetite for excellence, too. While we work every day to produce new goods and to create new wealth, we

---

* To hear the deliberations on the act, visit: http://americanarchive.org/catalog/cpb -aacip-15-18rbp7bm. Because, came the answer, *television* sounds better.

want most of all to enrich man's spirit." Johnson declared, "That is the purpose of this act. The airwaves belong to all the people."

* * *

Several years later, after various studies and meetings and jockeying for position, Congress allocated five million dollars to create the Corporation for Public Broadcasting, with the lion's share of the funds directed toward TV, and a sliver of that dedicated to radio. To determine what the transformation from "educational" to "public" radio might sound like, a small group of men who ran these noncommercial stations convened, creating the first board of what they soon incorporated as National Public Radio.

Together they agreed that their new service needed to produce some sort of signature show as its first offering to the stations that signed up as members—just as public television had begun creating premier offerings like *Mister Rogers' Neighborhood* and *Sesame Street*, which debuted on the air in the United States in 1968 and 1969, respectively.

Next, they needed to choose a leader. Among the candidates: respected, high-profile commercial broadcasters Eric Sevareid and Walter Cronkite; media historian Erik Barnouw; a former *New York Times* reporter named Robert Conley; Edwin Fancher, editor of the weekly *Village Voice*; and a veteran of educational media named Donald Quayle, who'd been keen to work on the public television side. Quayle got the nod.

A charismatic and paternalistic figure, Quayle had been the leader of the Educational Radio Network, where Susan had started out. He was the kind of person who felt equally comfortable schmoozing at cocktail parties (despite his Mormon roots) as he did crouching to install carpet in the studio. Associates described him as someone who'd drive for hours in the middle of the night to help a friend or colleague whose car had stalled out. He relished the technological challenge before him with NPR, linking up noncommercial stations into a cohesive network so they could share programs.

To serve as National Public Radio's first programming director, Quayle, in turn, chose one of the station managers, a former high school guidance counselor and speech teacher named Bill Siemering. Growing up in rural Wisconsin, Siemering had listened to and later worked at the station believed to be the paragon of educational broadcasting, WHA, headquartered at the University of Wisconsin. Since 1931, the station had produced a *School of the Air*, programs featuring stimulating fare like *Journeys in Music Land*, *Afield with Ranger Mac*, and *Rhythm and Games with Mrs. Fannie Steve*. The idea was to enrich students enrolled in the more than six thousand one-room schoolhouses across the state.*

Siemering embodied President Johnson's belief that the airwaves belong to all. His notion that radio was an agent for social change came alive when he was tapped to serve as the first professional general manager at WBFO-FM, at the University of Buffalo, in New York. Until he arrived, the station, in the hands of students, had aired only a few hours a day. Quickly, he won acclaim for his innovations, like airing twenty-eight hours of ambient sound of the Buffalo cityscape, taking listeners inside factories and cafeterias they might not otherwise visit.

Creating a storefront studio off-campus, in the heart of the Black community, Siemering encouraged volunteers to talk about the issues that concerned them, as well as to play and discuss music, allowing the station to reach not only the Black audience, said volunteer Ed Smith, "but the whites, too, who had never heard our perspective before." Along with giving voice to people of color, Siemering innovated coverage of campus tensions surrounding Vietnam by opening up the microphones to administrators favorably inclined toward the war as well as to angry students. "The idea," Siemering said, "was that there is not a single truth here."

In the aftermath of the new Public Broadcasting law, Siemering

---

* To hear some samples, visit: http://www.portalwisconsin.org/archives/wsahistory feature.cfm.

wrote a piece for a trade magazine that articulated the collective hopes and fears of everyone who'd worked in educational media. They felt now like Cinderella, about to be transformed by a fairy godmother from a "drab, colorless hard-working poor stepchild." Would this new attention prove a boon, or reduce them to the base level of commercial media—"utility grade meat devoid of taste and low in nutrition" which united people in a "common banality"? It was essential, Siemering believed, that public broadcasting unite the nation in a "common humanity."

A crucial element in doing this, he continued, was the inclusion, as had been done in Buffalo, of the views and voices of minorities. Siemering was dismayed that news on commercial media represented just one voice, that of the white male from New York. Radio, he wrote, offered a powerful tool for creating a more equal nation: "Racism and hate will not disappear with more high-rise apartments or larger police forces, but through meaningful conversation."

As we now lived in an age of information overload, Siemering continued, noncommercial media needed to redefine news beyond the car crashes, murders, and muggings that had become the hallmark of television news reports: "We need a more accurate barometer of what the public wants than top 40 charts and sales of cigarettes and acne lotion."

But how to achieve these lofty goals? That's what he and Quayle, and a handful of others, had to sort out in the year 1970.

* * *

As the framework for the new public radio system was under construction, Susan—over at one of those stations that would soon become a charter member of it—worked happily away on *Kaleidoscope*, her nightly alternative magazine show. A new manager had doubled the paid staff at WAMU and added new programs, including children's plays, language enrichment classes, and an inventive classical music show. The broadcasting day now extended from dawn to midnight, and thanks to the purchase of a $35,000 stereo transmitter, the station's signal could be heard as far as seventy miles away, increasing the potential audience to two million.

All this caught the ear of local reviewer Tina Hope Laver at the *Washington Star*, who extolled the virtues of WAMU in a feature report. There was more heft to this alternative than the music, punctuated with pleasant voices, that was available on commercial AM radio, she wrote: "WAMU-FM provides an outlet for the seldom-heard, frequently grating voices in the Washington community. Anyone tired of commercials, jingles and single-sound stations might want to move the FM dial to the left."

The story offered particular praise for Susan, the "statuesque, dark-haired intellectual with a New York City twang" who said she loved working in an environment where she could bask in her irreverence and air different ideas—though she'd no doubt earn more if she'd gone to work at a commercial station. Attending Barnard, she said, had taught her to believe she could do anything—even in the male-dominated field of broadcasting.

While Susan loved her job, the new spotlight on public radio already had led to change. The new manager was skittish about offending the audience—and potential sponsors. Fresh concerns had been expressed about language in the Public Broadcasting Act that restricted political commentary. Susan was warned that some of her contributors were "too radical" and might jeopardize the station's future. To show the breadth and depth of her guests, she compiled a three-page list of those she'd had on the air, which included actors and authors and yippies and professors and representatives from the DC League of Women's Voters, poverty elimination groups, the Martin Luther King Memorial Arts Festival, and the National Trust for Historic Preservation.

Still, *Kaleidoscope*, it was announced, would be replaced by an alternative, a wooden reading of local listings called *Kalendar*. The station's mandate of public service, in Susan's estimation, was becoming subservient to "public relations," no longer "a forum for free expression of community interest and opinion" but, rather, a place governed by "managerial fear of free speech."

Though she was disappointed and angry with this new direction, she had a new project to tackle: a baby. What started out to be a maternity leave turned into her resignation, which she explained publicly in a letter to the editor of the *Star*.

In the early part of 1970, as Susan embarked on the joys and challenges of motherhood, she received a letter from a former colleague, Al Hulsen. He'd just joined the brand-new Corporation for Public Broadcasting as director of Radio Projects, and he'd read the story about her departure. "Several new radio developments are about to take place in Washington . . . and I hope, when junior permits it, you can become part of them," he wrote. "Radio still needs expert and talented assistance." Susan would be the perfect addition to this new National Public Radio team, he continued—as soon as they figured out what, exactly, they were doing.

CHAPTER FOUR

Linda

There wasn't much to the *Current-Argus*, published five nights a week and on Sundays in Carlsbad, New Mexico. On average, the paper was comprised of about eight pages each issue. Wire services provided national and international news. Local reports appealed to the population of this town in southwest New Mexico: weather forecasts on the front page for ranchers and farmers, a key part of the economy; the daily visitor count to the area's jewel of a national park, Carlsbad Caverns, its limestone caves bedecked with magnificent natural stalactites and stalagmites; tidbits of gossip (who in the community was recovering from an appendectomy or emergency tonsillectomy, who'd filed for marriage licenses or divorces at the courthouse, the towns where locals had ventured to visit their relatives, and the relatives who'd come calling on them); and other matters of civic import (like the upcoming door-to-door sale of brooms made by the blind). Win or lose, the Carlsbad Cavemen, the high school football team, always received prominent play.

The newspaper, like its publisher, Floyd B. Rigdon—a goat-roping rodeo man who hailed from Oklahoma—was politically Democratic, but, as Rigdon proclaimed, concern for the community would always trump party politics. "Fair to its readers and fair to its advertisers," was the paper's motto. Rigdon elaborated:

> Your daily newspaper is noted for its civic spirit. Always ready
> to support any enterprise worthy of backing and publicity,
> the *Daily Current-Argus* sounds the keynote for every civic
> enterprise. Critical of anything that would hurt the common
> welfare, the *Current-Argus* stands ready to attack and expose
> any condition which might tend to retard the city's growth
> and development.

The dusty, wide-open landscape of the Pecos Valley had been evolving rapidly ever since an entrepreneurial rancher named Charles B. Eddy engineered a magnificent irrigation system that tapped the mighty river and bolstered farming, and then platted out the streets to form a town. For his efforts, the town as well as the surrounding county had been christened "Eddy" with a bottle of champagne at an official ceremony in 1888.

The arrival of the Pecos Valley Railway on January 13, 1891, heralded a new industrial era, allowing ranchers to export their abundant cattle and sheep more easily. A development company, seeking intrepid souls brave enough to relocate and avail themselves of the opportunities on these hundreds of thousands of acres of wide-open space, advertised free trips to prospective residents in neighboring states. Once years of politicking yielded statehood for New Mexico in 1913, colonists from as far away as Switzerland and Italy arrived at the behest of an ambitious industrialist who'd traveled overseas to tout the region's virtues.

Besides the splendor of the caverns, there was much richness to be discovered underground. Healing mineral springs inspired citizens to change Eddy's name to that of the famous resort town Karlsbad, Bohemia, whose waters were similarly enriched. Next, a prospector struck black gold. The search for another oil well revealed an additional bounty: massive deposits of the versatile potassium-rich mineral potash. Three hundred miles of tunnels were subsequently blasted underneath the earth, and a thousand men arrived to mine this multipurpose treasure, swelling Carlsbad's population. During World War II, the railway transported it by the ton to Santa Fe to be used for gunpowder. Potash, it turned out, also served a useful purpose in the creation of fertilizer and crystal tableware and, later, was to be a part of a booming business in the manufacture of television tubes.

* * *

Despite all this richness, this speck-in-the-desert city was otherwise proud of being ten years behind the rest of the world—a peaceful, pleasant place abundant with yucca, ocotillo, and dotted mesas; where no one locked their doors; and where each family sounded their own whistle or bell to summon their kids, playing, carefree, in the streets, home for supper. In Carlsbad, everyone knew everyone and could trace one another's family history back three generations.

During the ominousness of the war years, the pages of the *Current-Argus* reflected the travails of New Mexicans anxiously following the faraway battles, eager for news of the heroics or demise of their own. Wire reports brought news of the actions of "the Japs" and Hitler. Families placed ads thanking the community for condolences over loved ones lost. Note to citizens: Save those tin cans so the government can turn them into trench mortars, flame throwers, tanks, and bombers.

Another admonishment:

Help! Help! Housewives!
Be sure and use all of your A B and C ration stamps before they expire on March 31st. Your grocer needs all of the ration stamps you can possibly spend this month in order to build up a large allowable working inventory, which is to be determined by how many stamps he receives during March and control his purchasing power for the duration.

This was particularly important in a self-contained oasis like Carlsbad, 150 miles away from the nearest city. One of the town's grocers was among those scrambling to stock provisions for an anxious public when, smack in the middle of the war, in March 1943, a more personal item about him appeared in the daily paper:

Girl Born to Cozbys: A daughter, Linda June, was born Friday at St. Francis Hospital to Mr. and Mrs. Miller Cozby 512 North Alameda Street. She weighed 7 pounds 10 ounces. Cozby is the manager at the Jackson Food Store.

Vernon Miller Cozby, born in Lewisville, Texas, in 1910, had attended Lubbock High School and studied electrical engineering at Texas Tech University. He'd then made his way to New Mexico and the pleasant, peaceful Carlsbad, where he embarked on a career in the grocery business. His wife, June, a native of Loco, Oklahoma, became involved with the Carlsbad Woman's Club and the Concert Listener Lectures, a group committed to bringing more music to the town.

When Linda was three, her father took the bold step of becoming a business owner. From the widowed Mrs. Morrison, he purchased her eponymous grocery store at 414 N. Guadalupe (phone number: 174). Back in 1929, the Morrisons had pivoted from the furniture business into groceries, expanding a market they purchased and, eventually, built out at a larger location. Cozby, as the new proprietor, placed an ad in the *Current-Argus* to announce that "I wish to continue serving the cash and credit customers in the same faithful way that Mrs. Morrison has for many years. I will be happy to make your acquaintance and welcome many friends I once served."

So committed was Vernon to his work that he'd sell the turkey he'd reserved for his family if a last-minute patron requested it, leaving roast beef as the centerpiece of his own Thanksgiving celebration. No way would he purchase a bird from another store. His younger daughter, Nancy, might cry in anger at how unfair this was, but the point was clear: He put a premium on customer service.

A month before Christmas, Linda's mother would dutifully bake fruitcakes, the good kind, thanks to the family's ability to purchase pineapple, cherries, lemon extract, pecans, and brown sugar wholesale. After these delicacies were removed from the oven, they were doused with bourbon, wrapped in towels, and stored until being gifted to clientele. Linda admired her mother's skill in the kitchen: her "soft spot for overripe fruit and very dark red beef," as well as her foolproof eggs, "tender and soft, kind of a cross between poached and over easy," the kind, she said, that "go on top of a plate of asparagus, or a stack of red chile enchiladas, or a salad. Because the yolks are soft, they become like a sauce."

But June Cozby was more than a cozy, comforting mother who sewed her daughters' clothing and insisted on excellent manners. Concerned when she learned about unequal conditions for Black students, she pushed for the integration of local schools before the federal mandate. From her mother's tenacity, Linda saw that, despite being a girl, "there were lots of things I could do and, that if somebody got in my way, I should get them out of my way."

On Saturdays and in the summers, Linda would help out by delivering groceries, taking care, if no one was home, to open the unlocked door and deposit the customer's ice cream in the freezer and their milk in the fridge. In her spare time, she'd find herself walking through "that beautiful park in the center of Carlsbad in the bright summer sunshine and finding the dim, cool place full of books." The library was not just for new discoveries, but a source of answers.

Once, while foraging in the yard, she and her friend Mary discovered some unusual bugs. Eager to learn more, they stashed the catch in a pillbox—the modern convenience of a plastic bag didn't yet exist—and proceeded directly over to the kindly librarian, Mrs. Helen Melton. As a kid growing up on a nearby ranch, Mrs. Melton had done her own homework in this very same library Linda now enjoyed. A scholarship job at the University of New Mexico library had made it possible for her to finish college—and planted the seed of a career. That day, she directed the curious girls to the entomology section, offering pointers on how to research using the books they found there. Linda consulted with Mrs. Melton again and again as she grew into the joys of Austen, Dickens, and the Brontës.

Being brainy might not have been the premium at Carlsbad High School, but Linda couldn't help herself. She routinely made the scholar's list and spent the long, hot summers under the air-conditioning unit, reading books.

But "Coz" was no sheltered bookworm. She was active in the Order of the Rainbow for Girls, a youth service organization; placed second in a "I Speak for Democracy" contest; served on the Eisenhower Junior High Student Council; taught Sunday school at First Presbyterian Church, where her dad served as deacon; attended Carlsbad Community Concerts, which she'd been doing since she was old enough to stay up late; and participated in the "Mummers" theatrical troupe.

Linda's earliest political memory was a fiery debate with a friend, when she was eight, over whether Truman should have fired General MacArthur. (She felt that he should have.) Another: sitting by an irrigation ditch that ran past Roosevelt School with Mary, engrossed in a discussion about presidential candidate Adlai Stevenson and his chances for victory. The seeds of her interest in the subject had been planted around the cherrywood dinner table her dad had made by hand. There, the family dissected New Mexico state affairs. The drama of the vast corruption provided more fun than a movie at the Fiesta Drive-in, which boasted the largest neon sign west of the Mississippi.

When it came to keeping up with current events, the curious grocer's daughter eagerly awaited the arrival of *Time* magazine, assembled in New York. Though the *Current-Argus* had moved into a fancy new building and installed a state-of-the-art press in 1951—the largest in New Mexico—the lure of news and deeper analysis from faraway was strong. So, too, was the ephemeral medium of radio, though there were few options available: KAVE-AM 1240 or KPBM-AM 740, the religious station. Her dad liked to listen to Paul Harvey and country-and-western music; her mother favored news and entertainment. The great newsman Edward R. Murrow enthralled Linda. Blanketed by his worldly timbre, she dreamed that one day she might become his assistant.

Television's march would soon make Murrow and his ubiquitous cigarette a familiar visual in the nation's living rooms, but it had taken the medium a while to arrive in southwestern New Mexico. During the contentious Army–McCarthy hearings, citizens eager to tune in had to drive to Texas in order to watch. After numerous delays, in 1953 a monster of a signal finally began crackling over a 790-foot tower installed on a 250-foot hill southwest of Roswell by southwestern oil tycoon John

Barnett, who boasted that it was "138 feet taller than the Empire State Building, and that's pretty tall." Up until now, the closest stations, in Albuquerque and El Paso, wouldn't, as KSWS-TV Channel 8's general manager explained, "put a snow job" on a local set. Now viewers from Clovis to Portales to Hobbs to Lovington, all the way west to Carlsbad, would be able to experience the marvel that had captivated much of the rest of the nation.

Appliance salesmen, aware that locals would be skeptical about the technology, promised ninety-day guarantees on the purchase of a receiver. In newspaper ads for their products, department stores such as Carlsbad's Gambles printed the TV schedule next to pictures of the magic boxes. From four to eleven in the evening, viewers lucky enough to own a set could tune in to a hodgepodge of programs, like *Natchuk the Eskimo Pianist, Old American Barn Dance,* a live agricultural show called *Your Home and Land,* and the *Frigidaire Frolics: TV Talent Search,* which welcomed auditions by anyone from age 3 to 103. With all that entertainment available from your couch, the Fiesta Drive-in seemed superfluous.

Later, at a cost of a million dollars, Barnett amped up his might and installed a tower that soared twice as tall—the highest man-made structure in the world. A curious pilot from El Paso flew his piper plane around it and observed that it looked like a stiletto dagger smashing the lonely, dreary desert skies.

The stunning power of TV hit home in late November 1955, when NBC's *Wide Wide World* allowed millions of viewers to dip eight hundred feet beneath the earth for a look inside the natural wonder of the Carlsbad Caverns. It had taken weeks, three thousand miles of cable, and seven thousand feet of power lines to electrify and illuminate the underground chambers at the park known as "the Big Room" and "the King's Palace"—all for a hefty price tag of two hundred thousand dollars. A special booster tower allowed for transmission from the remote location. Two hundred locals stood in as tourists, while a technician shot a water gun at a stalactite so that it would drip dramatically on cue.

This technological feat paled in comparison to a different vision that caught young Linda's eye one night on the news while her mother ironed and she lounged in her dad's recliner.

"Mom," said the incredulous Linda, gesturing toward the reporter on the screen. Her name was Pauline Frederick, and from a spot on the steps of the United Nations headquarters in New York City, she was recounting a story about tanks rolling into Hungary. "That's a *woman*."

"Very good," her mother responded, wryly.

That a woman was reporting the news was, Linda said later, the "biggest thrill of my life." In the short time she'd been watching television, she'd never seen a woman delivering the news before. Suddenly, her ambitions shifted. "To hell with being Edward R. Murrow's secretary," she thought. "I'm going to aim higher."

Until the moment she saw Frederick, she said, "I didn't know women could do that."

* * *

Women didn't typically "do that." Indeed, Pauline Frederick had toiled for years before she earned the distinction of becoming the first female journalist to appear on network TV news. Indeed, it had been a struggle for her every step of the way.

As a precocious high school student, Frederick had found herself dazzled at the sight of her name in print after her school essay was published in the local paper. But that thrill wasn't enough to inspire her to accept the offer the paper later made for her to serve as women's editor. The society and fashion stories were pure drivel. Instead, she opted for a scholarship to study at American University in Washington. There, a college professor tamped down her ambition to practice international law, cautioning her how difficult it would be to break into the field. He encouraged her to instead focus on her original passion, journalism. After writing, and selling, a series of profiles of the wives of foreign ambassadors, Frederick landed a job as assistant to prominent radio commentator H. R. Baukhage. Though he valued her intellect and trusted her immensely, he informed her that she'd never make it on the air. The words of a broadcasting executive echoed his admonition: Women simply did not possess the "authoritative personality that men do," he said, and "that's good. Who likes an authoritative woman anyhow? Any woman who could manage this would sound too much like a man. So why not hire a man in the first place?"

This chauvinism, which drove the belief that women were of lesser authority and intellect, extended to print. Even when she managed to wrangle an invitation to travel the world on a once-in-a-lifetime postwar tour for journalists, as they arrived in far-flung locations, Frederick got more attention for the fact that she was a woman than interest in the stories she pitched. What did her husband think, asked curious reporters in China, who were shocked to hear the answer: "I don't have one." (She felt herself unmarriageable because of an emergency hysterectomy as a teenager. How could she be a wife if she was unable to reproduce?) Even when she masked her sex by using her initials, her stories didn't yield any takers.

The steady drumbeat of rejection and diminishment—including a snub by Murrow himself, who said he could call neither her nor her material "distinguished"—took a toll. "At times, it was so discouraging, I thought I'd just say, 'the heck with it,'" Frederick said, "but then I'd get just enough dander up to say I wasn't going to give in." She'd relieve the stress with a good, private cry and soldier on.

Her perseverance was not misguided. At age forty, Frederick finally got her first big break: a contract job as a reporter for ABC Radio. She was so happy to have the steady pay of $158 a week and a foot in the door that she didn't balk at being relegated to the women's beat.

One of her first assignments involved covering a forum on "How to Get a Husband," a lesson, she quipped, that she hadn't mastered. Another report looked at women's wartime quest to find that rare commodity, nylon stockings. When she pressed to cover hard news, her editor reminded her of what she'd heard time and again: "A woman's manner is not suited to news and serious discussion."

Ironically, it was because of her sex that she got the break that set her on the path to fame. One day, the assignment editor had two stories on the docket and one reporter. Sending Frederick out to cover a trucking strike, where there was the potential for violence, was too fraught. The other story involved an important meeting of foreign ministers who were working to hammer out a peace treaty. Luckily for Frederick, she'd earlier met some of the men involved, through her work for the columnist and commentator Baukhage. Here, her keen interest in international affairs served her well. The story she filed was so good that she kept being sent back to cover the talks, which ultimately would lead to the formation of the United Nations. A beat was born, and Pauline Frederick had been present at its creation.

Journalism might have been a man's world, but this tenacious, patient woman finally cracked into the sanctum. Covering the "ten-ring circus atmosphere" of the United Nations, she said, was to her an irresistible delight. Broadcasting live from the headquarters each day, she scored one exclusive after another.

At television's dawn, like most serious reporters, she'd expressed no interest in the medium. But the networks needed all hands on deck to achieve their promise of gavel-to-gavel presidential convention coverage in 1948.* Both parties were to hold their important gatherings in Philadelphia, a city wired with coaxial cable, which would allow for maximal national broadcasting transmission—eighteen stations in nine cities.

Frederick scrambled to prepare. What should she wear? How to style her hair and makeup for the visual medium? Even the experts at Elizabeth Arden's salon could offer no wisdom or tips on which cosmetics might work in this new medium to counter the impact of the early television cameras and the scorching lights.

On top of that, the blistering heat in the convention center proved

---

* Except for during *Howdy Doody*, which aired at 5:00 P.M. on Tuesdays and Thursdays. (When the puppet character announced he was running for president, NBC was deluged with nearly one hundred thousand requests for campaign buttons.)

particularly vexing for a woman, melting the makeup Frederick did apply, and wilting her hairdo. She found herself doing double duty to help her on-air guests, wives of lawmakers and the eight female members of the Eightieth Congress, in their own quest to be camera-ready. The visual medium also posed a question about eyeglasses—to wear or not. Some advised Frederick to keep hers on, for the specs made her look more official. Others voted no; they looked too frumpy.

Coverage of the conventions convinced network executives of television's potential as a news medium, but it didn't convince Frederick, who remained enamored of radio—and who preferred covering the United Nations to politics. Still, her assignments multiplied: In addition to six daily radio reports, now she was expected to deliver three television newscasts—and remain on standby for a host of others.

The requisite "glamour laws" of television, as Frederick called them, irked her to the heavens. "A man can look like Bela Lugosi if he is talented," she observed. "When a man stands up to speak, people listen, then look. When a woman gets up, people look; then, if they like what they see, they listen." Preparing for broadcast no longer meant reading, reporting, synthesizing, and writing; it required waking up hours before her male colleagues to primp and preen. Inevitably, in the middle of an unfolding news story, she'd have to drop everything and waste valuable time attending to her grooming.

Still, for the first lady network television correspondent, whom magazines described as a "tall lissome brunette of mellifluous voice and photogenic figure," as "capable as she is lovely," the investment was a necessary evil that allowed her to do what she loved.

As the United Nations grew, so did Frederick's stature. In fact, she became so synonymous with the institution that when, in 1961, UN secretary-general Dag Hammarskjöld died in a plane crash, the public flooded her mailbox with condolence cards.

Frederick's ascendance, though, hardly threw open the hiring gates for other female broadcasters. Surely, network executives maintained, lady viewers would be envious when beholding a "goddess with the right hairdo, makeup and dress, plenty of poise—and a brain besides?" But at least one young woman in southwestern New Mexico was anything but envious. Linda Cozby was inspired. She had no idea how to get where she wanted to go, but she figured education was the first start.

* * *

When students at Carlsbad High School chose to attend a four-year college, they typically ventured to Albuquerque to enroll at New Mexico State or the University of New Mexico. Linda, who'd won a prestigious National Merit Scholarship, had initially set her sights a bit farther away—on a private liberal arts school, Occidental College in Los Angeles. Her mother favored Mills, a women's college in Northern California. All Linda knew was that to achieve what she wished, she had to get the best possible education. The men's Ivy League schools were off-limits to women, but Mrs. Charles Feezer, a neighbor in Carlsbad with ties to the prestigious "Seven Sisters," considered the "women's Ivy League," convinced her to apply to three of them. Linda won a scholarship, choosing Wellesley, in a suburb of Boston.

That day in 1961 when she headed east on a train with her enormous trunk in tow was the first time she'd ventured farther from home than Oklahoma. The journey took three days and two nights—the first leg from Carlsbad to Las Cruces, then on to Chicago on the *Santa Fe Chief*, and from there to the magnificent, sprawling wooded campus she'd inhabit for the next four years. With its spectacular Lake Waban, its ponds, and its matrix of meandering paths, all skillfully coaxed by noted landscape architect Frederick Law Olmsted Jr., the Wellesley campus resembled an arboretum, or the English countryside.

Greeted by soaring maple and oak trees and the sweet smell of rhododendrons blooming outside the library, Linda settled into Bates dormitory, on the east side of campus. A mural of amber waves of grain honored its namesake, alumnus Katharine Lee Bates, class of 1880, who'd written the patriotic ode "America the Beautiful." In every corner, the school burst with pride and a sense of possibility.

It hadn't immediately felt that way. The East Coast girls laughed at Linda's southwestern twang, her speech peppered with country expressions like "fixin' to," and her use of two syllables for the word *striped*. Her clothing was just as out of place. That trunk she'd hauled from back home was loaded with bright dyed-to-match sweaters and skirts that wordlessly trumpeted to the refined denizens of the East Coast Establishment that she was not from around these parts. Her outerwear was similarly awkward. Her mother had taken an old hand-me-down alpaca coat and relined it with fake fur to insulate against the frost of New England. It was so clunky that Linda's arms couldn't lie flat. But at least it was warm, and when she slipped on the ice, it cushioned her fall.

The culture shock was offset by Linda's delight in inhabiting a place where women ruled the roost. Wellesley's president, Dr. Margaret Clapp, herself an alumnus of the school, was a historian who'd won the Pulitzer Prize in 1948 for her PhD thesis, which had been turned into a book, a biography of journalist and diplomat John Bigelow. Though she was not married herself, Clapp believed that married women should work outside the home to meet the needs of modern society. A liberal education, she said, was essential for women who became mothers, so they could "make the homes of this nation centers of activity, not retreats from life."

The same conflicting messages that haunted Barnard's campus a few years earlier during Susan's tenure continued here at this sister school: Achieving professionally might be important, but equally so was how to snag the right man to ensure one's future. To that end, Wellesley featured a "Marriage Lecture Series" that tackled matters of birth control, the psychology of male-female relationships, and navigating finances. Beyond the status of women, other social concerns were addressed. To participate in the "national effort to aide Negroes," Miss Clapp (who disdained the honorific "Dr.") invited eight Black women from southern schools to spend a year at Wellesley as "guest juniors." Lamenting how difficult it had been to attract qualified women of color to enroll at the school, the president hoped this would prove a helpful experiment during the national campaign for civil rights.

There was no avoiding other tumults of the 1960s. Teach-ins about the conflict in Vietnam were plentiful. During the Cuban Missile Crisis, Linda crouched in the corridors of the dormitory, away from the windows, as passing airplanes rumbled by, "afraid that we were listening to the end of the world."

Nestled in this oasis, where study and the habit of inquiry were encouraged, where critical thinking and writing clearly were valued, smart women ruled. Back in Carlsbad, except at her family's dinner table, "disagreeing had been disagreeable." At Wellesley, engaging in such debate was a prized part of the education. In the face of "dazzling" classmates, she felt cloaked in the sense of the possible. "You may have to work your ass off to do it," she learned, "but you can do it, whatever it is. You know, you want to become a rocket scientist? Fine. You want to write novels? Fine." Or even poetry. She contributed a plaintive villanelle to the *Wellesley Keynote*, the school's literary journal, but her sights were set professionally on broadcasting. That there might be obstacles on that path never occurred to her.

* * *

Linda never forgot her roots, or her longing for the good enchiladas she could get only back home. Midway through her sophomore year, she returned to the great Southwest for her coronation as Sun Princess in the annual Sun Carnival, riding on a float in an extravagant parade through the streets of El Paso, Texas, on New Year's Day. Later, she was seated with princesses from other area towns at the Sun Bowl football game and then danced the night away in black chiffon at a fancy ball.

Neither did she forget her father's admonition that she and her sister must learn to support themselves. It was a family joke that he believed neither of his girls would find men who would. So, that summer, despite the fact that she was an English, not a political science, major, she landed a paid internship in the DC office of New Mexico senator

Clinton Anderson. As crucial as the summer earnings of around seven hundred dollars was the front-row seat she had to the machinations of government—even if it did involve scut work: receptionist duties, running errands, operating office machines. She also got to witness what she called the "subtle facts of politics" and the "antics of Congress" as she peered in curiously on crucial committee hearings, heard Attorney General Robert Kennedy testify on civil rights, and mingled at parties with other students in the capital for the summer. Having had this experience allowed her to leapfrog into an advanced political science seminar back on campus that fall.

Come spring of her senior year, after the traditional hoop-rolling on the college lawn—the winner, it was believed, would be the first lucky girl to marry—the class of '65 listened as Mrs. Maurice T. Moore, class of '24, imparted her wish that the new graduates help conquer poverty and never stop learning: "I hope windows have been opened to you on too many vistas so alluring that you can't cease to explore further."

* * *

The vista presented to Linda was exactly what she'd hoped for: the dazzling chance to fly to London as part of an exchange program to learn the inner workings of the vaunted British Broadcasting Corporation, landing her one step closer to her goal. To raise money for her plane ticket, she worked in New York as a temp for a while.

Once overseas, she was assigned to work at the BBC News Service, which transmitted news from Britain to all corners of the empire via the largest shortwave radio network in the world. Her job, as a production secretary, involved carrying a clipboard and following a producer around—the kind of entry-level worker who, as she described, "does whatever she's told to do." While she learned the fundamentals of radio broadcasting, she couldn't help but notice the number of women in the halls. Most, she observed, were remnants of the war years, when women had to be brought in to work while men served on the front lines. Once the soldiers returned, they'd refused to leave.

Finding a workplace chock-full of female colleagues would not be her experience after her seventeen months overseas were through and she landed back in New York City, the center of the news business. The economy was booming, and finding a job wasn't the problem. It was finding a job you actually *wanted*, one that utilized your brain. Linda might be ready to graduate to the next level, but employers didn't wish to allow it. The law passed in 1964 had not caught up with reality. At NBC, a prospective boss offered to introduce her to a lady staff member who'd been a researcher for a decade; wouldn't she be happy in *that* role? Linda threw a fit. Smart aspiring reporters knew that "researcher" was code for a go-nowhere job where women were parked until they got themselves a husband, at which point she'd inevitably quit.

"It was in neon," Linda said. " 'This is the only job a woman can have.' "

Eventually, she wedged her toe in the door of WCBS Newsradio 88,* which had recently debuted an all-news-and-information format designed to compete with WINS, another all-news station in town. Commercial radio, recognizing its lot as a stepchild to television, had amped up its utilitarian role, opting to showcase snappy news, rat-a-tat-tat style, replete with an endless stream of time, traffic, weather, and the latest sports, all designed to hook the listener. Ads blanketed the city to trumpet the local station's "dimensional" reporting, everything from live breaking news transmitted by field reporters carrying walkie-talkies and shortwave mobile units to editorials, weather forecasts, Broadway reviews, and of course, sports, sports, and more sports.

For a self-described "flat-chested, brainy" woman who didn't wear makeup or a watch and didn't carry a handbag, radio seemed the perfect medium. Linda, imbued with the luster of having worked for, as some called it, "the Beeb," was permitted to write and produce the features that aired at the back of the morning newscasts. The front-of-show hard

---

* To hear what WCBS News sounded like in its early days, visit http://www.nyradionews.com/wcbs/index.html.

news was reserved for men. She hungered to cover that news herself, as an on-air reporter.

While her male colleagues were kind enough, and happy to teach her the ropes, she couldn't help but notice that the few other women in the newsroom with more experience were still relegated to second-class status—like the pugnacious Liz Trotta and Mary Panga-los, "brave, aggressive, ferocious" dervishes in the field who "spilled their blood and guts" only to have, Linda observed, their voices cut out of the stories. "Loophole women," the second-wave feminist writer Caroline Bird called them, window-dressing to "prove [that men] weren't barring everyone else." Their presence did not, in fact, mean that women were considered equal or had the same possibilities for career growth.

Pangalos had worked her way off the women's beat at the New York paper *Newsday* the way women typically did: by pitching a great story and executing it well. With the eyes of the nation tilting toward space, her idea was to convince NASA to let her take the astronaut's test—and she became the first woman to do so. After that five-part series, she wrote another, on the tribulations of Black performers in Hollywood, which landed her an invitation to speak on a television program. When an executive heard the plucky, attractive woman frankly dissecting racial discrimination in the entertainment business, he made her a dazzling offer: Would she join the powerful New York City network affiliate WCBS as its first female reporter?

The answer was a resounding yes. Who wouldn't jump at the chance to enter the glamorous world of broadcasting? But almost as quickly as she'd embarked on her broadcasting career, Pangalos realized she'd made a terrible mistake. Compared to print, this kind of reporting was shallow. The cameramen ganged up on her, because of both her sex and her youth. Someone muttered that her breasts were her best assets. Executives used their dislike of her voice as an excuse for cutting her out of stories. When she landed a coveted interview with prizefighter Muhammad Ali, her producers arranged for a man to do the honors. She'd have been better off staying at the paper.

Witnessing Pangalos's struggle dismayed aspiring reporter Linda. Being smart and tough and not worrying what people thought of you were clearly essential ingredients to survival in the business of journalism. But such tenacity and fortitude alone weren't enough. For women to get the jobs they desired, much less the respect, seemed an elusive dream.

CHAPTER FIVE
Purposes

A detour from Linda's ambitions arrived in the form of a man. She met Fred Wertheimer through mutual friends. He was born and raised in Brooklyn, the son of an accountant who "believed in playing by the rules" and a mother who had a "great sense of fairness and justice." He'd followed his older brother to the University of Michigan, where he proceeded to coach the swimming and water polo teams. Next, he was admitted to Harvard Law School. To avoid the draft, he enlisted in the U.S. Army Reserve.

When he returned to New York, he spent six months looking for a job on Wall Street. He wasn't the sort to gaze inward, but he wrestled with his inability to find work: Maybe he simply didn't have what it took to succeed. Then again, maybe *they* were wrong.

Deciding to focus on the latter possibility, he bolstered his confidence and relocated to Washington, where he landed a job working at the Securities and Exchange Commission. From there, it took three years of writing letters to members of Congress before he found the work he wanted on Capitol Hill. His position as legal counsel and press secretary to Massachusetts representative Silvio Conte offered a crash course in politics.

After Fred and Linda married in New York in June 1969, they left their jobs to embark on a three-month driving tour of Europe, traveling all over the Continent in a little Volkswagen. Back in Washington, Fred rejoined Conte for his reelection campaign. After a year, he decided to take a break; it was Linda's turn to find work. Through a friend on the Hill, Fred had heard about a start-up radio network spawned by the Public Broadcasting Act. The founders of National Public Radio had decided to locate the network in Washington, DC, to be close to the FCC and broadcast lobbying operations. The new network was currently hiring for an as-yet-unnamed magazine show that would feed out daily across the nation to ninety member stations.

NPR had moved into the Cafritz Building, at 1625 I Street NW, an architecturally revolutionary structure that featured an interior garage at its core, allowing tenants the modern convenience of driving directly to their floor so they could park just steps from their desks. Fortunately, given the noise this generated, these were only temporary quarters.

There were many factors to be determined about the new venture, but this much was known: About ninety stations across thirty-two states had qualified as charter members of the new network by dint of their reach and professionalism. These stations, in turn, had been promised that at 5:00 P.M. eastern time, on May 3, 1971, a ninety-minute program would begin. The choice of length was pulled out of the sky. An hour seemed too skimpy, and two hours seemed too long a time to fill each day. The time this show would air required more thoughtful consideration. Though mornings were the most popular time for listeners to tune in to radio, most noncommercial stations didn't get around to turning on their transmitters until noon. Besides, staffing an afternoon show was logistically easier than one that aired in the A.M., which would require workers to arrive, at the least, in the middle of the night.

Who would be the star of the show? Program director Siemering disdained the "white male voice of authority" tone of commercial media, the "plastic, faceless men" who starred in the network television news—the type of person who would typically be cast in such roles. To that end, he pushed back against the suggestion from the Corporation for Public Broadcasting that NPR should appoint veteran ABC broadcaster Edward P. Morgan as host.

Morgan himself was no fan of broadcasting's status quo. Before he'd left the network that employed him for years, he'd signed off by chastising it for "fertilizing the wastelands of the airwaves with the manure of utter mediocrity." The output of commercial media was so bad, he'd said, that the ads were often better than the programs themselves. He'd taken refuge in public television, in one of its very first offerings, an innovative news program called *Public Broadcasting Laboratory*, which promised a unique blend of information, education, and entertainment. Yet even though his views were simpatico with NPR's and his experience vast, Siemering felt Morgan's name and voice were too familiar to audiences. Installing him in the host's seat would immediately spotlight the focus on him, not the wider mission.

Instead, a different white man who'd escaped commercial media landed the job. Though journalist Robert Conley had earlier been passed over for the position as NPR's president, he'd been hired anyway in an unspecified role, purely for his journalistic bona fides. Besides reporting for the *New York Times*, Conley had worked in Africa for NBC. The belief was that his talents could be applied somewhere in the emerging service. Quayle and Siemering decided he had just the credibility without the distraction of celebrity to serve as host of their broadcast.

In keeping with Siemering's wish to offer a diversity of voices, he also extended an offer to broadcaster George Foster, the first Black correspondent for CBS News, to serve as cohost. Minorities in on-air roles were as rare as women, much less in the starring role. But Foster turned down the chance to leave the vaunted network for an untested one. So, a single-host format it would be.

As for what this program would cover: Siemering could more clearly define what he didn't want NPR to sound like than describe how it should. In a poetic mission statement, he defined its purpose: to "celebrate the human experience" and "encourage a sense of active constructive participation, rather than apathetic helplessness." In no way should they mimic the screech and tone of commercial broadcasts, or attempt to compete with them. As envisioned by Siemering, NPR was to be quieter, more constructive, and more illuminating than what could be found on conventional commercial broadcasting—and should leave whoever listened "more responsive, more informed human beings and intelligent responsible citizens of their communities and the world."

What was known in the business as "hard news," a recitation of the day's headlines, did little to achieve that goal. In Siemering's estimation, that kind of reporting was actually "easy news"—grabbing handouts at briefings and news conferences, rewriting them, distilling the information into sound bites and headlines. The nuance, the digging, the production, the analysis, the *art*—that was more compelling, and what he imagined for his program.

There must be a balance, too, in the types of stories. Siemering believed it was possible to get a better idea of what was happening in the nation by covering cultural affairs and by talking to regular people, not just bureaucrats and policy wonks. Encouraging stations across the network to submit stories was a solid way to reflect diverse perspectives. Easier said than done: Most stations were ill-equipped to generate taped reports, and, besides, the only way to transmit them to the network was through the mail, hardly a means for timely submission.

For his staff in DC, he sought out potential employees with a variety of backgrounds. A wide pool of prospects simply didn't exist. Those with any experience in radio news were, for the most part, unwilling to risk joining a start-up that paid a third of what commercial broadcast outfits would. Someone simply looking for a job to pay their mortgage was of no interest, either. Siemering needed people who hungered to create something new, people who said, "God, I'd love to do this. I've been dreaming of this opportunity for a long time." As a consequence, he relied on word-of-mouth referrals.

* * *

Which is how a young woman named Linda came to, in the winter of 1971, sit before Siemering. She arrived with the appropriate eagerness, but her résumé raised a red flag. Wellesley College? That was an elite private school. Elite, rich—that kind of mindset didn't square with the populist appeal he was after. When Linda sensed his hesitance and explained that, in fact, she was a grocer's daughter from New Mexico who'd attended the fancy school on scholarship, his prejudice melted away. That she had experience at CBS, a commercial station, could be a minus—mimicking that kind of sound was just what he didn't want to do—but this was tempered by her time at the more august BBC. Plus, he couldn't overlook the fact that she knew how to edit audio tape, a valuable skill that involved razor blades, a grease pencil, sticky white tape, and exacting precision. One false move, and you could bloody your fingers—not to mention the work.

The title she was given, production assistant, wasn't meant to restrict her contributions. Siemering wasn't keen on titles, anyway. For the show to build the way he wished, he needed an all-hands-on-deck collective, like a repertory theater troupe, where everyone could play multiple roles. The organizational chart wasn't so critical as was having enough creative people around who could turn on a dime.

Linda considered using her maiden name, as more modern married women had begun to do. But, she said, Fred seemed to prefer that she use his. She didn't have a preference, so it was "Linda Wertheimer," not "Linda Cozby," who came to be listed on the staff roster as of March 1, 1971, two months before the show was scheduled to hit the air.

While Linda was unique in having had radio experience, she wasn't in another way. Half the people being hired were women: Diane Epstein, Gwen Hudley, Carol Kadushin, Kris Mortensen, Kati Wetzel, Carolyn Welch, Barbara Newman; there was even a female sound technician, Renee Chaney. In early April, another woman joined the roster, someone Quayle knew from his days at the Educational Radio Network, a new mother ready for stimulation outside the "goo-goo, ga-ga" of her now-sixteen-month-old son. Susan Stamberg agreed to come on board part time as an associate producer. She knew how to cut tape, too, and had more practical experience than just about anyone else on staff.

Hiring all these women wasn't a conscious decision. Siemering hired the best people he could find. If they happened to be female, good. It helped that some were subsidized by parents or husbands, which made them able to agree to the low pay he could offer. A man expecting to support a family on what NPR could pay couldn't make do.

Now it was time to zero in on the name for this new program. A contest was held among the staff. Suggestions included *Our Daily Bread*, *Give Us This Day*, and one borrowed from Siemering's old station, *This Is Radio*. Operations manager George Geesey, another former colleague of Susan's, submitted the winner: *All Things Considered*. This title, said Siemering, "conveyed the range of our interests plus our reluctance to draw conclusions."

Since furniture had yet to be delivered, and the studio equipment yet to be installed, the first staff of *All Things Considered* sat on the floor listening to stories and discussing what worked and what did not. What didn't, Siemering explained, was the preachy, stilted tone of commercial news they'd all heard before. The pace was too high-temperature, frenetic, rushed. On NPR, they must speak in regular voices, as regular people, not announcers, "in order to allow the country to hear itself."

It wasn't until two weeks before launch that equipment was ready for them to put theory into practice by creating mock broadcasts. Instantly it became clear that, despite all the ruminating, they were absolutely not prepared to churn out ninety fresh minutes each day. Linda lamented, "The pieces were all the wrong size, some too short, some too long. We couldn't put together a decent road map for the actual show."

It was also apparent that Conley, with his shock of white hair and his beautiful intonation, had a terrible problem with timing. He would run too long, or pause too long. When alerted to this, he'd throw up his hands in despair. Occasionally, he'd lean back in his chair and tip over, leaving him to read the lead-in to the next story while leaning in to the microphone from the floor. The man trusted to serve as the voice of the show appeared to be, Linda observed, "marching to a different drummer, one that no one else could hear."

To give some order to the chaos, Linda proposed an organizational suggestion borrowed from her time at the BBC: install a giant assignment whiteboard on which to lay out the show's rundowns, or "road maps." It seemed like a very reasonable way for everyone to see clearly what was expected, with the format and the cues and the scripts. By default, she found herself stepping into the role of director of the program. She became the "person with the whip" who went around shouting, "Where are your stories?" and logging the show's road maps on paper, which she stapled into three-ring binders. Timing the program to make sure it ended precisely at 6:30 P.M. was far trickier.

As each day elapsed, bringing them closer to their May 3 debut, no one felt any readier for launch. At least the telephonic and microwave technology that would allow member stations to receive their signal live was now operational. The system got a live test when NPR transmitted taped concerts from the Los Angeles Philharmonic and live hearings from the Senate Foreign Affairs Committee on the Vietnam War. Miraculously, the interconnection worked. It was magic—although not bulletproof, and hardly of the best sound quality.

Another preshow test came on Saturday, May 1, 1971, when NPR went live for three and a half hours to cover a massive antiwar demonstration that attracted thousands of people, including many veterans, to the capital. Military police stood poised to stop them.

"It's like Woodstock, a really groovy community," one protestor told a reporter. "But, of course it's the war and stopping it that matters."

The marchers vowed to stay around town till Monday in order to clog rush-hour traffic and shut down the city's operations. This meant that when *All Things Considered* debuted, there'd be a guaranteed lead story right outside their front door. That was a boost. None of the staff could believe their good fortune.

On Linda's bus ride to the office from her apartment near the waterfront, she found herself taken by the juxtaposing smells of a perfect May morning, "scented with spring flowers and tear gas," not to mention mace, chants, anger, and helicopters swirling over ahead.

That first day was a blur, a mad dash of editing and preparation. And as the clock ticked toward launch time, Linda panicked in the control room. Not one bit of tape was ready to go—not even the lead story. She was terrified, completely terrified; she'd learned in her short broadcasting career that the worst possible thing that could ever happen was dead airtime. But the affiliates were waiting; the show had to go on.

The engineer opened the microphone, and Siemering cued the host.

"From National Public Radio in Washington, I'm Robert Conley, with *All Things Considered*." The theme music swelled, a perky, modern, electronic trill (starring a Putney synthesizer) furnished by a University of Wisconsin composer and music director at WHA named Don

Voegeli.* Conley spoke again. "In the top of the day's news, the crush, catcalls, flux and flow of the demonstrations in Washington against the war in Southeast Asia . . . As a result of those demonstrations today, somewhere between sixty-five hundred and seven thousand protestors have been picked up by the police."

For the next four minutes, the premiere host of *All Things Considered* verbally tap-danced to fill the time, waiting for the tape to arrive, describing the mayhem on the streets as demonstrators clashed with law enforcement: thousands of arrests, the squadrons of police, the fires set by protestors—until, mercifully, finally, the piece arrived in the studio and got threaded up on the playback machine. The host was so caught up with his riffing that at first he didn't hear Siemering alert him that the tape had arrived and was cued up to play.

The reason for the tape's delay? The man cutting the piece was caught up in stitching together tape collected by three reporters who'd fanned out around the city. Another issue: The guerrilla-style documentary news story that was supposed to clock in at twenty-eight minutes wound up lasting only twenty-three. The editor, it seemed, had forgotten to bring his stopwatch to work. But the piece sizzled with action, energy, the voices of the defiant protestors chanting and clashing with law enforcement. "Today is another Saigon," said one disabled veteran.†

Once that tape played out, other stories trickled into the studio. A live conversation dissecting the protests followed; then a fifteen-minute piece from Canada on poetry and World War I. A nine-minute newscast summarizing the day's headlines was compiled and read by staffer Jack Mitchell. At age thirty, he was a pre–Public Broadcasting Act veteran of educational media from Michigan who'd been NPR's very first hire.

Filling out the program: a profile of an inventive barber in Iowa

---

* To hear the original theme, visit https://www.npr.org/2002/05/03/1142774/all-things -considered-a-lasting-theme.
† To hear the protest piece, visit https://www.npr.org/2020/04/14/820509208 /thousands-of-young-people-risk-arrest-in-demonstrations-against-war. The complete first episode is available in the Library of Congress as well as at the Paley Center for Media, in New York City.

who'd pivoted his faltering business, diminished because of men's preference for long hair—he'd started shaving women's legs, seventy-five cents for the first leg, a quarter for the second.* "This is the kind of thing that might cause a rush to barbering schools, don't you think?" asked the reporter, Wayne Olson, of affiliate station WOI, his voice tinged with just a hint of lasciviousness.

Staff production assistant Gwen Hudley offered a chilling profile of a twenty-six-year-old nurse now addicted to drugs.

Poet Allen Ginsberg and his father talked about the impact of recreational drug culture on youth.

At twenty-five minutes after six, five minutes before they were scheduled to end, they ran out of material and steam. Conley, exhausted, signed off, leaving affiliates to scramble to fill the time.

Getting through this debut had been an ordeal. From his perch at the other end of the radio in Wisconsin, one board member declared, "Our child has been born, and it is ugly."

Tomorrow, they'd all work to beautify their "baby," though it wouldn't get easier or smoother for a long, long time. Not a day would go by without a tape reel being hurled like a Frisbee into the control room at the last minute, or breaking during playback, and it was never quite clear who'd show up for work or whether there'd be enough stories to fill the time. Live production, fueled by adrenaline, was amped into overdrive as they created not just a new show but an entirely new sound.

Linda, the grocer's daughter from New Mexico, put it more succinctly: "A daily program was just like the dishes," she observed, "As soon as you've got them all washed and dried, it's time to eat again."

---

* The barbershop piece can be heard here: https://www.npr.org/series/5383780/all-things-considered-turns-35.

CHAPTER SIX
Nina

Several weeks before making his American debut in late 1935, Roman Totenberg, a "brilliant young violinist of excellent European reputation," performed for Italy's king, Victor Emmanuel III, at the Quirinal Palace in Rome. To appear before royalty, the twenty-four-year-old virtuoso was told, one must wear top hat and cape. Given that he possessed neither, the musician borrowed the necessary haberdashery from the ambassador of his native Poland. Roman was also instructed not to turn his back on the monarch, which was considered a breach of royal protocol. After his masterful performance of a selection of sonatas, he shuffled backward off the stage, fixing his gaze on his host and never allowing his eyes to avert, the exemplary picture of austerity and propriety.

That the United States was entirely different became evident the minute he arrived, as one "agreeable" and "efficient" woman after another assisted him in becoming situated. Back in Europe, this player of "uncommon sensibility" explained, important women often proved their mettle at the expense of their feminine charms. "You here are well put-together, well-balanced people," he observed. Estimable, competent, and attractive American women were almost as impressive to the young musician as the delectable dessert he discovered here, the ice-cream soda.

In Washington, DC's Constitution Hall on November 7, Roman brought down the house with what a reviewer called his "brilliant interpretation" of Beethoven's Concerto in D Minor. Selections from Mozart, Sibelius, and Mussorgsky were also on the program. The American socialite Mrs. Alice Dows, whom he'd met in Berlin and with whose family he'd been invited to live in France, had made the necessary introductions for this tour and arranged his passage. She even finessed his use of the Stradivarius that belonged to the late Nicholas Longworth, a congressman and amateur violinist who happened to have been her lover. For a musician of his stature to make his American debut in a city other than the acknowledged cultural center, New York, was unheard of. But Roman found an appreciative public in the nation's capital city: The DC audience demanded that he return for six additional bows.

Among those dazzled by Totenberg's masterful playing were President and Mrs. Roosevelt, who invited him to the White House to entertain at the second event of the 1936 social season, an official state dinner in honor of Vice President Jack Garner. While performers at such affairs were not paid, the mere invitation to appear was akin to being gifted a bag of gold: royalty, American-style.

Roman marveled at the informality. The First Lady personally served the meal to the eighty-eight guests seated around a horseshoe-shaped table adorned with bouquets of light pink roses and baby primula. The guest of honor was so relaxed he kicked off his shoes, and at one point, Mrs. Roosevelt sat on the floor.

The after-dinner entertainment program also included the soprano Lily Pons and the writer and actress Cornelia Otis Skinner, who lit up the guests with laughter with her monologue "A Nebraskan Being Presented at Court." Mr. Totenberg, Mrs. Roosevelt reported in her syndicated newspaper column, played "delightfully."

He'd come to the beauty of violin at age six in Moscow, where the family had moved for his father's work as an architect. Neighbor Alexei Ermolov, the elegant concertmaster of the Bolshoi Opera, detected nascent skill in his young pupil, taking to the streets with the boy and their instruments to busk during the ravages of the Russian Revolution. Passersby rewarded the entertainers with essential food staples difficult to find during this time of famine—bread and butter and sugar, which helped Roman feed his family.

The twin wonders of music-making and the thrall of an audience intoxicated the young musician, who was trotted around to perform at Communist Party meetings. An announcement would be made that "Comrade Totenberg" was about to play. When a boy emerged, the audience laughed. They weren't expecting a kid. But when the kid began to glide his bow across the strings, their amusement morphed into rapture.

A brief detour to study mathematics reinforced for the young prodigy that music must be his destiny. In his less than a quarter century on earth, Totenberg had graduated from these street-side serenades for survival to the heady thrill of entertaining world leaders.

After his successful appearances in the United States, he resumed his concertizing around Europe and even sailed to Brazil for a South American tour. All the while, he collected shelves of prizes and lists of patrons.

The war hastened Roman's decision to leave Europe for good. Frightening stories swirled about Nazis, beatings, fear; anti-Jewish riots erupted in his native Poland. He was grateful for the distinguished artist visa that allowed him, and eventually his mother, to safely relocate in 1938 to these great United States, the country he so admired—where ice-cream sodas flowed plentifully and where he continued to flourish.

As Roman adjusted to the clanking cityscape outside his apartment at the Wellington Hotel on Seventh Avenue and Fifty-Fifth Street in New York, he communicated in French until he added English to his wide repertoire of languages. Music remained his most beloved mode of communication. Joining the New Friends of Music Chamber Orchestra, he played frequent concerts at Town Hall and on the radio. Commercial work, advertising, background music, and Broadway allowed him to earn good money, some of which he sent back home to relatives and friends. The harsh reality of life there under the "nonstop fear and terror" of Hitler weighed heavily, even at a distance, especially now that his only sister and her family were nowhere to be found. (Miraculously, they were discovered several years later.)

During those dark days of devastation, the handsome young virtuoso received a "burst of light" when the niece of beauty impresario Helena Rubenstein invited him to a party at the East Side duplex of New

York senator Jacob Javits. Across the room, the guest who stood out was the dark-haired beauty Melanie Shroder, who worked as a fund-raiser for the Democratic Party and President Roosevelt. The smitten Totenberg asked for a dance and then boldly invited Melanie out to the balcony for a chat. She wasn't interested. He persisted: Would she come for cocktails at the apartment he shared with his mother? Another no. Respectable women didn't visit a man's home alone. But, he assured her, other friends would be there, too. She caved.

They married eight months later.

Aside from the physical attraction, Melanie proved the perfect match for this rising star: She herself had studied piano at Juilliard and understood the commitment it took for a musician of Roman's stature to succeed. She made friends easily, could hold her own at parties, and ably played hostess, too—especially once Roman schooled her in the Polish custom of providing guests an abundance of food and vodka.

With the scourge of war scuttling concert tours of Europe, the newly minted husband earned income in other ways, taking a job as chamber music director at WQXR, the city's classical station, appearing live on the air as part of the house quartet and for other programs, playing for hire on Broadway and Radio City Music Hall.

Melanie delivered their first child, Nina, on January 14, 1944, thirteen days after Roman's thirty-third birthday. At his father-in-law's insistence, the Totenberg family moved to the Turin, a twelve-story building on Central Park West at Ninety-Third Street. The thirty dollars in additional rent seemed steep, but the neighbors—artists, poets, intellectuals—made for a congenial community.

From early on, Nina's force of personality was on display. As the family maid slept one day, Nina ran wild in her bedroom. Hearing the fuss from his apartment, their neighbor, René d'Harnoncourt, director of the Museum of Modern Art, arrived to babysit.

After earning admission to a flossy private school, Nina threw a fit. "I think everybody here is a big doody in the pants," she whined, recognizing that school would mean separation from her beloved mother. As Roman walked his daughter back home in the rain, he asked why she had acted out. She responded, "Because I felt that way." So, he pushed her into a puddle of water.

"Why did you do that?" she demanded.

"Because I felt that way," he said.

Lesson learned. His parenting philosophy was clear: "Children are like dogs. They need to know where the fence is."

Despite or because of the rules, Nina and her two younger sisters adored their father. Though he was away much of the time performing, they longed for this warm, loving, incredibly sweet man to return. Their mother was no different: The girls were well aware of the love their parents had for each other. Their mother's eyes, they observed, would sparkle at the mere mention of Roman's name.

The violin he practiced for hours each day, they also knew, was no mere instrument; nor was playing it just a job. In the hands of their father, it was a "living vehicle of human expression." Music was an extension of his soul, a way of life.

Just as intensely as he was devoted to his craft, he was also filled with love and respect for this great nation that had given him refuge. He'd proudly taken the oath of citizenship. Nina and her siblings were raised to revere democracy, flaws and all. The lesson was made easier when letters arrived from Europe that had clearly been opened by censors.

The family's days glimmered with music and friends—blintzes served amid the bustle and glitz of the Russian Tea Room, dinners consumed in the dimly lit hubbub of Sardi's—before they decamped to the leafy, child-friendly northern suburb of Scarsdale.

At Fox Meadow Elementary, Nina appeared as Maid Marion in the third-grade production of *Robin Hood to the Rescue*. The most disruptive of antics that occurred in this bucolic burg involved dodging firecrackers tossed at her and a friend by rogue boys. As Nina grew, it became clear that she possessed an operatic voice, like her paternal grandfather, who himself had longed to be a professional singer. "A superlative soprano," her classmates called her. But just as her mother had dropped piano, neither was her eldest daughter interested in the hours of daily practice necessary to become a great performer, the commitment she saw in her father. She was more attracted to a career as a cop, which she knew, for a girl, was not an option.

Searching for a role model who was both successful and assertive, Nina found herself magnetized to Nancy Drew, devouring the novels she discovered in the local library featuring the fictional girl detective. Nancy was the quintessential modern young woman, "as cool as Mata Hari and as sweet as Betty Crocker," as one writer described her. Not only did Nancy have a handsome boyfriend, Ned, but she also owned a fabulous car, a roadster, which she proudly and competently fixed herself. The perceptive young Nina observed that Nancy's mother was dead, "so she didn't even have to compete for her father's affections." That, and she solved all kinds of mysteries. This was something Nina was certain she herself could do.

At Scarsdale High, she contributed to the school's literary magazine, *Jabberwock*, and served as student director on a production of *The Diary of Anne Frank*, staged on a dazzling set; their performance won a rave from the *Scarsdale Inquirer*: "[I]t is still hard to believe that high school students and not scarred and seasoned sufferers breathed so much life into this play."

The star of the show was Nina's young classmate Liza Minnelli, daughter of the famous and legendarily troubled actress and singer Judy Garland. From her early days as a child performer on the vaudeville circuit and alongside elfin Mickey Rooney, Garland had become a movie star after playing a defining role as Dorothy in the 1939 film *The Wizard of Oz*. Her fame didn't offset her troubles, though. Over the years, she'd suffered a nervous breakdown, had attempted suicide, and undergone electroshock therapy.

Nina's perceptiveness struck again. Though she was just a few years older than Liza, she was sensitive enough to notice that her classmate was emotionally frail, so she invited her home to Fox Meadow Road for a dose of Melanie, her adoring and kind mother. Nina was happy to share.

* * *

Besides motherhood, among many other concerns competing for Judy Garland's attention during this period was a headline-grabbing libel suit she'd filed against the *New York Herald-Tribune*'s Marie Torre. The journalist had risen from a secretarial job at another paper, bypassing the usual purgatory of the women's pages and eventually talking her way into the job of "amusements editor," though she was given neither the salary nor the title of the man she replaced. Overseeing TV listings and coverage of the then-new medium was a big improvement over having to write about ballgowns. Torre treated her work with the gravity of a world affairs correspondent. In fact, she broke so many stories that her byline frequently appeared on the front page, which led to her becoming a hot-shot syndicated radio-TV columnist.

On January 10, 1957, Torre spotlighted the recent travails of Ms. Garland, who hadn't delivered a promised high-profile special to CBS. Why? Torre asked. An unnamed executive explained, "I wouldn't be surprised if it's because she thinks she's terribly fat." Two months later, just as Torre returned home from the hospital with her brand-new baby boy, a lawyer from the paper arrived to inform her that the star had filed a $1.39 million lawsuit against CBS for libel and breach of contract—all because of Torre's column. A District court judge was now ordering the reporter to reveal the name of her source.

He must be "foggy in the crumpet," she exclaimed. No reporter worth her salt revealed the identity of a confidential source. It was part of the journalistic code that enabled reporters to gather information. Divulging the name of someone who had spoken to you on the record, without attribution, posed a threat not just to "press freedom but also to the American way."

There were twelve states in the nation that provided immunity to journalists who refused such an order, Torre discovered, but New York was not one of them. The suit dragged on, and eventually she was ordered to serve ten days in prison.

Arriving at the Hudson County Jail in Kearny, New Jersey, she had in her possession two juicy, door-stopper novels to keep her company in her seventh-floor cell: *Dr. Zhivago*, by Boris Pasternak, and John O'Hara's *From the Terrace*. Celebrities such as Desi Arnaz and Jackie Gleason volunteered to write her column while the "Joan of Arc of journalism" was locked up.

"I have great hope," she said, as she began her sentence, "that this will lead to legislation protecting a newspaperman's sources."*

* * *

Nina, aspiring Nancy Drew, followed the plight of Marie Torre with great curiosity, intrigued by the daring of the gutsy lady journalist who defied authority and the plight of her school chum's famous, troubled mother. But she had nary an inkling that the Torre/Garland incident would foreshadow an experience in her own future. She was still trying to sort out how she'd arrive there.

Journalism seemed as close to detective work as she could imagine. Canvassing door-to-door in support of John F. Kennedy's presidential campaign unlocked her intrigue in politics, as did reading the gritty, page-turning account of that political battle by Theodore H. White, the bestseller *The Making of the President: 1960*. But working in government wasn't her goal. Observing the action was. Her desire to have a "seat at the table," to become "a witness to history," set aflame, she confessed that a more honest title for her aspiration might be "professional gossip."

---

* Torre's fame did indeed soar as a result of her imprisonment. Doubleday paid her a fortune to write her memoir, and she landed a job as a television personality in Pittsburgh.

Off she went to study communications at Boston University, where her father, coincidentally, had just been hired to teach. "Nina, we're both freshmen," he told her.

While Professor Totenberg excelled as a teacher, student Totenberg decided almost instantly that college was not her cup of tea. Sitting still made her "itchy," and studying for tests seemed a waste of time; she cut classes "like mad." She was, by her own admission, more of a doer than a "profound thinker."

She consulted with her beloved mother. At a time when few women even attended college, Melanie had graduated from Pembroke, the women's affiliate of Brown University, in Providence, Rhode Island. Despite Nina's legacy advantage, she hadn't herself been granted admission. With "lousy, lousy SAT scores," she felt "way too stupid."

Though Melanie believed her daughter's interest in a profession so unfavorable to women was the "dream of a torn-off head," Nina was surprised by her guidance. Drop out, her mother advised, and work for a few years. "The worst you can do is not succeed," she said, "in which case, you can always finish."

But for women, it wasn't as simple as will or talent or liberating oneself from the classroom. Nina got turned away by the first paper she approached because women simply weren't hired. When she did land an entry-level job, at New England's largest daily paper, the *Boston Record-American*, she was assigned to the only place where aspiring female reporters were allowed to work, the women's pages, the repository in the paper for issues of relevance to women: society news about who wore which gown to what event, fashion shows and recipes, and wedding notices. Only one female reporter at the paper was allowed to cover hard news, and she was a "tough broad," Nina observed—exactly what she herself aspired to be.

To prove her mettle, Nina assigned herself a story on a controversial topic: oral contraceptives. At the dawn of the sexual revolution, in polite society, the mere discussion of premarital sex and pregnancy prevention was taboo. When these issues were addressed in the media, psychiatrists typically got included in the coverage, in order to dissect the damaging emotional consequences of physical intimacy on the youth who dared to engage in it. The first birth control pill had been federally legalized in 1960, but questions loomed over its safety and morality. Some states still outlawed it, and typically, only married women could receive a prescription. Clinics on some college campuses, nonetheless, were beginning to make it available.

Nina got to work, making appointments to find out how college women obtained "the Pill." With enough preliminary "string" to pitch the idea, she wrote a memo to Eddie Holland, who started at the *Boston Record-American* as a copy boy in high school and, by the time Nina arrived, had worked his way up to managing editor.

His response: "Nina, are you a virgin?"

Yes, Nina answered.

And so, he replied, "I can't let you do this. Have you ever had an internal examination?"

No, Nina said.

He repeated his refusal, and that was that. It didn't occur to her to fight. To be a woman, particularly a young woman trying to establish herself in a male-dominated field, meant choosing one's battles.

Desperate to graduate from the "girly" beat, she volunteered to work for free in the evenings after her regular shift. In the twisted logic of discrimination, volunteering on an evening shift was allowed, while working for pay was not. She had the opportunity to cover crime, chase ambulances, report on murders and, on occasion, a bit of local politics, such as school committee meetings. Her byline never appeared on the stories; she was expected to serve as the eyes and ears in the field for the men who wrote them. But to Nina, this anonymity, not to mention the twenty-hour workdays, were a worthy exchange for invaluable field experience—especially if it rescued her from the social pages.

Cruising around town with a staff photographer, the radio tuned in to the police and fire scanners, Nina kept a keen ear for a bit of news, and the duo would head where the action took them. While her colleague snapped pictures, Nina would scribble down the details for the copy.

Along with honing her powers of observation, working in newspaper newsrooms ultimately allowed her to develop another useful skill: reading upside down and backward. This helped her guide the men in the press room who painstakingly set each word in hot lead type for printing. Peering overhead, she could figure out precisely where to trim an inch from a story that might be too long.

* * *

Eventually, a weekly community paper in a small city north of Boston, the *Peabody Times*, gave her a job. With a circulation of just several thousand, it was the kind of place that didn't care whether a reporter was a man, woman, or hedgehog, as long as he, she, or it could produce, nonstop. Some weeks, Nina would wind up writing every single story on the front page. She loved it. Fueled by the adrenaline not just of the chase but of the resulting byline, she liked to call herself a "deadline Dick."

One day, she heard on the police scanner that a robbery was under way at a local bank. She dialed up the branch and identified herself to the man who answered the phone. He responded, "This is one of the robbers." Flummoxed, the bad guys took off with the loot—and got busted. Nina's account of the botched heist antics made the front page—although, truth be told, it probably would have no matter what she wrote.*

Then there were the unpleasant parts of the job, like the time she was dispatched to the home of a little boy who'd died in an accident in order to request a photo for the paper to publish alongside the tragic story. She was relieved when a priest (and not the parents) answered the door and helped her get the picture she needed.

Eager to break into a bigger market, next she pitched stories about the upcoming presidential primaries across the border in New

---

* The *Peabody Times* attracted another intrepid reporter following Nina's departure. After being denied a press pass to board the U.S. Navy's oldest ship purely because of her sex, reporter Ruby Litinsky sneaked on board by wearing men's clothing.

Hampshire to a start-up publication in Washington, DC, called the *Examiner*. The paper's founder, O. Roy Chalk, was an ambitious and eclectic entrepreneur with a wide-ranging portfolio that included real estate, a Caribbean airline, and the Spanish-language paper *El Diario–La Prensa*. After a failed bid to take over the New York City transit system, he landed the contract to run the District of Columbia bus system.

The captive audience of 150,000 commuters tantalized the marketer in Chalk. To create a tabloid that would be distributed free on board each Thursday, he hired a young editor named Jack Limpert. With marquee gossip columnist Walter Winchell as the paper's star, it seemed a guaranteed home run. Best of all for Nina, here was another employer who cared not a bit about her sex; he was far more interested in her willingness to work. This was just the kind of place where a rookie freelancer could excel. Writing meatier stories that reached a wide, urbane readership was worth far more than the measly twenty-five bucks she got paid per piece.

Chalk had grand plans for his baby. He intended to expand it to daily publication, and to take it to New York.

The ambitious experiment encountered troubles from the start. The Associated Press and United Press wouldn't license the paper its wires. Then came the charge that Chalk was using transit funds to subsidize the paper's operations. When the paper shut down, leaving Nina with no outlet for her freelance reporting, this was her cue to skedaddle out of Massachusetts and head to the center of the action. Thanks to an aunt in Washington, she had a place to stay as she got situated in the capital city and began to search for work.

One-stop job hunting for a journalist could be had by cruising the halls of the fourteen-story National Press Building, at Fourteenth and F Streets, blocks from the White House. Erected in 1927 to centrally house bureaus for all manner of regional, national, and international news organizations, the place was so large it had been assigned its own zip code.

As she made her way around the hallowed marble halls, knocking on doors, begging for someone to hire her, she'd pause in the bathroom to cry. Her aggravation was amplified when she learned that the top two floors of the building were off-limits. This was the sacred head-quarters of the National Press Club, where women remained unwelcome. Members continued to believe the presence of a female would alter, if not destroy, the character of the institution. "Start mixing the sexes and you know what you'll wind up with?" riddled one member. "Babies." Groused another, "We don't ask to go to their beauty parlors. Why should they ask to come to our club?" A third: "They wouldn't know what to do with equal rights if we gave it to them."

The blockade still stood, too, at the exclusive Gridiron Club, which each year staged a rollicking white-tie men-only event filled with booze, skits, song, and elbow-rubbing. Newsmen and newsmakers alike rushed to attend this star-studded party, a sine qua non for every-one from the president to Supreme Court justices, cabinet members, and diplomats. Only once since its formation in 1885 had a woman been invited, and that was back in 1917, when the first female member of Congress, Jeanette Rankin of Montana, attended.* After that, it was back to stag.

Efforts to open up both the Gridiron and the National Press Clubs intensified along with the rallying cries of women's liberation. None other than First Lady Eleanor Roosevelt had been an early crusader. Just days after her husband's election in 1932, she'd swallowed her innate shyness and, at the suggestion of her friend Lorena Hickok, a reporter for the Associated Press, launched a weekly women-only news confer-ence to help support the then-pint-size female press corps, comprised mostly of women's page writers. As a syndicated columnist herself, the First Lady maintained membership in the Women's National Press

---

* Rankin was elected before national suffrage, as men in Montana voted to grant women the right to vote in 1914. Lest that state seem progressive, neighboring Wyoming had allowed women to vote since 1869.

Club. The only thing more scandalous than the wife of a president deigning to speak publicly* was Mrs. Roosevelt's motivation in doing so: By giving lady reporters something to write about other than state dinners and ballgowns, she'd help boost their relevance. And in this way, she'd also help America's women, still relatively new to the vote, to form a "general attitude of mind and thought" beyond domestic concerns.

Though the First Lady promised in her press briefings to steer clear of political matters—her husband's obvious domain—she couldn't help herself from commenting. One week, she might encourage passage of legislation that would allow the United States to take in thousands of refugee children. Another, she'd speak out against bills wending their way through state governments that would prohibit married women from working.

And each year when the Gridiron Club held its dinner, she staged a gala counter-party in the East Room of the White House for the "Gridiron Widows," with more guests and at least as much raucous gaiety as could be found at the men's affair, including off-the-record comedic sketches and supper served at midnight. One year, she declared it a costume ball and dressed as a Romanian peasant, while five lady reporters decked themselves out as the famous Dionne Quintuplets.

Now, decades later, amid the thrilling and expansive enlightenment of women, the tradition continued. Hundreds of counter-revelers, including men sympathetic to the cause, marched with picket signs declaring, "Gridiron, Grow Up!" and "Let My People In," as dignitaries arrived at the fancy Statler Hilton for their chauvinist "do." Afterward, they decamped to the Mount Vernon College gym. The one thousand tickets available, at a cost of $7.50 each, sold out, with the proceeds going to support an advocacy group called Journalists for Professional Equality. As a blue-jean clad bluegrass band performed, the partygoers played games such as "Pin the Tail on the Male Chauvinist Pig"

---

* Mrs. Warren Harding wouldn't even reveal the guest lists for official White House dinners to women's page reporters. Mrs. Calvin Coolidge had been warned by her husband not to speak to the press.

while enlightened supporters like CBS newsman Dan Rather sold "non-sexist" kisses at a kissing booth.

Among the liveliest and most vocal of the protestor-revelers: an ambitious newcomer, a relative newcomer to the DC press corps, Nina Totenberg. Loud and clear, she shouted out to arriving partygoers, including Supreme Court justice Thurgood Marshall, *"Shame!"*

CHAPTER SEVEN
Ms.

The lofty promise of equality guaranteed to all in the 1964 Civil Rights Act still had yet to catch up with the legislation. Change had come only in a trickle. Want ads continued to be segregated by race and sex, and unspoken barriers, such as the edicts that kept women off the air as newscasters and confined them to jobs where there'd be no danger they'd serve in a superior position to men, prevailed in many professions.

Workplaces remained unfriendly to women. Getting married or pregnant could mean losing your job. Women with children were routinely refused work or denied promotions. Married women bold enough to ask for raises were routinely told by their employers that they didn't need the money or that men deserved more for the same job because, well, they were the main breadwinners in the family and, in most states, obligated by law to support their wives.

Outside the workplace, denial of liberties abounded. Obtaining a bank account, much less a loan or a credit card, was impossible for a woman on her own, no matter her financial situation. And if she was married, the man's name always came first. Women who wished to use their birth name after marriage were ridiculed. "I do not understand why any virtuous woman would not wish to have her husband's name," said Senator Sam Ervin of North Carolina.

Women who traveled alone were believed to be prostitutes. A woman who dared wear trousers registered as subversive, rude, or immoral, though, ever so slowly, this casual wear was becoming somewhat acceptable in certain situations (as long as it did not hug the form).

As it had with the civil rights movement for Black Americans, a growing consciousness and anger over the denial of equal rights for women had given rise to a steady display of activism. No longer was this "radical" concept of equality for women the exclusive domain of angry, militant feminists. Singer Helen Reddy's number-one hit anthem, "I Am Woman," became a touchstone—even to doubters of the movement who mimicked the lyrics with a wink.

Arresting visuals helped bring the issues to the headlines, though sometimes at the expense of the cause. In 1968, marchers set up a trash can on the Atlantic City Boardwalk, just outside the annual spectacle of the Miss America beauty pageant. Into the bin protestors dramatically tossed "women garbage," oppressive and unnecessary inventions such as false eyelashes, bras, and girdles. Though nary a garment had been torched, suddenly advocates of "women's liberation" became known as "bra burners." (Had they called them "girdle burners," quipped one of the protestors, every woman in America would have joined the movement in an instant.)

Marchers carried signs decrying the competition as both degrading (judging women for their looks was barbaric) and racist (only white women were allowed to enter). A few of them managed to sneak a bedsheet into the hall during the big show and unfurl it just as the previous year's queen handed over the reins to the new winner, Miss Kansas. The interlopers then proceeded to shout out the words written on their makeshift sign: "Women's Liberation." It felt rude to interrupt during the pageant's big moment, confessed one activist, until it felt great.

Soon, the simmering women's lib movement was churning like a tornado through the daily fabric of existence. In March 1970, *Newsweek* published a cover story acknowledging its emergence. Oh, the irony: Given that women at the magazine weren't allowed to rise to the rank of writer, the story had to be jobbed out to a female freelancer.

The very same day the attention-grabbing issue hit the stands, the savvy *Newsweek* employees dropped a bomb they'd been constructing for months, filing a federal class-action suit charging their incredulous employer with gender discrimination. (Katharine Graham, *Newsweek*'s owner, confessed she had no idea whose side to take.) They were tired of being held back in dead-end jobs as they watched less qualified men sashay onto the premises and advance in their careers. And they were fed up with being called "dollies."

Also that week came more media activism as over a hundred women crowded into the office of the (male) editor in chief of *Ladies' Home Journal* and sat there for eleven hours until he promised to let them produce a special edition that addressed the real issues of the day.

In their hands, the plain vanilla pages of the *Journal*—typically filled with pablum like recipes for show-off desserts, how-to pieces on creating or commissioning elegant window treatments, and expert wisdom on headache cures—offered readers a healthy dose of "radical" thinking. Meaningful change and true advancement for women, the guest writers declared, would be achieved only when sex did not determine one's destiny. It was time, they wrote, to discard the "gigantic conspiracy" that marrying and having children was all a woman need aspire to, time that society accepted women as equal members. "Women! Come out of the house!" they said. "You have everything to gain!"

A few weeks later, a hundred liberationists ferried out to the majestic Statue of Liberty in New York Harbor, denouncing the absurdity of a lady representing freedom, and unfurling a banner at her base that declared, "Women of the World Unite." It proved the perfect visual to accompany the day's other headlines: New York City mayor John Lindsay had signed a law that banned male-only bars and restaurants. But the far greater news came from Washington, where the unrelenting U.S. representative Martha Griffiths had finally succeeded with passage of the Equal Rights Amendment. After years of previous failures, she deployed the seldom-used (and rarely successful) "discharge petition" to force the bill out of committee and onto the floor. The powerful House minority whip, Hale Boggs, had appeased her, saying he'd sign on when she collected 200 signatures—never imagining that she would. Just after she obtained signature number 199, she rushed to his office and made him live up to his promise. With the addition of his name, she easily got the buy-in of the eighteen others she needed for the necessary majority.

And a few weeks after *that*, on August 26, 1970—the fiftieth anniversary of the ratification of the Nineteenth Amendment, which granted women suffrage—thousands of protestors took to the streets in a hundred cities around the nation as part of a "Women's Strike." In New York, they marched on Fifth Avenue, demanding the completion of the "unfinished business of equality." The time was now, they cried, for educational and employment opportunities to be equal, for safe abortions available free on demand, for twenty-four-hour day care centers to be provided for mothers where they could safely leave their children while they worked.

"This is not a bedroom war, this is a political movement," roared Betty Friedan, author of what many saw as the guiding text of the movement, *The Feminine Mystique*, and cofounder of the National Organization for Women, or NOW, which had organized the protests. "Man is not the enemy. Man is a fellow-victim."

To jab at the absurdity of the women's demands, the *New York Times* ran a sidebar headlined, "Leading Feminist Puts Hairdo Before Strike." Friedan had been late to the march, the story explained, because she'd ducked into Vidal Sassoon to get her hair curled. "I don't want people to think Women's Lib girls don't care about how they look," Friedan had told the reporter. "We should try to be as pretty as we can. It's good for our self-image and it's good politics."

Because the news media frequently cast "women's libbers" as ugly, man-hating separatists—they mocked activists whenever they could for emasculating their husbands, denying them dinner, and aiming to steal men's jobs, and referred to the women as "braless bubbleheads"—this story was a change. Never mind that the first Pulitzer Prize won by the paper had been thanks to the deft and diligent foreign reporting of Anne O'Hare McCormick. Despite years of dutiful service as a freelancer who interviewed kings, presidents, and dictators, she'd waited years before being given a full-time job.

Women employees at the paper's every level had endured a range of insults common to the profession. One who'd dutifully worked as a researcher was told, when she asked for a shot at becoming a writer, "Why don't you go home and get married?" The powerful DC bureau chief James Reston had informed a well-qualified writer who dared ask for a job that she could work part time at the switchboard.

Of a young, token-female general assignment reporter, a public television crew filming a documentary about the paper asked, "How would you make this place better?" The vaunted paper was a great place to work, she told them, except for the fact that "There aren't enough women, there aren't enough blacks, there aren't enough Chicanos, there aren't enough American Indians." After the story aired, she got hauled into a meeting by management, who accused her of being a traitor. Anyone lucky enough to get hired by the *Times* was expected to display the appropriate reverence.

Aside from the anecdotal evidence, an analysis of union payroll data clued women into an even harsher reality: Nineteen male reporters at the *Times* each earned more than the most senior female reporter, a star whose stories frequently made page one. Perhaps even more bruising than the statistics was the discovery of damning notes tucked away in personnel files rating the looks and physical attributes of prospective employees: "Great legs, face only fair," "good figure and is not restrained about dressing it to advantage," "a very good worker but looks are not great."

Fed up, women banded together to form a "Women's Caucus" and composed a letter to management that questioned why, as women's voices were at long last being heard more loudly and clearly, "at the *Times*, we note little change in the basic situation of women. . . . [W]e call your attention to the twenty-one names on the masthead, editorial and business executives. Not one is a woman." The letter detailed the pay gap and reminded management that the 1964 Civil Rights Act behooved them to create a timetable for the creation of an affirmative action plan.

As a result, a few female employees received "equalization" raises, and a conciliatory meeting was held with the publisher, but with no larger impact. Joining their sisters at *Newsweek*, *Time*, *Reader's Digest*, and NBC, the women filed a suit against their employer to end the discrimination.

* * *

Allowing a woman to have a byline in print was one sort of progress. Permitting her to deliver the news over the airwaves was downright revolutionary. Yet over at one of the nation's newest programs, the prevailing concern wasn't the status of women. For the small staff churning out ninety minutes of *All Things Considered,* navigating the free-for-all chaos of the daily program was enough of a challenge.

It didn't help—in fact, it hurt quite a lot—that since the show's debut, no structure had been put in place. It wasn't always even clear who'd show up for work each day. Whoever arrived at the office first in the morning found themselves that day's producer—vetting breaking news, wrangling the reports gathered in the field, making sure they'd been spliced down and mixed and prepared for air, booking telephone interviews with guests (an inexpensive way to pad out the time), writing copy, sifting through the poorly catalogued pile of taped story submissions from affiliates in search of stories they might use, and assembling all the pieces into a loose-fitting "road map" so as to fill the promised ninety minutes. With so few staff reporters, everyone pitched in, assigning themselves whatever stories sounded interesting, with little direction or oversight and even less—make that no—editing.

A persistent struggle over the show's identity had emerged—a tug-of-war between those who wished it to serve primarily as a hard-hitting news-of-record daily report, a radio version of the front page of the *New York Times,* and those who wished it to be more reflective, with a feature-driven, analytical approach in the vein of the *New Yorker.* Just as writing a quick, breaking news story on deadline required an entirely different set of skills than a well-crafted, deeply researched magazine piece, "newspaper radio" was far less costly to produce than "artistic," long-form radio.

Neither approach was easy, or cheap. With fewer than thirty people, there simply wasn't the personnel, nor the budget, nor hours in the day. A million exhausting and exacting decisions were required to create an hour and a half of material every day. The reality of the elastic spirit of experimentation necessary to redefine news that had seemed so fun and liberating at the start had quickly worn thin. Each day, as they toiled to fill the time, it felt, one staffer lamented, like they were using a "teaspoon to fill the Grand Canyon."

Often, as it had on the very first day, the show would begin with nary a finished tape in the smoke-filled control room. Suddenly, a dozen reels would get hurled in there "like Frisbees," or a tape would break as it played, leaving the host to scamper in improvisation.

Working long, hard hours for a fraction of the pay earned by commercial broadcasters was hard enough, but was anyone even listening?

Even the radio start-up's location was a stark reminder of its puny stature. They'd moved from I Street into 2025 M Street—directly across the street from the broadcasting Goliath CBS, with its endless resources, hefty audience, and vaunted reputation for excellence.

The most pressing issue holding back *All Things Considered*, though, was neither its physical plant nor its lack of organization or listenership; it was its host. Robert Conley eschewed scripts, insisting on speaking extemporaneously, freezing in mid-sentence when Linda spoke to him from the control room to tell him he was running too long. Off the air, his brusque manner toward the staff didn't square with the collaborative vibe Siemering aimed to instill. After a matter of months, he'd been pushed off the air and replaced by two of the five reporters, Mike Waters and Jim Russell. With their attentions now devoted to hosting duties, this stretched the mettle of the already overworked staff even more.

Susan, thoughtful observer of the proceedings from her perch as a part-time associate producer, offered wise insights to the managing editor (a newspaper veteran with no radio experience) about the show's lack of "shape, form, style and personality." Listeners needed to be able to count on hearing similar types of stories at the same time each day, she explained. News should be summarized at various points throughout the broadcast, and shorter pieces were necessary, too. They'd fallen into the lazy, bad habit of "covering" press conferences, she observed: Why not, after briefly describing the press conference, talk to someone who's life would be *affected* by it instead?

She brimmed with ideas. Informed by her experiences as a working mother wading through her new and often daunting role, she pitched a program called *HouseBreak*, an afternoon show aimed at women that would provide an intelligent alternative to soap operas. There was little in any medium that appealed to her, a smart, educated woman concerned with issues surrounding motherhood and marriage and care for the elderly. Wasn't family a major institution that deserved to be covered? she wondered. The women's pages in newspapers, and the women's magazines, were vacuous. As much as management might have liked the idea, and Susan's occasional on-air contributions, there simply weren't the resources to make *HouseBreak* a reality. So, she contented herself with filing stories that addressed these issues as best she could.

One week, when the new cohost Mike Waters was about to head out on vacation, he encouraged Susan to sit in as his substitute; he liked what he had heard of her style in the stories she filed. Waters had his own unique approach. An acolyte of Siemering who'd come with him from Buffalo, he'd once narrated a "breaking news" report about a sunset. Another time, to approximate for a listener what it was like to ride in a barrel over Niagara Falls, he and a colleague sent a microphone for the ride. ("Sounds just like a toilet bowl flush," observed a bemused onlooker.)

On one of those days, while Susan served as fill-in host, the lead story centered on a topic near to her heart, India—an official state visit by Prime Minister Indira Gandhi. Next came a piece by Barbara Newman, a former print reporter; another from Kati Wetzel, a research assistant; and yet another from arts reporter Connie Goldman.

"That's too many women in the first part of the program," the day's (male) producer scowled.

What? said Susan. "Do you say the same thing when Walter Cronkite introduces Dan Rather to report on what Richard Nixon did today, followed by Daniel Schorr on Capitol Hill with Senator Hubert Humphrey?"

Why *shouldn't* the show factor in an abundance of female voices? Why did there have to be a scorecard? Why was it that the male voice dominated the airwaves, even here at NPR, as it did most everyplace else on earth? How come one half of the population was routinely shunted aside, included only as tokens? Why shouldn't women be heard in equal measure? They hadn't been in broadcasting till now. If any place was to reflect the new world order, the recognition that women counted, shouldn't public radio be that place? Wasn't that what Bill Siemering meant when he talked about featuring diverse voices?

It was. Diverse—and human. Susan didn't sound like an announcer. She sounded like a person. She spoke the way she wrote, in all caps and exclamation points and ellipses, with energy and enthusiasm, like she was gathered around the piano in her parents' living room on West Ninety-Sixth Street, inhaling that glorious nicotine, chatting up a gathering of friends as if at a salon.

Siemering didn't tell Susan about the derision her hosting had received from station managers in the small network of affiliates. News wasn't supposed to sound like this, they grumbled. News was supposed to be buttoned-up, delivered in stock broadcast inflection, by a man. A woman, as host? A woman whose voice was tinged with New York ("New York," of course, being code for "Jewish")? A lively woman, at that, laughing during convivial exchanges with guests. No one *laughed* during the news.

Even the big boss, Don Quayle, who'd known Susan from her previous job at WAMU, didn't think putting her in the host's slot was a terribly good idea. But at the time, there was a bigger issue: the organizational mess. Quayle insisted that Siemering appoint a steady producer to deal with that. Siemering, in turn, chose NPR's very first employee, Jack Mitchell, who was competent and organized and, having worked at an actual educational radio station before, had a sense of a format that might work for stations. (He'd also done some time at the British Broadcasting Corporation, having been dispatched by the Corporation for Public Broadcasting before NPR had even launched to observe their procedures.) Now he set about inventing and imposing a structure to make life easier both for the people who worked on the show as well as for anyone who bothered to tune in.

* * *

On a wintry day in January 1972, Susan found herself standing with Linda by the Xerox machine outside the tiny office they shared. Just as Susan had been appearing on the air, Linda had risen from her behind-the-scenes post as director, where her role had been to traffic cop the component parts of the broadcast and make sure the show timed out, to on-air reporter covering consumer affairs. On this day, the two women were photocopying portions of a new magazine that captivated their attention in order to prepare a special eleven-minute report about it. This publication wasn't like anything either of them had ever seen. Any woman could immediately grasp the significance of the cover illustration. It featured a multiarmed ancient Indian goddess clutching the accoutrements juggled by the modern working woman: a steering wheel, a frying pan, an iron, a makeup mirror, and a phone. The stories inside articulated Susan and Linda's own experiences and frustrations with the juggle and expectations faced by working women, inside and outside the home.

Even the magazine's simple name was resonant. *Ms.*, the publication was called—*Mmzzzz*—that "neutral form of address for women that obscured marital status," as Linda described it in their report. The honorific wasn't yet widely used. The women behind the magazine, it seems, had considered other titles—*Sisters*, or *The First Sex*, or *Everywoman*, or *The Majority*—but they'd chosen this simple two-letter word because it conveyed a complex concept. It announced, "I'm a feminist." The word itself was fraught, radical. If a person's sex shouldn't determine her fate, why should her marital status? Linda and Susan felt that if they were so enthralled by this magazine's ideas, their listeners would be, too.

Other magazines for women, *Ms.* cofounder Gloria Steinem had explained in a taped interview, offered "glossy, sweetness and light" fantasy, like a "Saturday afternoon at the movies." But *Ms.*, she said, had been designed to offer support, to raise consciousness, and to help women change their lives by telling the truth—instead of merely offering escapist fantasy.

In voices both defiant and proud, the reporters proceeded to tick through the issues raised by *Ms.*, as if they were reading a manifesto at a rally. Though *All Things Considered* now reached 130 stations around the country, up from the ninety at launch, and though there was no budget to commission ratings, the potential reach of a radio audience, even on the still largely undiscovered non-commercial airwaves, was far greater than would ever appear for the average protest.

"The Housewife's Moment of Truth," as the magazine's first cover story was called, examined the inequity of household chores and why men got congratulated when they bothered to pick up dirty laundry, while women didn't think to question why they shouldered the time-intensive chores of cooking, cleaning, and child care—even when they held jobs outside the home. (Liberation from, or at least shared responsibility over, such chores was a key component of the burgeoning feminist movement.) Another article questioned why girls excelled over boys when they started school but grew up to sabotage their success in order to supplicate themselves to men: "The cost of success was more dangerous than the cost of not succeeding." Another piece in the debut issue, "How to Write Your Own Marriage Contract," offered wisdom on equalizing the marital vows.

These "smoldering" and "dangerous" stories in this "text for a revolution," Linda and Susan announced to the audience, underscored this important truth: In the 1970s, a woman no longer needed to exist purely to support and bolster a man.

CHAPTER EIGHT

Scoop

Nina was finding, as she progressed in her career, that while her sex presented obstacles, it also had its advantages. She was fortunate to have stumbled upon a man like Sid Yudain, an inveterate bachelor who happened to like lady journalists. In 1968, Yudain hired Nina at his newspaper, *Roll Call*, launched thirteen years earlier with a grand starting budget of ninety dollars—the weekly take from his job as a congressional staffer. On Capitol Hill, a place where people flocked from all over the nation to serve their government and stoke their quest for power, he'd seen an unmet need for a "hometown" community paper.

"It just seemed logical to bring everybody together and let the people know who's who in which office, in the office next door to theirs, in the office down the street," he said. "I thought we needed to get a more human spirit there, a more human aspect to the thing."

The *Congressional Record* was a must-read for the minutiae of government, but *Roll Call* was essential reading for the soul. Yudain saw his creation as one-part newspaper, one-part fanzine, one-part trade rag, and one-part *New Yorker*—filled with juicy tidbits on weddings, birthdays, and who had caught a big fish. Anyone on the Hill who wished to contribute was welcome. Once, when he was vice president, Nixon wrote an obituary for a beloved congressional doorman. The *Washington Post* dubbed it a "house organ" that contained "all the gossip that's fit to print."

Whatever the weekly contents, the first thing anyone looked for in each issue was the "Hill Pinup" feature, spotlighting a young, fetching congressional secretary (carefully chosen from both sides of the aisle to reflect *Roll Call*'s bipartisan readership) posed somewhere in the District and captured by an official Democrat or Republican party photographer. (A vivacious woman stood out in the suited grayness of the town.) The accompanying text offered details on the woman's physical attributes, marital status, and job duties—"the pixie 106-pounder strikes an eye-catching pose in a bikini but she hasn't let it slow down her typing speed." So proud were the hometowns of these featured beauties that local newspapers mentioned the "honor" on their own pages.

The spirited publisher Yudain convened the community in other ways than with newsprint. By the time Nina arrived, he'd become famous for his Sunday suppers, where he served up his trademark short rib and sauerkraut soup. Even if there was no budget for travel, the connections a fearless young reporter could make at *Roll Call* were worth exponentially more than her seventy-five-dollar-a-week paycheck.

From the dingy basement of a row house blocks from the Capitol, Nina delighted in her job as *Roll Call*'s only staff writer. While the bespectacled, pipe-smoking Yudain schmoozed, and his sister sold ads, Nina was also expected to serve as editor, production assistant, and proofreader. (Once, in a frenzy to make deadline, she overlooked a misspelling of her own name.)

The fact that men ignored women, or refused to take them seriously, meant that sometimes they yammered on unfiltered, revealing to Nina things they shouldn't. Like the time Republican senator Norris Cotton explained that he hadn't partaken in a boondoggle travel junket to Asia because "Oriental food gives me the trots."

Every woman, particularly women working to make their way in professions long off-limits to them, seemed to have their stories. Once, when trailing a visiting female member of the British Parliament who needed to find the loo, Nina was the only lady around to accompany her there, which gave her the opportunity to chat with the dignitary one-on-one. Making friends with everyone and anyone was an essential ingredient for any reporter, especially for a newcomer to the city who wasn't attached to a blue-chip publication with cachet and ready-made sources.

Nina had attained her wish: a seat at the table, where she could witness history. Just as her father had immediately felt comfortable when he landed in the United States, Nina began to see her life take shape in the nation's capital. "This was a very tall mountain to climb," she said, "and the only way to get there was step-by-step."

From *Roll Call*, she graduated to another off-the-fringe publication, the *National Observer*, a weekly newspaper started in 1962 by Dow Jones, publisher of the *Wall Street Journal*. Intended to be edgier than the other, formulaic newsweeklies, *Newsweek* and *Time*, the *Observer* distilled the week's headlines in "sparkling, provocative and electric" prose—and even deigned to hire the occasional female writer, unlike its loftier parent.

Nina was assigned to hawk the legal beat, specifically the Supreme Court. That she hadn't studied law, much less finished college, didn't pose a problem. In fact, she started to believe this, too, was an asset. She wasn't a slave to legalese or the smugness of insiderdom. Hyper-aware that she "didn't know anything from Shinola," she was unafraid to ask questions of anyone, regardless of their position, and never for a minute was she concerned that in doing so she seemed ill-informed. She considered herself to be learning. Once, after reading a lower court opinion on a civil rights case that she didn't understand, she simply called the judge, John Minor Wisdom, who happily explained it. She was, she said, "too young and too stupid to know how outrageous that was." Wisdom became another contact to add to her files.*

And, in 1971, when she had questions about *Reed v. Reed*, the first Supreme Court case to declare sex discrimination a violation of the Fourteenth Amendment, Nina flipped to the front of the brief and sleuthed out its author, a professor of law at Rutgers University named Ruth Bader Ginsburg. The professor was happy to give this young reporter an hour-long lecture about why the amendment, which Nina believed covered only Black citizens, also covered women.

What Nina didn't know at the time was that this kind "tutor" a decade her senior had, just like her, experienced discrimination and

---

* A decade later, Justice Wisdom presided over Nina's marriage to former senator Floyd Haskell.

harassment in her chosen profession. In 1956, the Dean at Harvard Law School rebuked Ginsburg and the eight other female students in her class for taking slots away from men. After being rejected for a clerkship on the Supreme Court in 1960 because she was a woman, Ginsburg was demoted from another job for becoming pregnant. When she joined the faculty at Rutgers, one of a handful of female law professors in the nation, she'd been told her pay would be less than that of a male colleague because her husband had a good job.

Of all Ginsburg's ferocious opposition to inequality up till that point, perhaps the most groundbreaking (if most pedestrian) was the equality of her marriage. She'd fallen in love with her husband in college because he was the first man to treat her as if she had a brain. When administrators at her children's school called her about their kids, she reminded them that she had a job, too; it was their father's turn. Fueled by these experiences as well as her knowledge of the law, Ginsburg dedicated her career to the crusade for equality. And with Nina's inquisitive call to her, a friendship was sparked.

As Nina's career advanced, she kept choosing her battles, and charging ahead. Hardly any lawyer or justice she called refused her request for an informational meeting, where she could ask how they did their job. Ever mindful of promotion, she put them on the list for free subscriptions.

Getting to know the mechanics of the highest court in the land, unearthing details privy only to the principal players, was a thrill: how the justices convened in straight-back chairs at their weekly conference and were served coffee out of a silver urn as they sifted through the five thousand cases that reached the Court each year; how an argument before this august body lasted precisely an hour and was actually quite informal.

With every story she covered, every bit of knowledge she amassed, every new business card added to her address book, she chalked up another reminder of her admiration of and respect for that essential American promise: freedom of the press. When she traveled to New

York to cover a court of appeals decision on the publication of the top-secret Pentagon Papers, a document considered a matter of national security, she shuddered to realize what might happen in the aftermath. "This could be a very different country," she thought. "The free press could be a lot less free after this case."

While others might have found the legal beat restrictive, or even boring, Nina reveled in the wide range of subjects it required that she investigate and understand. Covering the individual justices of the Supreme Court is like "covering nine presidencies at the same time." One day, she might be reporting on school desegregation; the next, on abortion or antitrust. Then there were the longer pieces, like a fly-on-the-wall look at how, in the aftermath of the "overly male" 1968 political conventions, women in 1972 had committed to training other women to jump into politics.

"This year," she wrote, "the hand that rocks the cradle is rocking the political boat, too." Suffrage had been hard-won decades before, but since then, women's involvement in politics, not to mention their attendance at the polls, had been pitiful. One activist explained, "It's about time women grew up and stopped expecting men to provide all the leadership and happiness in their lives and all that stuff at the end of the rainbow."

As Nina waded deeper into the murky landscape of the beat, she began to break news. Working on a tip that President Nixon would nominate a Minnesota judge named Harry Blackmun to the Supreme Court, Nina flew north to gather material for a profile. The official announcement was made as she visited with Blackmun's elderly mother, who revealed that her son and the chief justice, who were old friends, spoke regularly. Blackmun was outraged and embarrassed to see this personal detail in print and even considered withdrawing his name for consideration.

He didn't. And in the aftermath, Nina wrote a sweet-as-pie letter inviting the newly confirmed justice and his wife to be her guests at the Women's Press Club's fiftieth-anniversary dinner—always good for VIP watching, she said—offering to help them house-hunt or even to be just "an extra pair of hands to help wash dishes." She also offered up a gratis subscription to the *Observer*.

Around the same time, Chief Justice Burger wrote a friendly admonition to his soon-to-be-colleague, welcoming him to the "snake pit" of Washington, where reporters possessed of a "psychotic passion for copy," particularly "the female of the species," were to be avoided, their sweet talk never to be trusted. "Like blackmail or heroin," he advised, once they get you on the hook, "they try to keep the victim impaled."

* * *

In 1971, Nina "set the White House on its ear" by revealing President Nixon's secret list of Supreme Court candidates. At not quite twenty-eight years old, she won recognition from the American Bar Association and high praise from her editor, Henry Gemmill, who described her as the hardest-hitting reporter on his staff—as willing as any of the men to "sit up all night pounding the typewriter to meet a deadline," someone who "rips hard right down the middle, evoking both cheers and catcalls." She was sweet when she chose to be, but "equally willing to throw the fishhook question at a member of the President's Cabinet, interview a burglar with a heroin habit, or claw her way through a pack of street demonstrators."

Gemmill, it seemed, admired more than Nina's tenacity. He'd propositioned her, too, repeatedly and over a period of months. "It was awful," she told the *Washington Post* years later. "There's no other word to describe it." Colleague Diane K. Shah, rattled by her own unwelcome encounter with the boss, commiserated with Nina. They knew there was little recourse. A woman lucky enough to land a job as a reporter could quite likely see her career killed if she complained. Besides, their boss was a superstar, so they felt it wasn't likely the powers that be at the paper's parent company, Dow Jones in New York, would listen or care or even believe them. It would be their word against his.

* * *

The burning desire to keep working trumped the harassment, so Nina plunged on. Nothing quite caught fire like her profile of that "master of political influence," the mysterious and pugnacious FBI director, J. Edgar Hoover. For the assignment, she interviewed more than a hundred sources and constructed a damning portrait of the man, enumerating his bizarre personal behavior and a litany of shockers, such as the fact that he had wiretapped Dr. Martin Luther King Jr.'s phones and intimidated him with information he learned about the civil rights leader's sex life; stationed FBI agents on college campuses in order to subvert left-wing groups; disciplined rogue agents by sending them to the equivalent of FBI Siberia, Butte, Montana; and tapped the phones of the owner of every Las Vegas casino except the one owned by his friend.

In the aftermath of the profile, Hoover wrote and demanded the editor fire Nina for what he claimed were "malicious lies, inaccuracies, distortions, and untruths." (Later, a memo revealed that he'd also privately referred to her as a "persistent bitch.")

Others began to suggest that there was only one way Nina could possibly be scoring such juicy stories. She must be sleeping with someone. Nina took such jealous sniping as part of the territory, an expected byproduct of being a woman who was good at her job. And while it stung, she preferred to revel in her victories: "I dare say I am the only Supreme Court reporter who ever asked" a justice to dance, she said of Byron White. "He was quite the gentleman as he waltzed me around the ballroom floor—lecturing me on the evils of Women's Lib."

But not every dance was so glamorous for this emerging superstar. Six months after the Hoover incident, she was assigned to write a profile of Tip O'Neill, who suddenly ascended to the role of House majority leader after Rep. Hale Boggs of New Orleans disappeared in a plane crash. In the finished piece, she borrowed a few too many quotes, without attribution, from a *Washington Post* article that reporter Myra MacPherson had written about the Massachusetts politician. This discovery cost Nina her job. The accusation that she'd plagiarized, she said later, "scared the holy beejezus" out of her.

* * *

Teflon Nina survived what could have killed a mere mortal who'd committed a similar transgression. Soon, she landed a job as the Washington editor of the twice-monthly *New Times*, a "sassy offshoot," as she described it, of *New York* magazine. The editors didn't seem to know or care about the *Observer* flap; they valued her reputation as a reporter. And soon again, her stories were leaping off the pages of their publication and into the news headlines.

No branch of government, she said, not even the FBI, was as veiled in secrecy as the Supreme Court. And she continued to lift that veil—whether by taking readers inside the vaunted institution by describing high-backed chairs and the mahogany table around which the justices sifted through documents on Wednesday afternoons and all day Friday as they decided which cases to consider; or describing how they wrestled with defining "obscenity" by screening "exhibit A" pornographic films; or by giving a shocking, in-depth description of the Court as the "last plantation," with its "antebellum" hiring practices that were more "mint julep than justice." The maintenance men and cleaning lady, she revealed, were all Black, while the skilled craftsmen (carpenters, electricians, and plumbers) were all white. All but one of the secretaries was white, and all the messengers were Black, as were the three elevator operators, including one who was fired for refusing to work at a private party at one of the justice's homes. So much for the Equal Employment Opportunity Commission: There was little chance for Black employees to advance in this "classically segregated work force," and not even an internal grievance process, although one had been instituted as soon as Nina started rooting around.

With her 1974 cover story that declared "The Dumbest Congress-man" (plus nine runners-up), she stirred another memorable sensation. To deduce the winners of this dubious distinction, Nina had polled two hundred people on the Hill. Among the "dumb"? Representative Earl Landgrebe of Indiana, who was so dumb he'd voted yes to a quorum call, a standard attendance roll. Sen. Roman Hruska from Nebraska was so dumb he'd actually said, "Mediocrity deserves a seat on the Supreme Court." (Two strikes: Hruska owned a chain of dirty movie theaters, yet had sponsored an anti-smut bill.) Then there was "Jumpin' Joe" Vigorito of Pennsylvania, who said he'd dreamed of being a congress-man because "you don't go from being nothing to being President." (So offended was he to have made Nina's list that he told a reporter who asked for his reaction, "I wouldn't dignify that prostitute by com-menting on her article.") And the man whom she'd crowned with the dubious honor of "King of Dumb" was Sen. William Scott, a Republican from Virginia who, when asked about SALT, the talks on arms control between the United States and the Soviet Union, began rhapsodizing about the mineral and its counterpart, pepper.

Right after the story hit the stands, Nina happened to be conducting an unrelated interview in the halls of Congress when a mob of report-ers rushed in her direction. At the head of the pack was NBC's Roger Mudd, who spoke for the group as they approached her. Senator Scott had called a news conference denying that he was the dumbest. Did she have any comment?

What could she possibly add to his stunningly dumb validation of her claim?

* * *

In 1972, Robert Zelnick, a lawyer employed as a legislative aide to Wis-consin congressman Henry Reuss, made a cold call to National Public Radio. He'd been a reporter in Alaska, had covered Vietnam, and now reported about the Supreme Court for the *Christian Science Monitor* and the Canadian Broadcasting Corporation. He liked what he'd heard on

All Things Considered on his drive home from work and figured it was worth a shot to see if they needed help.

As the blockbuster presidential scandal of Watergate unfolded bit by tortuous bit, the network was chronically short on on-the-ground talent to cover Washington. Even the basics, like obtaining credentials as a qualified news organization, could be a chore. With no budget for a dedicated White House correspondent, NPR certainly didn't have the funds to send someone to Vietnam. Being able to tap into a reporter with Zelnick's experience seemed worth the investment of the $175 they'd pay him each week in exchange for two days of work. (A rate, he'd soon discover, that was higher than what his envious colleagues earned.) For his part, it wasn't a bad deal in exchange for getting his foot in the door at a new outlet. NPR would allow him to juggle other freelance assignments to outlets where he was already a contributor.

As did everyone else at NPR at the time, Zelnick found himself dipping into a variety of subjects. Given his wide-ranging background, he served as a valuable utility player, filing reports on inflation, energy, and Watergate from the State Department, the Pentagon, and the Supreme Court. Though his voice wasn't the smoothest, he wound up working more days than his contract called for and got on the air practically every day.

But the bean counters decided that this extra cost was breaking the freelance budget. The next thing he knew, Zelnick was offered a job in management, overseeing the reporters. In that capacity, he enlisted an estimable contributor: the pioneering female broadcaster Pauline Frederick.

Frederick's reputation had landed her an offer to jump over to NBC in 1953, and after arriving at the network's mandatory retirement age of sixty-five, she'd been pushed out—learning about her departure only after a friend read a story in the *New York Times* announcing it. For a while, she'd enjoyed her time on the lecture circuit, but she was delighted when Zelnick, ever the hard-news man, hired her as a part-time contractor to report on the upcoming UN General Assembly. NPR could pay this accomplished pioneer the lofty sum of a thousand dollars a month. Frederick loved being back on radio, where "you can be concerned about what you're trying to say rather than how you look." After all the years she'd struggled to find acceptance as a female reporter, now she found herself up against a different "ism"—ageism. Zelnick pushed back against the staff, where people under thirty far outnumbered those over, who were put out by the presence of this elder stateswoman from big, bad commercial media even after it was explained to those who didn't already know that Frederick was perhaps the "greatest television reporter of all time."* Counting on the fact that there were those in the audience who would be impressed, NPR's public relations wing issued a press release boasting about this venerable addition to the team.

Besides this doyenne of the United Nations, Zelnick needed a workhorse reporter on the ground in DC. He had no time and little interest in the human-interest approach embodied by Susan. Around town, he'd encountered her opposite: Nina, a spirit as swept up in the swirl of political DC as Susan was repelled by it. Nina was impossible to miss. Women had made inroads, but the Washington press corps wasn't exactly crawling with them. Still, there wasn't anyone quite like Nina. She was brassy. She loved to drop the fact that her father was a famous musician. For every person who considered her "a major self-absorbed nightmare," there was someone who found her to be "a big-hearted loyal friend." One quality on which everyone could agree was Nina's unshakable confidence. When someone suggested she resembled the actress Bette Midler, Nina confidently retorted, "I'm much prettier." (She did allow, though, that she had a "duck walk," which she said her colleagues liked to imitate.)

---

* Frederick's reputation trumped her age when, in 1976, the League of Women Voters asked her to moderate the second debate between President Gerald Ford and candidate Jimmy Carter, making her the first woman to earn that honor. Her affiliation was listed as National Public Radio, bolstering the reputation of the network in front of eighty-five million viewers. The next year, NPR commissioned a half-hour weekly show she'd proposed, *Pauline Frederick and Colleagues*, an examination of international affairs. No other show on the airwaves at the time, on radio or TV, focused on the topic. "Foreign news" even got short shrift in the papers.

A man possessed of Nina's qualities would have been dismissed as direct and assertive—like Zelnick himself—but because she was a woman, the charge was "abrasive, tactless and arrogant." Whatever the assessment, few caught up in her whirl doubted that she was a "force of nature," as one law professor put it. "There's no stopping her. You can complain about it, but that is a very big mistake because it is going to rain anyway." This unstoppable energy and pugnaciousness were what helped make her an excellent reporter.

Zelnick's need for a reporter arrived at the perfect moment. *New Times* couldn't afford to keep a staff person in DC any longer; Nina was soon to be out of work. In late 1974, he offered her a job.

She had no idea how to hold a microphone, much less how to talk into one, but she wasn't worried. She'd made it this far by not being afraid to say she didn't know something. She just figured it out as she went. With each new work experience, she'd learned more, met more people, amassed more bylines. Radio seemed interesting. She had nothing to lose.

CHAPTER NINE
Cokie

From the start, Cokie Boggs was accustomed to getting what she wanted. When she was eight, her mother, Lindy, took her along while shopping for a larger house to accommodate the family—and her husband, Hale's, rising political star: A bigger home would offer more space for the entertaining that was part and parcel of life in the District of Columbia, where the family had lived half time since Hale's election to Congress in 1940. Eleven years later, after he lost a bid for governor back in Louisiana, the family resolved to commit more fully to life in the capital city.

Lindy believed it imperative that this new home feature a back staircase, to make for seamless handling of behind-the-scenes necessities for entertaining with a house full of growing kids. In the year after Pearl Harbor thrust the United States into the war, the capital ballooned with activity. A rotating cast of houseguests inhabited the Boggses' home virtually every night. Overnight visitors were common due to a wartime dearth of hotel accommodation and a slowdown in train travel. Even constituents from back in New Orleans were among those invited to spend the night.

In addition to the out-of-town visitors, there was the usual camaraderie and social swirl of the legislative crowd. Everyone in DC was originally from someplace else, and regardless of their politics, they felt invested in the bigger cause of the United States. Television had yet to assert its stranglehold on leisure time; instead, lively nightly engagements helped them while away the hours. "After the sun goes down, we're friends," Lindy explained. Shakers full of cocktails helped lubricate those friendships.

The property on Bradley Boulevard that Lindy saw that cold winter Sunday in Bethesda in 1952 felt like the distant countryside in comparison to Stephenson Place, the location of the family's current home in the District. Set on a capacious two-and-a-half acres, the house offered room not just for gatherings but even some space for Hale to indulge in his hobby as a gentleman farmer. Even better, the stately columns on the large white brick structure framed by weeping willows evoked the beloved and familiar landscape of their southern roots. It could have been perfect, except that the bathrooms and dining room were much too small, and there wasn't enough closet space; also, it lacked a back staircase. This house simply would not do.

Cokie, bundled up in a snowsuit as protection against the wintry weather, was distressed that her mother had dismissed this castle with which she herself had instantly fallen in love. She fell to the floor, splaying her body out in protest. "I like it here. I feel at home here. I want to live in this house, Mamma," she whined.

Lindy was well accustomed to the strong personality of her youngest child, which had been on display since, at three weeks old, she managed to turn over in her crib. Cokie came by her fortitude honestly. As a little girl herself, Lindy had threatened a sit-in when a shop owner in New Orleans refused to sell her mother a child-size mannequin she dearly wanted. Naturally, she'd prevailed.

Now Lindy patiently explained the deficiencies of the house to her daughter as if she would grasp the adult logic behind her decision. "I don't care what you say," Cokie had persisted. "I love this house. I'm gonna tell my daddy to buy me this house!" The next day, the enterprising Realtor dialed up Congressman Boggs's office on Capitol Hill and mentioned how much his darling girl seemed to cotton to this special property. Hale asked Lindy, his trusted adviser in matters great and small, why she hadn't told him about the place? She outlined its inefficiencies precisely.

Not long after, the Boggs family moved in.

* * *

Aside from having a strong will, Cokie innately understood adaptability. She deftly navigated and inhabited two distinct worlds: the surreal magical power center of the United States and the rich southern heritage in Louisiana, spiced with chicory and Tabasco sauce, scented with magnolia and gardenias, soundtrack provided by the honkytonk bustle and clanking streetcars of New Orleans. After Christmas, the five Boggs family members would pile into the car with their Black housekeeper, Emma Cyprian, for the two-day journey to Washington, where they would spend the first half of the year. Given Emma's presence, finding accommodation along the way was a challenge. Motels, like restaurants and gas station restrooms, were strictly segregated. "No sugar," Hale would say with a shrug to the family waiting in the car as he emerged from an establishment with the news that Negroes weren't welcome there. Lindy refused to stay separately. It irked her that Black people, especially such a "refined, educated, intelligent, polite, well-dressed" woman as Emma, faced such inequity.

As had most white women of the upper class in the South, Lindy had been attended since birth by loving Black caretakers. It was her first nurse, in fact, who gifted her with her enduring nickname when she declared that the little girl named Corinne resembled her father, Roland. "Rolindy," she called her.

The Spanish flu had claimed Roland's life when Lindy was just two and a half years old. After a time and a fleet of suitors, her mother announced her engagement to a wealthy landowner named George Keller. In a jealous fit, the little girl, with her "evil little mind," tried to preempt the union by feigning illness. "I decided if I could get sick, Mamma would have to stay up all night with me and she would look so ugly the next day George wouldn't want to marry her."

The wedding proceeded, and Lindy was the better for it. The family moved from the sugar plantation on which she was born to one of "Daddy George's" plantations, where she was raised with a butler, a maid, a cook, horses, a private tutor, and abundant, adoring attention. Lindy might have had a silver spoon in her mouth, her mother observed with pride, but it never went to her head. In fact, she had been instructed early on that "because everybody loved me," she must be nice to everyone.

The nuns who taught Lindy at the convent school where she was sent as a boarder when she was nine made sure of that. Along with a fierce devotion to God and Catholic doctrine, they instilled in their pupils a sense of social justice that countered pervasive hatred and segregation. There was also a sense of noblesse oblige. She was doing others a favor, she was instructed, when she gave them the opportunity to contribute to a good cause. The other gift the sisters imparted, at a time when women were just settling into the right to vote, was a belief that the so-called "fairer sex" was invincible. Observing the nuns and the graceful, unwavering skill and authority with which they ran schools and hospitals, Lindy felt there was nothing a woman couldn't do.

While she was imbued with the notion of her limitless potential, the reality was that a girl of her standing would never need to or be expected to work, for pay, outside the home. Her education was in the service of preparing her for a life as a supportive wife and mother, which included becoming a full and active participant in community affairs. For this young high school valedictorian, college was the next step. Perhaps it would prove an excellent path to an "MRS degree" as well. Daddy George saw to that: Instead of attending the state university where most of her friends were headed, Lindy attended Newcomb, sister school to the elite private university Tulane, "the Harvard of the South."

While her stepfather would foot the bill for college, it was, she liked to say, Mr. William Shakespeare who gained her admission. When she'd sat for an interview with the dean of Newcomb, he'd concluded by asking if she was sixteen, the requisite age for admission. She looked at him, sweet as pie, and answered, "To be or not to be. That is the question. But, to thine own self be true. Though thou canst then be false to any man." A pause, a bat of the eyelashes. "No sir, I'm fifteen," she added. It may have been one of the first times Lindy charmed a man, and it wouldn't be the last. He waived the rule.

In the midst of the Depression, rather than indulging in the lavish debut a proper southern young lady was expected to have, Lindy opted to apply her stepfather's resources to finishing her studies. She had lots of fun in the process. The vivacious belle's social calendar was crammed with two "shifts" of dates per evening, which she craftily and politely juggled so as to avoid bruising egos.

It was at a Beta Theta Phi fraternity function where she first encountered her future husband. As he and Lindy made their way across the dance floor, the tall, strapping man with dark blue eyes informed the beautiful young girl that he intended to marry her someday. She was already wise enough about masculine wiles to realize that this blustery, confident fellow no doubt used that line on every woman he met. "Who was that crazy boy?" she wondered.

Soon, she got her answer. Born in Long Beach, Mississippi, Thomas Hale Boggs had bootstrapped his way to Tulane on scholarship, arriving with infinite dreams and only thirty-five dollars in his pocket. What he lacked in material wealth and social standing he made up for in outsize charm and competence. To earn extra cash along the way, he dug ditches and sold Beech-Nut Gum and other curios. A skilled orator, he won debating awards, and his capacity for communication translated, too, to print. He'd been bit by the journalism bug as a kid, routinely winning the top prize from the newspaper (ten dollars) for best student editorial on a topical subject. Once enrolled at Tulane, he served as campus correspondent for the *New Orleans Statesman* and editor of the college paper, the *Hullabaloo*. And though he aspired to enter journalism as a profession, his leadership qualities elicited a nickname that suggested a grander and more important future: "Senator."

Lindy herself dreamt about the news profession, managing to snag the top post at the paper that a female could rise to: women's editor. Working as part of Hale's staff in the exciting days of Roosevelt's New Deal, she found herself in awe of his sophisticated knowledge of and interest in international and national affairs. But his interests also extended to pretty Lindy, whose preferred date was a medical student. To "keep the doctor away," Hale would place an apple on her desk in the *Hullaballoo* office. There was no danger of her choosing one man just yet. Women who married during school were expected to cease their studies.

Besides, she was consumed with wanderlust, especially when she learned the story of celebrated, pioneering war correspondent Margaret Bourke White, who traveled the world with her camera. White had managed to make a great life for herself, despite her biggest impediment—her sex. Lindy dreamt that she might herself have a peripatetic life, adventuring around in pursuit of stories, "learning about different cultures and civilizations, photographing people's lives and their habitats. I wanted to participate in great events and be where the action was."

That she would—but she never could have imagined just how.

* * *

When she and Hale married in 1937, Lindy had stepped in as a substitute teacher in the tiny town of Romeville, an hour north of New Orleans, after a friend got pregnant and had to leave the job; working while "with child" simply wasn't allowed. The man nicknamed "Senator" now nursed a loftier goal than the news business: He wished to serve in Congress. At the suggestion of one of his mentors, Hale had chosen law school over journalism and was setting up a legal practice in the city with classmates.

With a group of like-minded reformers, the new lawyer leapt into the jambalaya of Louisiana politics, intent on defeating the grip of the entrenched corrupt machine established by the late demagogue Huey Long. For Lindy, her husband's entry into the political underbelly of the state continued an age-old family tradition. Since her forbears first arrived on the shores of Jamestown, at least one member of each generation had served in public office.

Pregnant with their first child, Lindy enthusiastically joined her husband and his allies in support of their gubernatorial candidate. After their daughter Barbara was born, the new mother wheeled her baby carriage down the street, methodically ringing one doorbell after another and sweetly asking residents for their votes. She agreed to serve as a captain of the Fifth precinct in the Twelfth ward—after it was explained to her that "captain" didn't equal "police." The mere presence of women and ministers on Election Day, it was believed, might deter the voter fraud and thuggish intimidation rampant at Louisiana's polling places.

By the time her husband ran for office himself, in 1940, Lindy, though pregnant again, took on the job of campaign manager. In his brochures, Hale joked that unlike his opponent, the only "boss" he answered to was his baby.

That winter, the intensity of the race, along with care of a toddler and newborn, took its toll. On the marvelous winter day that her husband was sworn in as the youngest member of Congress, Lindy was on doctor-ordered bedrest. Still, it wasn't long before she was up and running and settling into the demands of a political wife in the capital city. Immediately, the other wives, like Mrs. Pauline Gore and Mrs. Lady Bird Johnson, instructed her in the strict protocols of Washington that were tinged with the lilt of a small southern town. Her privileged upbringing in New Roads, Louisiana, had equipped her well for these formalities. A legislator's wife was expected to make daily social calls on women whose husbands were senior to hers: Mondays meant paying visits to the wives of the Supreme Court justices; Tuesday, those of the House; Wednesday, the cabinet; Thursday, the Senate; and Friday, the diplomatic corps. When they weren't occupied thusly, the ladies planned parties and dressed up to attend them; participated in the PTA; plotted and executed important volunteer work; and prepared to engage in wise conversation at salons—all the while graciously tending to the needs of their husbands and families.

At her husband's congressional office, Lindy would serve Louisiana chicory coffee to visitors, restock the essential supply of Tabasco sauce on Hale's desk, and supervise the administrative staff, comprised of "Boggs belles," women from back home, each of whom Hale called the most beautiful on Capitol Hill (and who, in turn, voted him most charming member of Congress). His beloved Lindy was not merely a servile spouse, but, in his estimation, his equal partner. He recognized the asset he had in her kindness, grace, charm, and intellect, consulting with her on legislative decisions and insisting she sit in on pertinent debates. "He honored me by letting me help him make decisions," she demurred. (Eventually, he put her on the payroll, and when their son was college age, he was put on it, too.)

While Lindy obeyed convention, she refused to be flummoxed or stymied by the rules. Once refused entry to the Capitol, which issued no formal ID cards, she rushed to a department store, purchased a purple veil, draped it over her black velour hat, and announced to the same guard that she was "Mrs. Hale Boggs." In she went.

Still, when she traveled back to the constituents who'd elected her husband, she played the demure role of silent spouse, sitting on the porch in the rocking chairs with the other ladies, drinking lemonade. She knew the protocol: "Ladies don't make speeches in St. James Parish." And though she might not speak out loud, behind the scenes she wielded her influence, particularly as she pushed her man into a more progressive view of civil rights.

Together with their good looks and charm, Hale and Lindy became an unstoppable political force in the nation's power center—the "Franklin and Eleanor of Congress." Among those drawn to the young man was the venerable veteran lawmaker House Speaker Sam Rayburn, who mentored him in his ad hoc "School of Political Science." Lindy learned to accommodate the hail-fellow-well-met sensibility that prompted her husband to march an endless parade of guests to their home, often at the last minute, shuffling off to the farmers' market to amplify their crop of corn when he offered more to visitors than he'd grown. Or, as Lindy put it, "In cooperating with his tendency to dispensing generous hospitality, I learned to relax and enjoy it."

Blustery Hale, who loved his bourbon, could strongarm his way into assent, shuffle aside a speech prepared by an aide, and captivate an audience with extemporaneous elocution delivered in that "deep, mellow" southern drawl. And Lindy, the peacemaker, with a spectacular memory and infectious laugh, expertly finessed those whom Hale addled—whether it was while he was fortified with drink or not. Peacemaking was in her DNA, as was serenity. Women had been socialized, she believed, to be compassionate, gentle keepers of the culture, to calm the waters. There could be no better antidote to Hale.

As different as their personalities was the manifestation of their patriotism. Hale never ceased marveling that, in these great United States, a poor boy from Mississippi could win election to the great legislative body. With each passing day, Lindy found herself falling more enamored of what she called the "constitutional miracle" of the United States. Some nights, when she went to fetch her husband at the Capitol, she'd pull the car over and gaze at the shimmering, magnificent dome, "pink as a wedding cake at sunset." The very beauty of Congress, she said, inspired all who gazed on it to a sense of mission, one she was proud to serve.

* * *

As long as she'd been conscious, Cokie had been keenly aware of the intractable union between family life and politics. In Washington, her mother would wake at 5:00 A.M. to bake treats for her father's staff. At their home in New Orleans, the giant dining room table was perennially stacked full of campaign materials, ready to be folded and stuffed in envelopes in preparation for mailing. Parades, rallies, openings, blessings, and meet-and-greets filled the days of the three Boggs children, who served as built-in auxiliary staff, trained from an early age to deliver speeches, hand out literature, post signs—and rip down those of the competition. Cokie's excuse for not learning long division? On the day the nuns taught that lesson, she'd traveled to Baton Rouge to hear her father defend himself against charges by a bitter political rival that he was a Communist. (Countered a different rival, who leveled the only charge more egregious, "Hale Boggs ain't no Communist. He's too good a *Catholic* to be a Communist.")

And while she also joked that animosity toward "senators and Republicans" was the only permissible prejudice in their home, the reality was more ecumenical. Republican Gerald Ford and wife Betty were dear friends of the family. Meanwhile, Cokie's best friend was the daughter of a political foe of her dad's, the Republican congressman Bill Miller. Brother Tommy offered a pithy take on the family dynamics: "Dad never said anything good about anybody, and Mom never said anything bad." Add them up, and you get the middle path. Those were the bipartisan happy days, when civil discourse and disagreement were part of the Washington scene. You might think someone was wrong, Cokie learned from watching her parents, but you never thought they were evil.

In addition to their political training by osmosis, the children of lawmakers roamed the halls of the Capitol, the consummate playground, becoming as intimate with the hideaways as with their own backyard. For their comfort, a members' family room was provided, replete with couches and desks. Security guards and staff served as de facto babysitters as kids rode back and forth and back again on the world's shortest railway, the wicker cars that connected the offices to the magnificent dome, and then fortified themselves in the members' dining room.

As much as she looked forward to her seventh birthday party there, under the watchful supervision of the kindly headwaiter, Ernest Petinaud, Cokie's biggest gift that day was waking up with the knowledge that she was finally old enough to enter the public gallery. (Restrictions relegated youngsters to the Family Gallery, which Cokie found downright insulting. After all, she was considered capable of giving tours to visiting constituents. Why couldn't she go where the adults could? Her indignation over age discrimination didn't, however, extend to sex. She wasn't disturbed in the least that girls weren't allowed to become pages.* It had never occurred to her to aspire to that, she said, any more than she would think girls should be priests.†)

The indelible imprint of the Capitol's nooks and crannies was as deep as the bonds Cokie forged. With Walter Little, factotum for the House Ways and Means Committee, which her father chaired, she shared a secret. At the eightieth birthday party her parents hosted for

---

* Girls were allowed to become pages as of May 13, 1971. The Robertses even wrote an article for *Seventeen* magazine about what Cokie called this "off-the-charts" development.
† Cokie's philosophy on this changed. Later in life she said she thought women should be ordained.

Illinois congressman Tom O'Brien, she and Little conspired after they dropped the cake. Cokie used her giant green-and-white-checked skirt to conceal her friend as he furtively patched up the icing. *Shhh.*

As if all this weren't enough to make the Capitol feel like a second home, Lindy would point to a painting in the grand Rotunda that depicted the arrival of the *Mayflower* and proudly remind her children that they were descended from the little boy depicted at its center. Cokie didn't like the boy's looks and didn't wish to have anything to do with him. She preferred to fantasize that she shared lineage with the subject of a nearby artwork: Pocahontas. That the girl had been baptized "Rebecca" left a lasting impression. Cokie vowed to give that name to her first daughter.

Of all the pomp and formality that governed the congressional chambers, her favorite of all days was when members were sworn in, their families streaming onto the floor in their "Christmas velvets"—babies squirming as props in the arms of their awkward fathers. Inevitably, she noticed, they'd cry, and a mother or sister would rush in to rescue the squalling child.

And while she delighted in this rarefied playground over which she had free rein, there remained no place like home in Bethesda, which readily served as backdrop for the annual Boggs garden party for fifteen hundred; a tea for the Women's National Democratic Club, at which she'd serve canapés; or the family's frequent solo guest, House Speaker Rayburn, whom she addressed as "Mr. Sam." Her sister, Barbara, observed, "Some people have antiques and jewelry around the house, but we had the Kennedys, and Humphreys and Rayburns."

One day, when Cokie's pet chicken, an Easter gift, was devoured by a rogue neighborhood dog, Lindy suggested they hold a proper funeral. Cokie's brother, Tommy, teased her as he dug the grave and sang the Dragnet song: *Dum, da-dum-dum.* The little girl ran inside, crying over the irreverence, and into the arms of her surrogate grandfather, Mr. Sam, who was relaxing with her father over a cocktail. Distressed to see little Cokie in tears, the mighty Democratic leader retreated to the yard and sang an appropriately solemn hymn.

* * *

Just as the U.S. government was comprised of three branches, there were three branches of influence in the life of Cokie Boggs: her family, Congress, and the Religious of the Sacred Heart of Jesus. Since age five, she'd been indoctrinated in the story of Rose Philippine Duchesne, a privileged yet intrepid woman from France who'd survived a shipwreck and mutiny on her way to the United States in the early nineteenth century. Once there, she started the first free school west of the Mississippi. In both New Orleans and Washington, Cokie attended schools established by this order.

She reveled in the underpinnings of their teachings: an obligation to social justice, to intelligent action, to a spiritual life; a commitment to intellectual fun; and the expectation of a student that she would do her best. (Though as reverent an admirer as she became, she once bit a nun who put a chalk-covered hand over her mouth and refused to remove it.) Society in the 1950s might not have taken girls seriously, but not so the nuns.

This didn't mean Cokie was all work and no fun. A 1959 issue of *Ingenue* magazine chronicled the life of this "typical" American teenager: Cokie being sewn into her pale green prom dress by her mother (the better for chastity, she later quipped); Cokie sprawled on her parents' bed chitchatting on the phone with her girlfriends about boys; Cokie peering adoringly over her father's shoulder as he sat at his desk perusing his work; Cokie, singing her heart out at a choir practice led by Sister Claire Kondolf.

While Barbara opted to attend the Sacred Heart's Manhattanville College, in New York, known for its integrationist stance and progressive politics, Cokie headed in a different direction when she graduated high school in 1960—much to the consternation of both Lindy and the nuns. She chose Wellesley, one of the Seven Sisters colleges, allied with Harvard but not across the street, as Radcliffe was. (Boys were said to pay less attention to 'Cliffies.) The promise at Wellesley was to teach its students to embody the motto "Not to be ministered to, but to minister"—to make a difference in the world. It wasn't like her parents, but they drove her all the way up to Massachusetts, helping her settle in on a rainy day. After they bid her farewell, Lindy began to cry to her husband in distress, "We've left our baby in a Yankee, Protestant, Republican school."

There Cokie joined the Wellesley Widows, an acapella singing group, rising to become president, while other students, like Linda Cozby, a class behind her, whispered about the lineage of this pretty political science major. "Oh, she's the daughter of the House Majority Whip, she's Hale Boggs' daughter."

In August 1962, between her sophomore and junior years, the privileged and beautiful daughter of Hale Boggs experienced a lifechanging encounter on the campus of Ohio State, where she'd gone to attend the annual congress of the National Student Association (NSA), a fifteen-year-old confederation of student governments from across the United States. Sessions ran morning till night and covered a wide variety of subjects, like "Campus Communications and Freedom of the Press," and "Northern Civil Rights and Human Relations Problems." During a break, Cokie, age eighteen, spotted a boy she thought she recognized from back east. As she got closer, she realized it wasn't, in fact, *Marc* Roberts from Harvard, whom she'd met during freshman year. The man's name tag identified him as *Steven* Roberts of Harvard. Yes, he explained, he was Marc's twin.

He, in turn, recognized *her* name. "Are you Barbara Boggs's sister?" Barbara, too, was a regular at these student association confabs. As Cokie and Steve chitchatted, a "click" occurred, and during the hours and hours of workshops and sessions that followed, that click morphed into full-on flirtation in the safe form of passed notes.

"You're so efficient," Steve, nineteen, flattered Cokie.

"I'm the youngest child of an insane family," she wrote back, "somebody has to be efficient, or we'd starve."

Besides her good looks, Cokie also boasted pluck: She dared to speak at the gathering. Good girls in the early 1960s might attend coed student gatherings, but rarely would they stand up and address them. (For her trouble, she was upbraided by the civil rights activist Stokely Carmichael, who called her a "white, racist, imperialist stuck-up bitch.")

That fall, the young lady with the large, blue-gray, almond-shaped eyes and throaty, infectious laugh just like her mother's boldly called the Harvard boy who hailed from Bayonne, New Jersey, and whose father owned a mobile home park, to invite him to the Wellesley Widows' junior show. After all, their schools were just a dozen miles apart. Steve arrived to watch her perform. Afterward, they decamped to the restaurant at Howard Johnson's. Later, safely back at the dorm, she found herself dancing up the stairs, singing that song from *West Side Story*, "I Feel Pretty."

And then, she declared, "in the manner of obnoxious boys," she didn't hear from him again.

* * *

It wasn't just that this beautiful, intelligent descendent of the American equivalent of royalty intimidated the young, ambitious man of more modest means. All members of the female persuasion set Steve's nerves to flame. As much as girls tantalized him, they also terrified him; he never called one twice. On a rare date in high school, he'd practically passed out at the sight of the young lady seated across from him at the pizza parlor when he noticed how her sweater highlighted her bosom. But aside from his abject fear of the opposite sex, there was another enormous reason to avoid this woman in particular. Cokie was Catholic, and he was Jewish. People of different faiths did not intermarry. An acceptable mixed marriage, Cokie later noted, was "between someone of Irish and Italian extraction."

Back in Bayonne, when Steve developed a crush on a Catholic girl named Gigi, he knew even one date with her wouldn't be right. At the same time, there was something alluring about girls he wasn't "supposed" to go out with, as opposed to the girls he "should," girls with last names like "Posnack" and "Turtletaub."

Maybe it was that with a non-Jew, he could start with a blank slate—as his ancestors had done. Though he'd grown up acutely aware of the horror his elders had faced back in Russia because of their religion, his family didn't observe a single Jewish holiday. His mother hadn't ever attended a seder, much less held one for her own children. When Steve and his brother were ten, they implored the family to join a temple. They both wished to be become a bar mitzvah, or "son of the commandment."

The roots of Steven's confused identity traced back to his name. When his grandfather Abe—Americanized from "Avram"—first arrived from Russia, he'd lopped off the -sky from his surname, "Rogowsky." After Steve's father, Will, began a family of his own, he sanitized "Rogow" one step further, to the all-American "Roberts," infuriating his wife. Bayonne was hardly a place where one needed to mask one's ethnic heritage. Everyone in town was Russian, Polish, Irish, or Italian. (Steve quipped that he grew up "thinking WASPs were a minority group.") But his father's aspirations floated far beyond his hometown; he wished to be a writer, and for a time he even published children's picture books using a pseudonym fused from the middle names of his twins: Jeffrey Victor. The books were devoted mostly to teaching kids how things worked: *The Train Book*, for example, was based on trips to the local station that Steve and his twin brother had made with their dad. A more generic name might allow him to reach a wider audience.

Further consternation: Steve would have happily traded the first name he'd been assigned with the one his twin brother, born ten minutes after, had been lucky to get. "Marcus" was the name of his grandpa Abe's brother back in Russia, the dashing intellect who'd risen to become an editor at *Pravda*. It wasn't fair that Marc got the honor of being named for the journalist in the family, as it was *Steve* who aspired to become a newspaperman.

Yet brother Marc also got something Steve was quite fortunate not to—polio. The limp that resulted from the disease made it impossible for him to engage in the sports his twin savored. Instead, Marc became obsessed with model airplanes and books, and developing his intellect.

From their bedroom window, the two could gaze at the majestic Statue of Liberty and see beyond it to the starry promise of Manhattan. A wider world beckoned. How would they ever get there?

* * *

When he wasn't playing basketball, the thumping game he felt provided the "heartbeat" of the city, Steve was pursuing his journalistic dream by editing the high school paper, the *Bayonne Beacon*. For two hours each weekday and four on Saturdays, he earned a dollar an hour at the town crier, the *Bayonne Times*, where his job was to write up TV highlights, movie timetables, and local obituaries, which helped refine his capacity to spell the ethnic surnames so common among his fellow citizens.

Only a quarter of his classmates at Bayonne High School were destined for college, most likely state schools. (Girls were more likely to attend secretarial school, after which they'd "be condemned to a lifetime sentence in front of a typewriter.") Steve himself might have stayed local, were it not for another hometown boy who'd escaped: Barney Frank.*

Back in Bayonne for a visit, Barney ran into Steve at the Jewish Community Center and suggested that the bright "twinnies" consider applying to the school he was attending, Harvard. Barney had headed north after his brainy elder sister entered its companion school for women, Radcliffe. Neither Steve nor Marc had ever traveled as far from home as when they rode the bus to Cambridge, Massachusetts, for their college interviews. Arriving in Harvard Square, Steve innocently queried a stranger about the location of the school.

"All around you," was the bemused reply.

Steven and Marc were comforted to learn that the admissions officer had spent the war at the Bayonne Naval Supply Depot; this man was

---

* Frank was first elected to the House as a representative of Massachusetts in 1980.

familiar with whence they'd come. It seemed a miracle, but, that spring, both boys received admission letters. (Later, Steve began to suspect that might have had something to do with a study being conducted at the school on twins.) As great a miracle was the fact that their father, after years of privation, was now earning enough to pay for their education. Having given up the writing dream, Will had forayed into the lucrative business of mobile homes.

Marc, who aspired to become an astrophysicist or aeronautical engineer, was thrilled to have won a golden ticket to what he saw as an intellectual paradise, a "fairyland." But Steve wavered about the offer. He was eager to carve out an identity away from that of his brother, especially after Marc beat him for the chance to represent their high school at the prestigious student government conference, Boys State. After building a masterful campaign platform, which included a recommendation that the state operate drag strips for teenagers, he won election as the group's president and, with it, the chance to attend the national conference in Washington. Steve seethed with envy. There was no way he'd go to Harvard now.

Will intervened to talk sense into his son. Not attending the most prestigious university in the nation would be a tremendous mistake he'd regret. Harvard was big enough for the two of them, he told Steve. Go.

In short order, Steve discovered that the place his brother viewed as nirvana was, for him, purgatory. Surrounded by prep school boys in madras shorts and docksiders, sans socks, nonchalantly popping beers and puffing on cigars, Steve, clad in shirts his mother had bought for him at a discount store, felt his socially awkward worst. When he peered out the window into Harvard Yard and witnessed Sen. John F. Kennedy, the famous alumnus and presidential candidate, flitting by, he was sure he'd landed on Mars. Till now, the most famous person with whom he'd come into contact was Bayonne's native star, the child actress turned bombshell Sandra Dee (whom he'd first encountered when they were both kids, when she had yet to ditch her birth name, "Alexandra Zuck.") *This* was most decidedly not Thirty-First Street and Avenue A in Bayonne.

In this strange new stratosphere, absent the Good Humor trucks, Dido's Pizza, and stickball games, he'd lost his mooring. This Harvard thing was a very big mistake.

While some students might find solace in joining a sport or a fraternity, Steve beelined to his own house of worship: the offices of Harvard's daily paper, the *Crimson*. There, to prove his mettle, he underwent the newspaperly version of a hazing ritual and was assigned to interview the college's gruff dean, McGeorge Bundy, about a building project. The story he filed passed the test, and he was invited to join the celebrated paper.

Now he possessed that ineffable prize: an affiliation with a respected journalistic institution. This gave its bearer a license to show up in places mere mortals could not, to ask questions in the name of committing journalism.

He plunged into a diversity of subjects, writing book reviews, theater critiques, sports wraps, articles about panty raids in the Radcliffe quad, and the emerging civil rights movement—he even wrote a story about taking a girl on a date to a football game. Having never ridden on a plane before, he found himself flying south to Philadelphia to cover a Harvard basketball game.

That spring, he began earning an even fancier byline after being hired as campus stringer for the *New York Times*, the paper that served as a bible for all erudite residents of the New York metropolitan area, including his grandpa Harry. The first story he filed was about the sport of crew, a subject unfamiliar to a nice Jewish boy from New Jersey. For the best vantage point, he arranged to ride along with one of the teams, although his clever scheme collapsed when they won and everyone partied for an hour before coming ashore. On land, a messenger from Western Union jumped frantically up and down, pleading for the rookie's copy so he could swiftly ferry it back for transmission to the paper's newsroom headquarters in New York. Here was his debut in the big leagues, and he'd blown his very first deadline.

Back in New Jersey, Steve's father received, and devoured, the *Crimson*, occasionally even writing a letter to the editor in response to his son's stories, and he was thrilled when his comments made print. Having abandoned his own writerly dreams, now he was devoted to the unbridled success of his sons. When Steve scored his first byline in *The Nation*, an unfulfilled youthful dream of his own, Will drove the boy around to newsstands in Manhattan in search of it and snapped up every copy.

What father wouldn't delight in watching his children flourish at the country's preeminent college? But Will's pride and his ability to subsidize his sons' expansive experience was tinged, a bit, by envy.

The twins' mother, for her part, offered leveling wise words of wisdom in the face of their glide path to success: Slow down. Stop and get to know yourself. With every second filled and new experiences to savor, this didn't seem an option for Steven—or even desirable. This rarefied air that at first had seemed so asphyxiating portended his fate.

* * *

In March 1963, Steve caught a ride with friends to DC to attend another political gathering. It involved a project to which Cokie's sister Barbara had been assigned: the creation of a domestic "Peace Corps" to serve the nation's most impoverished corners. After college, Barbara had worked as a recruiter in a Catholic volunteer program, then landed a job in the White House as a special assistant in President Kennedy's Office of Presidential Correspondence. The burning ambition of this popular blond, blithe spirit, onetime Cherry Blossom Princess and queen of the Mardi Gras Ball, was to "find a good husband and raise six to twelve children." But till that happened, this meaningful work would do.

Students asked to discuss this burgeoning volunteer corps had been invited to stay at Barbara's family's home on Bradley Boulevard. Hale and Lindy each quipped (and Hale sometimes worried) that the place was becoming something of an "underground railroad" for student activists, "friends of their children, and children of their friends," heading down south for civil rights marches. (Don't let out that you were here, a trepidatious Hale said to one of them.)

When the car arrived in Cambridge to fetch Steve, who planned to write about the meeting for the *Crimson*, there in the backseat sat Cokie. Instantly, he felt a pang of regret for not having called her.

After that night's meeting at American University, Steve was assigned to Cokie's childhood bedroom, where he would sleep in her old bed with a crocheted canopy. A terrible cough kept him up, and in the wee hours came a knock on the door. Mother Lindy, an apparition resplendent in her flowing peach chiffon nightgown, had arrived to administer what she called "a little restorative toddy." She'd learned the medicinal powers of whiskey as a girl, when she'd been sent to convent school with a few bottles for the nuns.

The next night, after a post-conference party, an element of danger lurked in the air as Steve and Cokie sat up in the kitchen talking late into the night, just the two of them, while fixing scrambled eggs.

All the way back up to school, they smooched in the car—never mind the other passengers—but once they were back in their respective dorms: again, the deafening roar of silence.

* * *

Until, one night, when the housemaster at Eliot House poured sherry in honor of a visitor, and the booze emboldened Steve to pick up the phone and dial Cokie, whom he told with excitement and a bit of braggadocio that he was soon to appear on a panel at Radcliffe. He was seen, he was proud to say, as a progressive in the matters of women. He felt they should be taken more seriously, and thus an invitation had been extended to speak.

The uninhibited Cokie invited herself along, and Steve heard himself gulping out a "yes," adding that they should go out after the talk. The $5 he earned for each *Times* story he filed would easily cover their $1.99 dinner for two at Cronin's, plus tip.

And with that, a romance was officially off to the races, back and forth over the 12.6 miles between Eliot House and Cokie's dorm at

Wellesley, Tower Court. Fortunately for the young lovers, Harvard's "parietal rules" governing female visitation had recently, and controversially, been loosened, extending the hours men were permitted to entertain women in their dorm rooms till midnight—as long as the doors to the rooms remained open and one foot remained on the floor. The idea, explained a school administrator, was to allow students a chance to "enjoy each other in a private quiet place at no extra cost"—a development Harvard's dean and other educators shrieked was the beginning of moral ruin for all. The issue of campus sex was the subject of much scrutiny in the popular press that fall: How much should school police student behavior? Did premarital sex inflict lasting damage? Cokie, as a devout Catholic enrolled at a Protestant school (who also happened to be the daughter of a congressman), was invited to speak on a panel about "Sex and Morals," along with a Harvard psychiatrist, Yale's chaplain, and two male students on the David Susskind–hosted educational television show *Open End*.*

But the immediate morality of their relationship was hardly their concern. The bigger picture daunted them: Their religious differences made a future together impossible. Neither of them would ever convert, nor would either expect it of the other. They masked their fears by assuring themselves that this was just a spring romance. Over the summer, Steve even dated another girl, and Cokie accepted an invite from another boy to the Harvard-Yale game.

In the fall of their senior year, with the semester well under way, came the shattering, unfathomable news of President Kennedy's assassination. A pall fell over the Harvard campus at the murder of their treasured alumnus. Life stood still as the community collectively grieved the loss. A planned concert in DC that weekend by the Harvard Glee Club transformed into a memorial tribute.

Over at Wellesley, friends flocked to Cokie's room, assuming that given her family's connections, she might know more, or be able to offer particular comfort. Lindy had planned the president's inaugural ball,

---

* Sadly, a tape of the appearance does not exist.

which Cokie had been lucky enough to attend, and her father had, just weeks earlier, delivered a searing speech in New Orleans denouncing the haters of this president he adored. Not wanting to deal with the outpouring of others' grief during this moment of tragedy and sadness, Cokie turned to Steve, and together they headed up to a friend's cabin in New Hampshire, where they spent the weekend mourning, missing the marathon, unprecedented television processional that riveted and informed the nation.*

In the midst of this wrenching time, Steve received encouraging news about his future. He'd been invited, after graduation, to begin work at the Washington bureau of the *New York Times* as assistant to James "Scotty" Reston, the Pulitzer Prize–winning columnist. The son of the paper's owner, a classmate and fellow *Crimson* staff member, had tipped him off to the job—a referral amplified by a raft of A-list recommendation letters, including one from Lindy Boggs, who, lucky for him, considered the esteemed journalist Reston a family friend.

As Cokie's own graduation approached, she hardly shared in the joy. After all, the unofficial motto of schools for women was "a ring by spring or your money back." So many of hers and Steve's friends were engaged—even most of Steve's roommates.

The casual, carefree frivolity of Wellesley's May Day hoop-rolling on Severance Green in the final weeks of her college career was bittersweet. Tradition held that, like the lucky woman who caught the bouquet at a wedding, the winner of the race would be the first to be married. For Cokie, the possibility of an engagement, not to mention marriage, seemed a mirage.†

Just as rain had marked her arrival on campus, the weather was gloomy for commencement. By the time of Harvard's own grand

---

* Hale Boggs was asked by President Johnson to serve on the Warren Commission, which investigated the murder.

† In more recent years, it was believed the winner would be first in her class to become a CEO; today, it's said the winner will be the first to "achieve happiness and success, whatever that means to her."

commencement processional a few days later, though, the skies had cleared. It hadn't rained for that occasion in over forty years.

* * *

Fresh diplomas in hand, college graduates and conflicted sweethearts Steve and Cokie made their way to Washington together—sort of—and toward an uncertain future: he to an apartment downtown, she to her beloved family home, to which he now became a frequent visitor. Their postgraduate lives began just as the ink was drying on the 1964 Civil Rights Act, newly enacted into law. And though the act outlawed discrimination on the basis of race, creed, religion, and sex, the world Steve and Cokie were entering was anything but equal, yet.

Steve settled into his work at the vaunted *New York Times*, and Cokie managed to land a job herself. Thanks to the Wellesley College placement office, she found work at a local TV production company that had been started by Wellesley alumnus Sophie B. Altman, a woman who had it all: husband, kids, and a thriving business.

Born in Springfield, Massachusetts, in 1913, Sophie Robinson had attended Wellesley on scholarship, and then headed next to Yale, where she became one of the first women ever to earn a law degree. After moving to Washington and working as a lawyer in the Roosevelt administration, she met and married a fellow lawyer, Norman Altman, with whom she had four children.

She'd long had an interest in journalism. During World War II, she'd written a column about women's contributions to the effort, titled *Women at War*. This led her to a job as an associate producer on a popular weekly NBC radio show called *Meet the Press*, which she helped move onto television when the medium blossomed after war's end.*

---

* *Meet the Press* traced its roots to another formidable pioneer, Martha Rountree, whose first radio show featured career women offering advice on romance, called *Leave It to the Girls*. This led to a connection to the publisher of *American Mercury* magazine, Lawrence Spivak, with whom she'd launched the weekly show, which had originally debuted on Mutual Radio Network in 1945.

With her growing family, Altman wished to find a way to work from home. Television stations, she knew, needed to fulfill government requirements for public service programming. She conceived some family-friendly fare, an acceptable focus for the rare woman in the male-dominated world of television—such as a parenting advice program, *Report Card for Parents*, and *Teen Talk*, a discussion show, which, coincidentally, Cokie had appeared on once in high school. Recognizing that some young people felt uncomfortable speaking frankly about themselves, Altman had next created a quiz-show format that prompted smart kids from area high schools to compete with their brainiac peers. *It's Academic* launched in 1961 and became so popular that Altman licensed the format to stations in dozens of other cities. Cokie worked as associate producer on the show, but was soon pressed into service on another Altman youth-focused creation, *Meeting of the Minds*, which ran locally on Sundays before *Meet the Press*. Here, the new college graduate served as on-air host, leading a panel of international students as they quizzed a newsmaker on a wide range of subjects. While family lore held that Cokie had inherited her mother's distinctive laugh, her appearance on television showed that she'd inherited from her father his peerless ability to speak extemporaneously.

One week, joined by young people from Korea, Israel, Italy, and the Soviet Union, Cokie, recent college graduate, confidently quizzed Sen. Eugene McCarthy of Minnesota about the Central Intelligence Agency. "With all respects," said the novice television interviewer, "you're putting the CIA on the same level as the State Department. In my view, the CIA should be just a tool in the hands of the State Department and the White House." The girl who'd been taught her whole life by her politician parents to be skeptical of the press—the girl who learned from an early age to say "off the record" when a reporter called the family home—was now not only dating a journalist, but working as one, too.

Sure, her job was glamorous and interesting, but it didn't fill the tremendous void she felt as she trundled from city to city to serve as bridesmaid to one delirious, dazzled friend after another. Cokie wouldn't consider herself successful or happy until she donned a wedding gown, too. It didn't seem to matter to her that, without even trying, she'd landed a job that other ambitious women had aspired to and that so few had attained.

On the heels of Pauline Frederick's success, each of the networks had hired a woman to cover serious news, but that's where it stopped. One of these journalistic unicorns became the subject of young aspiring reporter Steve's second official byline for the *Times* in January 1965. Nancy Dickerson, a onetime junior high teacher from Wauwatosa, Wisconsin, had arrived in the nation's capital in 1950 as Nancy Hanschman, with zero secretarial skills or family connections, but with a dream that she might change the world. After much maneuvering, she managed to land a job as an assistant at the Senate Foreign Relations Committee. The vast Rolodex she assembled there trumped the impediment of her sex to score her a slot as a producer for the CBS public affairs program *Capital Cloakroom*. Through a combination of tenacity, grit, and charm, she eventually became the first female correspondent on the air at CBS and a favorite of President Lyndon Johnson's. "She managed the very difficult business of being authoritative without being masculine," a network executive told Steve.

Nancy's intense good looks (not to mention her high-profile position) allowed her to attract dashing men of power. She'd even dated the pre-Jacqueline Bouvier senator John F. Kennedy. Reluctant to alter her fast-track lifestyle, Nancy delayed marriage as long as should could, even after meeting the wealthy industrialist whose proposal she ultimately accepted.

Now, bouncing her eighteen-month old son on her knee in her elegant town house, she explained to this young would-be reporter, Steve Roberts, the key factor to her eventual success in Washington: meeting as many people as possible. "There's nothing better than working in Washington," she exclaimed, "and there's nothing more exciting than to stand there with a live mike, watch someone wave his hand, and start talking."

Steve's Cokie had all the trappings of this Nancy Dickerson: the looks, the confidence, and by dint of her heritage, built-in connections, the kind it had taken Nancy years to build. But with each passing day, Cokie became more distressed—frantic, even. She felt like a carton of milk, whose "use by" date was about to expire. After all, she was twenty-one.

* * *

Fresh good news arrived for Steve that made Cokie's situation even more dire: a promotion. The dream job as staff reporter meant moving to the *Times* headquarters in New York City, where he'd been assigned to the Metro desk. Even less desirable to Cokie than the limbo of being a girlfriend and not a wife was a long-distance relationship.

At a rest stop on the New Jersey Turnpike, she delivered an ultimatum: If he didn't propose, she was running off to California. She was wasting the best years of her life. How did Steve know she was serious? At a time when women were trained to give the best of everything to their man, Cokie, for once, took for herself the most delectable part of the pastry they were sharing.

Inevitably, in the past, their conversations about marriage had swirled into a never-ending spiral of despair. There seemed no way to resolve their religious differences. This conversation was no different. There was no question for Steve that Cokie was "the one"; everything felt better when she was around. But with his new job, the timing just wasn't right—and the timing would never be right to explain to his parents that he was marrying a Catholic girl.

Looming large for the couple was Cokie's sister's recent experience. Barbara had been engaged for a year to the charismatic activist Allard Lowenstein, a man possessed of a "demonic intensity" and whose opinions and attitudes, said a friend, "were often as outrageous as his habit of scheduling a midnight appointment, then arriving four hours later and pounding indignantly on the door if you'd fallen asleep." For his capacity to mobilize supporters, some called Lowenstein the "Pied Piper."

They'd met, as Cokie and Steve had, at a summer meeting of

the National Student Association. But Al was a decade older than the twenty-one-year-old Barbara, whom he described as one of the funniest people he'd ever encountered. For her part, she was taken with his sense of mission, his commitment to unity among all races. Very quickly, they committed to marry.

They could flirt with the notion of spending their lives together, Barbara said, "but for the sword, the dear old sword there," of their fractious religious differences. Never mind his erratic behavior. Barbara was consumed by the operatic intensity of her feelings, the courage he gave her to love. When they were apart, she felt as if she were missing an arm.

Though Al visited his prospective in-laws to convince them of how intense his feelings for their daughter were, they refused to support the union, insisting to Barbara that it was not his faith but his instability that was the concern.* Neither did Al's own family offer the couple their blessing. At the wedding of his sister to a non-Jew, Al's stepmother held Barbara's hand and cried hysterically.

Though nuptials were planned for September 1962, pressure from Hale led Barbara to call off the ceremony three weeks before. On the day they were to have been married, Barbara wrote Al a plaintive letter, elaborating the "fundamental differences between us" that were so great they would have made their union impossible.

Still, lasting love was around the corner. In short order, Barbara reconnected with Paul Sigmund, a man she'd known over the years, also through the National Student Association.† A whirlwind courtship led to a wedding in January 1964, at which Hale's brother Robbie, the priest, performed the ceremony, and Cokie served as maid of honor. Afterward, the newlyweds and a thousand guests, including the president and First Lady, decamped from the church to Bradley Boulevard

---

* Whether Hale was aware of Lowenstein's rumored bisexual tendencies, much less his alleged connections to the CIA, isn't clear. Lowenstein did eventually marry and have children. He was elected to Congress in 1969 and served one term. In 1980, he was murdered by an obsessed former student.
† Paul Sigmund had, in a twist, been Steve's professor at Harvard.

for a reception. On the menu: red beans and rice with mounds of ham, purchased on sale at the local Giant supermarket and prepared weeks in advance in the Bradley Boulevard kitchen under the supervision of Lindy. As her husband the inveterate entertainer said, "We don't do things in a country club."

Barbara had her husband. Cokie was in limbo.

Faced with her ultimatum on the Jersey Turnpike, and terrified of losing her to California, Steve acquiesced: "Oh, all right, Cokie."

The clumsy nonproposal aside, Cokie insisted that her groom-to-be ask her father for her hand in marriage, as was tradition. Over at the majestic house, as Hale tended his tomatoes, Steve had to practically be pushed out the door to the garden. He shuffled before his impos-ing future father-in-law and acknowledged that he was aware that their religious differences would be a hurdle.

"Yes, I do think you'll have problems," said Hale, as he gave his blessing, "but not as many as I'll have if I tell her who to marry."

When Steve informed his mother of his plans, she cried—and the tears weren't sparked by joy. His father, with whom he'd had a running discussion and exchange on the matter, made it clear that emasculation was in his future: No Jewish man married to a Catholic woman could ever be the "dominant male" in the family.

Steve's twin, Marc, intervened on behalf of this Romeo and Juliet, and eventually the family relented. Deep down, they knew there was no woman better suited for their son.

* * *

Negotiating the details of the wedding was no easier or more pleasur-able than getting to the engagement. In a meeting with her local priest, Cokie explained that her future husband's relatives were loath to enter a church. The local bishop dispensed permission for her to marry at home. But satisfaction for one family member came at the expense of another. To devout Lindy, a backyard wedding wasn't a wedding at all. "That's a party," she said with a frown.

How to include a Jewish presence in the ceremony? As her sister had, Cokie chose her uncle Robbie the priest as officiant, but finding a rabbi willing to perform an interfaith marriage turned out, she said, to be "like looking for an abortionist." The White House rabbi turned them down. So did several others they approached. When they learned that an elder statesman who happened to be Jewish was an acceptable substitute, they reached out to a Boggs family friend, the former Supreme Court justice Arthur Goldberg.

Next was the matter of the guest list. This wasn't just a wedding, after all. It was a political occasion. Along with extended families and friends and Washington insiders, including the president and Mrs. Johnson, the party grew outsized, to fifteen hundred. As she had for her older daughter, Lindy kept her kitchen busy in preparation for weeks in advance.

Everything seemed in order, except for one crucial matter. A license was needed to wed. On the Thursday before the big Saturday, the happy couple trekked to the Maryland county seat of Rockland, only to learn that obtaining a marriage license required a forty-eight-hour waiting period—and the office was not open on the weekend.

"Sorry, you'll just have to get married on Monday," said the clerk, unmoved by Steve's name-dropping from their star-studded guest list, headlined by President Johnson, who'd be inconvenienced. Desperate for a workaround, Cokie reluctantly enlisted the help of her brother the lawyer, who sleuthed out a circuit court judge willing to grant a waiver.

Undeterred, the bride-to-be marched into Justice Thomas Anderson's office the next morning just before court opened at 10:00 A.M., prepared to state her case. Guests were arriving from all over the country, she explained. Among the attendees who'd be inconvenienced was no less than the president. Grudgingly, the judge signed an order waiving the requisite waiting period. If she'd come at any other time on Friday, he scolded, he'd never have been able to bend the rules: He had eighteen cases that day.

An aide in Hale's office found the whole situation so amusing she tipped off the press. The wires trumpeted the story across the land, applauding the lawmaker's daughter for her tenacity. "Some gals might have caved in," wrote the reporter, "but Miss Corinne is made of sterner stuff."

* * *

At long last, the moment had arrived. A large tent had been erected on the property, replete with dance floor below and chandeliers bedecked with flowers from the garden above. Arrangements of Cokie's favorite flower, the lily of the valley, lit up the grounds. A white latticework chuppah under which the couple would exchange their vows reminded anyone who wasn't aware that this Roman Catholic wedding was infused with a Jewish twist. The festive cake came direct from the Senate Dining Room. Chauffeurs who ferried the VIPs to Bradley Boulevard were invited in for sandwiches and beer.

The minute President Johnson arrived, Hale coaxed Cokie, still primping in the bathroom, to get on with it. A trumpet sounded Purcell's Voluntary, and the wedding party began its procession up the aisle. Almost immediately, it stalled. Guests among the throngs of attendees whispered: Had the bride had a change of heart? With most of those attending standing, but for the VIPs and elders in their chairs, it was difficult to see.

Something differently dramatic had occurred: Ribbons, it seemed, had come loose on the satin pillow carried by the bride's young nephew, the ring-bearer, and Steve's wedding band—inscribed with the words "Forever Spring," a nod to that first season they'd fallen in love—had been tossed onto the grass and out of sight.

Cokie's father offered his daughter his own band as a placeholder, as did other guests in the immediate area who'd witnessed the snafu. But a petulant Cokie refused to proceed without the correct ring to place on her husband's finger.

"Daddy, the symbolism is just all wrong," she whined, as Barbara, her matron of honor, laughed.

Her father responded sternly. "Cokie, don't you think there's enough symbolism going on here for one night?"

A Secret Service agent saved the day, borrowing a pocket flashlight from the president's doctor to aid him as he combed through the lawn in search of the missing gold. Hale convinced his daughter to keep marching, and miraculously, the retrieved ring allowed the show to go on.

Cokie, as usual, had stood firm and gotten exactly what she wanted.

CHAPTER TEN
"Not even slightly a feminist"

After the fairytale, reality took a bite—and it was painful. For the honeymoon in Puerto Rico, the groom forgot to pack a bathing suit; on arrival, he threw out his back. The nuptial bliss continued when the happy couple arrived at their first marital home in New York City, the rent-controlled apartment Steve had secured for them on West Seventy-Fifth Street, four rooms for $185 a month. Cokie burst into tears as soon as she walked in the door. The ugly interior was made worse by the view of a brick wall.

And then there was the matter of how she would fill her days. There had never been any question that she'd give up her job in DC, which paid a tiny bit more than Steve's, in favor of his. She wouldn't have asked or considered any other way. Her main job now was to be his wife, to support him in his career—just as her mother had always supported Hale in his. But faced with those long, empty days in this ugly apartment, she found herself wondering: What exactly did tradition leave for her?

She began the search for some meaningful way to spend the time while her husband was at work. Politics was out of the question. To enter the "family business," she believed, might compromise her husband's journalistic career—and his needs came first. Pursuing some aspect of journalism just seemed simpler to do than anything else. She did like to write, and she believed she was good at it; she also enjoyed talking to people and learning what they had to say.

Time and again, though, she hit a wall, just as Linda and Nina had in their job searches: There were no jobs for women, or the company already "had its woman." (On occasion, the rejection was delivered by a man who put his hand on her thigh.) A steady pipeline of well-educated women flowed into *Newsweek*, to servile, dead-end jobs, while men with similar degrees waltzed in as writers and then raced up the corporate ladder. How about being a *researcher*? And oh, did she take dictation? How fast could she type? The pages of the campus papers at elite women's schools were filled with ads for secretarial courses that promised to equip these well-educated students for the working world. Had she wished to be a secretary, there or most anywhere, she'd have had a job in a snap.

When a prospective boss told her that the women who held those dead-end jobs loved them, she bristled: "I knew an 'Our servants are so close they are actually members of our family' statement when I heard one.'" Though she'd never have considered herself "not even slightly a feminist," facing down the belief that a woman could not perform the same job as a man boiled Cokie's blood.

Waiting at home for Steve to return each evening, cooking elaborate meals in their awful kitchen, she began to feel like a "basket case," as if she were dying inside. She was certain that her beloved husband didn't grasp her despair. In 1966, there were no illusions that men and women inhabited the same universe, with the same opportunities.

To combat the depression, she talked herself into a daily herculean task: running an errand. One day, she mustered the presence of mind to return a wedding present. She threw a coat over her nightgown and made her way to the fancy store Georg Jensen. Just her luck, standing next to her at the counter was the man whose wife had chosen the very gift she was returning. After laughing at this unlikely coincidence, he invited her to join him on his next stop, which happened to be the swearing-in ceremony of Nelson Rockefeller as governor at his Manhattan office. Holding her coat closed as tightly as possible, she tagged along. Her loneliness trumped her inappropriate attire.

Occasional pleasures, like exploring the city with Steve—up to Arthur Avenue in the Bronx or down to Katz's Deli on the Lower East Side—provided her temporary respite from the feelings of emptiness. Only when Cokie commiserated with other women did she realize she wasn't crazy, or alone. She'd never heard anyone talk about this sensation before. Weren't you supposed to, the minute you were finally married, feel fulfilled and complete? For her, the "happily ever after" feeling had yet to come.

After eight months of searching, finally, she landed a job as a writer and editor on a business newsletter published by the Cowles communications empire. When that folded a year later, she scored another gig, at local independent station WNEW, where a longtime acquaintance of her father's served as news director. As a producer assigned to the "Action News" segment, Cokie was charged with helping to solve seemingly insurmountable issues for the city's downtrodden and aggrieved citizens who wrote in with their tales of woe. She absolutely hated this job. While Steve was out all day crisscrossing the city, covering the important beat of housing and urban renewal and occasional politics or antiwar protests, she was trapped with what she felt was the "phony" futility of trying to help in the name of local tabloid TV news.

Besides, now that she'd been working, a new yearning had begun to consume her: She was desperate to have a baby. Her doleful longing to be a mother dominated (and ruined) the couple's first anniversary, which they'd gone to celebrate in Rome. Over a bottle of Asti Spumante, she cried and cried.

Steve was no readier for children than he had been for marriage, but becoming a father would actually solve a big problem: It would offer him a draft deferment, an escape from service in Vietnam. Cokie was not only terrified at the prospect of losing her husband to the devastating and protracted conflict. She also hated the idea of Steve having a "major experience that she couldn't share." To avoid being called up, he'd been halfheartedly attending graduate school at night. When the school caught on, he was kicked out.

To Cokie's delight, she discovered she was pregnant. The draft rules had changed, though, and Steve was called up anyway. A diagnosis of elevated blood pressure—probably generated by sheer terror, he acknowledged—saved him from service.

For Cokie, the only downside to expecting was the realization that she'd be stuck in the terrible TV job a while longer. No one would ever hire a pregnant woman. She'd be lucky if they'd let her keep working when she started to show.

By the time she cashed in a week's vacation to accompany her husband to the 1968 Democratic National Convention in Chicago, her pregnancy was supremely evident. But her father was in charge of the party's platform committee, and she wished to be present to support him. The gathering was the capstone of an incendiary period in the nation's history. Tensions flared that year with North Korea's capture of a U.S. intelligence ship; the bloody surprise of the Tet Offensive in Vietnam; the assassinations of the Rev. Dr. Martin Luther King Jr. and Sen. Robert F. Kennedy. Chaos ruled inside the convention hall and out as antiwar protestors rioted in the streets. Inside, her mother did her usual behind-the-scenes power-brokering, even sitting down for lunch at the fancy Pump Room with musician Sonny Bono, who gave the belle an uncensored verbal tour of the debauchery of sixties rock concerts and his plans to register voters at them.

As mayhem reigned on the streets, a policeman tried to rush Steve and Cokie along, pushing a club into her back. The mother-to-be turned around, exposing her massive belly, and barked, "If you don't leave us alone, I'm going to have my baby right here and now."

They did, and she didn't. But on a Friday night back in New York weeks later, as Steve screwed knobs onto a freshly painted dresser in the newly prepared nursery, Cokie, who was prepping dinner, announced that the time had come. Ever organized, she'd planned to wash her hair the minute she went into labor. That now seemed folly as they rushed across town to the hospital.

Marching into the delivery room with his surgical mask, the quintessential modern dad, Steve felt like a "kid following the high school band." He wasn't merely about to become a first-time father. He was there on assignment for *Good Housekeeping* magazine, documenting the experience of childbirth from the man's point of view. The story would pay twelve hundred dollars, the price of the hospital bill. An enlightened modern husband didn't just help make the baby; he helped his wife have it, too, having sat by her side in a dance studio on the Upper East Side for a class in the Lamaze breathing technique, equipping him to accompany her as coach in the delivery room. The finished magazine piece featured a photo of the beaming new parents and bouncing baby boy with the headline "WE had a baby."

The very next day, after situating his brood back at the apartment, Steve returned to work, where he received another life-altering bit of information. The paper wished to reassign him to the strange foreign land of Los Angeles. Heading to the other coast was nothing he'd ever considered; he'd trekked west of the Mississippi only once, just the month before, on a reporting trip. Wizened New Yorker that he'd become, he copped to suffering from an "advanced case of Eastern myopia, that the center of the world is somewhere around Fiftieth Street and Madison Avenue in Manhattan." His dearest wish was to be called back to Washington so he could cover politics, DC being the power center not of just the United States but of serious *Times* journalism. A posting in California was like being sent to Timbuktu. Yet new mother Cokie had had her fill of the Big Apple. Since their marriage had precluded her following through on her threat to leave Steve and head west, they might as well go together. She was happy to put life in New York in the rearview mirror, especially now that the city streets had been overtaken by a garbage strike—never mind that the merchants at neighborhood shops had become so fond of her they'd showered her with baby gifts. Navigating the city streets with her first child would surely be less joyful than fraught.

And so, they packed up their rundown Ford Falcon, loaded the baby in the back seat, and started driving west to the land of the counterculture, farther from home than either of them had ever lived. To maximize the experience, they purchased a zippy burnt-orange Karmann Ghia sports car and rented the quintessential California house, in Malibu—an ultra-romantic but utterly inconvenient abode in the glorious hills of the Santa Monica Mountains, three miles in one direction from the nearest store, five miles in the other to a place that stocked the

Sunday *New York Times*, and a half-hour commute to Steve's office. It was worth the hassle for the chance to gaze out their windows at a long, endless stretch of the Pacific Ocean.

Here in California, Cokie's eyes continued to widen with wonder at the emerging sixties pathos that seemed to waft through the smoggy air—LSD, free love, feminist consciousness, Charles Manson, earthquakes, brush fires, a permissive culture of divorce. While researching a story on the rise of pornography, Steve even brought his adoring wife along to several hard-core porn theaters, where the presence of a lady startled one proprietor so greatly that he sat her in a special chair in a corner.

When he returned home from a trip to Northern California with a poster of some counterculture group called Jefferson Airplane in tow, she indifferently tacked it over the baby's changing station. The psychedelic nature of it all held little appeal for either of them. "Women's lib," Cokie assumed, meant acceptance of any path a woman chose. Instead, she felt judged by these California radicals for having taken a traditional path. And yet, her reverence for those traditions was tempered by her anger toward women who wouldn't speak up. When she joined Steve at a seminar at the Aspen Institute, and the wives of other participants sat silently in the balcony, she insisted that they be included at the table in at least one of the sessions.

And she bristled when they socialized with her husband's colleagues, who immediately dismissed her as "just" a wife and mother. Thankfully, though, she could counter that she did, in fact, have a job, even if part-time. Altman Productions had sold a version of *It's Academic* to a Los Angeles station, and another educational kids' show, *Serendipity*, was in development. It was the perfect setup for this new mother—a little work, a lot of flexible time. Another opportunity emerged when Steve enlisted her to research some freelance magazine stories, one on venereal disease, another on teen pregnancy—for which she was rewarded with a byline as coauthor. On a piece about the pleasures of Los Angeles, for instance, they extolled the virtues of whale watching from the Palos Verdes Peninsula and shrugged over the "stars" on the disappointing Hollywood Boulevard. ("You won't recognize nine-tenths of them," they pooh-poohed.)

Occasionally, when Steve was away on one of his frequent reporting trips, living his dream life, she'd fantasize, as she hauled out the garbage, about finding a partner who was home more often. Then it would occur to her—if she were on her own, she'd always have to do *everything* by herself.

Together and separately, the couple waded through the murkiness of the changing world and their roles in it. In the midst of this, a new baby arrived, a daughter. As Cokie had wished since childhood, she named her Rebecca.

CHAPTER ELEVEN
Woman, Ascendant

Campaign season, 1972: Hale and Lindy tirelessly crisscrossed the nation in service of the Democrats. With no opponent for Hale's seat in New Orleans, they could dedicate themselves fully to the needs of other candidates. Though he could never say so in public, Hale despised presidential nominee Sen. George McGovern and was certain the staunch antiwar candidate would lose. With the passing of his beloved mentor, Sam Rayburn, Hale had ascended to the position of House Majority Leader. Politics being what it was, the dynamic Boggs duo committed themselves to doing whatever they could to bolster the success of their party brethren.

Their travels took them briefly to California, where, while Lindy was off conducting business, Hale spent a rare day with Cokie and the kids at the hotel pool. It was the last time they'd ever see the commanding patriarch again.

The last years had been tough on the Boggs household, personally as well as politically.

For his rousing, unplanned speech against racism and his "yes" vote on the 1965 Voting Rights Act, Hale had been pilloried by his fellow Dixiecrats. The divisiveness followed him back to New Orleans, where a cross had been burned on the lawn of their home. Then there was the social ostracism, said Lindy: "We would go to a party and someone would get tight. There would be a dispute, and it would be embarrassing and we would have to leave."

It had been a radical political shift for Boggs, who'd been described as "as liberal as any deep southerner could be" while managing to hold on to his power, particularly against conservative Republican challengers. Previously, he'd voted against the 1964 Civil Rights Act and even signed on to Strom Thurmond's "Southern Manifesto," which denounced the Supreme Court ruling outlawing segregation. Politics trumped ideology or conviction.

Lindy and their children had pushed for a public transformation. She couldn't help but think of "the black women who had raised me and had helped me raise my children, women who had been prevented from voting because of their color." At times it felt as if she and Hale were neither southern enough nor northern enough.

But geographical dissonance was only part of the issue. Drinking was another part of Hale's troubles, and friends noticed a change in his behavior beyond the alcohol. He'd been diagnosed as manic-depressive, but he didn't like to take the lithium he'd been prescribed. Other issues dogged him: a brutal reelection campaign in 1968, where a Republican challenger received an uncomfortable margin of the vote; a federal corruption probe into his use of a contractor to remodel the house on Bradley Boulevard. He began to give rambling, long-winded speeches, charging in one that FBI director J. Edgar Hoover had wiretapped his personal phone and demanding Hoover's ouster for his Gestapo-style tactics. (Other lawmakers echoed the complaint, but the chances of ever proving that, one member of the House told *Newsweek*, were "slim as hell.") At the Gridiron Club Dinner, a brawl erupted in the bathroom after Hale cursed President Nixon and a former Republican lawmaker decked him, causing him to bleed all over his crisp finery. At another official dinner, in Florida, Hale nearly came to blows with a local dignitary. The hosts locked him in a room away from the main banquet area and told the assembled crowd the guest of honor was ill. Next thing you knew, he appeared and rose to speak, denying he'd been sick.

As reports of her husband's drinking grew more widespread, about all Lindy would say was that the five parties a night they sometimes attended in the swirl of social season were not conducive to sobriety. DC insiders whispered that while Hale was a brilliant orator and legislator, it was Lindy who'd propped him up all these years.

Fighting exhaustion after the grueling campaign season, Hale kept his promise to stump with a junior congressman, Nick Begich, back in the man's home state of Alaska. Lindy had been scheduled to go along, but decided to stay put in Bethesda, where she did her part for the party by tying up the phone line dialing up southern governors during the commercial breaks in a football game to solicit their support. When Hale's call finally got through, he told his wife he'd be home after a fund-raiser in Juneau.

Lindy settled in at the kitchen table to tackle her mail. It was a comfortable, cheery room with a large open fireplace and a bay window from which she could peer out at her husband's garden. With her terrier, Cody, sleeping at her feet, the warmth of the room induced drowsiness. The ringing phone startled her alert, and the dog jumped up on the table, as if he knew something was terribly wrong.

The House Speaker, Carl Albert, was on the line, apologizing for the message he had to deliver. The plane Hale had been riding on was missing. Surely, he'd be found soon.

The news wires hastened the spread of this development. Soon, a reporter appeared at the back door. Friends, family, neighbors, and strangers began to arrive. A psychic from Ohio called, offering to help find the plane. As a devout Catholic, Lindy needed to consult with her priest about whether it was permissible to receive supernatural guidance. She was desperate enough that she'd take any help she could get.

As storm and fog lifted, the air force mobilized the largest search-and-rescue operation ever mounted, deploying the latest technology over Portage Pass. Lindy was certain it was just a matter of time before her husband and the other men would be found; she could just hear Hale complaining, "What took you so long?"

Cokie arrived from California, only to be told that the family would now head back west to participate in the search in Alaska. What good could it do? she asked her mother. Lindy reminded her that if *her* plane had gone missing, her adoring father would have been at the scene in an instant.

For thirty-nine days, the rescue workers continued. Despite the prayers and their presence and even a bit of that psychic assistance, neither the aircraft nor the bodies were found. Rationally, Cokie knew that ice must have caused the plane to plunge and plummet deep to the bottom of Prince William Sound. This deeply unsettling reality didn't help her process the shock and pain of the sudden loss, but only intensified it.

Hale, so beloved and yet missing and presumed dead, was easily reelected come Election Day.

* * *

When Congress convened on January 3, 1973, Boggs's seat was officially declared vacant. It was impossible, even months after the fact, for Lindy to accept that her husband would never return. Surely, he'd materialize someday. This belief, along with Mass every morning, helped soothe her. "I know it's an oversimplification to say that I know wherever he is, he is with God," she said. "But that is how I feel."

Aware that her husband's were formidable shoes to fill, she found herself deciding to run. No one knew their district better than Lindy. After all, as her son said, she'd done everything in Congress but vote. Even her archbishop offered encouragement, suggesting that running was a "natural extension" of her life. If she won, she vowed, she'd finish the work Hale had begun. At the very least, she rationalized, if she were the one inhabiting his seat in Congress, she could gracefully step aside when he did reappear, so business could resume as usual.

Wags accused Lindy of running to keep the seat warm for her son, who'd lost his own bid for Congress a few years before. No, she retorted, she was keeping it warm for his ten-year-old daughter.

Her dear friend the former First Lady, Lady Bird Johnson, no stranger to the difficulties of politics, asked Lindy a logical question: "How could you run for office without a *wife?*" They both knew—any wife of a lawmaker knew, especially one like Lindy—that the spouse was an essential ingredient to a man's success.

* * *

Nineteen seventy-three. Women, ascendant forces of strength and change, their names leaping out of the society pages and into the headlines:

Argentina's Isabel Perón elected vice president while simultaneously serving as First Lady. Israel's prime minister Golda Meir meets
with President Nixon. Tennis champion Billie Jean King triumphant
in the Battle of the Sexes match against Bobby Riggs. *New York Times*
women's page editor Charlotte Curtis tapped as op-ed editor, the first
female on the paper's masthead. At Yale University, Hanna Holborn
Gray installed as the first lady provost. The navy graduates its first co-ed
class, and female pilots are permitted to train. Though the Equal Rights
Amendment as championed by Martha Griffiths stopped short, the
feminists score a victory with the Supreme Court's landmark ruling on
abortion rights with *Roe v. Wade.*

And Lindy Boggs, who'd been a crucial force in the rise to power of
her husband, easily defeats Republican attorney Robert E. Lee to win
the seat she'd helped her husband occupy for thirty years. And as she
becomes the first woman to represent Louisiana in Congress, she makes
it clear that she's representing not only residents of her district, or even
her home state, but women, everywhere, who need a voice.

Transcending her immense personal tragedy and her grief, she
settled into the job for which she'd been unwittingly preparing herself
for years.

* * *

The next year, Steve and Cokie and their two young children traded
the mountains of Malibu for a house surrounded by citrus trees on St.
Sophie Street in the suburbs of Athens, Greece, where Steve would serve
as the bureau chief for the *Times.*

Cokie didn't mind saying goodbye to her part-time television work
in exchange for the chance to embark on this foreign adventure with her
family. But she knew herself well enough now to recognize that she'd
need to find some kind of work. On a layover in London, while Steve
shopped for the requisite Burberry trench coat in order to be appropriately costumed for his new role as foreign correspondent, Cokie was left
watching the kids. This bit of thoughtless dallying caused her to miss

an appointment at NBC that could have yielded freelance contacts. She managed instead to find some at CBS, where she was outfitted with an audio recorder and instructed in its use. News producers loved these smart wives of ex-pats, low-obligation freelancers who could tap into the fully stocked offices of their husbands and add to their coverage, without saddling the network with the obligation to subsidize a full-time employee.

Athens, Cokie and Steve decided, possessed little of the charm of Paris or Rome, but it did have an abundance of Greeks, whom they discovered could be "maddening," but for their ability to enjoy life as it came—a quality they believed was lost to Americans. The Roberts family now received a crash course in souvlaki, falling in love with the cafés around Kolonaki Square, small and quiet, where you could sit for hours splurging on a feast of stuffed mussels and shrimp shish kebab. Dazzled by the olive groves and beaches northeast of the city, they concluded that farther north, the beach was even better, but the food not as delicious.

In California, they'd launched a new family tradition, instigated by none other than devout Catholic Cokie, which they now continued: the celebration of Passover, the annual seder. Here in this ancient city, she dispatched Steve, whose family had never developed the tradition themselves, in search of unleavened bread, matzoh. To her consternation, he returned with the most Jewish food he could find: cheesecake.

As they roamed the Continent, Cokie graduated from Steve's research assistant to cowriter for the travelogues they crafted, including the one on the joys and hazards of hitting the road with young children in tow. Once, on the island of Santorini with their family and a nanny, Steve exclaimed as they enjoyed a beautiful meal, "We're on assignment for the *New York Times*! We're getting paid to do this!"

The transcendent feel of this endless vacation was tempered by reality when serious news erupted: the overthrow of the government in Cyprus by a military junta. Steve darted off to the island to service the expectations of the *Times*. The phone soon rang, too, for Cokie: CBS was calling, for the first time, asking her to put that recorder they'd given her to use. She woke up the sleeping nanny and told her she was off in search of reaction to the news.

For the next several days, she'd collect sound in the field, and as the availability of phone lines permitted, she found herself unscrewing the receiver and affixing "alligator" clips to it, which allowed her to transmit her audio back to the States. The CBS News staff rang up Representative Boggs's office to request a picture of Lindy's daughter. Why? Lindy wondered with concern, until they explained that nothing was wrong; they merely needed a visual to post on television with her story, which would run on that night's *Evening News with Walter Cronkite*.

On July 23, 1974, the most trusted man in America appeared in black-and-white glory and announced in his trademark timbre that the exiled former Greek premier had returned to Athens, where he was received by jubilant crowds. "Late this evening," Cronkite said, "Cokie Roberts filed this audio report from Athens."

And so, in an appearance that lasted not quite fifty seconds, a novice broadcaster made her network debut, invisibly: A slide of a map popped up on the screen, with her name below it.

"Crowds have been jamming the streets around the Parliament building, singing dancing and hugging in happiness and anticipation," Cokie reported. "America's support of the military regime here is less popular than ever tonight . . ." The strains of the Greek national anthem rang loudly in the streets of Athens, she continued. "And shouts of *Eleftheria* and *Demokratia*. 'Democracy and freedom.' Cokie Roberts, CBS News in Athens."

Over the next week, as the crisis unfolded, Cokie's voice floated over the CBS Radio affiliate airwaves across the United States. Friends were so surprised to hear her distinctive voice that they pulled their cars to the side of the road. By the time Steve returned, Cokie had been transformed from someone who "didn't know squat about being a radio reporter" to wizened "veteran foreign correspondent."

For her efforts, the network rewarded her with an offer of regular work. Committing to a steady assignment just wasn't possible. Steve had to travel often for his job. It would have been unfair to their children for her to always be on the road, too.

Sometimes, though, she'd tag along with him, recorder in hand, so she could file the occasional story. This posed a bit of a problem for him. When he pitched ideas on a similar topic, the editors back in New York might already have heard Cokie talking about something similar on CBS Radio during their morning commute.

The lessons? Number one: Broadcast media, no matter how brief a report, trounced even a prominent print publication for sheer sizzle. Number two: The joy of one's own byline? Priceless.

No longer was she merely the wife of a foreign correspondent. Cokie herself was now a reporter, too.

* * *

They hoped for another baby—they'd even chosen names—but that was not to be. Still, another form of excitement loomed for the Roberts family: a new posting. First, it seemed like Israel would be their next stop, and then came word that they were heading to Thailand, to live in Bangkok for a while. Cokie was dying to go. She loved the ex-pat life, plunging into a new place by learning all there was to know about it, the perfect blend of mothering and work, she'd discovered. Much to her consternation, though, Steve turned the opportunity down. The peripatetic life of a foreign correspondent was keeping him away from his family.

Then came a heady surprise U-turn. Steve received an offer to return to the Washington bureau. After all these years feeling off the radar in Greece, he was thrilled by this invitation; the capital city, especially in the aftermath of Watergate, was the quintessential high-profile assignment, the vaunted bureau where news of power broke daily.

Cokie, for her part, wasn't excited one bit. To her, the mere prospect of returning to her hometown left her feeling as if she were being buried alive. She knew if they went back, she'd never leave the city again. Added to her litany of woes was the fear of not being able to find work in

Washington. She'd just sold her first story to *The Nation*, about Turkey, and with the freelance radio work, she was finally in a groove. The prospect of begging for a job distressed her as much as having to face the "ridiculous" ostracism of not having an answer to "What do you do?," the question invariably posted in status-conscious DC. With the cost of living soaring higher in Washington, and without the financial support awarded to families on foreign assignment, she also knew she'd need to find full-time employment for practical reasons, not just for her soul.

She wasn't just depressed; she was a "first-class witch" about the move, "kicking and screaming the whole way." Off she went for a walk to try to shake her depression, stopping herself from buying a dress that was costlier than her usual purchase. Steve marched out to the store and brought it home as an olive branch—a consolation prize for disrupting the family, and her life, once again.

* * *

The logical place to land when they returned to DC in August 1977 was the family house on Bradley Boulevard. To celebrate their homecoming, which coincided with their eleventh wedding anniversary, Lindy threw a grand party, replete with Greek food.

Each day, as Steve left for the *Times*, Lindy left for Congress, and the kids left for school, Cokie had nowhere to go; she found herself gripped by that sense of despair, that emptiness again.

Having been bitten by the thrill of a byline, a reporter is what she wished to be. Once she was back on native soil, CBS made it clear that the sweet overseas freelance gig she had enjoyed would not translate into a steady job. The woman problem, all over again: Most newsrooms already had their one female reporter; there was no need for another. It might have been illegal now to say these things, but that didn't stop anyone.

At the *Times* bureau, the coworker at the desk next to Steve's was a new hire named Judith Miller. Faced with that class-action discrimination lawsuit by its female employees, the paper had been pushing to bring in more women, and not just the Ivy League men, like Steve, who'd forever been their mainstay. Miller had made a splash around town and caught the eye of one of the bureau's editors, landing herself a coveted reporter's slot that, until recently, would have been off-limits.

Steve chatted with his new colleague, asking her where she'd worked before.

National Public Radio, was her answer. She'd been covering national security at the network, and her stories had been appearing on the air most nights.

What's that? he wondered. He and Cokie had lived in California during NPR's earliest and most invisible years. Their car radios were more likely to be tuned to the poetic Paul "Panther" Pierce's traffic reports on KMPC-AM 710. Despite an industry push to get the FM band included on all new radios, most cars and many home receivers weren't equipped with the capacity to tune it in. This had been the bane of FM-dwelling non-commercial radio's existence, since, with most of radio's robust action on AM, there wasn't much incentive for people to upgrade.*

No matter the size of its audience, any radio network at all sounded like the perfect workplace for Cokie. Steve was desperate to help her land a job. He couldn't bear his wife crying herself to sleep every night. Miller told him that her former colleagues, perennially understaffed, were looking to replace her, and she suggested he call a woman named Nina Totenberg. Having settled in at the network herself, Nina was particularly eager to make sure NPR kept hiring women. After all, women had struggled for so long; they needed to support one another.

The next morning, to save his aggrieved wife a trip into the city, Steve walked over from the *Times* office on L Street to NPR's studios on M Street, with Cokie's résumé in hand. Nina met him outside on the sidewalk to retrieve it. All they could do now was hope.

---

* Proponents of FM had been arguing for pretty much the entire decade that they deserved parity with TV. The government had been insisting since 1964 that manufacturers enable televisions to receive both VHF and high-on-the-dial UHF stations, which had been a boon to the independent and education stations on that fringe.

CHAPTER TWELVE
Transition

Even before the full extent of the scandal that was Watergate unleashed endless dissection of the actions of President Nixon, the president had amped up his warfare against the "Eastern liberal press" that, in his estimation, had been hounding him for years—from the *New York Times* and *Washington Post* (which had deigned to publish the top-secret Pentagon Papers, allowing the world to peer into the true magnitude of the Vietnam War) to that dogged, pugnacious reporter at CBS, Daniel Schorr (who clocked in at number seventeen on Nixon's enemies list).*

The president's enmity for Schorr never quite rose to that of his hatred for syndicated columnist Jack Anderson, whom the president and his aides despised so intensely that they conspired to plot his murder. (Mercifully for all, this remained in the realm of sinister fantasy.) The chief of the White House staff of four employed to review newscasts and clip print publications on behalf of the commander in chief wondered "how the hell he can sit there and take this shit day after day." Disgusted with the network practice of deploying reporters and commentators to dissect the president's prime-time speeches immediately after they were delivered, the White House decried this "instant analysis." CBS puzzled others in the press when it cowed to the pressure and announced it would do so no more.

In a nation founded on free speech, Nixon could do little to silence the intrepid reporters eager to expose and dissect his every move and transgression, except to bitterly complain about and attempt to discredit them. The "unelected elite," as Vice President Spiro Agnew sneeringly called the press, was an "unrepresentative community" of a dozen or

---

* Aside from ranking number seventeen on the fabled enemies list, he was referred to internally as "Daniel P. Schorr." The *P*, he learned, stood for "prick."

so men scattered across the "geographical and intellectual confines of Washington, D.C. or New York City" who used the airwaves they'd been allocated by the government to commercialize and then dictate the news forty million Americans received each night. There was, however, one aspect of media over which the government did wield a modicum of power: the purse strings of public broadcasting. Documentaries like *Banks and the Poor*, which exposed discrimination against the nations' neediest by commercial lenders, and the erudite, offbeat humor of the weekly satirical variety series *The Great American Dream Machine* boiled Nixon's blood.

The heat overflowed with the announcement of a new news program that PBS officials explained would explore "the growing deterioration in relations between the press and the government." It was to be hosted by former network broadcasters Robert MacNeil and Sander Vanocur, another journalist whom the president despised. In Nixon's mind, Vanocur had unduly grilled him in 1960, in that first-ever televised debate that was widely believed to have decided the election in favor of the more telegenic John F. Kennedy. To Nixon, this new show was tantamount to a declaration of war. What the hell was going on?

"Get the left-wing commentators who are cutting us up off public television at once, indeed, yesterday, if possible," the White House screeched. This, clearly, was "nothing but an attempt (on the part of PBS) to become a fourth major network . . . a liberal-base for an attack on this administration."

As retribution, the president resolved to silence the Corporation for Public Broadcasting by flat-out canceling its funding. An aide explained that this move was both illegal, given public broadcasting's charter, and a potential public relations firestorm. Kill public television, and with it its beloved, sacred offerings *Sesame Street* and *Mister Rogers' Neighborhood* and *Masterpiece Theater*? Talk about political suicide.

A president could have no say in the shows produced by public broadcasting, but Nixon recognized that the administration could try to stack the decks by appointing friendly members to its board. Despite

President Johnson's admonitions, the oversight of public broadcasting thus became politicized. *Los Angeles Times* critic Cecil Smith wrote that he'd been sure this "emasculation" of the system was inevitable. "The President is capable of anything, no matter how petty, to put television right where he wants it—under his thumb."

Amid all this Sturm und Drang and maneuvering, not a single word had been uttered about the radio component of public broadcasting. National Public Radio, with its daily ninety-minute news magazine and various musical offerings, was still a low-wattage blip. It wasn't clear the president even knew it existed.

* * *

As this drama was unfolding, the two beloved men most indelibly linked to defining National Public Radio at its start had disappeared from the premises. In late 1972, NPR president Donald Quayle had fired program director Bill Siemering, shocking those in editorial who revered Siemering and his courtly philosophy. He was too much of a big-picture visionary, Quayle believed, in a lean shop that needed more of a brass-tacks daily helmsman.

Six months after that, Quayle himself had left, "kicked upstairs" into a more bureaucratic role at the Corporation for Public Broadcasting. He'd bequeathed his job as president to his handpicked vice president and longtime ally, a career educational media administrator named Lee Frischknecht. (Later, Quayle would say giving up the position was the worst mistake of his career.) The two men had grown up together in Utah, where they'd been raised in the Church of Jesus Christ of Latter-day Saints. While Quayle himself was not an observant practitioner, Frischknecht credited his Mormon faith with imbuing in him a "direction and stability that's difficult to shake."

But direction and stability were qualities that eluded the service Frischknecht now found himself running. And though the contents of *All Things Considered* were often a bit offbeat and a tad too contrarian for his personal taste, that was the least of his problems.

A faction of the network's founding fathers, men who had toiled in educational radio for years, fiercely opposed the direction and the pace of NPR. The network wasn't creating new programs fast enough, in their estimation; nor did they feel that its leaders were lobbying hard enough to bring attention to the medium. Hoping to inject new, big-picture thinkers into their midst, they splintered off the already brittle public broadcasting infrastructure to create their own rival service, the Association of Public Radio Stations.

In the meantime, Frischknecht's low-key nature and perceived passivity addled the mood in the already tense NPR halls. It was one thing to work hard, and for peanuts, but to work hard in a vacuum was triply exhausting and debilitating. How demoralizing to tell one prospective source after another where you worked, only to be met with silence or a blank stare: "What? Who?"

At one all-staff meeting, Frischknecht even appeared to gloat about NPR's below-the-radar status—what a relief it was that public radio had slipped beneath the fiery gaze of the administration that had engulfed public television. A staffer rose to express outrage at his boss's apathetic ambition. "Let me see if I can get this straight? You're suggesting that invisibility is an asset?"

In an attempt to combat the dysfunction and paralysis, Frischknecht commissioned a pricey management study, hoping it might help him dig down to the root cause of the problems. The consultants spoke plainly about their conclusions. The free-for-all disorganization at National Public Radio, they said, rendered it "the nation's largest unlicensed Montessori school," which survived purely thanks to the "federal tittie." The place was little more than an afterthought, a "private toy," a "pimple on the ass of public broadcasting." In short, NPR was in desperate need of an overhaul, and the consultants proposed just the plan to fix it: a complete reorganization, which included playing down the news, particularly news of the inside-the-Beltway variety, and giving a giant boost to cultural programming.

As word of the plan's details spread among worried *All Things Considered* staffers, tensions soared in the hallways and conference rooms.

One reporter physically shoved someone from the cultural department out of his way. Nina swiped memos off desks and leaked them to the press.

Most staffers were surprised the press even cared about their operation, particularly when the *New York Times* reported on the proposed shift in programming from the news to more subjects of human interest, like job satisfaction and astrology. Member stations, the story said, were hoping to fashion themselves as more of an alternative to commercial broadcasting.

With that, a war of memos, flow charts, and confusion pierced the heart of NPR. Half the journalists threatened to quit in defiance of these invasive outsiders who, in their estimation, "didn't know dog shit about news." And when the mass walkout didn't materialize, a push to unionize emerged among workers in search of a 25 percent pay raise to offset their paltry salaries, which hovered around $18,000 a year.

Zelnick, whose management job was recast as a result of the changes, wrote a five-thousand-word critique of the overhaul and demanded that Frischknecht pay for it to be copied and distributed to each and every member station. When the president refused, Zelnick paid for the copying and postage himself—and then quit.

Frischknecht was deluged with angry responses from station brass and listeners alike. The audience might not be vast, but they'd come to depend on *All Things Considered* as an alternative to commercial broadcasts. "If the news were watered down, where on earth will those of us be who are sick and tired of the pap and crap all around us," wrote Mrs. Jo-Ann Goldfarb of Atlanta. "I am appalled."

While the foundation of NPR quaked in distress, without design or focus group, the founding mothers of NPR continued to emerge.

* * *

They rose in concert with the escalating cries for "women's liberation." Just as the world of Hollywood began to smack of female power, reflecting society's transpositions—subservient June Cleaver replaced by crusty Maude; Gidget transformed into Norma Rae—so, too, did the surreality of broadcast journalism begin to change.

Women began to slide across the local news set, from the weather map to a seat at the news desk. Still, they typically played second fiddle to the main, more serious anchor, a stentorian man. And rare was the television newswoman who didn't look like she'd stepped out of a lineup of beauty queens. (Some, in fact, had been so crowned.) Had *Washington Post* society page reporter Sally Quinn not been a bombshell blonde, network television executives would never have made the promise to her of a slot on a national morning show that would "make her a star." (Despite her looks, she flamed out in just a matter of months.)

A young deejay named Terry Gross, newly arrived in 1975 at Philadelphia's public radio station WHYY to host an afternoon jazz and talk show, lamented that the lone female voice she'd heard on the radio while growing up in Brooklyn was that of a sultry seductress known as the "Nightbird," aka Alison Steele. For Gross, a woman who'd previously lived on a commune and hosted a feminist show on educational radio in Buffalo, New York, the dearth of women role models was galling.

Flits of change were in evidence even in fictitious newsrooms, where actress Mary Tyler Moore—who once portrayed a giggly, suburban wife and mother on *The Dick Van Dyke Show*—now played a single, thirtysomething television news associate producer, whose travails embodied the plight of the modern working woman, replete with man troubles and a hip bachelorette pad (and a neighbor, Rhoda, a New York City transplant in similar straits).

By 1976, twice as many women ran local TV and radio newsrooms than the year before, though still not a lofty number—under 10 percent. A raft of victories was declared in those class-action gender discrimination lawsuits against media giants like *Reader's Digest*, *Newsweek*, and the *New York Times*, which goaded along a tiny bit more diversity, if not equality, in the nation's newsrooms. The women who crashed through what came to be known as the "glass ceiling" still registered low in numbers, but at last they were present.

Equality moved along mightily when the communications giant

AT&T, the nation's largest employer and keeper of the vitally important infrastructure that allowed for the transmission of news in every medium, was ruled in violation of the 1964 Civil Rights Act. Soon women landed higher-paying jobs previously reserved for men. Equality worked both ways: Now men could be hired, if they wished, in low-level jobs once deemed the exclusive domain of women. The verdict served as a warning to all other employers: The walls of gender discrimination must come down.

All this was reflected in the wider culture. Surveys of young women underscored their evolving ambitions. Previous dreams of marrying well and serving the family as a happy housewife became subjugated by hopes for a professional career. Women comprised a full 40 percent of the workforce now, many of them mothers of small children—women who'd previously been banned from employment or who'd self-selectively sat out wage earning due to middle-class cultural norms. (It had long been a matter of pride for a man to earn enough so his wife didn't "have" to work.) And yet, despite the growing presence of women in the workforce, the income gap continued to widen.

Woman's economic plight got a mighty boost with the Equal Credit Opportunity Act, first introduced by New York congresswoman Bella Abzug. Its passage meant that women, too, could finally obtain credit and mortgages on their own, regardless of their marital status and without being subjected to invasive questions about their use of birth control. (Even for a married couple who wished to factor in a wife's income in order to qualify for a loan, the going had long been difficult. The Credit Act outlawed the accepted practice that stipulated that they provide a "baby letter" from their doctor, attesting to their sterility or use of approved birth control, as pregnancy meant a woman was likely to lose her job.)

Other barriers crashed down, but not without incident. Though women had been allowed to attend the White House Correspondents' Association Dinner since 1962, they were still wildly outnumbered in May 1975, when Nina brought along as her date to the event her young NPR colleague, host Bob Edwards. A milestone was on the agenda:

Veteran United Press wire reporter Helen Thomas was to be installed as the group's first female president in its sixty-one-year history. For the entertainment portion of the evening, superstar comedian Danny Thomas (no relation to Helen) had been hired. When his time arrived, he launched into a sexist Vegas-style routine laden with demeaning "ding-a-ling" one-liners. The women in the audience hissed and booed as the tone-deaf comic finished his act and slinked off the stage. (Afterward, when two women reporters asked him for his reaction, the comic threatened to buy their newspapers and have them fired.)

The Gridiron Club voted to admit women that same year, four years after men at the National Press Club finally agreed to allow women to descend from the balcony where they'd long been sequestered and take a place on the main floor as full-fledged members. Introducing the first-ever female speaker at the club—referring to Australian feminist writer Germaine Greer as "the saucy feminist even men like"—UPI's Sam Fogg sounded as surprised as he did condescending when he remarked that the women-filled hall sounded like a "Schrafft's tea room."

The outspoken author and activist Greer proceeded to lambast the roomful of journalists for their paltry coverage of stories about, and important to, women. While newspapers were quick to highlight the achievements of men, she observed, women still appeared mostly as window-dressing in advertisements—typically, for products that addressed such "trivializing and demeaning" invented problems like vaginal odor. "The first move that any women's movement must make is to raise the self-image of women the same way the Black movement found it could accomplish nothing without raising the self-image of the Black people," she told the crowd. "We must keep as our first priority the spreading of the movement on the widest possible base."

Before decamping to the club's bar to drink beer with her acolytes, the bemused feminist was presented by Fogg with the club's customary speaker's token of appreciation: a blue-and-gold necktie. "Well, that should be pretty useful," she said, her voice dripping with sarcasm. "It'll keep my hair out of my eyes in demonstrations."

* * *

As the leadership at NPR struggled to define the network, newly anointed producer Jack Mitchell tinkered to find the right sound for *All Things Considered*. National Public Radio was not CBS, and he knew the show he'd been entrusted to lead shouldn't aim to mimic it. There were enough bloviating men on the airwaves, that whole "voice on the mountaintop" sound of the networks. To build an audience, creating something different was key.

To Mitchell, the answer to his problem was right in front of him: Susan. It was despite, not because of, her sex that he chose her to be the cohost. What Mitchell was drawn to was Susan's resemblance to the perfect diplomat's wife—not in the white glove, pinkie-finger-in-the-air-while-sipping-tea way, but because of her authentic and inherent interest in everyone she met. Yet the very qualities that excited him were exactly what unnerved both management and member stations. Mitchell pushed back on the pushback, all the while shielding Susan from it, not wishing to dash her confidence.

Susan herself had worried a bit about her "funny, awful voice," which was laced with the geographical marker of her native New York City, but she concluded that, like a beautiful face on TV, a voice was "just what's up front; it doesn't do the job." Indeed, it was her unique sensibility that did. Bill Siemering's mission statement had perfectly articulated what Susan believed radio should be—a celebration of human experience. She preferred to tell listeners the meaning of the news, not to merely recite the headlines; to explain how those headlines came to be and what their impact might be. It was nothing like conventional news, anywhere.

When the Apollo 17 crew landed on the moon, she interviewed a farmer in Ohio who believed it was a hoax. When TV's Rhoda got married, Susan talked with a radical feminist about which honorific the fictitious new bride should use. When Squeaky Fromme took aim at President Ford, Susan spoke to filmmaker Robert Altman about an assassination scene in his 1975 movie *Nashville*. And when President

Nixon began releasing transcripts of his Watergate tapes, Susan and the staff offered dramatic readings of them so listeners wouldn't have to wait to read them in the Sunday newspaper, the usual repository for such items of record.

Career politicians and their spokespeople, with their pat, predictable scripts, bored her. Similarly, she had no desire to speak with Hollywood celebrities. Artists, yes: performers, writers, composers, dancers, people who created the great works she loved to consume and that she assumed her listeners craved, too. Radio was a bridging device, a way to put people around the world in touch with one another, she said: "All of us are part of a community that lives in a very confusing and difficult world, and we need to understand it together." She considered it a joy, a gift, to jump into someone's life each day and to distill their ideas for others.

She adored radio for being the exact opposite of the passive, stationary medium of television, which required lights, elaborate crews, makeup, the "self-consciousness of the contrived." On TV, it was so difficult to convey ideas because the image was the star. On radio, there was warmth and a depth that invited participation, that activated a listener's imagination.

And while there was little out there to emulate, she learned from what she didn't like, from the "garbage," as she called it, of chasing ambulances, screeching, and collapsing complex subjects down to bits. Never would she engage in that treacherous line of questioning for which local TV news had become infamous ("Mrs. Kennedy, how does it feel to be a widow?"). If someone began to cry, she immediately turned off her tape recorder. She did not wish to make her living off someone else's pain.

Susan sizzled in this medium she seemed born to inhabit. She had a capacity to ask the questions curious listeners might have wished to ask but might never have thought to; a capacity to talk about dance and visual artwork so vividly that a listener could practically *see* it. She loved sitting down to read and think about the best way to stitch together information, plotting out the best line of questioning, and then assembling the results, like pieces of a puzzle, into a clear account. It was just a matter of geography, not her state of mind, that her physical presence happened to be inside the Beltway.

But with her lofty perch as a woman behind a microphone—the first woman to cohost a nightly national news program—came a responsibility. She found herself, as she put it, "eternally on gender watch," vigilant and persistent about seeking out women as experts to interview whenever possible, though finding those experts wasn't always so easy. Few women had risen through the ranks to achieve expert status yet. So, she continued to push for stories that dealt with the issues she faced every day, about families and child-rearing; stories that consumed her personally; stories that elsewhere would have been relegated to the women's programs or pages.

While she reveled in her role as pioneer, she refused to believe she was a token: "I'd like to believe that the reason I'm cohosting the program is because I'm the best possible person to do it. Not just cause I'm a goil." Every night, just before 5:00 P.M., this "goil" would enter the studio armed with her cigarettes, some orange juice, and, just as she had back at the start of her career, her lipstick.

* * *

With a new voice as its star, affirmation for this "magazine format brimming with light and serious subjects and intermittent music ranging from Bach to rock" began to stream in, signs that listeners out there in Radio Land not only were tuning in to the program but appreciating its inventive approach, the measured tones devoid of the clutter and noise of ads for creams and potions that marked commercial newscasts.

When Susan put out the call to listeners to send in pictures of themselves, a carton of letters arrived—a true, if unscientific, indication of a devoted audience. She attributed her steady stream of personal fan mail—each piece faithfully answered—to the fact that listeners didn't like the "plastic people" who proliferated on other airwaves. Accolades for *All Things Considered* almost always spotlighted Susan's "aggressively conversational" style, which, as one reporter described it, smacked of the "kind of informality that one might expect at a cocktail party that's run out of liquor but not out of ideas."

Amused by innumerable interpretations of her last name, this one-time visual arts student clipped the botched attempts from the envelopes and assembled them into a collage. A newspaper headline mused, "Hamberg, Steinborg . . . Who Is Susan Stamberg?" More and more people could answer the question, even if they got the spelling wrong.

There were, it seemed, two types of listeners: those who had an image of Susan seared in their minds, and those who could not conjure one. "Whatever you think I look like," she winked, "that's what I look like!"

Her fame was the best kind: adulation cloaked with a veil of privacy that allowed her to go out in public looking as she pleased. Once, as she picked up her son at day camp, no one paid her any notice until she lost a quarter in a vending machine and shouted at the machine in anger. "I know your voice," exclaimed another mother. "You're *Susan Stamberg!*"

The *Iowa Press-Citizen* published a love letter. Women's movement be damned, wrote William Mueller: He had a crush, plain and simple. "She sounds sexy in a way which doesn't make you feel guilty. . . . In this day and age, she can still make men feel warm and attractive while still admiring her as a real pro . . . feminine and sharp, emotional and yet shrewd, wise but sensitive. She doesn't deliver the news. She delivers humanity."

The humanity Susan delivered boomeranged back in her direction. If her voice sounded tinged with a cold, worried fans called in with concern—or sent chicken soup. Her beloved son, Josh, a budding performer, sang a song on the air, and they sent gifts for him, too.

When, to fill time created by a shortage of tape or a mistake in backtiming the show, she verbally tap-danced, it never sounded like cutesy, TV news happy talk, probably because she genuinely sounded like the lady under the hair dryer next to yours showing you pictures of her kids—not like some made-up beauty queen reading a script she hadn't written. "I think broadcasters should be able to share themselves with listeners, to show we're not special or set apart, to show we have the same concerns," she said. "My child and husband are a very important part of my life."

Indeed, even after her ascendance to the host's chair, she continued to pre-tape parts of the show so she could leave every night at five thirty, right in the middle of the broadcast, in order to be home for dinner with her family. As a homey touch, Susan continued the tradition she'd started on *Kaleidoscope*, trotting out the formula for her mother-in-law's cranberry relish; the bitter fruit turned a Pepto Bismol-color with the addition of sour cream, onion, and horseradish. One man's "yuck" was another's culinary adventure. Each year forward, her signature dish made its way onto the show.*

When revered CBS newsman Charles Kuralt called *All Things Considered* the most interesting program on the air—not just on radio, but on the airwaves, period—Susan knew that she, and the show, and NPR, had risen one step closer to the big time. Outdoing that rave, the godfather of broadcast news, former CBS president Fred Friendly, declared that the program "towers over the competition on commercial radio and television."

But the ultimate affirmation for Susan that she'd personally infiltrated the zeitgeist arrived in an issue of the magazine that had long embodied her raison d'être, the *New Yorker*. A cartoon by the Minnesota-based artist Dean Vietor shows a husband relaxing over a newspaper, and his wife answering the phone. "It's Susan Stamberg, at National Public Radio," she says to him, cupping the receiver, "she wants to know if you want to defend yourself on the airwaves tomorrow."

---

* She would learn later, years after she'd propagated the recipe, that it wasn't an original family recipe but, in fact, one her mother-in-law had swiped from a Craig Claiborne cookbook in 1959.

* * *

"It's Only a Radio Program" read the sign Susan hand-painted for a colleague who was nervous before a difficult broadcast. Sure, it wasn't brain surgery, but radio had become, adjacent to her family, the centerpiece of her existence. Despite her insistence that she not take herself seriously and her assertion that she was "very much like most people"—meaning like everyone else who juggled career and a family, getting by thanks to assistance from a part-time housekeeper from Uruguay—Susan was now someone who could invite Dave Brubeck to her home to play piano for a segment (for there was no piano yet at the NPR studio), instead of merely sitting in an audience as a fan. This was her job? This was a spiritual experience! "An Elvis fan seeing The King risen from the dead, couldn't approach what I felt," she said. Mere mortals didn't get to sit for a long chat with the likes of the great writer Joan Didion, or the great artist Helen Frankenthaler, or the great stage actress Helen Hayes. Even if she still changed the water in the goldfish tank, there was nothing ordinary about this life.

When, in 1976, ABC lured Barbara Walters away from NBC to cohost its nightly news—her $5 million salary the highest ever paid anyone in television news and 150 times what Susan earned—the pioneer public radio broadcaster's ego began to mightily poke through. To set the record straight, NPR took out $16,000 worth of newspaper ads in the *Washington Post*, the *New York Times*, the *Los Angeles Times*, and the *Boston Globe*:

We Love you too Barbara
BUT
You're not the first woman to cohost a national news
    program.
Susan Stamberg has been co-anchoring a national news show
    since 1972.
(And Susan does it without pictures.)

In response to this boast, *Broadcasting* magazine upbraided the network. "Big deal," the magazine's editors wrote. "That's the kind of footnote that might have been worth a few calls to radio editors, but isn't worth a nickel of the public's money." On second thought, they continued, perhaps the money hadn't been misspent: "It did call attention to something we hadn't realized: that Miss Stamberg and *All Things Considered* have been on the air for four years without making a dent in the public consciousness." Ouch! Though its reach was still nothing like that for commercial broadcasting, its audience did continue to grow.

Absent a dogged agent like a celebrity television personality would have, Susan began to fend for herself and demand her due. Lofty salaries commensurate with her notoriety were but a dream—her salary would keep Barbara Walters in taxicabs for a week, she quipped—but she could continue to demand that other great commodity: time. Why must she have to work on Thanksgiving, Christmas, New Year's? Couldn't more junior staff fill in? She'd autograph their overtime checks, she quipped.

And while she was well aware of her value in distinguishing the show with her specialty, what she called the "rich dessert of conversation," she also knew that every cast relied on supporting characters. Increasingly important were those who produced the news that was the show's "bread and butter."

And the person buttering the bread most consistently at NPR these days was that young reporter whose mainstay was the kind of good, old-fashioned, shoe-leather reporting from the trenches of DC that was of little interest to Susan.

* * *

From her perch on the justice beat, Nina continued to dig, and connect, and root out stories. With each passing day, her fame eclipsed that of her violinist father. This self-proclaimed "deadline Dick" kept managing to land the name of the sleepy little network for which she worked, as well as her own, in the papers—the surest mark of validation around. Usually, broadcasters borrowed from print, a medium with typically more robust resources. She ferreted out one scoop after another, from President Ford's leading choice to fill a Supreme Court vacancy ("according to a report Friday on National Public Radio") to the FBI's destruction of Lee Harvey Oswald's letters ("Reporter Nina Totenberg on NPR's 'All Things Considered' said . . .").

Unwittingly, Nina's stories, time and again, embodied the old maxim "Advertising is what you pay for, and public relations is what you pray for." All the ads in the world couldn't have matched the publicity her work was generating.

In the spring of 1977, she struck again with an unprecedented bombshell from the Supreme Court. The justices, she reported, had voted to refuse to review the Watergate burglary convictions of Haldeman, Attorney General John Mitchell, and White House counsel John Ehrlichman. The announcement of this had been delayed because the chief justice had hoped to change his colleagues' minds.

With this insider news, the reporter herself became the headline. The question loomed: Just how had Nina managed to crack through the impenetrable armor of the highest court in the land with this information from a private session? The intimation, in the papers and on the street, was what it had been before: sex.

Nina balked at, but wasn't surprised by, the suggestion that the story had been leaked to her by a man with whom newspapers reported she had had a "close relationship," Justice Potter Stewart. Sniffing at the derision, she explained that leaks were the lowest way to score news, reserved usually for A-listers at the most prominent publications. "I had seven different court sources for the story. It was not leaked to me at all. I wouldn't have gotten the story if I didn't go after it," she said.

This wasn't the first time she'd had advance notice of the Court's inner workings, she told reporter T. R. Reid of the *Washington Post*, but in those cases, she added, she hadn't bothered reporting the stories because "there's no profit in it except self-glorification"—as if the secrets from the highest court in the land were as trivial as gossip she heard while getting her nails done. Clearly, she continued, these inquiries were sexist.

By now, she was accustomed to envious whispers that her scoops were connected to the deployment of her feminine charms. A newsroom colleague even sent her a dozen roses, suggesting that whatever she'd had to do to get the story had been worth it.

She took it in stride.

Yes, she was a rabble-rouser. (For stealing those memos during the reorganization mess, she'd gotten suspended for a week.) Yes, she was unabashedly frank. (Once, while substitute-hosting for Susan, she waved off a script as gibberish and began laughing on the air, saying, "I can't read this damned thing," and cueing the director to go ahead and run the tape. "Had I been a seasoned pro, I would have realized this, but I wasn't a seasoned pro, and I was furious at being handed it so late," she explained. "You could have said, 'We're having technical difficulties,'" reprimanded her boss, news director Robert Siegel, who instead of "woodshedding" her, wound up laughing.) But no one could deny she was a tireless reporter, through and through—the kind of person who'd wait up till 2:00 A.M. to call someone on the West Coast just as they walked in the door after a night out. (This was well before answering machines and cell phones allowed for phone calls to follow you, at any hour.)

After the latest firestorm flamed out, she wrote Stewart a letter of apology: "I just wanted you to know that I am terribly sorry for the embarrassment I have inadvertently caused you. . . . You and I know perfectly well this sort of speculation would never have occurred had a man broken the story."

CHAPTER THIRTEEN
Frank

By the spring of 1977, NPR was still inching its way off its training wheels and desperately seeking an identity, still hounded by behind-the-scenes bickering and jockeying for power. New technologies and the public's expanding appetite for broadcast media were morphing the communications landscape at warp speed. Satellites now spun above Earth and with each orbit were beginning to change the way information flowed and humans connected. Plans were in the works for NPR to engineer its own essential system, a monumental feat akin, described one board member, to building a battleship. Decisions made about the best way to do this, beyond the grasp of all but the most ardent technophiles, would change, for years to come, how stations were connected and programs transmitted.

But before it could head into the stratosphere, NPR had to pull itself out of the muck. Commissioning ratings still wasn't a financial possibility, and to some it was unseemly, besides—the ugly lot of commercial broadcasters that had caused that realm of media to devolve into a "stinkhole." A third of the country still couldn't receive NPR, and even in cities and towns that could, it was hardly a chart-topping influencer. In its eternal quest for a bigger slice of the public broadcasting pie, public radio faced a reckoning. If the two rivals didn't merge forces, as one executive put it, public "television was going to eat their lunch."

This harsh reality proved enough to prompt unity. In front of a blackboard easel at a gathering in Phoenix, each side laid out its terms. Priority number one: The old management had to go. New blood, new leadership, was critical now. It should be someone with the ambition and the drive to take the network to the next level, someone who possessed the right blend of glitz and political finesse.

And so, NPR's hapless second president, Lee Frischknecht, found himself pushed aside. A new board was formed, half of it comprised of "originals"—people (mostly men) who had been at the network since its creation, whose roots traced back to the homespun, mediocre old days of educational radio, when reading books out loud on the air was a mainstay of programming. Outsiders to public media made up the other half. This included the widow of none other than Edward R. Murrow, Janet, who had herself been a reporter and now devoted her days to a variety of philanthropic efforts along with advancing her husband's legacy. Also brought on: an Atlanta-based businessman named Edward E. Elson, who was about to play a crucial role in NPR's fate.

A brash, self-confident "master of the money-power-success game," Elson had multiplied his fortune by expanding his family's magazine distribution business into the "Tiffany" of newsstands—hundreds of shops that purveyed not just periodicals, but pricey tchotchkes, too. Well-placed real estate deals Elson made in conjunction with the influential senator Herman Talmadge had added to his millions.

High-profile civic involvement dazzled Elson more than the machinations of business, which he said he found boring. As a Jew who'd come of age in the segregated South, he was proud to serve as chair of the Georgia Advisory Committee to the U.S. Commission on Civil Rights, boasting that he had personally "desegregated Georgia." He remembered the days of quotas at the fancy private schools he attended, when college fraternities remained off-limits to Jewish students.

He also recalled when *Sports Illustrated*, a magazine Elson's company distributed, featured the black Dodgers catcher Roy Campanella on its cover. Some stands refused to carry the issue, a bald-faced illustration of racial inequity. "I always felt that the Civil Rights Movement would help the Jews," Elson said, "because the blacks would be accepted before the Jews were. And that would pave the way for Jews." Once equality had been won, Elson said, Atlanta's number-one priority had become bolstering the city's reputation as a great climate for business: "The only color that the city of Atlanta really cared about," he said, was green.

Unbridled altruism was not always the sole impetus for Elson's civic engagement. Through his connections to Senator Talmadge, he managed to get appointed to the President's Commission on Obscenity and Pornography. Given that his newsstand chain distributed materials like *Playboy* and *Hustler*, which were outlawed in Georgia, he had a vested interest in how the government recommended the handling of sexually explicit materials. After years of review, the group concluded that there was no evidence that such materials played "a significant role in the causation of delinquent or criminal behavior among youths or adults."

One day, Elson was asked to serve on the board of an agency whose name he didn't recognize—something to do with public broadcasting. Flattered by the ask, and believing, perhaps, that it was the prestigious and high-profile Corporation for Public Broadcasting that was calling, he found himself agreeing to join and, not long after, charged with helping to hunt for the new president of NPR.

More than 350 applications arrived from a formidable assortment of candidates, including several university presidents. Among this wide pool of possibilities, none possessed the star power, much less the creativity or energy, that Elson and his hiring committee were hoping to find.

As a prominent Georgian, Elson was familiar with the players in the newly installed Carter White House; budget director Burt Lance was his neighbor and friend. He turned to him next for guidance. This led him to the head of the White House transition team, who passed along a list of VIPs who wished to work in the administration but for whom a place had not yet been found.

A few of the names leapt out at him—those of basketball star Bill Bradley; Sen. Edward Zorinsky from Nebraska; and Frank Mankiewicz, a political operative who'd forsaken the glitz of the Hollywood into which he was born for the heady power of media and politics. "My god," Elson said to himself as he took a closer look at Frank's background, "if we had to go to Central Casting and find the perfect vitae for this job, it would be Frank Mankiewicz!"

Mankiewicz's father, Herman, had been a pioneer in entertainment as it leapt off the stage and into new, uncharted media. A theater critic for the *New Yorker* (and among the funniest of wits to inhabit a seat at the fabled Algonquin Roundtable), Herman had moved the family west, when Frank was but a toddler, on a starry dream: to script radio dramas and to corral other writers to the burgeoning business of Hollywood. This had led to his most celebrated achievement: winning an Oscar with Orson Welles for *Citizen Kane*, the fictionalized story of Mankiewicz's pal William Randolph Hearst.* (So disdainful of Hollywood was Herman that on the night he won Best Screenplay, he was lounging at home with his wife, half-listening to the Oscar ceremony on the radio.)

A keen sense of showmanship had been baked into his son, whose childhood skill at public speaking earned him acclaim as the "boy orator." But even more to his father's delight, Frank had expressed zero interest in trading in the manufactured reality of Hollywood. Actual reality had proven far more compelling. After joining the infantry in World War II, Frank fought in the Battle of the Bulge. Following the war, he enrolled at UCLA, where he served as editor in chief of the *Daily Bruin*. He next ran a newspaper in Santa Monica, and then earned a master's in journalism at Columbia. He studied law at UC Berkeley, later cutting short his career as an entertainment lawyer in Beverly Hills when he decided, along with his wife, Holly, "If I stayed with the firm, within ten years we'd have this terrific house and a lot of money, but nobody would care if we'd lived or died, except perhaps our mothers."

Frank's quest for meaning led him to the newly formed Peace Corps, where he put his fluency in Spanish to use in Peru and, later, as chief of the Latin American region. The experience of leading part of this volunteer service program, he said, had radicalized him. Late one night, he trekked to the airport in Panama to greet the visiting American dignitary Sen. Bobby Kennedy, whose plane had stopped for

---

* Whether Welles actually wrote a single word of the screenplay has long been in dispute. See Pauline Kael's "Raising Kane" in the February 13, 1971, issue of the *New Yorker* to learn more about that claim.

refueling. Reporters lurking outside the airport had been told there was to be a press conference. Given the hour, Bobby was relaxing in bed on the plane.

"Who gets hurt if I don't go see them?" Kennedy asked Frank. "Do the reporters get hurt or the owners of the papers?"

"Well, probably the reporters," Frank responded.

"Well, that's what I thought, so let's go." Bobby dressed, and with Frank by his side as interpreter, he met with the press—even though there wasn't anything to say.

Weeks later, the call came from the nation's capital: Would Frank be willing to serve as Bobby's press secretary? Though Frank was then up for a formidable position as the president of San Francisco State College, and though he wasn't sure exactly what a press secretary on Capitol Hill did, this new, heady offer trumped the other. He was so enchanted by the man that he would have sorted the mail for him.

Quickly, the two formed an intense bond over their shared love of words, of writing—a marriage made in heaven, observed Bobby's brother Ted. While the shy senator carried snippets of poetry and philosophy in his pockets, sneaking a look at them when time allowed, garrulous, outgoing Frank, with his witty one-liners, could always make him laugh.

One day, after returning from a reporting trip to Vietnam, CBS newsman Walter Cronkite asked to pay a private, off-the-record call on the senator. Cronkite was so disgusted by the protracted conflict in Southeast Asia that he had an urgent request: "You must announce your intention to run against Johnson," he implored the senator, "to show people there will be a way out of this terrible war."

Until then, Bobby had steadfastly refused to challenge the sitting president, his avowed enemy. Vietnam had divided the Democratic Party, as it had the nation, into doves and hawks. But amid the fanning flames of antiwar protests and civil rights marches, he acquiesced, catapulting Frank into the manic, heady chess game of a presidential campaign. It felt like the logical next step in Bobby's professional career—and in Frank's.

With each passing day came yet another startling turn of events: President Johnson's announcement that he would not run for reelection; the murder of Martin Luther King Jr.; Bobby's resounding triumph in the California primary less than three months after declaring his candidacy.

That glorious night in June, Frank was helping Ethel Kennedy step down from the podium after her husband's acceptance speech, assisted by their hired security man, Bill Barry. Given that Secret Service agents weren't assigned to protect candidates, the campaigns were on their own. Despite the assassination of his brother, Bobby eschewed cops as escorts. Frank and the guard were among the few in on his secret: that Mrs. Robert Kennedy was several months pregnant.

Having helped Ethel safely down from the rostrum, Frank and Bill Barry rushed to catch up with the candidate. As they did, they heard the crackling sounds, like the ones that had startled them the night before, at a rally in San Francisco's Chinatown. Firecrackers, they figured.

Then they heard the screams.

Every November hence, on Bobby's birthday, Frank braved the cold to visit Arlington National Cemetery to pay his respects to his beloved friend, whose death it had been his job to announce to the world. He knew that whatever he'd accomplish in his life going forward, that terrible task would lead off his epitaph.

To manage the initial waves of grief, Frank plunged further into his work—cowriting two books about the menace of Nixon and another about Fidel Castro, whom he'd interviewed over thirteen hours in Cuba, the first interview granted to a U.S. crew in fifteen years. *Playboy* purchased the rights to publish his Castro book, but shopping the film footage proved far trickier.

Navigating the surreal world of Castro was nothing compared to the bureaucracy of network television. CBS agreed to buy his film only if he arranged for their star reporter, Dan Rather, to shoot additional material. The experience taught Frank the many pitfalls of being an indie producer, and led him to conclude that "people are being deprived of a lot of news by the rigid policy of the networks. So many people depend on television for news and they are being shortchanged." The television special that finally resulted, *Castro, Cuba and the USA*, almost bankrupted him.*

When the staunch antiwar candidate Sen. George McGovern called and asked Frank to join his presidential campaign, he dropped a political column he was writing and a television news show he was hosting to serve as the candidate's political director. The lure of the frenzied campaign trail, plus the potential to influence history, was too intoxicating to pass up, even if it offered a fraction of the money his other work did.

Remembering the visit paid to Bobby Kennedy by Walter Cronkite years earlier, Frank proposed the television anchorman as McGovern's running mate. His team nixed the idea instantly. "Everybody said, 'Don't be silly. He'd never accept. We'll look bad if we offer it to him and he turns it down, because everybody will know that.' So, let's go to a more mainstream politician."

That, they did. The disastrous choice of Missouri senator Thomas Eagleton, whose mental health struggles came to light shortly after he accepted the nomination, tanked their already tenuous quest for the White House.

By the time Elson paid Frank a call in the late spring of 1977, Frank had just finished his fourth book, *Remote Control: Television and the Manipulation of American Life*. That watching television had become the second-most-popular activity in the nation (after sleep) deeply troubled him. The medium's main purpose, he observed, was not "to educate or entertain or inform or titillate or even to tell a story, but simply, at all times, to deliver the maximum possible audience to the advertiser."

Indeed, Frank seemed primed for public broadcasting, even though he hadn't heard of, nor did he listen to, NPR. This invitation to apply for a job to run it that had just landed in his lap seemed the perfect and logical plot twist in his starry life.

---

* Declassified government documents show that Mankiewicz may have carried a message from Secretary of State Henry Kissinger to the Cuban dictator, inviting him to secret negotiations (which halted as abruptly as they began). See Peter Kornbluh's National Security Archive: https://nsarchive2.gwu.edu/NSAEBB/NSAEBB494.

* * *

From his years of nonprofit service, Edward Elson had learned that it was best to present just one qualified candidate to the board for its approval, rather than offer a list of choices. If they vetoed Frank, they'd simply return to square one. But there was no question in his mind that Frank was the perfect person for the $65,000-a-year job as the network's third president.

And so, on the late afternoon of July 11, 1977, in the Chancery room of the Embassy Row Hotel in Washington, the assembled board of National Public Radio was introduced to the number one, and only, candidate for network president, the quick-witted, jut-jawed man with storied roots and circles under his eyes who'd been on both sides of the news business. Frank's looks belied his ability to lift the network to glossier heights. But this was the strange, ego-driven hyperspace of radio, a medium where, it had been said, a fat man could play Hamlet and where a woman, even a woman with a decided New York accent, could be the star of the flagship news show.

Someone asked the candidate, "If you were president of NPR, what's the first thing you would do? What do you think's most important?" And Frank, confessing that he hadn't known of National Public Radio's existence until he'd been told about the job, answered with his trademark, charming self-confidence: "To do whatever was necessary so that people like me would have heard about it."

Down the hall he was sent, to await the board's verdict, nervously smoking his way through a pack of cigarettes. Members of the board expressed confusion. They spent most of the meeting questioning why no one else was being considered for the job.

Elson, in a cheeky retort, handed out actual bullets to colleagues in whose hands NPR's fate now rested. Bite this ammunition, he quipped. "Hold your nose. *Vote*, then critique," he advised. He did not want to take no for an answer. The choice of Frank would trumpet the dawn of a "new momentum and visibility" for public radio, which stands on the threshold of a "new era of service to the public."

Could this man Frank Mankiewicz, possessed of a face one columnist described as "smooshed like a boxer," the man whom writer Hunter S. Thompson called a "scurvy, rumpled treacherous little bastard," be the illustrious soul who could elevate public radio to the big time?

Though the old guard wasn't convinced the big time was where they wished or needed to be, the verdict was a unanimous yes.

* * *

It was unseasonably warm that late August in 1977 when Frank, three weeks on the job, paid a visit to the campus of Florida State University. There, he poked around the modest 2,500 square feet on the fourth floor of the Diffenbaugh Building that housed radio station WFSU-FM. Having just quit his three-pack-a-day habit, and still longing for a cigarette, he made the rounds with station manager Jim Irwin, who puffed on his own trademark smoke, a cigar. The night before, Frank had appeared as a special guest on a local show, answering questions about his intentions for the radio network.

In the seven years since NPR had incorporated, the number of stations that had professionalized enough to qualify for membership had doubled. Slowly but surely, stations were transforming from the homespun educational radio days, when professors delivered Spanish lessons or lectures on Shakespeare, into slicker operations intended to serve an audience beyond the perimeter of campus. This particular affiliate, in Florida's capital city, Tallahassee, was a sparkling gem in the public radio system. Picking up the rights to air the all-important Florida Seminole football games had propelled WFSU to become one of the most-listened-to public radio stations in the nation. A $70,000 grant from the government had also allowed the station to pump up its signal from 3,000 watts to 50,000, multiplying the potential audience to include the entire metro area.

The stronger the NPR affiliates got, and the wider their reach, the more critics emerged, leveling charges of elitism. Public radio, in the estimation of one local critic in Tallahassee, was not some "community-oriented . . . alternative" that deserved taxpayer support, but a "plethora of slick, bourgeois imitations of commercial shows, which function, fundamentally, as ideological organs of Tallahassee's white ruling class (the people that have money to donate to hear eighteenth century European music.)"

It still wasn't clear how many people actually listened. Across the land, public radio faced a conundrum at the confluence of the old philosophical saws "If a tree falls in the forest, does it make a sound?" and "Which came first, the chicken or the egg?" With scant marketing and that FM tuner problem, how could NPR reach listeners who didn't know it existed and who might not even own a radio equipped to tune in to one of the stations that carried it?

His tour of these modest facilities complete, it was time for Frank to press the flesh of the five other managers of public radio stations from around the Sunshine State who'd trekked to its capital city to meet this mythic figure. Most Americans, if they hadn't seen or heard him deliver the news of the death of Senator Kennedy, had devoured books in which he'd appeared, such as Theodore White's epic *The Making of the President: 1968* and Hunter S. Thompson's *Fear and Loathing on the Campaign Trail '72*. (Had Mankiewicz really attacked the gonzo journalist with a tire iron?)

To those who wondered what this unabashed DC insider whom they'd seen so often on the news was doing at the helm of a largely invisible, government-subsidized public radio network that was supposed to be politically agnostic, Frank had a ready and politic response that deftly skirted the question: "I'm like the guy selling shoes. When they ask, 'what do you know about it?' I tell them, 'Well, I've been wearing them all my life . . . I've been listening to radio for 40 years.'"

He intended, he told the assembled station managers, to be highly visible, to be involved in every aspect of NPR, from the budgeting to the programming and development. He knew very well that it wasn't his "non-existent experience as a broadcast executive" that had been his calling card, but his very name and pedigree. His purpose was to "make waves—to raise less corn and more hell."

"I didn't take the job because I wanted to be president of something," he explained. It had been years since he'd held a "regular" job, the kind where he was expected to show up at the same place every day, and he definitely wouldn't have accepted this one had it involved running some established business or industry. No, he'd accepted the offer because it came with the chance to shape an entity, "a wide-open opportunity to reach a helluva lot of people, to do something that might make a difference. Besides," he added with self-deprecation that masked his unerring confidence, "I haven't really decided what I want to be when I grow up."

* * *

While the *Washington Post* reported, in the aftermath of Mankiewicz's appointment, the fluffy fact that he'd gone out and bought himself a 1968 Mustang, in smaller papers around the country the stories zeroed in on the meatier dilemma: "Appointment of Mankiewicz Questioned," bleated the headline of a column by radio critic Magee Adams in the *Cincinnati Enquirer*. How would the new network president's political past square up with public broadcasting's commitment to nonpartisanship? His appointment, said the columnist, would "sharpen the watch for political footprints."

Another writer, in Oregon, observed after hearing Frank interviewed on the radio, "One would think that he was still managing Sen. George McGovern's presidential campaign," for "some of his comments were far from the type that one would expect from the public-owned broadcasting organization." These comments, the columnist continued, were "not called for. . . . Let's hope that he will tend to the job and keep away from his first love—politics."

But, to Frank, the twin sports of media and politics were indelibly entwined. He liked to say he knew everyone in Washington, that half of them owed him something, and the other half, he owed. As evidence of this, he arrived on his very first day toting a massive Rolodex. (This spectacle led newscaster Noah Adams to observe, "That's why we hired him.")

To the frontline journalists at NPR, eager to put the internecine warfare of the past years behind them, this new high-profile chief was more good news than worrisome. Neither of his predecessors had been the sort who'd amble into the newsroom, fingering the wires as they curled off the teletype, asking about stories and offering up sources, corralling them for lunch or drinks or coffee. Nor would they have declared a desire to turn their shop into the finest newsroom the world had ever known, as this new boss had. Frank instinctively grasped the trenchwork that was essential to journalism, for he himself had inhabited it; he declared his respect for the staff's travails and for their product. He stated his belief that if more people could hear them, they'd be fans, too. (Truth be told, he did think *All Things Considered* could sometimes edge toward a bit too cute.) A higher profile for the network was his goal, and that of course would translate into a higher profile for every one of them. The new boss's sweet notes of respect and understanding were welcome music to the journalists' ears.

At long last, they had hope.

* * *

And so, NPR's new president stepped headfirst into a world of obstacles, where factions raged—the member stations were angry, wishing for more programming, and annoyed that stacks of taped reports they'd submitted for use on *All Things Considered* sat unaddressed, collecting dust—where charges of elitism dogged the system; where the ongoing absence of FM in car radios still proved a major problem in attracting new listeners; where hoisting NPR up to the long-in-the-works satellite was an enormous and expensive undertaking that promised, ultimately, to improve sound quality while connecting stations at a new, space-age level; and where the budget was simply never big enough.

And then there was the internal strife, including the pathetic pay and poor working conditions for the staff, who, despite having voted to unionize, hadn't managed to negotiate a contract. Linda welcomed the new boss with the pithy greeting, "Hi. I'm shop steward. We're striking you next week." A month later, Frank negotiated an agreement that improved the paltry wages, at least a tiny bit, and left the beleaguered troops feeling that at least they and their work were valued by the new man in charge.

Frank, the relentless optimist, demanded positivity. The once-reserved culture of "can't" transformed into one of "yes." Company credit cards were issued for the first time. Though the budget was still a fraction of what was spent in television network news, now when they were out in the field, staff could stay in hotels paid for by NPR, instead of having to crash on the couches of friends.

Finding new sources of revenue was another crucial priority, a way to become less reliant on the funds provided by the Corporation for Public Broadcasting than the 97 percent they now received. Frank wished to get that number down to zero, aiming for self-sufficiency so as not to be at the whim of the administration. Corporate underwriting, the public broadcasting method of inserting commercials that craftily didn't resemble commercials, was sensitive and tricky, but Frank intended to pursue it. That and donations from the "bedrock American do-good charity establishment, people who supported things like the symphony, the art gallery, the public library."

Maybe, in addition to news and cultural affairs programming, he mused, NPR could offer programming related to his truest love of all: sports. An inveterate fan of baseball in particular, he floated the idea of the network running a "game of the day." Make the place less "brie and Chablis" and more bowling—that would stick it to the critics who thought NPR too elitist. (Still, one of the first deals he signed was to broadcast the San Francisco Opera's season.) In fact, he was willing to try anything "but the world's oldest profession" to get the network's name out there and for it to achieve financial independence.

Change would take time, but that was okay. He planned on being at the helm for a good, long while, he said. But, he warned, the results would not come immediately. Indeed, he predicted, "It will be five years before you can look at the system and say, 'By God, it's a lot better than it was in '77.' "

* * *

Frank's first bit of handiwork became evident on February 8, 1978, when Linda took her place at a microphone in the front row of the radio-television gallery of the Senate and announced to NPR's network of affiliates around the nation, "Today is the first time in our two-hundred-year history that the debates in the Senate will be heard far beyond the chamber and its visitors gallery." On deck were two treaties that would determine the future of the mighty Panama Canal, the body of water that, for decades, had allowed ships to travel from one coast to the other by bypassing the tip of South America. Would lawmakers hand the governance of this important artery over to the tiny nation? There was no clear-cut outcome.

For at least a decade, as other elected bodies around the world began to allow electronic media to broadcast their inner workings, U.S. lawmakers had stalled in their ongoing deliberations over opening their doors to cameras. Wary of the edits and tweaks made by commercial broadcasters, and fearful of how being on display would change the business of Congress, they'd routinely shot down such proposals.

Democratic majority leader Robert Byrd presided over the passage of a resolution that allowed these debates to be broadcast in this one-time-only instance. Technical difficulties made television transmission impossible—not that commercial television would ever have dedicated so many hours to a decidedly undramatic legislative matter.

Frank had negotiated the details, such as the right to rehearse in advance, and to fade in and out of the proceedings as they wished. It helped that a few years earlier, the Senate had installed one hundred microphones to improve acoustics in the chamber. Also lucky for Frank, Byrd, the "gentleman from West Virginia," was a bigtime bluegrass fan. As a devoted listener to member station WAMU, he was familiar with public radio, and when the senator learned that the engineer for the Panama Canal proceedings coverage would be none other than Gary Henderson, the host of his favorite bluegrass show, a yes was a cinch. Ever the negotiator, Frank threw in a bonus: "I've assured the Senator he can have a guest shot anytime. He can come on and play his fiddle." Byrd said he'd be happy to have an edge when he called in to the show to make special requests.

As for the larger historic import of the Panama Canal broadcast, would hearing the voices of their elected officials inspire respect among the American populace? Sen. Alan Cranston allowed, "That of course will depend on how well we handle the treaties and how individual senators comport themselves in the course of the debate."

Just as much under the microscope as the senators themselves was Linda. Frank had taken some flak for choosing her as the "play-by-play announcer" for this historic debate. It was the same old trope that Mitchell had heard about Susan: A woman's voice was too shrill, too unbelievable, to use on the news (or, at least on news that was "important"). Covering politics, the White House, the courts—that was the domain of *men*.

"This is a sexist town," Frank acknowledged. "You can tell because people in Washington talk about equality more here, which means there's less of it. Then, too, when a woman is called 'charming,' society puts a little spin on the word. It means she is more guileful than attractive. Like a 'charming pitcher,' it means she doesn't have a fast ball." The discrimination was doubly confusing to Frank, given that, by now, the voice most linked to the network was Susan's.

Everyone knew that Linda was a diligent worker, a good study, and besides, Congress was her beat. Who *else* was he supposed to assign to this task? Around Capitol Hill, she'd become a familiar presence, as had her husband, now a lobbyist who routinely challenged Congress through Common Cause, the governmental watchdog group he led.

("Are you related to *that* Wertheimer," asked Rep. Wayne Hayes of Linda. "Yes, by marriage," was her answer. His retort: "That's the only smart thing that bastard ever did.")

A woman in anything but a servile role was still so uncommon that Linda's presence flummoxed the elders. Sen. James Allen of Alabama insisted on addressing her as "Little Lady," to which she'd routinely respond, "Big Senator," after which he'd apologize. She'd come so far from those days, not long ago, when she was, as she described it, the "lowest form of life at the BBC—the person with the clipboard." In just a few short years, she'd successfully graduated from her thankless behind-the-scenes job as director, to reporting on consumer affairs, to general assignment, and then on to covering politics and Congress. During the Watergate hearings, she'd had the thrill of being present for a scoop as she sat in the room where the judiciary committee voted to impeach President Nixon—and the frustration of not being able to claim a scoop because *All Things Considered* didn't air until 5:00 P.M.

There was some advantage to having to wait for her chance in the spotlight, Linda confessed—her voice was richer now. She'd certainly shed what there had been of the midwestern twang. "When you turn thirty," she told a reporter, "you're in better shape than when you're twenty-three." She was now a month shy of her thirty-fourth birthday.

Obviously, the reporter concluded, this Linda was "top-flight" and had been tapped for this assignment "not because of her beauty," though she did have "more than her share, a fresh-faced statuesque blonde who could wow the natives without difficulty, but through hard work."

As if she were back cramming for finals in Carlsbad, the onetime Sun Princess from New Mexico prepared for weeks, reading three books on the Canal and a three-foot-tall stack of materials provided to her by the Senate.

Would anyone out there in Radio Land bother to tune in to the drudgery of government proceedings? "If NPR ever had any listeners," remarked a skeptical unnamed senator to *Broadcasting* magazine, "they're going to lose them."

* * *

That winter Wednesday, with Linda Wertheimer's opening words, NPR listeners around the nation were instantly transported into the hallowed halls where so much of their lives was determined. For the first time since Vice President John Adams called the Senate to order in 1789, average citizens could tune in as their lawmakers engaged in the work they'd been dispatched to Washington to perform.

It was a distinction only the most diligent students of government procedures would have known: *Hearings* had been aired before—when NPR first flipped the switch on the service on April 20, 1971, the first sounds it transmitted were from the Senate Foreign Relations Committee hearings on ending U.S. involvement in Vietnam—but never a *debate*.

From his office, Frank sat beneath a prominently displayed photograph of Bobby Kennedy and a framed poster of an Albert Camus quote that read, "I would like to be able to love justice and still love my country," and eagerly tuned in for the big show. Listening to it gave him goose pimples.

In just the first ten minutes, NPR received twenty-five calls from people asking Linda to stop talking over what she'd presumed would be, to the average listener, boring introductory blather. The audience did, it seemed, have an appetite for the procedural rules of Congress.

Linda did her best to translate the bizarre language of senatorial procedure—such as the words of treaty opponent "Big Senator" James Allen: "As to an article and to have a vote on such article before amendments of any sort to the next succeeding article could be offered or considered in the Senate. I ask unanimous consent that the documents, quote, documents implementing the Panama Canal Treaty, close quote. And the, quote, other documents, quote, identified on page . . ."

What the heck did *that* mean? "It was just by the grace of God," said Linda, "that I was able to explain what those things were."

For the next thirty-seven days, fueled on little else but high-protein breakfasts to start the day, pound cake throughout, and a continuous

flow of adrenaline, Linda performed the play-by-play of these important debates, announcing the names of lawmakers as they spoke—how
else to distinguish all those male voices from one another?—filling
time with guests she lined up when quorum calls created unseemly
silence in the proceedings, and wrapping it all up every night in a
"post-game" show.

There was only the occasional glitch, usually when a senator,
unaccustomed to technology, stuffed the microphone into his breast
pocket, muffling the sound. Linda noticed that some lawmakers were
self-conscious about the fact that their words were being carried far
beyond the chamber, and this seemed to focus them. Yet those who
were typically quiet were suddenly grandstanding. When she noted on
the air that the number of legislators on the floor totaled only five or
six, all of a sudden, more bodies appeared: "I think they were a little
mortified to think their voters out in, wherever they were from, knew
that they were not there, so they came."

By the end of the proceedings, Linda had presided over two hundred hours of broadcasting; she was certain that she'd heard more of
the debate than the lawmakers themselves. A deluge of calls and tele-
grams arrived at NPR's headquarters: People loved being able to peer
in on the action of Congress. Linda's voice was now familiar to millions
of listeners across the nation. As her sister sat in the dean's office at
New Mexico State, she remarked about the voice she heard on the radio:
"That sounds like my sister."

"That's Linda Wertheimer," the dean responded; hers was a voice
he'd come to know.

"Then it *is* my sister," came the response.

Other high praise was issued by the lawmakers themselves. Senators Allen and Byrd, who, though they came down on opposite sides of
the issue, agreed on this: They owed Linda a debt of gratitude for quietly
and modestly taking the nation on a "guided tour of the United States."
(Byrd also sneaked in a plug for the bluegrass show.) Later, Linda
learned that even the leader of Panama had tuned in at the embassy,
angrily shouting at the demeaning descriptions of his nation. At one

point, he got so angry that he jerked the radio out of its plug and threw it out the window—then called for someone to bring him a new one so he could keep on listening.

But the best validation of all came from the two crucial sources who'd inspired her to get into the business years back when she was a grocer's daughter in Carlsbad. NPR board member Janet Murrow, widow of her earliest idol, wrote Linda an effusive complimentary letter. About the only input that could have topped that was what she heard from Pauline Frederick, the vaunted, pioneering newscaster who'd embedded Linda with the dream she was now living—and who was now her colleague. On a trip into the DC office, Frederick thrilled Linda by offering her congratulations.

As for NPR's new president, he knew he'd hit a home run with the $200,000 in network money he estimated he'd invested in the Panama Canal debate coverage. The residual benefit was priceless. What would he do for an encore now that he'd convinced the Senate to allow a live broadcast? How about an even more impenetrable body: Perhaps he could convince the Supreme Court to allow NPR to broadcast its proceedings.

CHAPTER FOURTEEN
Star Wars

That day in the early fall of 1977 when Steve Roberts handed Nina his wife's résumé out on M Street, she ran back into the newsroom. When Linda saw it, she wondered, "Is that Cokie Boggs?" Cokie Boggs from Wellesley?" Cokie didn't know Linda, but everyone on campus had known Cokie.

Linda and Nina had a vested interest in making sure the open reporter slot vacated by Judith Miller went to a woman. Having been stymied by the good old boy network, they were eager to amp up their own parallel effort. Now that they had the jobs they'd long angled for, who better to do so than them?

When Cokie walked in the door for an interview, Nina and Linda were there to cheerlead her on, and a mutual admiration society immediately formed: Cokie felt herself drawn to this place because of them—even if it was an also-ran of a network.

At first, she was hired as a contractor, an unsettling, uncertain arrangement. She and Steve were still searching for a house, using her childhood home as a temporary base. Buying one that wasn't way out of town, on his pay alone, was going to be a stretch. Though one producer at NPR wasn't so keen on her voice, Cokie filed stories every day. Still, the security of a salaried job wasn't offered.

The presence of a sitting congresswoman's daughter inside the building, not to mention her appearance on the air, caused consternation among a few of the executives, including one career public media man who stormed around slamming doors at the mere suggestion that Cokie might be awarded a staff position.

For once, the argument wasn't about her sex. Here, the issue was lineage. Could the daughter of career politicians really serve as an impartial journalist? With the constant fear of government defunding looming, hiring someone with such entrenched DC roots seemed like asking for trouble, a political hot potato—on top of the newly arrived political hot potato that was network president Frank Mankiewicz. This kind of attention and possible controversy was the last thing NPR needed.

As far as Frank was concerned, Cokie's connections were a major asset. The fact that her husband was a rising star at the nation's most important paper was another chit in the plus column. Not to mention her prominent, powerful brother, Tommy, who'd moved on from his failed congressional campaign to practically invent modern lobbying. Congress, at budget time, might be more favorably inclined toward NPR—even more so than toward him, since his own connections ran deep. The profile of Congresswoman Lindy Boggs had been soaring ever higher since she'd first won her own election; in 1976, she'd been tapped to chair the Bicentennial Commission and the Democratic National Convention. Her name was even floated as a potential vice-presidential candidate (although even she knew that her unwavering pro-life stance would scuttle her from a nomination).

Everything about Cokie that his colleagues considered a liability was, to Frank, an asset. She was the perfect "ornament" for the network, he said. Another force pushing back against the dissenters? Linda and Nina.* They collectively advocated for their new friend, and after months of wrangling, Frank finally gave Cokie the plum staff job she was after.

It wasn't like they were handing the job, as low-paying as it was, to someone with no qualifications. Cokie had experience, after all. She'd reported for CBS. She'd written for *The Nation*, a variety of magazines, and, with her husband, the *New York Times*. She'd been a producer and even a host of youth-oriented television shows.

There was, as far as Frank was concerned, only one problem with his newest hire: her name. It was far too cutesy, too preppy. Didn't she have another she could use?

Well, yes, she responded. How about her actual name, Mary Martha Corinne Morrison Claiborne Boggs Roberts?

---

* Robert Siegel and Robert Krulwich, Cokie's editors, were also boosters.

"Okay," Frank shrugged. "We'll stick with Cokie."

And with that, the woman whose distinctive childhood nickname had served her quite well up till now landed her first staff job in a newsroom. Lindy agreed to sell her daughter and Steve the beloved family property on Bradley Boulevard for a cool $235,000 and move to a condo closer to the Capitol. Everything was falling into place.

Good politician that he was, Frank dashed off a letter to the congresswoman. "I just wanted to let you know how happy I am that Cokey [sic] is on board full-time at NPR," he wrote. "She will be a fine addition to the staff here, and a first-rate journalist. Professionally and personally we are delighted to have her here." Frank added a postscript that evidenced his inside-the-Beltway mettle: "I'm sorry I couldn't make your Mardi Gras party." While the boss might consider Cokie an ornament, he was a pretty fine one himself.

* * *

With her plunge into full-time work and her first job as a staff reporter, Cokie was now a full-fledged woman of the 1970s, a working professional tending to a career with unpredictable hours as demanding as her ambitious husband's while juggling the needs of school-age children and a commute with the fundamental, pressing need to put dinner on the table.

It had been one thing back when she had flexible part-time jobs, such as when her daughter was just ten days old and she'd left her and her two-year-old son with her visiting mother at a hotel, so she could scurry off to a taping for *It's Academic*. Now the acrobatic demands would be her lot every single day.

Her new colleague Susan had been dealing with this for years, adding to her part-time hours gradually as her son grew, and grateful that she could afford to hire domestic help to assist her. People who said the juggle was easy were lying, Susan said. Something always went on the back burner. Time was always working against you. There was always something pulling and getting short shrift. Raising a child was the hardest thing to do.

A configuration of assistance came for Cokie thanks to a neighbor-hood teen and a few young relatives with newly minted driver's licenses. Once the Robertses were able to import the Scottish nanny they'd employed in Athens, that offered relief, too, but it didn't allay Cokie's guilt over the long hours, missed weekends, or measly two weeks of vacation she got as the newcomer on the workplace totem pole. Her daily life was vastly different from the one she'd witnessed her mother handle. "You have to give up something," she said, "and what it is, is sleep." She recited the motto of the nuns, *Hic et nunc,* "here and now," as her guiding light: "Do what is necessary."

At long last, alongside what she considered to be her number-one jobs as wife and mother, she was carving out an identity of her own. Even when the kid's show she worked on back in Los Angeles had been nominated for a local Emmy, the commendation had read "Mrs. Stephen Roberts"—with his first name spelled incorrectly. Yes, her husband worked for a more prestigious news organization, and yes, he made more money. But now they each found themselves consumed with similarly demanding jobs: "And Steven couldn't walk in the door at the end of the day and plead for mercy from the worries of household and family. We walked in the door together."

The intoxicating power of having her own career came with an even greater bonus: a public persona. She adored this medium, though she admitted journalism wasn't the most "mature of vocations," what with the ego stroke it provided, of having one's voice heard. "It's that business of being able to tell something at length, the freedom to tell the story the way it needs to be told," she told writer Nicholas von Hoffman of *Channels* magazine.

On the job, NPR's newest reporter gravitated toward stories about schools, family, and other issues of concern to working women. When the Pope came to town, the devout Catholic was sent to chronicle his visit—although when she called home and Steve tried to guilt her about how one of the kids had had an accident, she snapped that he should just call a plastic surgeon. She'd noticed for years now that while women went ahead and juggled the tasks before them, men felt the need to announce what they were doing, as if they deserved a prize for handling the matter.

"Stepping up" was her unspoken mantra. When news broke of the partial core meltdown at Three Mile Island, Cokie, as one of the few staff reporters, volunteered to go. It wasn't because she had any desire to enter a nuclear danger zone, but because, first, she was done having children, so the environment would be less risky for her; and second, she could drive a car, unlike many of her colleagues. Linda had had an accident, long ago, and as a result, didn't drive. A detached retina had diminished Nina's eyesight, and the few other reporters there had grown up in Manhattan and therefore had never learned.

By the time she embarked on the two-hour trek to Harrisburg, Pennsylvania, Steve's *New York Times* bosses had asked him to cover the story, too, but he refused—with two young children, they couldn't very well *both* head to the scene of an unfolding disaster. For the very first time, his work was accommodating hers.

As she settled in at the network, she'd studiously avoided the beat that seemed most obvious for her to cover. It was at the suggestion of Linda that Cokie tiptoed into reporting on politics. At any other time or place, or with any other person, the daughter of a grocer from New Mexico might have been ferociously envious of her coworker who'd been "born in the boiler-room" of Congress, the institution Linda herself had spent so much time and energy studying and learning to understand. In fact, back during the Watergate hearings, depleted by exhaustion, Linda had recoiled when a female colleague arrived to relieve her, ferociously pushing the woman away in order to protect her turf.

But Cokie, she was different. Her mother was a member of Congress, for god's sake. Linda's own mother, the grocer's wife, once heard her daughter grill a lawmaker and chastised her in the aftermath— she hadn't raised her to speak to people in that tone! Linda could see plainly that her new friend and ally knew politics better than anyone, had absorbed it for decades—little details that were of enormous help, the fact the clerk in the congressional takeout joint knew the lawmakers' schedule better than the majority leader. Many of the people Cokie had known when she was a kid still roamed the halls. (When she'd first returned, a man who'd worked at the Ways and Means Committee who'd watched her grow up exclaimed, "Baby, you're back. I mean, *Miss Baby*.")

While Linda had had to teach herself how to decipher the convoluted language of Congress, it was Cokie's native tongue: "I don't even know how I knew it, but I knew it," she said. It wasn't just that she knew it; she had a gift for *explaining* it. It seemed silly for her to continue her resistance to the beat. There was enough of Capitol Hill to go around for both women. In fact, they became a team and soon could finish each other's sentences. House Speaker Tip O'Neill paid them a high compliment: "I give youse girls from NPR everything."

The way to cover Congress, Cokie said, was "to live, breathe, eat and sleep Congress, period." For her, it was neither a stretch nor a hardship. Indeed, it was difficult to imagine or believe that Cokie hadn't aspired to this job.

There was just one source that eluded her, and that was Representative Lindy Boggs, who addled her daughter by being "disgustingly discreet." Still, Cokie loved, after driving into work with her husband, running into her mother in the halls of Congress and confiding in her, during a late-night session, her fears about her kids back at home with the nanny while she was still at work. ("They're fine," Lindy assured her, even if Cokie was still dubious.)

The Capitol felt like home for both of them, almost as much as their wonderful property on Bradley Boulevard. Sometimes, as Cokie meandered this grand building she'd first come to know as a child, she'd flash back to her childhood—and at the right angle, she was able to imagine her beloved daddy, long lost to the icy waters of Alaska, zipping around the corner.

Frank, who knew a star when he saw one, commissioned newspaper ads to tout his gem. "The House Is Her Home," read one headline. Somewhere along the way, the old maxim that women "didn't have the authority to cover the news," a belief that had held them back for so long, began to melt away. Just as Susan had imprinted NPR with her distinctive voice and carved out an identity for the network with her humanistic view of the news, now, despite initial objections, Linda, Nina, and Cokie carved out identities for themselves in the establishment world of politics. Women—or, as Susan began to call them, "the founding mothers"—had morphed into NPR's greatest asset.

* * *

Because of the nature of their work and their obsession with the machinations of Washington, Cokie, Linda, and Nina forged a particular bond. Fortifying their might was their geographic proximity to one another at the office: They inhabited a cluster of desks situated near the front corner of the building. When they weren't out chasing stories as star representatives of the growing network whose reputation they were helping to bolster, they were inserting themselves into its machinations.

Any staff member beckoned back to their area and asked to take a seat on their yellow ochre sofa knew that something was up—would they be reprimanded, praised, asked for a favor, or prodded for gossip? Sometimes, the founding mothers would play matchmaker. Other times, they'd scold. When they heard about a gentleman staffer who was planning on having a baby out of wedlock, Nina and Cokie marched over and expressed their displeasure. "Your children will be called bastards," they cautioned.

Neither did they hold back regarding hiring and union matters and management issues. Nina, the screamer; Linda, the rational one; Cokie, ever tactful. They weren't women *in* power—though, had they wished, they could likely have seized it—they were women *of* power. They preferred the loftier perches they inhabited; influencing from a distance, never hesitating to weigh in on their needs or concerns or opinions. They asked for what they wanted, and they got what they asked for.

If Cokie had to run to a parent-teacher conference, Linda, who did not have children, might cover for her. If Nina unearthed one of her famous scoops, she'd run it past the other two for their input. Together, they'd grouse about their personal lives. Cokie and Linda, hearing Nina working the phones, digging for sources, would marvel at her courage and tenacity. Nina and Cokie revered Linda for her persistence and attention to detail. And Linda envied Cokie's even temper.

If the three of them were nowhere to be found, their editors (back when cell phones were but a fantasy) considered a few possibilities: They might be out in the field, reporting; or they might have sneaked off to Cokie's house to can tomatoes; or perhaps they were out to lunch, gossiping with Frank and a handful of others lucky to be asked to tag along. Frank would gleefully listen in to their chat—not girl talk, he emphasized, but "women's language."

Why, people would ask him, did he have so many women on the staff? Because, he'd say, "you get more bang for the buck with women." The women groaned and, as they always had, kept working.

And networking—with a group of other Washington women who'd made inroads into journalism, they'd get together for an extension of their own personal "girls' club" lunch each month; if anyone needed anything, like a job, they'd leap into action, working the phones to make it happen. Their very presence on the scene was changing everything, and they believed it to be their responsibility to speak up.

"Nobody reported on the widespread philandering of President Kennedy," observed Nina of the not-very-long-ago era of underrepresentation. "Some of us at this table might think that that's because there were virtually no women on the campaign plane."

The force field increasingly extended well beyond their jobs and office politics and into their personal lives. When, in 1979, Nina married the former Colorado senator Floyd Haskell, Linda and Cokie served as her attendants (with Judge John Minor Wisdom, earlier a source, performing the ceremony). With their husbands, the friends became regulars at Cokie's annual (and growing) "shiksa seder." Most Saturday nights, they'd all grab dinner at the Pines of Rome, in Bethesda, a white-tablecloth neighborhood Italian joint owned by Cokie's next-door neighbor, before heading to the movies.

When someone in the press corps gossiped about how Steve Roberts of the *New York Times* was having an affair with that reporter from

NPR, they all laughed. Didn't they catch that they both had the same last name?

Gossip, Nina, Linda, and Cokie style, involved trading observations about the cads of Capitol Hill. Linda had been chased around a desk by a senator, but he was so old that she knew he'd never catch her. Cokie talked of her innocence in believing that a wedding ring on her finger would provide armor against other men's advances. Said Nina, "You knew who was a bottom pincher and which Senator not to sit near," or when it was best to dress "like a nun." Scenes could be avoided, for the most part, if you moved away; the man usually knew better than to push it. *Usually.*

They'd tolerated this kind of behavior for years, gritting their teeth and repressing their anger. Yet, now that they found themselves united together, they drew a collective line in the sand to show they were done with being regarded as second-class. To wit: When the producers of the Miss America pageant, looking to infuse some intellect into the competition, inquired about having host Bob Edwards interview the contestants about current events, the women intervened with an emphatic "go away." A beauty pageant was a cultural force with which they did not wish NPR's name associated.

For all this, a bemused male coworker christened the women, and their corner of the office, with equal parts admiration and derision, the "Fallopian Jungle." Yet those who sniffed at the ladies of the jungle did so at their own peril. The women had all lacked allies and friendship for so long that they were unabashed in their delight in having found one another—and this work. No longer did they need to gaze at or be at the hand of the old boy network. They were firm and proud leaders of the hard-won old girl network they'd hatched.

Not, however, universally. While they might be quick with advice and praise, one talented but volatile female reporter was so reviled by this trio of star reporters (and they by her) that a wall had to be erected to separate her desk from theirs. And though there were countless admirers in the audience who kvelled with delight at the sound of strong, smart women delivering their news, there were, of course, the inevitable detractors. One listener in Missouri wrote to Frank that he found the women insufferable, blasé, didactic, and elitist. *All Things Considered*, he said, should be renamed "All Things Condescended"—jettison the "trite, rhetorical" format that treated listeners as if they "were grade school kids at a mandatory assembly at an eastern boarding school."

Let the critics say what they wish, said the women. Triumphant, they stood watchfully over the barricades they'd busted down. There was no going back.

* * *

One unseasonably cold Saturday morning in early October 1979, Susan's husband, Lou, fetched her from an early morning appointment at the beauty parlor for an important date at the White House. This was an unusual end to another week of daily toil. On Tuesday, she'd interviewed an advocate for prostitutes' rights; on Wednesday, South African writer Nadine Gordimer. Thursday brought a chat with a *New York Times* writer in Belgrade about a Czech playwright with citizenship troubles. She'd been doing this so long now, she innately understood the flow: "Like cars on the assembly line, news programs get better by Wednesday . . . Thursday tends to be the best broadcast day of the week . . . the words are flowing well, originality takes up residence in typewriters and behind microphones," she explained. The days marched on, sometimes labored and slow, sometimes with lightning speed, and on occasion, the rhythm was punctuated by a thunderbolt of excitement, as would be the case today.

Though it required working on a weekend, a day she typically jealously reserved for her family, today she would be broadcasting from the nicest studio she'd ever seen—a makeshift one in the Oval Office, hosting a rare event: a special two-hour call-in talk show with President Carter. Thrilled with the home run he'd hit with the Panama Canal debate broadcasts, Frank had made the official ask and gotten a yes.

There was no question that the honor of conducting this high-profile production would be awarded to NPR's biggest star, even though Susan was on the record as being less than enamored of the Washington zeitgeist. When Carter had first arrived on the national political scene, she'd been more interested in learning about his distinctive smile than his politics, and she had found, in inimitable Susan fashion, clues to his personality in an interview with his dentist. (He was unerringly conscientious, the man reported.)

It was unusual for the nation's populace to hear the president speak extemporaneously, and certainly not on the airwaves. The folksy peanut farmer from Georgia was considered the first "television president," employing a former network producer as his consultant to help him wade through the ever-intensifying impact of electronic media. But news conferences with the press corps weren't routinely televised; networks were loath to interrupt regularly scheduled (and lucrative) programming for the routine business of government, which seemed of little appeal to the average citizen. The inhabitant of the highest office in the land was too busy with the work of governance to speak directly to the people, much less to interact with them. Except for major addresses like the State of Union, his media presence was limited to sound bites on the evening news.

This fact elevated the appearance on NPR to the realm of news, not just stunt. For his part, President Carter said he liked fielding unrehearsed questions from people outside the press corps. He believed the questions to be more heartfelt. He'd done this sort of program once before, with Walter Cronkite.* Susan called the "maestro" of broadcast news to ask for his wisdom, never expecting he'd take the call from an obscure outlet like NPR. To her utter delight, the man known as the most trusted in America flattered her when he said he'd heard her on the air and told her she didn't need any advice. But, he cautioned, Carter could be long-winded and somewhat convoluted in his responses. For

---

* Cronkite's presidential conversation was parodied on *Saturday Night Live*: https://www .youtube.com/watch?time_continue=5&v=-68iTvhWNBo&feature=emb_logo.

Cronkite, this presented a problem: He hated interrupting a president. Confident Susan knew that tamping down Carter's loquaciousness wouldn't be an issue for her.

The big day arrived. Stuffed in Susan's corduroy bag were her prep notes and that sign she'd made a few years back to calm the nerves of a colleague, now a reminder for her and her very special guest: "It's Only a Radio Program." That might be true, but this day in radio would be a special one.

At a time of historic inflation, crippling budgetary crises vexing the nation's cities, gas rations, and rising crime, fifty thousand letters from Americans eager to voice their concerns arrived at the White House each week. For the Cronkite/Carter radio call-in, nine million viewers had jammed the lines and swamped AT&T's system. This time around, a new system was implemented. Potential questioners had been instructed to write in and were told, "Don't call him, he'll call you."

Ten thousand postcards arrived at P.O. Box 19369, Washington, DC, sorted solely by zip code, with no other prescreening. (One man confessed to having sent in 250 cards to increase his chances.) The happy task of informing the sixty people whose cards had been chosen that morning fell to NPR secretary Jennifer Gomez, who said, "There were shrieks of delight, and you could hear clamor in the background from other family members once they knew who was calling." She instructed them to sit by their phones from noon Eastern Time to 2:00 P.M.

Susan admired the bookcases in this glamorous makeshift studio, which included the complete works of Jefferson and a bust of Harry Truman. Her husband stubbornly refused to turn on the heat until Thanksgiving, regardless of the weather, but here in the Oval Office, Susan felt toasty warm. Striped couches had been moved, a white sheet laid out on the floor to protect the carpet, microphones perfectly positioned in front of the rust wing chairs before the fireplace. Soon, the president entered the room and took his seat beside her, as photographers snapped photos to capture the moment.

As the switch allowing their voices to be transmitted to the nation was flipped, Susan explained in the conversational style that was her hallmark, "We're kind of strolling around the country by phone, and we're doing it for the reason that citizens from many parts of the nation want to have a chance to speak with the president. We want to give them that chance."

Over the next two hours, she introduced those citizens and moved the conversation along as President Carter fielded a wide range of questions from all corners of the United States—Philipsburg, Montana, to Weston, West Virginia, to Fallbrook, California. The topics were as diverse as the locations, encompassing solar energy, the Equal Rights Amendment, inflation, the rising costs of health care, and the treatment of Native Americans.

Susan found herself less interested in President Carter's answers and more absorbed by the changes in his complexion and in his eyes as they talked. Occasionally, she'd sneak in a question of her own, nodding to his struggles—he faced flagging approval—and that of the nation, which was in the grip of a recession and still recovering from the scourges of Vietnam and Watergate.

"Our basic institutions that we sometimes doubt—government, the presidency, the Congress—have survived and have prevailed," said the president. "And I don't think our system of either economics or our social system or our government system has any equal anywhere on Earth. We ought to remember that."

The two hours flew by—just another day in Radio Land. Susan wrapped up the show and tossed back to the studio at headquarters, where Linda would now host a wrap-up analysis of the president's remarks. Was this the highlight of her career? people asked Susan later. Not at all, she said. Every word uttered by the president had been uttered before. That's politics.

But the broadcast itself was excellent theater. With his own characteristic flair, Frank had scored yet another victory in his ongoing campaign to raise public radio's profile. The entire operation had cost two thousand dollars in phone line installation and long-distance time. The publicity it yielded was priceless. The story made the nightly news and landed on the front pages of the papers the next morning.

* * *

Again and again, Frank embodied what the slogan on the promotional tote bags he'd commissioned pithily promised: "NPR Means Business." The number of stations carrying the network had tripled from the start, now up to 267. Most cities, he explained, didn't have a decent newspaper, and *All Things Considered* offered them a chance to find out what was really going on—unlike television news, which he professed to be the broadcasting equivalent of Chinese food: "In an hour, you're hungry for more."

With Edward Elson at his side, Frank visited Capitol Hill to boast of the progress he'd made. "Not long ago," he told lawmakers on the House Committee on Interstate and Foreign Commerce, "there was a sense that radio was hopelessly old-fashioned—television without pictures. From its roots as an unconnected system of discrete, primarily low-powered, largely instructional stations, often operating as extra-curricular activities much like student newspapers, public radio has grown into a system of stations servicing their communities at least eighteen hours a day, every day."

On the strength of his arguments, Frank managed to route a larger slice of the public broadcasting pie in the direction of radio, from 17 percent up to 25 percent. Out of thin air, an unexpected onetime bounty of $15 million arrived from the Corporation for Public Broadcasting, for the pet project of Frank's choice. He didn't hesitate for a minute about what he'd do with this found money: He'd launch a new show during the part of the day most important to radio, mornings. It had been easier, when NPR started, not to have a show that aired then, but now with its growing reputation and audience reliance on the service for news, it seemed a necessity.

To help figure out what this new program should be, Frank first hired psychologists to answer the question: What did listeners want to hear when their eyes first fluttered open in the morning to greet a new day? A person's first impulse, it seemed, was relief that they were, simply, alive. How better to do that than with a news show that indicated that the world had continued as they slept. Old habits would die hard. Convincing member stations that their listeners wished to hear something other than classical music first thing in the morning would be a challenge.

The already strapped staff of *All Things Considered* also did not greet news of a new show as a positive development. The announcement incited everything from skepticism to resistance to envy. "Fix us first," Susan shouted, "we don't have the resources" for the ninety minutes they were already producing, much less two hours more. At last, they were consistently proud of what they'd been producing. What if this new offering stepped on or outdid what they'd been building for years?

The Fallopian Jungle roared at the prospect of having to contribute to another program. Filing stories twice a day? Forget it. They were already working hard enough. "We can't . . . I mean, we're having a hard enough time doing what we're doing," Cokie said. "How are we going to do two programs a day?"

You won't have to, she was told. "We'll bring in people."

But "people" didn't equal more reporters, who were needed to create more stories to fill the additional airtime. Frank did, however, hire a new news director—a rising star plucked from the *Washington Star* named Barbara Cohen. Thanks in part to a minority and women hiring initiative at the paper, Cohen had risen through the ranks, beginning as a copy editor right out of graduate school and climbing all the way up to managing editor—one of the first women in the nation to hold such a position. Bringing in a woman manager with serious journalistic chops helped Frank counter searing criticism of public broadcasting for what several reports had called its "appalling" track record on hiring women and minorities, particularly in management.*

---

* The report, called "A Formula for Change," can be found in its entirety here: https://files.eric.ed.gov/fulltext/ED172269.pdf.

SUSAN, LINDA, NINA & COKIE

At first, Cohen hadn't been convinced a leap from stalwart print to flighty radio made sense, although ownership changes at the *Star* helped goad her along. Never mind that at the fancy restaurant where Frank took her to woo her and impress upon her the benefits of the medium, he'd forgotten his wallet, and she had to pay. His enthusiasm for the future, and for NPR, proved infectious, though, and she acquiesced.

Staffing up the principals for the new morning show proved just as challenging as it had at the start of the network. The pool of candidates simply wasn't much larger. The producer who was eventually hired, from commercial radio, horrified the troops when he attempted to institute a no-jeans dress code. Worse, they complained, he ran his news meetings with all the panache of an actuary.

Then there were the hosts, decidedly off-key. Chirpy, cheery—they sounded as if they'd made a wrong turn from the nearest all-news radio station. The disastrous state of the new show inspired much gleeful schadenfreude among the existing staff. The pilots were so bad, so opposite of what they'd worked so hard to build, the member stations expressed outrage.*

But the show had been promoted and advertised, and there was no choice but to go on. How could it be rescued, with just days to go? Several inside staffers got hooked for the assignment—two producers and two on-air hosts, Barbara Hoctor, a newly hired weekend host, and Bob Edwards, the self-described "newsy Catholic male" counterpart to Susan's "artsy, Jewish New York female."

It had taken some time for Edwards, a disciple of Edward R. Murrow, to make personal peace with not working at the mighty temple of news across the street, CBS, and to overcome what he described as his "Mr. Prig" attitude about his cohost, Susan—what was this *woman* doing at the helm of a news show? The fact that Susan had top billing and made more money than he did *and* got to leave early to tend

---

* Despite the unceremonious end to their time in public radio, the pilots' hosts, Mary Tillotson and Pete Williams, wound up doing quite well for themselves in their careers, she at CNN and he at NBC.

to her family didn't help tamp down the professional resentment. But each night, as he'd sat in the studio with her, he graduated from the old-school spoon-feed-the-news approach, where men were the voice of god, and began to respect and even find himself awed by her utter and complete control of the medium. She was also, in his estimation, smarter than anyone else in the newsroom.

With the morning show in dire straits, Edwards and Hoctor each figured they'd step up as team players and agreed to help out for thirty days, to get the show off the ground. And just as it had when *All Things Considered* debuted years earlier, big news occurred as *Morning Edition* was about to debut. This was particularly dire: a hostage crisis in Iran, which proceeded to drag on and on—in the process, training listeners to tune in each morning to hear what had happened overnight.

It wasn't until six months into the program that the Fallopian Jungle and others on staff tabled what Hoctor had called their "savage" and "bitter" resistance to the show. An aborted attempt to rescue the hostages, plus hours of protracted coverage, along with the realization that listeners were tuning in, pulled the staff together. Besides, it was clear *Morning Edition* wasn't going away, and because it was branded with their network's name, the women felt lending their names and voices to it would improve the program. Cokie noted that when she walked into Congress each day, two thirds of the members seemed to have listened. Still, mistrustful of this morning crew and its editors, the founding mothers asserted their power when they submitted stories, cautioning that nary a word or a moment of tape should be altered. (That didn't mean that they weren't.)

* * *

Delighted by the launch of his new creation, mastermind Frank kept at the scheming, the politics, the innovation. His coauthor on the Nixon books, James Reston Jr.—the journalist son of Steve Roberts's first mentor at the *New York Times*—arrived with a motherlode of tapes retrieved from the Guyanese compound of cult leader Jim Jones. In the aftermath of the mass suicide there, it had been discovered that the wicked leader had recorded hours and hours of chilling talks, including his followers declaring their commitment to die as plainly as if they were discussing what they'd eaten for lunch. Reston needed a home for the rich and disturbing audio. Frank, in turn, assigned producer Deborah Amos and host Noah Adams to work with Reston to create an audio documentary that vividly brought to life Jones's unfurling madness. With a budget of fifteen thousand dollars, they crafted a chilling documentary, *Father Cares: The Last of Jonestown*. Critics heralded it as "one of the great achievements in this history of broadcasting."

Just as the show was airing, a newly installed presidential administration, Ronald Reagan's, focused public broadcasting in its crosshairs. A 20 percent cutback in funds was announced for the next budget, to begin in 1983, ratcheting up the urgency for new sources of dollars.

Not every seed yielded fruit. Excited over his successful broadcasts with President Carter and Congress, Frank managed to get himself invited for tea with Chief Justice Warren Burger, who explained that while he admired NPR, he had no intention of permitting broadcasts from the chambers of the highest court in the land.

When offered the chance to take a popular variety show produced in Minnesota on a national scale, Frank turned it down.* *A Prairie Home Companion* was, in his estimation, the *Laverne and Shirley* of public radio—he found it offensive.

And though he seriously considered the offer of a donation of the financially faltering wire service United Press International from newspaper publisher Scripps-Howard, he ultimately concluded that folding it into the NPR newsroom would be unsustainable.

The installation of the long-heralded $17 million Westar satellite system gave Frank starry hope. Not only did it improve the audio quality of NPR's programs, which till now often sounded like a scratchy

---

* His rejection of *A Prairie Home Companion* allowed rival production service Minnesota Public Radio to flourish.

long-distance phone call—the signal was so clear, Frank joked, that he had to ask the engineers to introduce static on the line so listeners would believe the transmission was actually coming from two separate locations—but the satellite would save NPR from the pricey tape-dubbing and mail delivery of the non-news programs. No longer would the network be a radio service that "depends on the goddamn post office," he said. Last, and most lucratively, in these early stages of satellite deployment, the system would prove a cash cow. NPR could rent out unused bandwidth for big bucks. Frank got permission that allowed him to sign on with a telephone paging firm angling to create the nation's first nationwide service.

As a glitzy showcase of this invisible but essential technological improvement, Frank set his sights on reviving a grand old, mostly fallow tradition: radio drama. A long-standing theatrical public radio series out of Wisconsin called *Earplay** proved too low-key for his taste. He needed a splash.

It had never been far from his mind, watching his dad work with Orson Welles and the Mercury Theatre troupe when he was a kid. Back then, before the invention of audiotape, all radio had been performed live. Actors gathered at the Mankiewicz home in Beverly Hills on Sunday mornings to rehearse in advance of their performance.

A key member of the Mercury troupe, producer John Houseman, developed a particularly close relationship with Frank's dad. It had been Houseman's job to take Herman into the desert and keep a watchful eye (over him as well as the booze) as he finished his masterpiece, *Citizen Kane.†* As Houseman aged, he'd moved on to a storied acting career. Now he was teaching at the University of Southern California, devotedly listening to his old friend Frank's NPR, when Frank called with a question. Who better for NPR's chief to ask about radio drama than the man responsible for possibly the most famous one ever produced—the

---

* You can hear many of the *Earplay* performances here: https://www.oldtimeradiodown loads.com/drama/earplay.
† Houseman knew the truth of Welles's claim to have been cowriter of the film.

terrifying, realistic alien attack drama *The War of the Worlds?* The one-hour live program was said to have panicked listeners who believed the dramatic plot, that the planet was under siege by extraterrestrials.

Houseman, in turn, posed Frank's query to Richard Toscan, the head of the university's theater program: What should Frank do? The answer was simple: "Create a scandal." Scandal was Toscan's code word for "splash."

What constituted a scandalous splash in radio drama? It just so happened that the blockbuster director George Lucas was both an alumnus of the University of Southern California and himself a fan of public radio. KUSC, licensed to the school, was the dominant public radio affiliate in the market. Also, as it happened, Lucas's film *Star Wars* had become, as *Variety* called it, the "all-time box office champ." For the grand sum of a dollar, Lucas sold the rights to adapt the story into a thirteen-part radio series. This was exactly the sort of popular and populist splash that suited Frank's fancy.

Science-fiction writer Brian Daley was hired to craft the action. Two of the movie's original actors, Mark Hamill as Luke Skywalker and Anthony Daniels as the heroic borg C-3PO, signed on to reprise their roles. Lucas even agreed to turn over sound effects and music from the film to sound designer Tom Voegeli, who would painstakingly edit them with razor blade and tape.

Now all they needed was the money. The BBC agreed to pay 40 percent of the $200,000 budget—the first time the "Beeb" would make such a major investment in an American public broadcasting production. The director general of the BBC even appeared at a news conference with Frank as he announced this "spectacular first step toward expanding National Public Radio's dramatic activities."

By the time the series hit the air in March 1981—expertly timed to seize the buzz surrounding the starry film premiere of the sequel, *The Empire Strikes Back,* and coinciding with local station fund drives—the BBC had bowed out of the deal. It wasn't quite clear where the funds were obtained to finish the show. Still, to amp up the drama, NPR's publicity department revved into overdrive, arranging for Darth Vader to arrive at NPR headquarters to pose for a promo shoot with Frank's two main news stars, Susan and Bob. Ads promoting the series promised, "You may think you've seen the movie. Wait till you hear it!" and "Radio drama is making a resounding comeback."

Critics affirmed the hype. James Brown of the *Los Angeles Times* declared the finished product "a flashy smorgasbord of space hardware and otherworldly characters constructed like a symphony." The producers, Brown said, had taken the "theater of the mind that radio drama was in the past and infused it with technological wonder."

A glitzy gala premiere listening party was held high above Los Angeles, at the Griffith Observatory, replete with a starry light show that accompanied the first episode as it blasted out to the crowd over loudspeakers. The giant "Hollywood" sign in the hills nearby harked back to Frank's roots. His life had been filled with glamour and drama of his own making. Recasting his beloved medium of radio for a modern, mobile society, he exclaimed, was "like the lungs of someone who has just quit smoking" not only surviving but regenerating.

Ten thousand letters arrived on M Street, and forty thousand phone calls jammed NPR's phone lines; *Star Wars* was an unparalleled success. There had been three million listeners when Frank Mankiewicz arrived in public radio in 1977, and in the five years he promised it would take to make a splash for the network, those numbers had tripled. The founding mothers had established NPR as an important source for news; Frank had taken it to a new level.

What could possibly go wrong?

CHAPTER FIFTEEN

The Drive to Survive

A newsroom is a curious workplace, unlike any other—a waystation where information streams in from points near and far; where it is filtered with alacrity, ego, and angst through the odd lot of individuals entrusted with collecting and reconstituting it and then distributing it out to an audience eager to connect to and make sense of the world beyond. While each newsroom is slightly different depending on the medium and the people who inhabit it, fundamentally—as Tolstoy said of happy families—all newsrooms are alike, propelled by a common goal, the race to deadline, and, perhaps, by a dollop of belief that somehow, in the endless hours of toil, just perhaps, you're collectively serving the common good.

At 5:40 A.M. on Wednesday, November 17, 1982, nine days before Thanksgiving, the newsroom at National Public Radio's headquarters at 2025 M Street pulsed with the caffeinated tension of the predawn hours. Different day, same noise (the click of the keys on the state-of-the-art, tanklike IBM Selectric typewriters) and clutter (reels of tape and hulking machines on which to play it; push-button telephones perched on desks and shelves, silent, given the hour; and stacks of newspapers and old scripts and fresh blank pages and torn scrolls of white paper bearing urgent transmissions ripped off the persistently ticking wire machines). Along the back wall of the newsroom, a giant whiteboard—as useful a device as back when Linda first insisted on installing one twelve years prior—alerted the staff to work in progress. On it, producers had scribbled in black Magic Marker the "slugs" of stories in the pipeline ("Drugs in Florida," "Vaudeville Economics," and "Motorcycling through China"). The décor of the room was, to be charitable, latter-day college dorm: dingy walls papered with staff lists and schedules; a perk of nature provided by a fading bouquet of flowers sent, by the looks of its droop, days ago; a head shot tacked, pin-up style, of the boyish blond star Bob Edwards, titled "America's Foremost Host"; a reproduction of a print ad for NPR that promised more than snippets of sound-bite journalism: "presenting news on the radio that doesn't stop when it starts getting intense."

Trash bins, yet to be attended to by the janitor, overflowed with discarded scraps of wire paper now deemed dated and obsolete. Scattered on desks, for fortification, were cans of Tab and Coke and Styrofoam cups, some reincarnated from coffee receptacles into ashtrays; and everywhere, cigarettes aflame, even in places where a No Smoking sign admonished against their use, wafting the pungent slow burn of nicotine into air already thick with deadline pressure. Only a cocktail party, bar, or racetrack might have been as polluted with as much smoke. And along with the caffeine, nicotine, and adrenaline was as was true in so many newsrooms, an undercurrent of sex. "You didn't need office parties in those days. They had edit booths with no windows on the doors," said Edwards. It could be hard to keep up with the affairs. "You had to remember who was seeing whom."

The sturdy hands of a large white Favag clock, a timekeeping system synced to the Naval Observatory's Master Clock and so reliable that Europe's trains depended on it to keep to their schedules, lorded over the room, ominously counting down the minutes to showtime.* The Casio watches on the wrists of many a staffer were a nifty digital invention, but not precise enough for network broadcasting. Nineteen minutes to go and not a second to spare. In the control room, a director cued up the perky twang of the theme song from the TV show *The Beverly Hillbillies*, leavened in tone by the plaintive sophistication of the theme for a different program, *Hill Street Blues*—irreverent and catchy musical "buttons" having been a signature flourish since back when Bill Siemering programmed flute sonatas and folk songs to bridge

---

* The Favag came in handy during World War II, before international telephone hookup was possible, allowing Edward R. Murrow in New York and William Shirer in Berlin to seem as if they were conducting a conversation with each other in real time when they were actually just speaking precisely timed comments.

between stories. (They helped, in a panic, to fill the empty airtime.) Newscaster Carl Kassell, the oldest person on the shift and the only person at this hour wearing a tie, strained to hear the sound of the *CBS World News Roundup*, obligatory morning listening for any journalist. A staffer jammed pieces of pastry into his mouth; another, his porridge, both working and chatting all the while. No time to pause for breakfast.

On this particular day, the unfolding action was captured by visitors wielding video cameras. They did their best to stay out of the fray—a challenge, given the clunkiness of their tripods and gear. They were there on behalf of a four-year-old television channel, the Cable-Satellite Public Affairs Network, better known by its acronym, C-SPAN—the brainchild of an inspired onetime congressional staffer and telecommunications reporter named Brian Lamb. As concerned as the lawmakers had been about the mediated filter of network news and how they altered the public's perception wherever they trained their lens, Lamb had fought to provide viewers a live, unedited stream from the halls of Congress.

Since 1979, a year after Linda's Panama Canal debate broadcasts, and thanks to funding from the burgeoning cable industry (eagerly seeking municipal approval to wire the nation's cities for their utility) and the long-debated approval of the House of Representatives, Americans could now, from the comfort of their couches, occupy a ringside seat to the inner workings of democracy. (It would take the Senate several more years before its members voted to allow in cameras.) Though it aired around the clock, C-SPAN, with its pure-play public service mission, was far different from the new all-news channel that had debuted a year after it: cheeky playboy Ted Turner's all-news service Cable News Network, which, by offering news at all hours, was upending the news cycle and roiling the establishment.

When lawmakers weren't active, special programs and chat shows filled the C-SPAN airtime in the service of illuminating other essential elements of democracy, such as the inner workings of the almighty fourth estate, which grew in importance as the media landscape expanded. By turning the lens on a news operation, C-SPAN's producers could provide viewers with an unvarnished look at how, as journalists liked to joke about their product, the "sausage" got made—though the "sausage" made by NPR was consumed by an audience a fraction of the size of that of the television networks (about three million a week) and "tasted" entirely different from the more conventional fare.

The C-SPAN footage being recorded today would not mark the first time NPR appeared on television. Thanks to an arrangement Frank had made with PBS, the network had done a turn on the tube earlier in the year, with a special called *All Things Considered . . . on Main Street.*

The mere announcement of the TV show angered the NPR board of directors—for one thing, because they'd learned about it in the newspapers and not directly from Frank himself; and for another, because they feared that its production would impact the core product on which member stations relied. The audience already erroneously confused and conflated public radio and public television as one and the same—wasn't all public broadcasting fed from the same bank account? The two were cousins, sure, but their operations and their finances were completely independent of one another—just as the stations around the country that carried NPR's programs were completely separate financial entities from one another and from the network.

Surely, said board member Bill Kling in a memo, this venture would further add to the confusion. "Television tends to wear out formats and personalities," he wrote, citing the pangs of regret that radio's early stars expressed when they leapt to television. The visual element changed the very nature of a show. "What is radio's gain in exchange for the inevitable 'cost' of a television version?" was the question he said he hoped Frank would answer. "What are the risks?" Besides, Kling added, while being on the tube might be good for NPR, what benefit could it possibly have for the member stations? Pissing them off was ill-advised. They needed each other. Without them, who would air their programs?*

---

* Of course, in the age of podcasting and streaming, the equation is different. But in 1983, there was no other way to receive the programming.

Production proceeded nonetheless, and in January 1982, *All Things Considered . . . on Main Street* debuted, with a cheerful animated open that offered fans a visual of their beloved Susan, alongside her latest cohost, Sanford Ungar, an accomplished print journalist who'd been hired after Bob Edwards decided to stay put on *Morning Edition.* Just as it did on the radio, the TV version featured a wide range of subjects: a report on discrimination against refugees, a profile of young politicians, a feature on Cajun music, and another on the social impact of the shopping mall.

For at least one reviewer, though, the crossover fell flat. "There is supposed to be an element of irreverence in the humor, but for the most part this serving of *All Things Considered* is about as naughty as a liberal bishop," wrote *New York Times* TV critic John J. O'Connor, who wondered where the money was going to come from to continue this experiment. He had other questions: "Where are the personnel going to be recruited? Would the radio version be dumped? Have the last ten years of success been only a prelude to 'making it' in the big pond of television?" NPR, he hoped, would proceed with caution.

TV critic David Bianculli echoed these concerns: "A lone tape recorder placed quietly on a teacher's desk can give a more accurate representation of grade-school activities than all the disruptive cameras of *60 Minutes.*"

For her part, Susan told a reporter from the *Washington Post* that she found TV "extremely cumbersome." Talking into a microphone was one sort of artificial, but speaking to a camera, quite another. It felt fake and phony and struck her as absurd. Some people might have had a wonderful flair for it—say, NBC's Jane Pauley and Bryant Gumbel of the smiling fluff the *Today* show—and maybe, with practice, one could develop the skill. But she didn't want to.

Others shared her disenchantment. A fan wrote with a piercing, one-line pan in the aftermath of the special, advising Susan to "Stick to the Marconi."

* * *

Still, the lure of TV was hard to resist. When the kindly, cardigan-wearing children's TV darling Fred Rogers asked Susan to join him on a special series, she agreed, then waffled. By speaking to her in the guise of one of his characters, Daniel Striped Tiger, Rogers persuaded her past the fear. ("I know you're frightened," Daniel said, promising that she'd get whatever help she needed to succeed on the program. The persuasion worked. "By the end of the conversation, I was practically sucking my thumb," Susan confessed.)

The dynamic congressional duo of Cokie and Linda themselves leapt at a plum part-time gig: the chance to cohost a weekly PBS show called *The Lawmakers* alongside veteran DC-watcher Paul Duke, host of the well-regarded *Washington Week in Review*. An alumnus of commercial television, Duke had deep concerns about the impact of round-the-clock news on broadcasting, which, in his estimation, had devolved into "brief and snappy" reporting devoid of substance—and thus, a disservice to the people. While the networks invested in resources to cover the White House—a tedious, spoon-fed beat Cokie personally considered her idea of "hell on earth"—they all but ignored the 535 men (and handful of women) entrusted with crafting the nation's crucial legislation. On the contrary: Congress was more than "just another Hill story," he said, but rather, the "heartbeat" of the city.

Who better to help Duke convey this than these two younger, attractive, fiercely knowledgeable women? Duke, an older white man, embodied the old school; Cokie and Linda exemplified the new. In the past, they'd offered analysis from time to time on PBS's news coverage with Bill Moyers, but this time their names would be plastered on the credits as costars.

The *Chicago Tribune*'s Marilynn Preston commended the "glib and gifted" women who, she said, "know how to handle the straight, standup reporting that we're used to seeing on TV, but more important, they know how to handle the nuance, the context, the behind-the-scenes subtleties we're *not* used to seeing on TV." In contrast to the superficial headlines served up by commercial television, Preston continued in her praise, Cokie and Linda "don't just give reports. They tell stories."

Linda and Cokie had been discovering the power of their microphones superseded the sexism. The letters after their names, NPR or PBS, and the promise they offered, of airtime, were more important than their sex. If "you were polka-dotted with three heads . . ." Cokie observed, "they'd say, 'Sit down, have a cup of coffee, or would you like three?' They didn't care about your sex or anything else, really." She loved to tell the joke "What has two legs and is attracted to light? Any elected official."

Attention-seeking politicos such as Congressman James Scheuer of New York shared the secret to a successful television appearance: Being seen on camera was as important as, or more important than, what you said. "All you have to do is express yourself intelligently, show a sense of humor, and be well-behaved," he said. "Five minutes later they wouldn't know what you were talking about, but they know you were there."

Though there might be pointers, or even a formula, for making the most of an occasional television appearance, it was impossible to manufacture the ineffable presence necessary to stand out amid an endless parade of talking heads. And from the get-go, it was clear that Cokie possessed that particular star quality. She lopped off some of her straight "gym teacher" hair and, adorned in her proper DC businesswoman attire, embraced the game. With her no-nonsense beauty and a voice tinged with just the perfect hint of a southern lilt layered with just enough gritty edge—better than a classic broadcaster's voice; distinctive—the cameras brought her vividly alive in another dimension. It was as if television had been waiting for her to sail onto the screen.

* * *

But spotlighting the reporters in the field, those staffers who got the glory and the voice, wasn't the object of the C-SPAN crews documenting the action at NPR on this late fall day. Allowing viewers to peer behind the scenes at headquarters was. And, as the cameras rolled, NPR staff faced a dilemma that had hounded anyone who'd ever worked in daily news. It was, simply put, a dud of a news day. "How is it we've got a sports story in A?" some cynic hanging around the control room asked, referring to the lead story, which was about a resolution, arrived at late the night before, in the seven-week-long NFL players' strike.

On the other side of the glass separating the control room from the host, Bob Edwards chimed in over the microphone in the voice a newspaper reporter once described as "mellow-roast." Despite the punishing schedule of the graveyard shift—into the office by 2:00 A.M., asleep by 7:00 P.M.—Edwards had fallen in love with his role as star of this show, and millions of listeners had become accustomed to waking up to him each day. Ever since his cohost left after just a few months, he'd been a solo pilot.

"You try to find a story out there today," he said. "That's good."

"What about that large truck delivering a length of greased rope to Lech Walesa's home?" quipped the cynic, in retort, about the Polish leader.

Even when it didn't cross into breaking news, the topic of sports had been creeping its way into the newscasts—to Frank's delight. In his retirement, the fabled baseball announcer Red Barber had been enlisted as a commentator.

Frank knew plenty of smart listeners were just like him, rabid about their cherished teams. (His was the St. Louis Cardinals; when he was growing up in California, Missouri was as far west as professional baseball reached.) From the campaign trail to the newsroom, he routinely deployed quippy baseball-speak in his conversation. Rumors had even been circulating around Washington that he was in the running to replace baseball commissioner Bowie Kuhn.

The clock's second hand showed one minute to six. The woman directing the program, Cindy Carpien, spoke the language of radio, her words a baton: "Stand by with one. Ready. Hit it." The theme music rolled, and as Carpien went about her behind-the-scenes business, Edwards spoke into the microphone, cigarette in hand, alerting America that another day had begun.

"Good morning. Leaders of the Soviet Union and China say they're seeking a normalization of relations . . . [T]he foreign ministers of both countries held long talks in Moscow. This is Wednesday, November seventeenth, and this is NPR's *Morning Edition.*"

* * *

With the show under way, the C-SPAN cameras now relocated to a tiny conference room to record the morning news meeting. Here the staff would plan for tomorrow. At the end of the table sat producer Jay Kernis, casually shuffling through the day's papers, waiting for his colleagues to arrive. His star had continued to rise after he'd stepped in to help rescue *Morning Edition* days before the program's debut.

It was this same sort of happy, transformative accident that had drawn Kernis into the medium in the first place. An article about his prodigal skills as editor of his high school newspaper in Bergenfield, New Jersey, had caught the attention of the general manager of an educational radio station licensed to the Riverside Church in New York City. The man had called up the ambitious kid and enticed him to come to work for $1.75 an hour. This required a two-bus schlep into the city, but the commute proved a worthy haul. It was one of those jobs where Kernis did a little bit of everything: winding up the tapes of finished programs, duplicating them to ship to other member stations in the Educational Radio Network, writing copy, sorting the mail. And every last task conspired to make him fall further in love with the medium.

Early on, Kernis had recognized that his future wasn't in front of the microphone. His voice wasn't suited for that. What he loved most was writing, the piecing together of information into a compelling script. It was only logical, when he graduated from the University of Maryland in 1974, that he'd migrate to DC to work in educational radio's next incarnation. In his capacity as NPR's first audio promotions guy, he would sit in on meetings for the network's arts programs as well as the news, which gave him a 360-degree education into every aspect of the place and its people.

Still not yet thirty, Kernis had now been working in noncommercial broadcasting for practically half his life. And as his staff filed into the room to plot the next day's show, it was obvious to the C-SPAN cameras that Jay was not alone in his youth. Not only was this crew young, but about half happened to be women, as had been the case since the network's start.

Each of their backgrounds was unique. Some had completed just a few years of college, some had attended journalism school, others had earned degrees in unrelated fields like Greek or literature or chemical engineering—offering a wide swath of knowledge they could draw on, just as Bill Siemering had hoped in the beginning. (Though his wish for adequate minority representation had been dreadfully unfulfilled.) Everyone present here, regardless of their background or official title, was expected to lay out their ideas for the program. As was the case in most broadcast shops, those ideas most typically were sparked by stories culled from newspapers and magazines and the wires. Around this table, once they zeroed in on a list of stories, they'd riff on ways to NPR-ify what they'd learned. Cigarette smoke billowed up from a variety of hands all the while.

"Are we doing Reagan in Miami?"

"Tomorrow the Postal Service issues a twenty-cent stamp featuring Stravinsky. Wait. Is it a two-cent stamp?"

"Tomorrow is the Great American Smokeout. Smokers are encouraged to give up smoking. And as America found out this morning, this staff smokes like crazy. Do they have this every year? We need to ask the question, 'Do these work?'"

"We could make a Bob Edwards segment out of this by pairing with Bobbie Ann Mason, the Kentucky writer who writes about people, who—people who watch TV and go to K-marts . . ."

"Real people . . ."

". . . real people who want to get out of Kentucky and who don't want to get out of Kentucky."

"We have been given a taped piece on Zimbabwe from Joe Frederick, on growing tensions there."

"Do we use the taped piece and put copy about Bush on top of it, or do we take the phoner that may or may not be planned? The taped piece isn't that long."

"The Parliament of Spain is officially doing something . . ."

"Opening."

"Great. Use Sandy Close's commentary on the Pope."

"Why?"

"Because there's a brief mention of his visit to Spain."

"We need to do something on the military budget. What kind of person, Congress, Defense—should we go for a Defense analyst? It would be good to get somebody who's a Republican."

"I want to hear from most anyone on Armed Services, either side."

Such was the confident chatter of those whose job it was to be in the know, to stay up on the movements and actions of world leaders, to be savvy to the hot spots and danger zones and upcoming votes and reports, as well as to the latest cultural trends and how to blend them together for a program balanced with substance and quirk.

And yet, as skilled and plugged in to the zeitgeist as these broadcast journalists might be, as aware as they were of the news unfolding in the wider world around them, they were completely unaware that, right beneath their eyes, a crack had emerged to threaten NPR's very existence.

* * *

Of course, their eyes had been wide open to the steady stream of cash pouring into the network since Frank waltzed in the door five years earlier. You didn't have to be a wizard of finance, much less have access to the books, to wonder what the heck was going on. Where was the money coming from?

Hiring independent producers from around the world for special projects, or commissioning field reports from freelancers in far-flung points where staffers couldn't reach, was rarely an issue or concern. Bills for those company-issued American Express cards handed to a quarter of the staff got magically sent to the back office—there was no policy against using them for personal expenses.

"Computers were rolling in here," observed one employee who'd been around long enough to remember the very first days, back before the first furniture arrived, when the idea of a desktop computer was but a figment of the imagination. Now a word processor sat perched on every secretary's desk, pricey Apple computers arrived in executive's homes (though they weren't quite sure what to do with them). "People were buying stuff like it was Going-Out-of-Business Day at Filene's." At the start of 1983, the NPR board even approved an outlay of ten thousand dollars to replace Frank's three-year-old company car.

The future they'd all been working toward gleamed bright with the promise of Oz—a vibrant, public radio fantasyland thrumming with excitement, achievement, and possibility. The profligate spending wasn't their concern; producing great radio was, and doing that, under the circumstances, was certainly more pleasant, particularly for those who'd been around a while. The budget had tripled; a hundred new staff members had joined in the last months. Notoriously short on reporters, now ones had been stationed in bureaus in Miami, Houston, Los Angeles, Salt Lake City, San Francisco, New York, and Chicago—and even at their first international outpost, London. Merit raises of at least 6 percent had been promised to 250 staff members.

Beyond *Morning Edition* and *All Things Considered*, the network offered its member stations more than a hundred hours of programs, from classical to jazz to opera, and special services for the handicapped. The *Star Wars* saga would continue that spring with a version of the blockbuster movie sequel *The Empire Strikes Back*, set to air in March 1983. An expanding array of regular listeners and luminaries alike dispatched their applause. Industry awards filled shelves and wall space.

Off the air, Frank's "Project Independence"—his goal of freeing NPR "from the government fix by '86"—continued apace. Stations willing to pay five grand a year could subscribe to a new music and information service called NPR Plus. (They got the main news programs for free.) Corporations were beginning to pony up cash in exchange for on-air "funding credits," polite public media–speak for "commercials." A new fund-raiser had been hired, charged with shaking money out of foundation trees.

Customers such as Muzak and the Mutual Radio Network rented unused space on the NPR satellite system. Telecom player Mobile Communications Corporation of America even cut the network in on the potential profits from its nationwide paging service, which Frank boasted could bring in millions in revenue. And speaking of that satellite, cutting the cord to the phone company and the U.S. Postal Service had eliminated the need for tape duplication and mailing costs that had already yielded annual savings of six hundred thousand dollars.

To keep track of it all, a chief financial officer noted for deploying a computer accounting system at his last job had been brought in to install a similar system at NPR. Just around the time the C-SPAN cameras rolled, that executive had dispatched a memo to Frank, warning of a budget shortfall of half a million dollars. Frank, ever the dreamer, was so sure the bets he'd made were soon to leave the coffers flush with cash that he figured this couldn't possibly be a problem.

* * *

By the time the ten hours of C-SPAN's *Day in the Life of NPR* footage aired on January 11, 1983,* that half-a-million-dollar figure had somehow tripled. But no one who witnessed the cinema verité glimpse inside the network, much less most of the NPR employees, had any inkling of these financial straits, yet.

Cokie, who had been invited to the C-SPAN set to kick off the special programming day, was seated next to the cable network's founder and host, Brian Lamb. He asked for her wisdom on the day's front

---

* The verité footage can be seen at https://www.c-span.org/video/?88365-1/day-national -public-radio. However, several hours are missing, including an hour-long interview featuring Frank Mankiewicz that aired that evening.

pages. " 'Reagan, Annoyed by News Leaks, Tells Staff to Limit Press Relations,' " he read from the headlines, holding up the morning's *New York Times*. What's that about? Pithy, knowing Cokie, answered non- chalantly: "You could fill in any president's name for 'Reagan.' " All presidents hated the press, she said.

Later in the day, Barbara Cohen, newly promoted to vice president, appeared on the air alongside host Bruce Collins to talk about daily operations. Was the footage they were seeing a typical day? he won- dered. Yes, she said proudly, but even since November, new programs had been added: afternoon and evening newscasts and a 4:30 P.M. daily show that zeroed in on a single topic. The channel's engaged audience dialed in with everything from praise to derision about lib- eral bias, curiosity about funding, and observations (by one woman) about how many women NPR employed and both delight and distress over the youthfulness of the staff. "When we don't know the answer," the ever-politic Cohen, all of thirty-seven herself, answered, "[W]e will go to a person who is over forty, over fifty, over sixty, to give us that perspective."

Back to the verité footage, which followed first to the futures meet- ing, where longer-ranged stories were hatched and assigned; and then on to the afternoon news meeting, where Susan would mention, given the impending Thanksgiving holiday, that it was time again to trot out her recipe for Mama Stamberg's cranberry sauce. (Frank, never at a loss for a pithy one-liner, had offered up a competing one: open can, *thump* contents onto plate, and serve.)

* * *

By February, the brewing hurricane had intensified to a category four when the network's CFO delivered more disturbing news: The $500,000 shortfall that had tripled to $1.5 million had now, it seemed, doubled, to $3 million. In March, the financial woes crept into the open when fifty-five employees, many of them recent hires, were informed that their jobs would be slashed. The panicked fear that grips a work-place when cutbacks occur spread through the halls like wildfire.

Who would be next? What was going on?

Despite the conflagration, Frank wasn't running for cover. "There is no deficit," he insisted to *Broadcasting* magazine about his $26 million annual budget. Blame the troubles on accounting. By the end of the fiscal year, he said confidently, we'll have a surplus, as always. Perhaps they might raise ample cash by imposing a fee on the member stations, who got the news for free.

Not so fast. Confronted at the annual Public Radio Conference in Minneapolis with the reality that the mothership's finances were in chaos, the leaders of member stations expressed shock and shrieked at the idea that it might fall to them to finance the bailout.

The union that represented NPR employees, the American Federation of Television and Radio Artists, dispatched "Sister Cokie" to serve as the "eyes, ears, voice and worried frown" of employees. "Cokes" reported back to her union brethren the latest revelations to the member stations: The $3 million deficit, it seemed, had suddenly ballooned to $6 million.* Chilling mentions of a "death spiral" and "bankruptcy" were bandied about. Bills had not been paid, including a quarter of a million dollars in back rent and a $20,000 phone bill. In order to make sure there was enough cash to make payroll, the CFO hadn't paid Social Security and unemployment withholdings for months, to the tune of $652,172. Not even the folksy, feel-good lunchtime entertainment at the conference, provided by beloved commentator Red Barber, could offset the pall that descended on the radio gathering.

What was clear was this: Making the next month's payroll would be impossible unless the Corporation for Public Broadcasting came to the rescue with an emergency loan. The necessary bankruptcy forms were drawn up to keep the creditors at bay. If NPR couldn't borrow more cash, the entire operation would have to be liquidated.

The radio Shangri-la, it seemed, had devolved into a horror show.

---

* About $15 million in 2020 terms.

* * *

What on earth had happened?

"Their eyes were so completely tilted toward the heavens," said the station manager of KUSC, "that they totally forgot about the details of the daily operations."

But hadn't anyone been watching? Apparently not. Every single one of them had been living in an "unreal world," a dreamlike state in which money was someone else's concern. No one had been paying attention to the tedious but crucial matter of balancing the books—even the people whose job it was to mind them. Even the members of the board of NPR had trusted that the system was moving along smoothly when, in fact, the finances had been kept like a kid's lemonade stand.

How to right this rapidly sinking *Titanic?* One action was clear: Frank, heralded only recently by the NPR board as a genius and a savior, would have to go, now. If any entity were ever to invest in the network going forward, if the stations were ever to trust NPR again, new leadership would need to be installed—and fast.

At a departure gate in the Minneapolis airport, an NPR original who now worked in public television ran into Frank, waiting to catch a flight back to Washington. Frank shrugged with resignation. "I've just been fired."*

* * *

Still, the man credited with putting NPR on the map didn't go quickly, or silently. He had to be practically pushed out of the office. The line was he'd stay on as a "consultant." Before announcing the news that Frank was no longer in charge of the day-to-day, Susan had been asked to tone down the angry farewell she'd prepared. Furious at the predicament

---

* For an excellent and detailed blow-by-blow of NPR's financial rescue, see *Listener Supported,* by NPR's first employee, Jack Mitchell.

in which he'd left her beloved workplace, she had wanted to announce to the audience, "We had a radio broadcast before Frank Mankiewicz came, and we'll have one after he leaves"—even though no one knew for certain if this was true.

Instead, she acknowledged that this was NPR's "brightest and darkest time" and listed the good Mankiewicz had accomplished: "Before he came, NPR was the best-kept secret in broadcasting. Frank let the secret out, with relish and style. . . . He gave us new pride in our work."

Politesse aside, now it was time to wade through the muck. A new, temporary regime stepped up to navigate NPR out of woe, led by a man who'd worked in public broadcasting for so long that he remembered its roots in plain Jane "educational media," before the shining promise of the Public Broadcasting Act.

Ronald Bornstein's love of radio stretched back to his youth in Michigan, where he'd switched majors from pharmacy to pursue his less practical passion, broadcasting, talking his way into a job at the University of Michigan's station. In his current position as the general manager of WHA in Wisconsin, the oldest and one of the most respected public media outfits in the nation, he was revered for his practical innovations and sense of mission.

When Ed Elson first discovered Frank, Bornstein had been chair of the NPR board and enthusiastically pushed to enlist Mankiewicz's swagger. Now this stoic, trustworthy midwestern Yoda had been enlisted to clean up the mess caused by his P. T. Barnum. To him, the journalism produced by NPR was worth giving up six months of his life to save. Plus, he said, he was a sucker for a challenge. "My job is not to affix blame," Bornstein said. "My job is to cure the problem, and that I will."

* * *

From the second Bornstein arrived, though, as he and the clean-up team he assembled confronted the disarray, he could see how overwhelming the task before him would be. "Anywhere you turned, there was trouble," he said. "Anywhere you turned, there was no answer."

Among the people he turned to for help was none other than Jack Mitchell, the same man who'd had the stroke of genius to elevate Susan as host. Mitchell had left NPR years earlier to work with Bornstein in public broadcasting in Wisconsin. To the first official producer of *All Things Considered* now fell the unenviable task of eliminating both programs and personnel—eighty-four more positions, in fact. "No amount of cutting," he observed, "could bring the budget into balance."

The landlord informed interim chief Bornstein that, for nonpayment of rent, he planned on evicting NPR. "I don't think so," Bornstein responded, calm, stern, menacing. "I don't think you want radio listeners to know [you] have thrown NPR out in the street. You can't do that." And he didn't.

Other bills, it seemed, had been filed incorrectly, invoices hadn't been sent, and stacks of checks—six thousand of them, totaling $320,000—were found lying around the office. The for-profit broadcasting service Frank had created to raise money turned out to be *costing* a million dollars a year. And that fund-raiser he'd hired? Not only had she not been informed of her goal, but she hadn't raised even half of it. Nina, upon learning this, screamed that she could have done a better job raising money herself.

As if sifting through the financial rubble weren't job enough, Bornstein faced the thorny task of convincing the Corporation for Public Broadcasting to bail out the radio service, while simultaneously managing the stress of member stations, all in shock and panicked about what they'd do if NPR did indeed disappear. After all, the service's programming filled at least a quarter of their airtime. And though many of them balked at the suggestion that they guarantee loans or pony up a lifesaving donation dug out of their own coffers, eventually Bornstein managed to extract promises of about $1.6 million from them.

Next, there was the babysitting necessary to manage NPR's board, which had been blindsided by the crisis and the ensuing blame for its lack of oversight. After heated words and maneuvering, some of the members simply quit.

And as if all of *this* weren't enough, Bornstein needed to grapple with the press, which was obsessively chronicling NPR's downfall—which, in turn, stoked the criticism of the existing foes of public broadcasting, who already despised that the government funded what they decried as impartial liberal media.

Day after day, plaintive headlines bleated out the troubles across the nation: "National Public Radio's Saddest Story Is Its Own," said the *New York Times,* followed a few weeks later with "What Went Wrong at National Public Radio?" From industry trade magazine *Broadcasting*: "NPR's Bad News Gets Worse." And the *Washington Post*: "Camelot in Crisis: The Dream Failed."

Newspaper editorial writers extolled the importance of saving the network, and an editorial cartoon in the *Cincinnati Inquirer* by Jim Boardman depicted *All Things Considered* cohost Noah Adams huffing and puffing it out on a treadmill connected to a generator, which in turn powered Susan's microphone. The caption for this Rube Goldberg apparatus: "NPR Financial Crisis."

Even NPR covered its own calamity. Shortly before Barbara Cohen bolted to a new job in television—pointing out that the elimination of her management salary would save two staff positions—she imported Scott Simon of the Chicago bureau. He'd recently returned from the front lines in El Salvador, and now he'd stand on the front lines of disaster in DC to produce a series on the NPR financial crisis. Working at NPR had been Simon's dream since, as a young television reporter, he first heard *All Things Considered.* He'd written to the network and talked his way into filing freelance reports, which eventually led to a staff job. Now here he was, outing his beloved family's dirty laundry. It felt odd, but he plunged in, even interviewing the ex-boss for his reports.

Frank tried to pin the woes on having underestimated the impact of the recession. Simon didn't buy it. "See, to some people, the question arises," he challenged, "how could someone who not only listens to the two daily news programs that National Public Radio does, but also . . . has a hand in them, be surprised by that?"

The situation was so bad, Scott explained to Bob Edwards on *Morning Edition*, that there wasn't any paper to be found in the newsroom.

NPR was so behind in its bills, the supplier had refused to deliver even the basics. Hearing this entreaty, the secretaries across the street at CBS sent over a ream. And on Capitol Hill that day, administrative staff who'd heard the report brought Cokie paper and other office supplies to spirit back to headquarters.

* * *

Of the many onerous tasks Bornstein faced, the worst of all was dealing with the bewildered, devastated staff, and their anxiety over this sudden implosion. Many took the financial transgressions personally. Some employees who'd survived the cutbacks stepped forward and volunteered to take a 10 percent pay cut, while others vowed to quit if their paychecks didn't materialize.

Farewell parties for pink-slipped employees punctuated the NPR staff's usual daily march toward deadline. Newsroom cynicism competed with the terror: Employees pooled their bets on just how gaping the financial hole would, in the end, turn out to be. There wasn't much in the way of a prize for the poor winner, who'd lost his job, so he took home a collage of photocopied business cards.

Irreverent NPR staffers released some steam with a parody they recorded early one morning, set to the tune of the title song from the Broadway hit *Camelot*, riffing on both Frank's Kennedy connections and his starry promises that were in danger of dooming NPR to a tragic end.

> *A budget made about a year ago here.*
> *Said we could go ahead and spend a lot.*
> *See there was just no limit to cash flow here.*
> *In Camelot.*
> *Spend-a-lot.**

---

* To hear this, visit https://soundcloud.com/marty-79/npr-xmas-tape-1983.

Bill Drummond, the same man who'd referred to the powerful cluster of women as the "Fallopian Jungle," started bandying about another pithy phrase, railing against management for taking his hardworking colleagues to the "guard rail of bankruptcy." Producer Jay Kernis wore a T-shirt emblazoned with the words that summed up the daily undercurrent of conversation: "Gossip. Rumor. Innuendo."

Their beloved leader had failed them. "I look out at [Frank] and think, 'Why did you let this happen to me?'" Kernis said to a reporter. To which Frank responded dismissively, "Jay is a dramatic fellow. He tends to personalize matters. He will, I assume, grow up some day."

Easy for him to say. Frank was still pulling in a handsome paycheck. As the clean-up crew scrambled to fix his mess, the deposed president simply refused to ride off into the sunset. He just kept yapping to reporters, often defensively: "My responsibility was not to spend all day checking financial reports. I had no reason to believe the shortfall existed. It is outrageous to suggest that I knew it and didn't do anything about it." To *Newsweek*: "It may be that I should have known all this, but I sure as hell didn't."

On ABC's *Nightline with Ted Koppel*, he had the temerity to announce, "It is not that bad, Ted. There are steps that can be taken." Other organizations had faced financial woes far worse than the nine-million-dollar deficit that was the latest NPR tally. He continued: "Warner Communications had a twenty-million-dollar loss in their first quarter, for instance. Atari thought it would make a profit and it had lost forty-five million. Now that's a miscalculation, isn't it? The USA is going to have a two-hundred-fifty-billion deficit this year, and *their* president is not going to resign."

To still others, he mulled that perhaps he might run for president, or write a novel. Then he pulled off a lucrative, if not theatrical, escape plan: He landed an executive job at Gray and Company, the DC public relations and lobbying firm.

* * *

While Frank kept yakking, Bornstein achieved the unimaginable: He finessed a half-million-dollar loan from a sympathetic local bank, and a million-dollar line of credit. *Phew!* Now he could make June's payroll.

The public radio Yoda also bravely took the heat, appearing before an angry panel of lawmakers at a House subcommittee hearing with a forensic auditor from Coopers and Lybrand whom he'd hired to help wade through NPR's financial minefield. They presented their findings, which corroborated Frank's assertion that the troubles at NPR were not due to "willful malfeasance," but rather, plain old-fashioned "grave systemic weaknesses," "bad judgement," and "mismanagement."

Two sets of books had been kept, he told the subcommittee, and both of them had been fiction. The computer system that was to have been installed to keep track of finances? It had never arrived. Later, it was revealed that the chief financial officer had been on medical leave for months. Closer investigation showed the deficit had climbed to nearly ten million dollars. Meanwhile, creditors kept pounding on the door.

"You said the next two weeks are critical. Exactly what has to happen?" asked Rep. Dave Obey, one Wisconsin man to another. Bornstein responded without drama. "We have to have an infusion of six million dollars, sir, within the next two weeks. And prior to the end of September, we have to have an availability of funds of three million." Without that immediate burst of cash, he continued, NPR would cease to exist.

* * *

As they steeled themselves for the end, everyone who remained employed by NPR leapt into action. Cokie and Linda scrambled around the House, rallying 110 representatives, led by New York congressman Thomas Downey, to sign a petition "expressing a strong commitment to NPR." Never mind that reporters were forbidden from lobbying. On top of their efforts, thirty-one employees signed another petition demanding that NPR executives avoid additional cuts to the news staff by raising more money—as if conjuring up money were a snap. "The damage to NPR's news and information programs would be enormous and irreparable if funding, staff and air time were to be reduced to the levels currently under discussion," the letter read.

What part of "NPR is nearly bankrupt" didn't they understand? Collecting signatures might be cathartic, but signatures, even ones belonging to important people, weren't going to keep NPR alive. The only thing that would was a very large infusion of cash.

Mysteriously, pricey full-page ads suddenly appeared in the *New York Times* and *Washington Post*, courtesy of a group called "Friends of NPR" and signed by a who's who of luminaries from modern broadcasting: CBS's Walter Cronkite; ABC's Barbara Walters and Ted Koppel; NBC's Tom Brokaw, Judy Woodruff, and John Chancellor; and PBS's Paul Duke, Bill Moyers, and Jim Lehrer. Rounding out the list: Linda's husband, Fred Wertheimer, of Common Cause; Hollywood director Carl Reiner; and writer George Will, who appealed to listeners to "act now."

Despondent over the possibility of losing her beloved network and her career, Susan, brimming with ideas that might now save it, had been zipping off memos as fast as she could, while simultaneously writing entreaties to management on behalf of treasured colleagues: Please preserve their jobs. (She also hedged her bets, taping pilots for a pop culture show produced by *New York* magazine editor Clay Felker.)*

Now, in the aftermath of Frank's departure, no idea was too small or too far out to save the network she'd helped build. Why not call the networks, newspapers, and magazines and ask them to pony up "sizeable checks in the form of loans or gifts"? CBS and the *Washington Post* would gladly contribute a million bucks each to save NPR, she insisted, wouldn't they? When a concerned listener wrote in with the suggestion that maybe the Hollywood superstar George Lucas might donate a day's worth of profits from *The Empire Strikes Back*, Susan vowed to track down the director and make the ask.

And while the temporary board hunted for a new, full-time leader,

* Called *Back of the Book*, it aired on PBS in 1985.

she offered another suggestion. Why not coerce Walter Cronkite to step in as president? Surely, installing the most trusted man in America at the helm would instantly bolster NPR's credibility and restore its tarnished reputation. He wouldn't even have to set foot in the place; just having his name attached would be a boon. Yes, she acknowledged, it's a wild idea. She offered to make the call herself.

And if Cronkite didn't bite, maybe they could ask another trusted pinnacle of impartiality, Brian Lamb of C-SPAN. On June 7, she appeared on the channel beside him. "Are you surviving the bad publicity and the difficult times?" Lamb began the show. "It's not bad publicity, it's bad *news*," Susan responded. "Whether we're going to be able to survive these bad times is something I sit about and think about like this," she said, crossing her fingers. Then she proceeded to turn the next hour into her own sort of pledge drive, as only she, its passionate founding mother, could.

"May I do an absolutely shameless thing," she asked, though it was clear she was going to do it even if the answer was no. "I happened to have brought along our address." She raised up a carboard sign on which she'd scrawled in Magic Marker, like a ransom note:

NPR
WASHINGTON, DC 20036.

After a lifetime in public broadcasting, here she was doing a commercial. "If listeners would just send in money as a vote of support for the kind of work we're doing . . ." she implored. "They say we have something like seven million listeners. My math isn't good enough to add up quickly what ten dollars apiece from each of those listeners would be, but it would clear up our debt."

Callers offered their own solutions: Why not pull the plug on NPR and just carry Canadian Broadcasting? (Um, because the CBC is Canadian, and NPR is American, was Susan's flummoxed reply.) Another caller, from Cleveland, denounced the five to ten minutes an hour on NPR's news shows "given over to fluff," meaning the quirky features that had become the network's hallmark. Still, he said he'd be good for one hundred dollars a year if it kept the network on the air. Another sniffed at how unbecoming it was for a news anchor to beg for funds. Wasn't there a better system?

"I'd like to say how much I enjoy *Morning Edition* and *All Things Considered*," said a man who hailed from San Francisco. "I'm not quite sure it's worth one hundred dollars to me, but I'd give fifty."

"We'll take it," Susan said.

But they couldn't, technically. NPR wasn't set up to receive donations directly from individual supporters. The only way a fund-raising appeal to listeners would work would be if donations got funneled through the member stations. Surely the stations, whose fates were indelibly entwined with that of the network, would help out.

A fund-raising drive was scheduled for three weeks out, August 2–4. They'd call it the "Drive to Survive."

* * *

By that time, though, NPR might very well be history. If a bailout agreement with the Corporation for Public Broadcasting weren't negotiated by July 28, the doors would be padlocked, the phones turned off, and paychecks would bounce to the high heavens. There was, it seemed, only twenty thousand dollars in the bank.

Negotiations had been stuck for months. One of the key issues: CPB was insisting on overseeing every single NPR expenditure until the loan was repaid. Bornstein balked at what in essence would mean handing over editorial control. Another sticking point: CPB wanted to seize NPR's most valuable, tangible asset, its satellite system. Bornstein knew better than to budge on that, for whoever had the keys to distribution maintained critical control over the public radio universe.

A resolution seemed impossible. Staff were instructed to take their personal gear home, while company-owned equipment was being tallied up for liquidation purposes. The end had arrived.

At three thirty in the morning on July 28, after a twelve-hour marathon session, acting president Bornstein and representatives of the CPB finally, miraculously, came to terms—with some particular goading by House telecommunications subcommittee member Colorado representative Tim Wirth. Until the loan was repaid, the satellite would be transferred to a trust as collateral. And with the required financial oversight came the explicit agreement that CPB would have no editorial control.

With a half-million-dollar check in hand, Bornstein prepared for the bank to open a few hours later so he might make the deposit to cover August's payroll. In the meantime, he cracked open a celebratory Amstel Light, relieved to have gotten through this part of the saga. The rest of the details would be worked out in the coming days.

NPR had, miraculously, been rescued.

* * *

The bailout kept the lights on, but it was hoped the Drive to Survive would raise additional money to stave off further cutbacks. Instead, it illuminated a thorny fissure: The vast majority of member stations, furious about the roller coaster of the last year and angry that the network was encroaching on its fund-raising territory, refused to comply. Besides, they'd already succumbed to Bornstein's strong-arming and had agreed to pitch in for the bailout.

Some station managers fretted that the on-air appeal would confuse listeners, already unclear about the convoluted identity of public broadcasting. When people donated to their local station, they believed they were giving money to the network. Still, fifty affiliates did agree to run the drive, including WHYY in Philadelphia, now run by NPR founding father Bill Siemering. Despite his having been pushed out of the place he'd lovingly helped create, he was still a sympathetic and ardent supporter of the cause.

During the segments where Susan and others made their impassioned appeals for cash, dissenting stations simply covered them up with recycled stories from the archives. This, in turn, angered some of their most devoted listeners, who were desperately eager to help save their favorite media outlet in its time of need.

Around the nation, other listeners were mystified by assurances that their money would be well-spent. "Well, what about the millions that had been frittered away?" countered John Price in the *Eau Claire Leader-Telegram*. He was still scratching his head over the notion that network leaders had just woken up one day and found its coffers empty. "I'll help prop up NPR, but I want to know what happened."

A congressional hearing would aim to get to the bottom of that soon. In the meantime, about $2.25 million flowed in over the three-day appeal—the participating stations kept half, and the rest went to the network. Not bad, but certainly not enough to pay back the loans that had saved it.

Was there any silver lining to this disaster? wondered those in public radio's orbit. If there was, it was that Frank got his wish, just as he'd promised when he arrived: Now everybody in America knew about National Public Radio. He could also update his eventual epitaph, said Bornstein—whose own would surely now include the words "savior of NPR." No longer was Frank Mankiewicz the man who announced the death of Bobby Kennedy. Forevermore, he'd be the man who brought NPR to prominence—and then nearly killed it.

EPILOGUE
Hollywood Walk of Fame

Rubberneckers are as common in Hollywood as dreams. In search of the slightest smidgen of celebrity, they'll troll the remotest thorough-fares, gladly forking over hefty fees to ride tour buses that promise star sightings, expectantly gripping their selfie sticks all the while. On the streets of Los Angeles, especially in the age of the smartphone, every-one's a paparazzo.

On the first Tuesday in March 2020, as the stock market plum-meted precipitously and the world was fanning shut in the grip of a deadly pandemic, not a cloud darkened the sky over a cheerful crowd gathered at lunchtime on Hollywood Boulevard. Passersby craned their necks to get a glimpse of what glittering specimen might be shin-ing behind the rope line. The Los Angeles Police Department's finest shooed them along a narrow path between stanchions: "Keep it mov-ing!" Invariably somebody wondered out loud, "Who is it? Who is it?" The cops shrugged. This was just another day's work. Then some know-ing soul in the throng piped up with an answer:

"It's Susan *Stamberg*."

A beat; no recognition, and then a bit more explanation:

". . . of *NPR*."

The tourists, still in the dark, looked at one another and shrugged, too. Who or what was *that*? Clearly, they were hoping for a Kardashian.

Those on the other side of the barricade knew quite well. Many in the crowd, in fact, could thank Susan for the flourishing of public radio that had led them to their careers.

How far NPR had come in the fifty years since it incorporated. Five decades had elapsed since radio had been cast aside as the "hidden medium" and men had to fight to get it included in the 1967 Public Broadcasting Act. From its first days as a "mom and pop store," as

Susan described it, NPR had long ago graduated to Bloomingdale's, a big-league, star-making brand and mainstream media powerhouse. Each week, thirty-five million listeners tuned in on more than a thousand stations, and the superstar hosts now raked in upward of a very starry half-a-million dollars a year. Devoted listeners proclaimed their allegiance to public radio as they would a religion. This wasn't just some media outlet you consumed, but a way of life—something you devoured.

While back in those earliest days, NPR struggled to find staff capable of artfully slicing tape into captivating radio news stories, now audio storytelling constituted an entire area of study at journalism schools. Students eagerly signed up to learn the trade in the hope of landing coveted jobs at the nation's member stations, unaware that those stations had once been dismissed as lacking staff to reliably generate air-worthy submissions. If journalism school graduates were very, very lucky, they might score a job at the network itself. (And if they were *really* in Lotto territory, perhaps they'd put their skills to use to create a hit podcast, yielding a movie deal or the mega-buck backing of a venture capitalist.) The audio medium had been morphing along with all of communications into this uncharted, digital, time-shifted landscape that proved to be far more disruptive than the arrival of television had been.

Decades after laws first mandated that hiring must be equal and gender blind, there was now nothing at all surprising or uncommon about a woman on the front lines of the news. The absence would have been more startling. That they were breaking ground for anyone but themselves hadn't occurred initially to the first of the founding mothers, Susan and Linda. They were just being themselves. They were just being, as Bill Siemering had instructed them, *human*. Then a stranger had approached them at a public radio conference and thanked them for "legitimizing the sound of women in serious news roles," and they realized that simply by appearing on the air and reporting stories of a serious nature, they were helping not just their own careers but the cause of women.

Susan remembered the collective thrill they'd all felt on that historic day in the summer of 1984 when Geraldine Ferraro, a member of

Congress from New York, was revealed as presidential nominee Walter Mondale's running mate. Hearing this groundbreaking news—the first woman named to a major-party ticket—Susan grabbed the phone to call Linda, who was covering the convention in San Francisco, to discuss this "massive door" that had swung open.* Linda relayed that she and Cokie had just walked past a female Mondale staffer, who mouthed the words "What now?" Getting there, as the founding mothers knew well, was only the lead-in for the next generations to the follow-up question: What next?

* * *

Among the cheerleaders in southern California that day in March 2020 was a young NPR reporter, Sonari Glinton. He'd led the charge to get Susan the honor they were gathered there to celebrate: a star on the Hollywood Walk of Fame.

Over the years, Susan had lamented the fleeting nature of her work, quoting comedian Fred Allen: "Radio is as lasting as a butterfly's cough." In several instances—on a wintry day, or when she spotted a construction site near the office—she'd rally coworkers to "play" Grauman's Chinese, etching their names and handprints in the snow or freshly poured concrete, mimicking the collection of footprints and handprints of celebrities outside the historic theater just up the street from where she was now about to be more permanently immortalized. (The only footprints hers would fit, she'd discovered on an earlier visit, were Fred Astaire's.) Immortalized now with her own marker, she wouldn't be standing in anyone's imprint. Just as she had in broadcasting, she had carved out her very own.

The bit of brass and terrazzo implanted into the sidewalk along the storied tourist attraction paled in comparison to Susan's actual accomplishments—chief among them that, in the evanescent (and

---

* Had Congresswoman Lindy Boggs not been a strict foe of abortion, she might have been Mondale's choice.

supremely ageist) world of media, she was not only still considered relevant, but she actually still contributed on the air at age eighty-one.

Way back when Susan was reciting poetry to embellish her weather reports at WAMU—and long before that, during sleepovers with high school friends she'd keep up all night chatting away, her own version of a Parisian salon—it remained in the realm of fluttering fantasy that she might one day see her name inscribed along a constellation of that of others who'd ascended to the lofty heights of fame. After all, her modest ambition at the start had been simply for a taxicab driver to recognize her voice when she requested a stop from the back seat.

So, too, did the financial worries that nearly collapsed the network back in 1983. After loans were repaid several years later, NPR had indeed extricated itself "off the government fix" (indirectly, at least), and the man who'd recruited Frank, Ed Elson, had ultimately helped the network create a foundation as another means of independence. In 2003, an announcement was made that Joan Kroc, the progressive, deep-pocketed news junkie heiress to the McDonald's fortune, had generously stoked the network's various coffers posthumously in her will, to the tune of $225 million, the largest gift from an individual the network had ever received—and, at the time, the largest to an American cultural institution.* (Insiders jokingly referred to the largesse as their "Kroc pot.")

Independent of that, member stations each year collectively raised millions of dollars—on top of the sponsorship dollars they raked in from advertisers eager to get their names in front of the well-educated and largely affluent public radio audience. What had begun as an idealistic venture to combat the pernicious power and influence of commercial broadcasting had itself become influential big business.

* * *

---

* Mrs. Kroc famously attempted to give half that money to public television, but when her staffer's calls were not returned, the entire sum was routed to radio.

To glitz up the ceremony, an actual movie star had been enlisted to appear, the actress Annette Bening. The trim, bespectacled woman looked more like a stylish librarian as she proclaimed to the audience, "Susan Stamberg is my hero!"* Susan's voice is so synonymous with NPR, Bening continued, it even greets you in the elevator at headquarters in Washington, DC: "Like many people, I feel I know her because of listening to what she said, how she said it, and what she invited me to pay attention to. *Her* curiosity became *my* curiosity."

Acknowledging Linda, Nina, and Cokie, Bening explained how they, along with Susan, had paved the way for women reporters everywhere. "Hosting shows, interviewing government officials without backing down, going to war zones, talking to survivors of natural disasters and shootings . . . These women bring the news into our lives and make it come alive by talking to people and listening to their stories."

Next up to the podium stepped Susan's handsome son, Josh, who'd made a career for himself these last twenty years (much to his mother's great pleasure and relief) in one of the few industries more cutthroat than journalism: entertainment.† Josh's father, Susan's devoted husband Lou, had been gone for over a decade now. Their only child had expanded the small family with two young daughters of his own. The kids sat perched in the front row as Josh relayed memories of the woman they called "ZuZu." (Susan was most definitely not a "Grandma.")

Back as a kid himself, when he'd visited his mother at the office, Josh said, innumerable delights enthralled him: the cough button and flashing lights on the audio console in the darkened studio, the thrilling

---

* Bening erroneously suggested that Susan's voice was now installed in the Library of Congress because the first broadcast of *All Things Considered* had been made part of the collection. Susan, however, was not in the first broadcast.
† Josh had in fact met Bening when they appeared together in a play at Los Angeles's Geffen Playhouse a decade earlier. The actress played a character based on the writer Germaine Greer.

magic of the hulking Xerox machine on which he made photocopies of his hand, the tanklike electric typewriter, a vending machine stocked with treats. Most of all, watching his mother "at the center of the universe," chain-smoking, drinking Tab, nibbling on almonds—sharing stories, charming the nation. She herself knew a thing or two about performing. ("It's a joke," she'd said long ago, "when people tell you there's no show business to this.")

Susan had practically raised Josh on the air, unabashedly so, grappling publicly with questions and dilemmas that faced every parent—from dissecting the best approach to temper tantrums with a child psychologist to poignantly sharing the emotion of the first day of kindergarten. (What are the rules, Josh had wondered sweetly.) To the famous director Elia Kazan, she posed a question on behalf of an unnamed "young actor" who'd been told of his resemblance to Brando. She loved "taking the personal and putting a professional lens on it—making the assumption that if it affects me, it must be affecting hundreds of thousands of other people." Her assumption had touched a nerve, and her humanity had made her career.

Josh couldn't have realized then how much his very existence had influenced her work, or the demands she had made to accommodate her family—a rare perk reserved for few in the working world, particularly in the demanding world of media. The aching balance of nurturing one's own ambitions while tending to the needs of the family was something few women before her had been able to achieve. He did know this: His mother's "passion for storytelling" had inspired his passion to perform.

It was time for the woman of the hour to speak. Susan rose, her tall frame clad in an eye-popping raw silk chartreuse pantsuit, her broad smile beaming, her mop of once-dark curls now silvery gray. "It's very kind that my name is on that star," she said. "But the honor really goes to NPR. I know it's an old-fashioned, old-fangled medium. But it's the medium of my heart."

* * *

It had been decades now since Susan herself had been front and center, the main voice of NPR. She'd stepped down as cohost of *All Things Considered* in 1986, three years after the financial crisis that almost destroyed the place. At the time, she'd attributed her departure to her need to "un-grind" from fourteen years of "daily-ness" and the hyper-organization necessary to juggle work and family. Though she'd negotiated a four-day workweek back before the dark period, had completed a two-month professional fellowship in Hawaii, and enjoyed time off to compile a compendium of transcripts of early interviews and segments into a book titled *Every Night at Five,* the show had become more a demand than a joy. She'd spent so many years clearing her throat at ten seconds before five, doing so had become a natural reflex.

"It's a goodbye to being the one who says, 'And for this evening, that's Susan Stamberg,' but it's not goodbye to public radio," she said. The staff presented her with a formidable token of her achievement: a three-inch-thick dot-matrix computer printout listing every single story she'd done. To soften the blow of her departure, she revealed that she'd soon appear on a new program in development, *Weekend Sunday.*

In the aftermath of her bombshell announcement that she was "tired of hauling the anchor," she preened that several people had paid her a compliment for it. " 'You know, it's amazing,' they said. 'You actually told the truth.' "

Actually, though, she hadn't—not entirely. There was more to her desire to step off the news carousel than the desire for a change. She had a secret. She'd been diagnosed with breast cancer. She knew herself well enough to know that had she revealed her illness more widely, she'd have felt pressured to "cheer people up or make them feel better." Ever the salon hostess, she felt the need to keep the party upbeat as the "bringer* of joy."* The monumental worry she faced was not one she wished to inflict on others.

---

* For a masterstroke of interviewing, listen to Terry Gross quiz Susan: https://freshair archive.org/guests/susan-stamberg.

Instead, after a lumpectomy and while she endured radiation, she plunged into work on a piece about the writer and adventurer Beryl Markham, the first person to pilot a plane solo across the Atlantic from Britain to North America. Immersion into the life of a faraway and long-ago adventurer was just the escape this founding mother needed. Only the keenest of detectives might have deduced something was wrong when she broke down in tears on the air after her last on-air chat with the longtime commentator Kim Williams, the Montana-based naturalist who was in the end stages of cancer. The segment occurred just as Susan learned of her own diagnosis.

* * *

It was not only the status of women that had changed vividly since she'd walked into that new radio station in Washington as a young woman long ago. So, too, had the media. News, once seen as an "eat-your-vegetables" offering that interrupted more compelling entertainment fare, had moved to center stage. The sheer number of news outlets (and, thus, jobs) had multiplied exponentially. More recently, in a digital world, news and information revved faster than a satellite in geosynchronous orbit, delivered right in the palm of your hand.

And with that speed came audience sophistication. Back in the 1970s, the average person flinched at the sight of recording gear, unsure of what to say or how to behave. Slowly, it seemed, the growing ubiquity of home-grade camcorders and the hum of TV had obliterated self-consciousness and trained the average citizen in the way of the sound bite. The culture of over-sharing and public self-reflection had been steadily chipping away at privacy and social decorum. (And that was long before the societally accepted practice of confessing your every mood, or meal, in a selfie or a tweet.)

By the 1990s, anyone and everyone was primed and ready for their close-up, Susan observed of the general public. "They know how to talk into microphones, they know how to be on TV and they know how to summon their strength in how to tell difficult things."

Sometimes, in the years after she gave up being the star, Susan had lamented her choice. The access that the host's seat had afforded her was unparalleled, and the adulation nourishing. She might not miss the nightly adrenaline rush, but she did miss that limelight.

Yet, all these years since, she'd written her own ticket. To be near Josh and his family, she spent the winter months in Los Angeles, dropping into the office at NPR West to file stories on topics of her choice. The creative mind remained far more compelling than the "titillations of yesterday's irrelevances"—the politics, the *news*. "I would choose five minutes with a performance artist over four hours with Paul Ryan any day," she said. Art in all forms would save us, she believed. Arts councils and other civic groups were happy to pay her speaker's fee to have her grace their stage and say so at their events—a humane reminder, in the growing, angry screech of media, of the "nerve synapse" she had represented for so many years.

After the wraps were pulled off the Walk of Fame's newest star and photographers had had their fill, select VIPs among the onlookers—varying generations of "Nippers," as the more vintage in the NPR crowd called themselves—made their way up the street to sip celebratory martinis at the classic Hollywood joint Musso and Frank. Susan had never achieved her dream of becoming a jazz singer in a smoky bar, wearing a red strapless dress with a long slit up the side, but life had unfolded on a different, equally starry course.

* * *

Susan's 1986 departure as host had forced NPR to a reckoning. Newspaper editorials feared the post-Susan era might be marked by the empty tone that dominated so much of broadcasting's sound-bite journalism. The perfectly cast successor to deposed president Frank Mankiewicz, Doug Bennet, an economist who'd worked in the Carter administration,*

---

* Coincidentally, Bennet had run the same agency where Susan's husband made his career, the Agency for International Development.

had been consumed with the daunting task of stabilizing NPR's finances. In his short tenure, Bennet had fundamentally altered the way the system worked. The new formula involved routing the Corporation for Public Broadcasting funding directly to member stations, who, in turn, paid sliding-scale fees to NPR.

Now Bennet had to face the thorny dilemma: Who on earth could possibly replace Susan? The clear heir apparent appeared to be Nina, since she most frequently sat in for Susan on her Fridays off. But, as Nina told the *Washington Post*, the glory and confines of the hosting chair were not for her: "I'm forty-two and not ready yet. I'm not ready to come in out of the cold. I'm delighted to substitute, but I'm a reporter and I feel like a prisoner in the studio. I get much more pleasure from reporting. It gives me such a kick!"

Destabilizing the show even more, Susan's latest cohost, Noah Adams, announced on the heels of her departure that he, too, was moving on—to host a variety show from rival service Minnesota Public Radio called *Good Evening*. The new team installed to replace the duo, Renee Montagne and Robert Siegel, received lackluster reviews. An important affiliate, KUSC in Los Angeles—the station that had co-produced the *Star Wars* radio series—dropped its membership, calling the news product that was being served up "mundane and dull, very traditional, very predictable." The new team's professionalism wasn't the question. To the critics, they just sounded like everything else in mainstream media.

This charge hardly disturbed the die-hard newsies in the place, who preferred this solid shift to "hard" news over the soulful, artful documentary experimentation that had once filled the time. Cokie was chief among those happy to wave goodbye to NPR's rap as antiestablishment: "I did not go to Woodstock, and I'm the right age," she said. "A lot of what went on here in the 'good old days' was too long and boring. Now we can tell it shorter. That might not be all that different and zany, but it is better journalism."

Linda, for her part, concurred. "I'm not nostalgic for those days at all," she said. "I don't want to be a sidebar to the world anymore or an intellectual magazine that twelve people read." Been there, done that.

Along with this more conventional, harder-news focus came the standard pollution of infighting and maneuvering that characterized most every workplace on earth. Montagne was yanked from the program. A new idea sprouted: to hire a cast of three, so each could take turns out "in the field"—no better way to showcase their chops as reporters and hammer home that NPR's hosts were not mere readers of news copy.

Under this new configuration, management played musical chairs with the staff: Weekend host Lynn Neary was announced as the new female weekday cohost, and reporter Margot Adler in turn got promoted to Neary's weekend job. Then, mysteriously, came the corporate backpedaling. After Neary returned from her honeymoon, she learned that Linda had been promoted to the job she'd been promised. The promotions were off.

What happened? Equal parts bad management and poor communication, it seemed, spiced with a hefty roar from the Fallopian Jungle. The *Washington Post* reported that Linda, angry that the job as weekday host hadn't been officially posted, filed a grievance with the union. The early-years network practice of filling new or vacant staff positions through personal networks—which was how most of the earliest NPR employees, including the founding mothers, had landed their jobs—had ended. This was hastened along by the arrival of the union, the creation of a Corporation for Public Broadcasting task force on minorities and hiring,* and a lawsuit filed in the late seventies by three Black reporters who charged "subtle discrimination employment practices." That case was settled by a District court judge.†

Nina and Cokie reportedly petitioned management on their friend

---

* While today, women are more equally represented at the network, minority representation remains an issue. In September 2020, SAG-AFTRA, the union representing NPR employees, called for vast and immediate changes to make NPR a more inclusive workplace.
† NPR denied claims that it had not posted job vacancies in the past.

Linda's behalf. Various coworkers said they heard that the star reporters threatened to quit if Linda didn't get elevated to the top spot. This, Nina denied. "If I talked to Bennet about it, it was *en passant.* I didn't threaten anything." Fearless Cokie: "I told him frankly what I thought, as I do with many hires. I would love for it to be true that I control the hiring, but I don't want to be management, and I am not."

As for president Bennet, all he would say is, "We did not handle that situation well."

And with that, a star reporter became the star host—at least, until 2002, when she was pushed back into the field as a correspondent and replaced by two younger women.

* * *

The bigger NPR grew, the more popular it became, and the higher the stakes, the thornier the office politics. Then came the Senate, digging into the books with an eye toward answering the impossible-to-quantify question: What is the commercial value of the current broadcasting system? That debate had raged on from back in the Nixon years, along with other questions: Was public broadcasting an "elitist enterprise" with a liberal bias, the perpetrator of "sensitive cultural or scientific reporting" on "controversial topics some people would prefer not to hear," or "a conservative sell-out with no principles on a par with the Pentagon?" There was, too, the never-ending debate over who should have the right to use public airwaves, and to what end? (Not helping matters was the endless confusion over NPR versus member stations versus rival production services.)

In the meantime, a 1991 government inquisition outed the top earners on NPR's staff. And while founding mother Linda had seniority over practically everyone, and was cohost of the signature program, she still didn't earn what her male colleagues in similar jobs took home.

Commentator Daniel Schorr, he of the Nixon enemies list, storied veteran of the House of Murrow, and refugee from CNN, was hired as a contractor at $100,025. Robert Siegel, who'd risen from newscaster to foreign correspondent to news director before ascending to the *All Things Considered* co-host slot, was earning $97,805.* *Morning Edition* show host Bob Edwards made $95,337. The yearly salary of the other *All Things Considered* cohost, Noah Adams, who'd returned when his variety show flopped, was $90,994, and *Morning Edition* news reader Carl Kassell made $90,953.

And, at the bottom of the top, Linda—among a handful of the original employees of the network, was now costar of the show, earning $90,921. (Susan, Nina, and Cokie didn't even rank on the list. In fact, Nina's salary of $65,000 had recently landed her a mention, alongside Mother Teresa, in a *Spy* magazine story on society's most underpaid people.)

Then, there was a vexing series of lawsuits, chief among them that of a longtime female contractor who'd been ping-ponging around the network for fifteen years, watching as a variety of men were hired from outside NPR to staff jobs she'd performed as a temp. After she charged NPR with discrimination and asked for $1.2 million in back pay and damages, lawyers for NPR derided her case for lack of merit. A judge settled the dispute for an undisclosed amount.

There might be powerful, terrific women reporters at NPR, the aggrieved employee told the *New York Times*, but if the network was "going to argue in Congress that they are a valuable institution to this country, then within their own hallways they have to treat people fairly and equally." After all, she added, they'd be the first to call out others when they did not.

* * *

A report on workplace injustice was about to elevate another of the founding mothers to a household name. Whispered allegations around

---

* Terry Gross on *Fresh Air* jokes that Siegel acted in the spirit of Dick Cheney when he proposed himself for the job as host. (She also thanks him for being part of the push to distribute her show nationally.) See https://freshairarchive.org/guests/robert-siegel.

Capitol Hill in the summer of 1991 piqued Nina's curiosity about Supreme Court nominee Clarence Thomas, onetime chief of the Equal Employment Opportunity Commission that had been established as a result of the historic 1964 Civil Rights Act.

Nina had already altered the course of history a few years before by revealing information about an earlier Supreme Court nominee, Douglas Ginsburg, that a background check had not: While working as a professor at Harvard Law School, he had smoked pot, a revelation that unleashed a frenzy of admissions by other public officials who said that in the past they had toked, too, and denouncements from others who said it was no one's else's business but their own. The very day after that piece ran, she returned to the airwaves to reveal another incendiary bit: that Ginsburg had inflated his résumé, overstating his trial experience. (*Vanity Fair* reported several years later that a *Legal Times* reporter was said to have given Nina this story in exchange for attribution he didn't get. Nina, for her part, said she'd learned the information on her own.)

Two days later, after innumerable mocking jabs in the press about the "*High* Court," Ginsburg withdrew his name from consideration. To the critics who accused her of digging up information they considered private, Nina responded (after admitting to having once taken a puff herself long ago) that the use of an illegal substance by a potential Supreme Court justice was not simply a case of youthful experimentation. It was essential information that the government and the public deserved to know. "Doug Ginsburg . . . was breaking the law while he was teaching it," she said. "Where are you going to draw the line? . . . If someone's a wife beater, a shop lifter, an embezzler or misused his brother's estate . . . you're going to find somebody who will think that it is private information and others who will not."

The Ginsburg story turned out to be training wheels for the conflagration unleashed surrounding Clarence Thomas's nomination. During the routine background check, a former employee named Anita Hill had accused him of ongoing and graphic sexual harassment. Like

Thomas, Hill was a Black, Yale-educated lawyer who'd bootstrapped her way out of poverty. Now a professor of law in Oklahoma, she'd informed the Senate Judiciary Committee that when she'd worked for Thomas at the EEOC, he'd subjected her to an onslaught of graphic talk about sex, including details of pornographic films he enjoyed watching and his supposed prowess in the bedroom.

Behind closed doors, the committee, led by Senator Joe Biden, dispatched the FBI to investigate Hill's charges, receiving a sworn affidavit from her, then dismissing the allegations for lack of evidence. Thomas's nomination proceeded. Somewhere along the way, a latter-day Deep Throat leaked the incendiary allegations.

Two days before a full vote in the Senate, reporter Timothy Phelps of *Newsday* broke the news about the nation's next Supreme Court justice in print. "While Thomas implicitly pressured Hill to have sex with him," Phelps wrote, his source said "he never told her explicitly that she would lose her job if she did not consent." Nor had she reported the harassment at the time. (What was she going to do? File a complaint with the EEOC?)

Nina had been hustling to get the story, too. Her curiosity had been piqued when she'd heard Senator Biden make a defensive remark about the nominee's character. A few hours after Phelps's story landed in newspapers across the nation, Nina's piece aired on NPR, including an added element: the voice of the accuser.

Hill told Nina she'd grant an interview if the reporter managed to get her hands on the confidential affidavit. This was a challenge she didn't have to hear twice. Daring Nina to sleuth out an elusive document she wasn't supposed to have was like "waving a red flag at a bull," she said. Time and time again, Nina enjoyed living up to that accusation by J. Edgar Hoover that she was a "persistent bitch" (or, at least, the persistent part).

On tape, the aggrieved lawyer explained in a voice just above a whisper, "Here is a person who is in charge of protecting rights of women and other groups in the workplace, and he is using his position of power for personal gain. . . . And he did it in a very—just ugly and intimidating way. But he is also really, in spirit and I believe in—in action, too, violating the laws that he's there to enforce."

The firestorm that Nina had anticipated after her report flamed far larger than either woman imagined. Switchboards lit up at the White House and the Capitol, "telephone gridlock" caused by an army of outraged women who also jammed the lines with faxes, furious that Hill's charges hadn't been fully investigated. In a dramatic display, seven female members of the House marched over to the Senate, demanding a delay in the vote as well as a hearing—which Nina wound up cohosting on PBS.

The resulting three days of testimony created what one wag called "the most riveting television drama since the infamous plot-line of the nighttime TV soap opera, *Dallas*, 'Who Shot J.R.?'" (Though, of course, *that* drama was fiction.) The hearings even trumped the World Series playoffs between the Toronto Blue Jays and the Minnesota Twins; more viewers tuned in to hear the Supreme Court nominee defiantly deny the allegations and insist that this was a "high-tech lynching for uppity blacks." Hill faced a firing squad of white male senators with unflappable grace, her voice never wavering as they peppered her with incendiary questions as if she herself were on trial. *Are you a scorned woman? Do you have a martyr complex? What was the most embarrassing of incidences?*

Observed columnist Mary McGrory of the shocking proceedings: "It was as if a river of raw sewage had suddenly been unleashed in the marble chamber, words forbidden in polite company and on the air-waves; X-rated phrases; vivid graphic references to large breasts and big penises and sex with animals."

This river of sewage seeped out of the chamber and blanketed the culture. The American people chose sides as they publicly confronted the long-simmering scourge of workplace sexual harassment. The blockbuster movie *9 to 5*, starring Jane Fonda, Lily Tomlin, and Dolly Parton, had brought the issue into the zeitgeist in 1980, but its depiction of boorish and abusive office behavior hadn't incited a fraction of what Hill's revelations had. Her treatment by the senators escalated the outrage.

Did you believe Hill, or did you believe Thomas? One of them had to be lying.

Television shows like *Murphy Brown*, *Saturday Night Live*, and *Designing Women* worked the divisive she said/he said story line into their scripts. *Cosmopolitan* editor Helen Gurley Brown exploded the debate with the revelation (in a *Wall Street Journal* op-ed) that at one of her first jobs, men chased the secretaries around the office in order to "de-panty" them. Much to her dismay, she was not one of them. Male columnists retorted in horror. There wasn't anything new about the thorny sexual politics of the workplace, especially for generations of women who'd gritted their teeth and endured it. What America had never seen before was such a graphic and public discussion about it.

For having given Hill a voice, Nina became both a hero and a punching bag. Many believed, as they had with the Doug Ginsburg revelation, that such information should remain private. Every morning, she'd arrive at the office to a voice mail overloaded with messages—some praise, some echoes of the tongue-lashing she took from Senator Alan Simpson on the television program *Nightline*. "Did you ever read the code of professional ethics?" Senator Simpson shouted at her in the parking lot afterward. "How about the part that says you respect the privacy and dignity of those you deal with?"

Nina responded in her operatic trill. "You big shit. *Fuck you!*"

Referring to how Ginsburg's nomination had been destroyed by Nina's reports, the senator sneered that she must be happy to have "brought another one down." But she hadn't. Despite the allegations and the public showdown, the Senate approved Thomas to the High Court, 52 to 48.

* * *

Thomas's confirmation hardly tamped down the consternation—or the feeding frenzy revolving around Nina, particularly after she revealed to reporter Howard Kurtz of the *Washington Post* that she herself had once been on the other side of a predatory man at the office. It was her long-ago boss at the *National Observer*, and unlike with Thomas and Hill, she added, "it wasn't just talk . . ." She didn't wish to dwell on it. "It happened. I left. That's all I'm going to say."

With this revelation, critics wondered why she hadn't recused herself from the story or, at the very least, from narrating the hearings for PBS. Another sexist jab, countered Nina (kind of missing the point): "Would you tell Woodward and Bernstein not to cover Watergate because they broke the first story?"

Then came another salvo. Columnist Al Hunt in the *Wall Street Journal* protested that the *Post* hadn't made enough of the *real* reason Nina departed from the *National Observer*—even if it was twenty years earlier. Her firing had had nothing to do with advances made by her boss. It was plain and simple because of that Tip O'Neill story. "Purposeful plagiarism is one of the cardinal sins of journalism," Hunt wrote. "There is no statute of limitations on that judgment."

In the aftermath of this dustup, the press vultures swirled. Interview requests piled up, including one from ABC's Sam Donaldson, Cokie's TV colleague. Cokie firmly counseled Nina against it. She knew the dogged reporter Donaldson was likely to dwell on the plagiarism and harassment elements of Nina's story, not on her heroics in having sleuthed out Hill.

In a masterstroke of spin control, next thing you knew, Cokie, Nina, and Linda were appearing on ABC, not with Sam but alongside a far friendlier Diane Sawyer (sister graduate of Linda and Cokie's alma mater, Wellesley College). Woman power! Sawyer cheerfully introduced viewers to "three women who inspire respect and their share of fear" around the nation's capital, despite the fact that they worked not for one of the big-name, old-guard news outlets, but "the formerly funky, gentle, offbeat" NPR.

The three women proceeded to growl about how "every woman of a certain age" had, in fact, experienced abuse in the workplace at the hands of a man. Maybe younger women found it shocking and impossible to believe, but it was all part and parcel of the way things used to be not very long before—back when the idea of flagging this behavior might very well cost a woman her career, or put her in the unwelcome spotlight Anita Hill found herself in.

All this chatter and attention might have left Nina feeling a bit like "hamburger meat" in a media food fight, but it was nothing compared to the punishment she faced now in the aftermath of her biggest story: the prospect of going to jail. A special Senate counsel, attempting to identify the source of the leak, ordered Nina and *Newsday* reporter Phelps to turn over their telephone records, or else risk imprisonment for contempt of court. Suddenly Nina was in the same position as her childhood hero, the newspaper columnist Marie Torre, who'd refused back in 1959 to name her sources in that Judy Garland case against CBS—and had served time as a result. Nina said she was prepared to do the same—anything to protect her pledge of confidentiality. She was, she said, taking this secret to her grave.

"I find myself a bit embarrassed to be wrapping myself so totally in the grandeur of the First Amendment," she said. "At the same time, I believe this is exactly the kind of situation the founding fathers had in mind when they wrote the First Amendment."

Editorial boards around the nation echoed the sentiments expressed in the *Hartford Courant*: that Nina and *Newsday*'s Phelps shouldn't be probed or punished. They had been obliged to follow up on the information they got after the senators refused to take such damning allegations seriously. By reporting on the confidential information they'd received about Hill's charges, they were doing what the Senate had failed to do: "[T]here would have been no leaks had the committee shown respect for open government in the first place."

Eventually, the subpoenas were rejected by the Senate rules committee, evaporating the concern over jail time. And the "queen of leaks," as *Vanity Fair* called Nina in a glossy celebrity profile, found herself inundated with offers to write books, give speeches, and even (for a side gig) act as a contributing correspondent for NBC News.

Every story that included her name, she boasted, turned out to be "like a press release for me." Deliveries of congratulatory flowers and candy arrived at the office, but, she said, "I had to throw the candy away. First, because I might get chubby. And second because it might be poisoned." At least she had a sense of humor to match her ego. "In the future, if someone has important information," she cried, "do you think they'll give it to the U.S. Senate? They'll give it to *me!*"

Whatever insecurities Nina might have harbored twenty years earlier, when asking for a job felt like asking for a favor, had melted away. "When I stand in any line of reporters at a big event that I'm covering," she told Ron Powers of *GQ* magazine, "be it a big Supreme Court argument, a trial or an election campaign, I am the star in the line." Her bluster masked her lack of confidence. Shielding herself in a coat of fearlessness seemed necessary to trump her biggest liability: that she was a female in a man's world.

Aside from her ascendance to the lofty perch of stardom, she'd always have the satisfaction of having trained a Klieg light on a thorny societal scourge. Reminders of that came often, whether from a flight attendant on board a plane who grabbed her hand and thanked her or when Nina delivered a speech to thunderous applause. "I asked Anita Hill to stand up, and it changed her life, it changed Judge Thomas' life," she told graduates of Chatham College in Pittsburgh, "it changed our country and it changed our politics."

Hyperbole this was not. In the year after the Hill incident, the number of harassment cases filed at the EEOC doubled, and more women ran for Senate than ever before—and won. Thanks to the plight of Anita Hill, 1992 became known as "the Year of the Woman."

* * *

It was also the decade of Cokie Roberts. *Spy* magazine had presaged Cokie's ascendance in 1990 with a cartoon flow chart jam-packed with the names of everyone who was anyone in media, power, politics circling her orbit, with the caption "Cokie Roberts: Moderately well-known broadcast journalist or *center of the universe?*"

The outer bands of her connections traced decidedly far outside the Beltway, showing the interconnectivity of the Cokie-verse that linked everyone who was anyone in television, publishing, newspapers, government, and politics to the stratosphere of celebrity that included rock stars like Led Zeppelin and Axl Rose and pop stars like Madonna.

As the decade progressed, "moderately well-known" didn't do her status justice. She was, suddenly, ubiquitous. ABC had wanted her so badly, they let her keep the radio gig, which she told them she didn't want to give up. "You can't do what you do on NPR anyplace else," she said of the long, thoughtful pieces that never in a zillion years would be possible on commercial television. What a reporter couldn't do at NPR, though—at least not then—was earn the salary she was about to command: a whopping half million a year.

To adequately accommodate the wardrobe she'd need for television, she indulged in an upgrade at the house on Bradley Boulevard—a giant closet. The least she deserved, if she was going to have to dress for the camera, were wrinkle-free dresses!

In no time at all came the accolades. Cokie's pithy, knowing chatter with the guys on Sunday mornings as she broke down inside-the-Beltway shenanigans was a hit. Readers of *George* magazine voted her their "Favorite Talking Head," and the magazine's publisher, John F. Kennedy Jr., described the almond-shaped gray-blue eyes of the woman who'd dined with his father before he himself was born as "an evolutionary adaptation allowing her to see more acutely than the rest of us."

What was it, exactly, besides those eyes, that made her a star? Was it the distinctive crackle in her voice? The lineage? Or was it what she had to say? Practical Cokie could precisely define her own appeal. Until now, "there wasn't anybody else just talking sort of commonsense, suburban-matron talk. Before, it had been much more of a male club talking about deep policy things without ever saying the emperor has no clothes."

Oh sure, her sex had scored her admission to the club, but it wasn't what got her promoted. She got promoted, she said, because she was *good*. Soon, she asked, and got the chance, to sub for Ted Koppel on ABC's *Nightline*, even though that meant committing the occasional social faux pas, like excusing herself to her seatmate at the White House

Correspondents Association Dinner, President Bill Clinton. Not even the commander in chief would stand in the way of a live broadcast.

But he didn't hold it against her family. Just as she was settling into her new role, post-Brinkley retirement, as cohost of *This Week*, the show that had catapulted her to television fame, President Clinton tapped Lindy, the devout Catholic from whom Cokie had inherited her religious devotion, to serve as his ambassador to the Vatican. For an eighty-one-year-old former congresswoman who slept with a photo of the Pope next to her bed, there couldn't have been a more perfect assignment.

Cokie got much mileage from the irony of her beloved, dignified mother explaining to her Catholic brethren why she was serving a rogue like Clinton. She also loved to joke that Lindy had traded the wild French Quarter, where she'd inherited a home, for the hallowed Holy See—both places populated by men who wore skirts. What she didn't love so much was that people were beginning to call the esteemed older woman "Cokie Roberts's mother."

"She thinks it's funny," Cokie said. "But I think it's ridiculous"— especially when she came face-to-face with the work Lindy had accomplished. Cokie knew well that what she herself contributed to the world was ephemeral; what her mother had done had changed lives. To wit: Cokie had recently refinanced the mortgage on the house on Bradley Boulevard, and as part of that, she had had to sign a discrimination disclaimer. Her mother had fought, while she served in Congress, to make sure that minorities and women would have equal access to loans. The banker dismissed the paperwork as nothing.

"This is not nothing! This is a law written by my mother," Cokie balked. The man promised he'd never say that again.

* * *

With her fame came the inevitable microscope—such as the time she appeared in front of a facsimile of Capitol Hill and pretended she was actually outside, bundled in a coat against the wintry weather. In fact, she was *inside*, and the coat was worn in the service of covering up her full-length gown, the requisite attire for the Washington Press Club Foundation Congressional Dinner she was to attend immediately after the news. Oh, how far she'd come from that day when, as a young, depressed newly married woman in New York City, she'd thrown a coat over her nightgown and kicked herself out of the house to perform a simple errand.

Then there was her growing side gig, delivering speeches for tens of thousands of dollars a pop—commanding more in one evening than the annual salary of an average reporter. One year, this ballooned her already ample income (according to media reporter Ken Auletta's calculation) by an additional $300,000. There seemed no end to the groups who wanted to brag that insider-observer Cokie Roberts had graced their "do." And it seemed that every single women's group and college on earth that could afford her services, particularly those with a Catholic affiliation, summoned her with invites—trade associations, corporate annual meetings, chambers of commerce, and Junior Leagues, too.

Like a skilled politician repeating his stump speech anew with each appearance, Cokie recycled her list of themes around women, politics, women and politics, and life in the strange, alien otherworld that was the nation's capital city.

One refrain—the tortured relationship of journalists and politicos: "Our interests are different and our mission is different. . . . It's also not our role to make problems worse."

Another: the media were helping to erode Americans' confidence in their government: "hating Congress is something that is as American as apple pie. It's a view we've helped foster in a negative way."

Audiences clambered to hear more of Cokie than they could get from her pithy, knowing Sunday morning television appearances. Rapt with attention, they "devoured her anecdotes about Strom Thurmond, her analysis of Jack Kemp, Iran-Contra and the National Debt." As one reporter at a Cokie event in North Carolina described, her mere presence soothed attendees: "They have come like children to be reassured that the world isn't as out of control as it seems."

As women had changed over the last decade, so, too, had the media. A cadre of purists raged against this new world order of celebrity reporters and speechifying punditry, and how this would surely destroy the credibility of the profession. It was wrong, they said, and rife with risk. "Those who collect fees are increasingly making those who don't uncomfortable," wrote Alicia Shepard in *American Journalism* magazine. "They say receiving large sums for speaking before groups with a vested interest in news coverage can give the appearance of a conflict. And it seems hypocritical for reporters to stuff their pockets with money from the same organizations they criticize for trying to buy influence on Capitol Hill."

But to Cokie, trotting around from bank to school to association, offering up variations on her insider anecdotes and female empowerment while collecting a hefty paycheck was her right. (It also stoked her generosity, as she was known to write checks to friends and family members in need.) Not for one second, she said, did she feel it impacted her ability to objectively report the news; nor did she feel the need to discuss it further.

Her husband had an explanation. "It's a classic free market," said Steve, who was sometimes one half of a bundled speaking deal. He'd given up his job at the *New York Times*, in part because of the paper's edict prohibiting its writers from appearing on television,* trading it instead for a column at the magazine *US News & World Report*, which encouraged them to. "I've often compared giving speeches to having a little stall in a souk in Damascus."

Reporter Jim Warren of the *Chicago Tribune*'s DC bureau was among the fiercest critics of celebrity journalism. He launched a regular column called "Cokie Watch," in which he called out Cokie, Steve, and others in the rarefied class of "reporter-pundit" for their paid gigs, which they rationalized, he said, "with a mix of sophistry and fervent self-righteousness." Just a jealous crank, sniffed Steve. "Reprehensible."

For her part, Cokie dismissed Warren as barely registering a blip in

---

* Though it's impossibly hard to imagine today, when a reporter must develop a personal brand to stand out from the rest, there actually was a time (not very long ago) when certain newspapers not only jealously guarded their reporters' time, but also did not wish them to flout their opinions on television or radio shows.

the tight-knit DC ecosystem. But somebody was paying attention: the Senate. Lawmakers winkingly passed a measure to push journalists on the congressional beat to disclose their outside income. Why not? observed columnist Mike Royko, who confessed that he never got paid "more than zero" when he himself gave a speech. "If teams of sleuths can trail politicians to see who they are sleeping with," he said, "what's wrong with asking the McGoofy Group how many thousands they were paid to get on a stage and make public fools of themselves?"

Of course, Cokie rarely did *that*—although she did confess a blunder to *Lear's* magazine that showed her confidence was not unwavering: Rising out of a relaxing soak in her remodeled bedroom, she got so depressed after catching a glimpse of her middle-aged physique in the full-length mirror that she tripped and broke a toe.

As for her husband, the man who'd aspired to be a journalist since his boyhood in Bayonne watched as his wife with the lofty lineage ascended, quite by accident, to the omni-media superstardom he himself had scraped up against but never quite attained. Though he wasn't one bit surprised by his wife's tremendous success, he did confess that it stung a little. "Is this situation totally free of tension and regret?" he said to a reporter. "Would I like to be on the Brinkley show? Of course, I would."

The advantage he'd had at the start of his career, as a white male reporter from the Ivy League, now worked against him. DC was teeming with smart journalists like him who wanted a seat at the table. Finally, it was the women who were in demand. And as a consequence, Cokie (along with a handful of her TV cohorts) raked in ginormous fees. It wasn't because they were "ten times smarter than me," he said. It was because she was *ten times more famous.*

Cokie's glittering star was about to rise even higher as she added "bestselling author" to her list of achievements. And no one, observed Linda, would have thought there was anything unusual at all about her fame had she been a man.

* * *

It traced back to Lindy, who was finishing up her memoir. Her editor asked Cokie if she was ready to write one, too. At first, she'd balked—she was fifty, she said, too young. But then it occurred to her: The theme of many of the talks she gave centered on the power of the modern woman and the endless juggle of work, family, friendships. "Women have played many roles throughout the course of time. For almost all women, it's the role of nurturer, whether for the planet or for one small creature on it," she told the College Club of Ridgewood, New Jersey. "We learned it from our mothers, both in word and deed, and we teach it to our daughters in the knowledge they must carry on."

Lassoing up wisdom like this in her 1998 book *We Are Our Mothers' Daughters* skyrocketed her to bestseller-dom, expanding her role on television and radio as Scolding Mother Hen of Congress into that of Relatable Acceptably Feminist Sage whose wisdom you could now store on your bookshelf. Never radical, always accessible, chiding men (when they deserved it) and celebrating women.

When she talked about the vexing responsibilities of motherhood and career, the sentiments resonated and soothed so intensely that you forgot she was, in fact, a highly paid daughter of American aristocracy. Because she knew of Cokie's privileged background, reporter Michel Martin admitted that she hadn't always appreciated the star journalist. Sure, she and others helped open previously closed doors for women in the next generations. But Cokie had arrived with the advantage of having grown up in the halls of Congress, while Martin herself was a newcomer, simply "trying not to get lost. . . ." Over time, as Cokie would suddenly appear in Martin's path during a rough spot with a big, kind, sisterly word of encouragement, Martin softened: "While I might not have seen myself in her, how lucky I am that she saw herself in me." Cokie seemed to see herself in so many others, observed Mary Louise Kelly. Because Kelly received notes of encouragement and praise from the superstar, she felt she and Cokie had a "super special relationship"—until she realized that others received notes and believed their relationship was super special, too.

The kind words flowed so effortlessly, like everything else about her: from the pithy analysis, to the perfection of her hair, to her non-chalant wrangling of several dozen guests for Sunday supper while prepping on the phone with her producer for her Monday morning radio segment, to the effortless notes of praise she sent younger colleagues, to her enduring, fabulous marriage to a man about whom, after all these years, she still found herself "crazy nuts."

Even, miraculously, after they started writing together on a regular basis. A weekly, nationally syndicated column they began gave way to a book project. The logical topic for this longtime couple: marriage. *From This Day Forward* flipped back and forth between the story and secrets of their union to that of other couples throughout history.

While researching a chapter on John and Abigail Adams, Cokie found herself inspired to learn about other women cloistered behind more notable men, women who'd been essential in building the nation. With various assistants, she dug through previously unmined stashes of archival letters in the service of elevating these women beyond the footnotes. The "Founding Mothers," she called them—and her book. The stories of women had been missing from American history—just as women had largely been missing from broadcasting before Cokie and her founding mother colleagues barnstormed the airwaves.

* * *

For all her wealth and fame and acclaim, what sustained Cokie through life's tribulations and joys was her family and dearest friends: the wrenching return of her sister's cancer—the two women wept in each other's arms, and Cokie cashed in vacation days to keep her sister company and help with her care; the death of Linda's mother; Susan's breast cancer and, much later, her husband's illness and demise; Nina's husband's fall and subsequent surgeries and decline, when Cokie and Steve made sure she was never alone for dinner, spelled her when she was on assignment, and diligently took notes at Floyd's doctor's appointments. You didn't want to *not* deliver the care you promised a patient when Cokie was present, Nina said.

When Cokie received her own cancer diagnosis, the founding mothers all took turns accompanying her to rounds of chemo and radiation. For years, she'd been notorious for materializing, with just the right words of support, in the hospital room of a friend who was ill or who'd just had a baby. Now they could be there for her.

After Nina's husband died, they all delighted years later at the news she'd found new love. Again, they stood by her side when she married—her new husband, surgeon David Reines, had painstakingly inserted his proposal in a fortune cookie. The ceremony was officiated by the law professor Nina had called decades earlier for clarification on a legal brief, with whom she'd become good friends. Now, Ruth Bader Ginsburg was known as *Supreme Court Justice* Ginsburg. And each year, the couple's anniversary brought them all together for a special feast at her home, concocted by Belgian-born chef Frederik De Pue.

To celebrate Roman Totenberg on his hundredth birthday, naturally it was Cokie who did the honors of narrating a special tribute concert at Boston University.* He died a year later, at age 101—a fact Nina lorded over the graduating class of Columbia Journalism School when she delivered the commencement address a few years later. Anyone who might have designs on her job, she told them, look out. Her father worked up until the last moment, and; she planned on doing the same—and matching his longevity. She might be in her seventies, but she wasn't slowing down.

In between the milestones and the speeches and the fund-raisers and galas and roasts were the ordinary Saturdays, like supper at the neighborhood joint the Pines of Rome. Every once in a while, someone would remember and laugh about that guy who'd called them "the Fallopian Jungle." Oh well. He mustn't have liked them. He didn't last at NPR long, they shrugged. The good old girls prevailed.

*   *   *

* "A Centennial Celebration of Roman Totenberg," December 16, 2010, https://www.youtube.com/watch?v=c885DT-9mps.

On the last Saturday night of August 2020, Susan, Linda, and Nina got together the way most people had to that summer: on a Zoom call. This one had five hundred eavesdroppers, fans who'd paid up to fifty dollars each to the hosting station, WFAE in Charlotte, for the chance to log on and spend an hour or so with these formidable women who'd provided a soundtrack to many of their days.

The deadly pandemic had persisted longer than most anyone had imagined; it had been an oppressive summer, where the aggravating heat had been intensified by dissent and uncertainty. A historic and contentious presidential election loomed. Alongside it had risen a fierce and impassioned debate about redefining journalism, its role in a deafening media universe. A smartphone allowed anyone to be a reporter and commentator now.

What is truth, whose facts are real—was it up to journalists simply to repeat what they'd witnessed, or was it their obligation to call out the lies? Why wasn't there more diversity, on either side of the microphone?

Out on the streets, respect for the profession of journalism had devolved into suspicious, scathing, angry derision. Within public radio itself, both at the network and at member stations, tensions raged about unfulfilled promises of diversity and inclusion. Critics pointed angrily to the 1978 report on bias that declared the public broadcast system "asleep at the transmitter." The task force had urged long ago that the voices of minorities and women not be excluded. Thanks in part to the founding mothers, at least women had a place at the table.

Still, there was no disputing that the world was in turmoil, turmoil that rivaled May 3, 1971, the day *All Things Considered* debuted with a lengthy report on the war protest clogging the streets of Washington.

Everything felt palpably different from the day Susan had made headlines just for taking phone calls on the air from the Oval Office with President Carter—back when it was delightfully quaint that the most powerful man in the world could talk, for an hour or so, directly to the people. Different from when Linda had first started trudging around the country with Cokie, taking the pulse of voters in diners and malls by engaging them in conversation, offsetting the sterility of polls. There was no better way to get a read on what citizens were really thinking than by gliding on the ice on ladies' night at a curling center in Wisconsin before a primary, Linda said, or by talking to women at a breast cancer survivors' group to get their take on how they'd write health care laws. No one had routinely asked women what they thought about politics before. It took women holding the microphone to make that happen.

One thing that hadn't changed was Nina's distinctive Supreme Court storytelling. She explained that her theatrical style of relaying legal matters had been born out of necessity: Despite's Frank's early queries years ago, taping the High Court for broadcast purposes still wasn't allowed. Then she recalled how Linda and Susan first showed her the ropes of radio, telling her not to cover her mouth. "That's the best advice I ever gave you, Nina," Susan said with a laugh, and you knew there had to have been plenty more.

Being forced to work from her attic these last months was driving Nina crazy. Listening to the oral arguments of the Supreme Court on a conference call wasn't the same, she told the group from a rental house in Cape Cod, not at all. She missed the collegiality of being out in the field, the water cooler at the office, and the gossip, she said.

Some people listening to this evening of reminiscences were just as nostalgic as the women. They'd been tuning in for years, starting back in the days when there'd been just a handful of news sources; when NPR sounded raw, experimental; when Susan was at the peak of her fame. Others on the Zoom call were journalism students with zero idea—no matter how much these esteemed, venerable women explained it—just how different the media landscape used to be before the news cycle became stuck in the always-on position. They certainly couldn't imagine life without cell phones, computers, the internet—or the right to complain if a coworker harassed them. Even the fresh-faced public radio host moderating this evening, her smooth-as-glass skin a stark contrast to that of her guests, asked whether they'd "believed in public radio" when they joined NPR. It was impossible for a young person to imagine that there'd ever been a time without NPR, much less that NPR hadn't always commanded huge audiences and respect.

The founding mothers happily meandered from story to story, expressing delight at the careers they'd been able to carve out for themselves. To get paid for being curious, to experience the world—what a gift. They marveled at the 24/7 news ecosystem that had flourished right before their very eyes as their careers blossomed. Complaining about having to service two shows a day back when *Morning Edition* began seemed such a quaint concern in the face of the nonstop, cross-platform news cycle journalists had to feed today. The times had changed, so much: Witness the founding mothers' younger colleagues who read bedtime stories to their young children over FaceTime, with nary a flinch, as they worked out in the field late into the night, filing for radio and Web and appearing on television, all the while finessing social media, never doubting for a moment their spouse's support. And they grimaced about Frank's long-ago explanation for why NPR hired so many women: "You get more bang for the buck." Today such a comment would have ended a man's career.

At one point, a virtual audience member raised his hand: Bill from Philadelphia. Susan lit up with a smile when she heard founding father Bill Siemering's voice, as he thanked them for their work, for defining the sound. How many times had she told the story about how Bill had bolstered her confidence, instead of dashing it, in the face of critiques from station managers who didn't want a New York woman in the host's seat.

Siemering's post-NPR career had been storied. He'd worked with another public radio pioneer, Terry Gross, as her fame grew at WHYY in Philadelphia. Siemering had even won a MacArthur "genius grant" in 1993 for his work with radio makers in developing nations, deploying the medium to help communities address social concerns. After years of lying fallow, Siemering's "Purposes" document had been revived and studied and circulated in recent years, like a Rosetta Stone. Now, on the Zoom call, his name known only to the insiders, Siemering acknowledged with pride how the founding mothers had paved the way for women everywhere.

* * *

There was only one thing missing from this delightful retrospective: Cokie.

Her absence was huge. It was best not to dwell on it. No one mentioned that it was almost a year to the day since they'd last gathered for dinner, that last Saturday night when they all knew that soon she'd be gone.

At Cokie's request, the founding mothers served as ushers at her funeral on that achingly beautiful day in September when she was memorialized at the Cathedral of St. Matthew the Apostle—the same storied church where President Kennedy's funeral had been held. House Speaker Nancy Pelosi had delivered the eulogy.* Like Cokie, Pelosi had grown up in the Capitol; her father had served alongside Hale Boggs. The women's families had been intertwined for decades, long before Cokie or Nancy could have imagined conquering the world as grandly as they had.

"Cokie Roberts is a national treasure whose passing is a great loss for America," Pelosi said, as Steve, in the front pew, reached for his handkerchief and wiped his tears. To the crowd of mourners, the groundbreaking first woman Speaker recalled how Cokie's mother had counseled her early in her own congressional career. "'Darlin', know your power and use it,'" she'd advised. "What Lindy wants, Lindy gets. So here I am," Pelosi said. The cathedral filled with laughter.

Cokie, Nancy continued, clearly also got Lindy's message. She'd used her power, too. In various ways, against a host of obstacles, women had been doing that for years. It took the combustible spirit of the times to take it to the next level.

What now? What would Cokie have made of the deadly pandemic sweeping the planet, and the way it had been handled? In the surreal, intimate glare of the Zoom call, Nina relayed the story she often told,

---

* The funeral service, which was streamed online, is here: https://www.c-span.org/video/?464579-1/funeral-mass-cokie-roberts.

how the founding mothers had helped her survive in times of anguish. They all backed one another up, Linda explained; that's what friends do. Friendship was more important than anything. Back when Cokie was on the road for a story and couldn't be reached, for instance, her kids knew they could call the other "mothers" with questions. "We advised them and talked them off the ledge when they got upset," Linda said, even though having not been a parent herself, she wasn't always certain what to say. "And we all waited for Cokie to come home and fix it."

"And she did," said Susan wistfully.

"And she did, yeah," said Linda. You could hear it in her voice, how much she missed her friend—and those old days.

A still photo flashed up on the screen to indicate the end of the program: a shot of all four women standing side by side, clutching bouquets like beauty queens. It was from an event held in their honor at the National Women's Museum, but that was less important than the fact that it was a rare picture where they appeared together. It perfectly punctuated the previous hour of nostalgia with a tinge of the bittersweet. Off-camera, the founding mothers of public radio cooed to each other privately—just like any other girlfriends presented with a snapshot of a happy memory—"I love that picture."

Acknowledgments

The idea for this project was born after I submitted the manuscript for my last book, the origin story of CNN, when I casually mentioned to my editor, Jamison Stoltz, that I planned to get an advanced degree in biography/memoir from CUNY. (I didn't mention the reason: Ageism and dwindling opportunities in journalism had prompted me to think it might be time to teach, and teaching without a master's degree was impossible.)

A few days later, he returned with an idea: What about a biography of Cokie Roberts? She had recently passed away.

I countered: What about the founding mothers of NPR? I didn't know much more about them than the fact that they were a powerful force. But as a woman who began her career in the 1980s and managed to make her way in the field despite the modest means from which I'd sprouted, I'd always been eager to learn the stories of the pioneers.

When I casually mentioned the project to a friend from public radio, Fiona Ng, she enthusiastically urged me to jump in. The milestone fiftieth anniversary of *All Things Considered* in May 2021 hastened along this mammoth project.

Though I've worked in and around public radio since 2004, I've never worked at NPR itself, except as a very occasional contributor. As a reporter and backup host for the show *Marketplace*, produced by American Public Media, which has its own intriguing founding story, I'd learned that the audience rarely understands the labyrinth of entities comprising the public broadcasting system—how they are interrelated and, more important, how they are not.

Because of a magical departure that took me to the Kingdom of Bhutan in 2008 as a volunteer at a brand-new radio station called Kuzoo FM, I'd been fortunate to meet the man known as the founding father of public radio, Bill Siemering. Becoming friends with Bill deepened my interest in understanding his contributions.

Later, after being asked to serve as afternoon drive-time host at public radio station KCRW in Santa Monica, I opted instead for part-time work as an arts reporter, which allowed me to be out in the field instead of locked in a studio. This also allowed me to keep writing books. When I dispatched myself to cover the story of a disintegrating sculpture of a nuclear mushroom cloud that had been anonymously gifted to the city of Santa Monica and discovered the donor was Joan Kroc, I found myself learning more than I ever imagined about this incredible, inventive, and underrecognized philanthropist, one of the greatest of a generation. Mrs. Kroc was seen as the savior of public radio for her landmark posthumous gift to NPR. Selling a book on her incredible life proved impossible until we learned that a Hollywood depiction of her husband was under way; after recasting the book with his name in the title, we found a publisher. All this is to say that, despite my having orbited public radio for quite some time now, I had little idea about the story you have just read until I embarked on this project.

Accomplishing this has been an enormous task in such a short period, one I've relished, particularly as an immersive diversion during this terrible time in world history. After decades of daily deadlines, I now revel in mining archives and digging deep into these important slices of American media history.

So, in addition to Jamison for sparking this idea, as well as Lisa Silverman, Sarah Robbins, and the entire team at Abrams Press for bringing it to life, I'd like to thank Dan Conaway and Lauren Carsley at Writers House, and:

Michael McCauley for his rich repository of oral histories with "NPR originals," as well as his important book about the early history of NPR; Jack Mitchell for his own excellent book and for sharing his memories; Mike Henry at the Library of American Broadcasting at the University of Maryland, a spectacular spot I'm happy to have visited before the pandemic shut it down; J. J. Yore for hiring me at *Marketplace* despite the opposition; the founding mothers themselves allowed this writer, unknown to them, to query them about events from long ago; Ron Bornstein; Jay Kernis; Bob Edwards; Robert Siegel; Art Silverman; Tom Voegeli; Susan Altman; Jim Russell; Jim Schelter; David Michaelis; Mary Lahammer; William Drummond; Barbara Cochran; Fiona Ng and Larry Mantle at KPCC for allowing me the chance to interview Susan live on their air; Andrew Schwartzman, as always, and Diane Luber, too; Rich Radin and Dan Pollack; Tom Thomas; Adam Clayton Powell III; Steve Symonds; Dan Trigoboff; Josh Mankiewicz; Joan and Jill Holtzman; Sydney Ladensohn Stern; Gay Jervey; Diane K. Shah; Skip Pizzi; Alesia Powell, for allowing me to camp out; Libby Lewis; Bernie Woodall; Jeff Kamen; George Hirsch; Richard Toscan; Johnathan Maseda Walton; Matthew Mirapaul; the Friday night Zoom call crew; Alison Berger, for research assistance and moral support; George "Code One" Moore, for the magic password; all my neighbors on Bunker Hill in downtown Los Angeles, where I have been swimming and writing for longer than I ever imagined; and James McGrath Morris, Brian Jay Jones, Sonja Williams, Michael Burgan, and everyone at that indispensable resource from which I've learned so much, the Biographers International Organization.

* * *

My beloved mother, Jane, tolerated and indulged my presence after I got locked down at her home in Florida at the start of the deadly pandemic. (If only I had worked so hard when I was a teenager at Midwood High School as I did during those three months. Who knows what I might have achieved in life?) Camped out in the home office that once belonged to my father, Vincent, I was surrounded by his Ernie Kovacs poster and other ephemera, testaments to his adoration of radio that offered me a bit of solace for not being able to talk about this project with him.

Then there is Ted, who, once again, with immense patience and love, tolerated living with me and my subjects and the deep toll this project took. I can never adequately thank him.

Timeline

September 7, 1938	Susan Levitt (Stamberg) born, Newark, NJ.
March 19, 1943	Linda Cozby (Wertheimer) born, Carlsbad, NM.
December 27, 1943	Cokie Boggs (Roberts) born, New Orleans, LA.
January 14, 1944	Nina Totenberg born, New York, NY.
August 28, 1963	Historic March on Washington for Jobs and Freedom is broadcast in its entirety on a landmark consortium of educational radio stations in the Northeast.
July 2, 1964	Civil Rights Act passed with inclusion of "and sex," leading to the creation of the Equal Employment Opportunity Commission.
November 7, 1967	The words "and radio" are added into the Public Television Act, which becomes the Public Broadcasting Act.
March 1970	Women at *Newsweek* file gender bias lawsuit; sit-in held at *Ladies' Home Journal* by protestors demanding more accurate depictions of women.
March 1970	National Public Radio incorporated with $3.5 million Corporation for Public Broadcasting budget; ninety member stations in thirty-six states.
August 1970	Women's Strike for Equality marks fiftieth anniversary of women's suffrage.
December 1970	Women's National Press Club votes to admit men.
January 1971	National Press Club in Washington, DC, votes to admit women.

January 1971	Hale Boggs elected House majority leader.
March 1971	Linda hired by NPR.
April 1971	Susan hired by NPR.
April 20, 1971	NPR's broadcasting debut features live hearings of Sen. William Fulbright's Senate Foreign Affairs Committee hearings on Vietnam War.
May 3, 1971	NPR debuts *All Things Considered* with host Robert Conley.
December 1971	*Ms.* magazine debuts as insert in *New York* magazine.
March 1972	Susan takes over as permanent cohost of *All Things Considered*, becoming the first woman to anchor a nightly newscast.
March 22, 1972	Congress passes the Equal Rights Amendment after Rep. Martha Griffiths' push. Having fallen short of the additional three state votes to ratify it, a renewed push to enact the amendment (after Virginia's passage of it in early 2020) is under way.
October 16, 1972	Hale Boggs's plane goes missing in Alaska.
December 1972	Bill Siemering leaves NPR.
January 20, 1973	NPR moves to 2025 M Street NW.
March 1973	Lindy Boggs wins special election to fill her husband's congressional seat.
October 1974	Equal Credit Opportunity Act becomes law.
1975	Nina hired by NPR.
August 1977	Frank Mankiewicz hired as NPR's third president.
1978	Cokie hired by NPR.
February 1978	After the Senate passes a special resolution to allow broadcast coverage, Linda hosts Panama Canal debate live over ten weeks.
November 1979	*Morning Edition* debuts with cohosts Bob Edwards and Barbara Hoctor.
October 1979	Susan interviews President Jimmy Carter live on the air in only the second such call-in of its kind.
January 1981	Cokie and Linda join the staff of *The Lawmakers* on PBS.
March 1981	*Star Wars* debuts on NPR.
January 13, 1982	PBS airs *All Things Considered . . . on Main Street* special.
May 1983	Frank is fired from NPR amid mounting financial crisis.
July 1983	NPR receives temporary bailout that saves the network.

1986	Susan leaves as cohost of *All Things Considered*.
May 1988	Cokie is hired by ABC News.
May 1989	Linda becomes cohost of *All Things Considered*.
October 1991	The Clarence Thomas/Anita Hill story propels Nina to the center of a public dialogue on sexual harassment in the workplace.
1993	Bill Siemering awarded MacArthur Fellowship, known as the "genius grant," for his work in establishing community radio around the world.
2002	Linda is replaced on *All Things Considered*.
October 2003	Joan Kroc leaves landmark posthumous gift of more than $225 million to NPR.
September 17, 2019	Cokie dies at National Institutes of Health Hospital, in Bethesda, MD.
March 3, 2020	Star celebrating Susan unveiled on the Hollywood Walk of Fame.

Notes

Prologue: Living Legend

1 antique cherrywood rope bed: Cokie Roberts, *We Are Our Mothers' Daughters* (New York: William Morrow, 1998), 129; and Chuck Conconi, "Cokie Roberts Looks Back on a Teenaged Photo Shoot," *Washingtonian Magazine*, August 1, 1998.

1 "gym teacher" hair: Alison Cook, "One Smart Cokie," *Lear's*, February 1993, 54.

2 "None of us had any ax to grind": David Brinkley, interview with Don Carleton, December 8, 1999, The Interviews, Television Academy Foundation, accessed online, https://interviews.televisionacademy.com/interviews/david-brinkley#about.

3 "magic wands waved against": Stamberg in "Hall of Fame: The Class of 1994," *Broadcasting & Cable*, November 14, 1994, 19.

4 "Cokie knows more about Congress": Brinkley, in Cook, "One Smart Cokie," 54.

4 "She looks nice": Paul Hendrickson, "Roberts Rules," *Washington Post Magazine*, June 20, 1993, N8.

4 "I get the feeling": Claudia Dreifus, "The Midlife Triumph of Cokie Roberts," *TV Guide*, June 19–25, 1993, 22.

5 A natural orator who understood . . . snow and sleet: Kurtz, *Hot Air: All*

NOTES

Talk All the Time—How the Talk Show Culture Has Changed America (New York: Basic Books, 1986), 182.

5 "If you interrupt too much": Cook, "One Smart Cookie."

5 "critical mass in cathode-ray": Hendrickson, "Roberts Rules."

6 "cancer returned?": Comments on "We Know that Trade Wars Create Global Recessions," Powerhouse Roundtable, ABC News, August 2019, https://abcnews.go.com/ThisWeek/video/trade-wars-create-global -recessions-cokie-roberts-65043717.

7 began to believe that modern women: Cokie said modern women were weak "sissies" in many interviews. Here's one: "Journalist, Historian Cokie Roberts Speaks at South Carolina Library Event," WIS News, May 12, 2016, https://www.wistv.com/story/31961865/journalist -historian-cokie-roberts-speaks-at-south-caroliniana-library-event/.

8 After six months of chemotherapy: Erin Kirsten, "The Real Story," *Cancer and You* 4, no. 3, Griffin Publishing Group for RiteAid (2003), 9.

8 She'd pray as she walked: Kerry Kennedy, *Being Catholic Now: Prominent Americans Talk About Change in the Church and the Quest for Meaning* (New York: Crown/Archetype, 2009), 26.

8 "little bit simpleminded": Mary Ann Walsh, "Cokie Roberts: Catholic Woman in the Public Square," *America Magazine,* November 18, 2014, https://www.americamagazine.org/faith/2014/11/18/cokie-roberts -catholic-woman-public-square.

8 In the afterlife, perhaps she'd encounter: Peter Slen, *In Depth with Cokie Roberts,* C-SPAN, December 6, 2015, https://www.c-span.org /video/?326445-1/depth-cokie-roberts&start=0.

9 After the Sunday show: Mark Zimmerman, "Noted Journalist Cokie Roberts Sang in Parish Choir," *Catholic Standard,* September 23, 2019, accessed online, https://cathstan.org/news/local/noted-journalist-cokie -roberts-sang-in-parish-choir-and-supported-her-catholic-school.

9 The valet parking attendants: Steven V. Roberts speaking at the funeral mass for Cokie Roberts, C-SPAN, September 21, 2019, https://www .c-span.org/video/?464579-1/funeral-mass-cokie-roberts.

9 "I'd see her on the other side": Nina Totenberg, "'The Personification of Human Decency': Nina Totenberg Remembers Cokie Roberts," NPR, September 17, 2019, https://www.npr.org/2019/09/17/761597458/the -personification-of-human-decency-nina-totenberg-remembers-cokie -roberts.

9 carry out the values of the document: Linda Wertheimer and Nina

Totenberg, on friend and colleague Cokie Roberts, *PBS News Hour* with Judy Woodruff, https://www.pbs.org/newshour/show/linda-wertheimer-and-nina-totenberg-on-friend-and-colleague-cokie-roberts.

Chapter One: Susan

11 Those voices, she believed, spoke: Diane Casselberry Manuel, "The Woman Behind 'All Things Considered,'" *Christian Science Monitor*, May 20, 1982. Also Susan Stamberg, *Every Night at Five: Susan Stamberg's "All Things Considered"* Book (New York: Pantheon, 1982), 9.

12 Her father, Robert, trotted her around: Susan Stamberg in Elizabeth Benedict, ed., *What My Mother Gave Me: Thirty-One Women on the Gifts That Mattered Most* (Chapel Hill, NC: Algonquin Books, 2013), 217.

12 "just as the voice inside put itself into you": Susan Stamberg, *Talk: NPR's Susan Stamberg Considers All Things* (New York: Random House, 1993), 7.

12 Still, Sue preferred to listen with her eyes open: Resourceful Women Symposium, held at the Library of Congress, June 20, 2003, 2003, Folder 9.0, Box 55, Susan Stamberg papers, 0009-MMC-NPBA, Special Collections, University of Maryland Libraries, College Park, MD.

13 "performer, joke-teller, schmoozer, narrator": Susan Stamberg, Resourceful Women Symposium.

13 She was accustomed to the presents: Stamberg in Benedict, ed., *What My Mother Gave Me*, 218.

13 She'd never seen anything like this: Deborah Ross interviews Susan Stamberg, Jewish Women's Archive, March 28, 2011, https://jwa.org/exhibits/dc/stamberg-susan.

15 "always had a weight issue": Stamberg in Benedict, ed., *What My Mother Gave Me*, 214.

15 "unerring good taste in sound and color": Sue Levitt, Barnard paper on "Music and Art: Social Classes and the Specialized High School," *Soc.* 1–2, January 7, 1957, 8.52.1, Barnard Term Papers, 1956, Folder 1.0, Box: 52, Susan Stamberg papers, 0009-MMC-NPBA, Special Collections, University of Maryland Libraries, College Park, MD.

15 "If we'd gone to some suburban high school": Tara Bahrampour, "La Guardia Reunion Celebrates Youth and the Arts," *New York Times*, June 14, 2000, B15.

15 "Cheery Chatter" column she'd written: Carol Horner, "All Things

Considered, Stamberg's Talk Is Magic," *Chicago Tribune*, May 15, 1982, 14.

15 It was at the paper where she collided: Stamberg, *Talk*, 187.

16 pockmarking their voices with "little prickers": Stamberg, *Talk*, 59.

16 "There is that in me": Susan Stamberg personal email to author, August 16, 2020.

16 Had she attended the area high school: Gus Dallon, "Two Great Schools, One Big Reunion," *New York Daily News*, November 25, 1983, 173.

16 he offered support unthinkable for a man: Ross interviews Stamberg, Jewish Women's Archive, March 28, 2011.

17 "cooperative" rather than a "dominant" position: Elizabeth Halsted, "Liberal Education for Women Urged," *New York Times*, October 3, 1953, 13.

17 This created, she observed, not just a war *between*: Susan Stamberg, "Some Aspects of Chapter Three in 'Women in the Modern World' Reconsidered," February 28, 1958, Sociology 32, 8.52.3, Barnard Term Papers, 1958, Folder 3.0, Box 52, Susan Stamberg papers, 0009-MMC-NPBA, Special Collections, University of Maryland Libraries, College Park, MD.

17 the first married woman to serve as president: Karen W. Arenson, "Millicent McIntosh, 102, Dies; Taught Barnard Women to Balance Career and Family," *New York Times*, January 5, 2001.

18 "less physical strength, a lower fatigue point": Margaret Pickel, "No Jobs for Women," *New York Times Magazine*, January 27, 1946, 110.

18 "ecstasies of intellectual discovery": Stamberg, *Every Night at Five*, 9.

18 "she was well aware that the opportunities: Stamberg, "Some Aspects of Chapter Three in 'Women in the Modern World Reconsidered.'"

18 just one of five of her classmates: Susan Stamberg, personal email to author, August 19, 2020.

19 onetime literary agent who'd switched to publishing: Jessica Weisberg, "Mavis Gallant's Double-Dealing Literary Agent," the *New Yorker*, July 11, 2012.

19 "I Miss Elvis Contest": Susan Stamberg, "Remembering When 'the King' Entered the Army," NPR, March 29, 2008.

19 job as an editorial assistant: Ellie Grossman, "Susan Stamberg: Radio That 'Takes You There' Like a Camera Does," *Napa Valley Register*, January 21, 1980.

20 suffer so intensely: Susan describing Lou's law school experiences in 5.2.55.47, Keynote address, given October 5, 2006, California Women Lawyers Annual Dinner Keynote, held February 2006–October 2006,

Folder 47.0. Box 55, Susan Stamberg papers, 0009-MMC-NPBA, Special Collections, University of Maryland Archives.

20 "Mrs. Miller, Mother of Two Small Children": Megan Rosenfeld, "The Golden Age of Helen Hill Miller," *Washington Post*, July 7, 1992.

24 "there were all those boys who certainly didn't": Randy Sue Cohen, "On the Airwaves with Susan Stamberg," *New Age Magazine*, December 1983, 34.

24 "enormous array of buttons and switches and cords": Susan Stamberg, report on the occasion of WAMU's fifth birthday, 1.2, India, 1966–February 1968, Susan Stamberg papers, 0009-MMC-NPBA, Special Collections, University of Maryland Archives.

24 "keep it up! Put a colon": "March on Washington for Jobs and Freedom: Interview with Susan Stamberg," *OpenVault*, WGBH, March 8, 2011, http://openvault.wgbh.org/catalog/A_D7D11865BB08470EB6471D923001EDB6.

24 "The franticness and excitement never stopped": Stamberg, *Talk*, 46.

Chapter Two: ". . . and sex"

26 "someone might get killed": David Brinkley, *Washington Goes to War* (New York: Alfred A. Knopf, 1988), 83; and Lerone Bennett Jr., "The Day They Didn't March," *Ebony*, February 1977, 128.

27 "conspiracy of men to keep women": Maurine H. Beasley, "The Women's National Press Club: Case Study in the Professionalization of Women Journalists," Paper presented at the Annual Meeting of the Association for Journalism in Education, August 1986, University of Oklahoma, Norman, https://files.eric.ed.gov/fulltext/ED271760.pdf.

27 This upstairs area was jammed: Gil Klein, "The NPC in History: Day Khrushchev Brought Women Down from the Balcony," The National Press Club, March 13, 2019, https://www.press.org/newsroom/npc-history-how-khrushchev-brought-girls-down-balcony.

28 "We find it hard to imagine": Maurine H. Beasley, *The Women's National Press Club: Case Study in the Professionalization of Women*, paper presented at the Annual Meeting of the Association for Education in Journalism and Mass Communication, August 1986, accessed online, https://files.eric.ed.gov/fulltext/ED271760.pdf.

29 confusion over which was the Washington Monument: "March on Washington for Jobs and Freedom: Interview with Susan Stamberg."

29   They worked the phones to line up: "March on Washington for Jobs and Freedom: Interview with Caroline Isber," *OpenVault*, WGBH, March 7, 2011, http://openvault.wgbh.org/catalog/A_168313257D594FA6912DED EF48AFF83A.

32   "bulldog with the jaws of a tiger": William "Fishbait" Miller, *Fishbait: The Memoirs of the Congressional Doorkeeper* (Englewood Cliffs, NJ: Prentice-Hall, 1999), 374.

33   "Men make the laws which govern": Nancy Seifer, "One Woman's Voice: A Simple Question of Justice," *Fond du Lac* (WI) *Reporter*, January 19, 1975, 12.

34   "a turning point in history": Lyndon B. Johnson, "Radio and Television Remarks Upon Signing the Civil Rights Bill," July 2, 1964, Documents, The American Presidency Project, https://www.presidency.ucsb.edu /documents/radio-and-television-remarks-upon-signing-the-civil-rights -bill/.

35   For a time, she even took on the role: Bernie Harrison, "One-Day Network Wonder," *Washington Evening Star*, May 13, 1965.

35   As it had for the March on Washington: "WAMU-FM on the March," (American University) *Eagle*, December 10, 1965, A-9.

35   "designed to be overheard": Ellie Grossman, "Susan Stamberg 'Invents' Radio," *Times and Democrat* (Orangeburg, SC), January 6, 1980, 8.

36   Radio was like a "wonderful novel": Tina Hope Laver, "Educational Radio: WAMU-FM is eight years old this fall. The station encourages an uninhibited policy—speaking out," *Washington Star Sunday Magazine*, November 16, 1969.

36   This was a preparatory trick she borrowed: Randy Sue Coburn, "On the Airwaves with Susan Stamberg," *New Age Journal*, 34.

Chapter Three: "The airwaves belong to all the people"

37   Through his work with the U.S. Agency: Rona Cherry, "WAMU-FM Program Director Going to India," (American University) *Eagle*, January 11, 1966, 5.

38   Susan's Voice of America work was becoming: This and other descriptions from Letter to Roger Penn, 1.2, India, 1966–February 1968, Susan Stamberg papers, 0009-MMC-NPBA, Special Collections and University Archives, University of Maryland, College Park, MD.

39   "marvelous, warm and mystifying busy-ness": Letter, July 13, 1967,

Susan Stamberg papers, Box: 4, Folder: 12.0, University of Maryland, College Park, MD.

39 Susan was thrilled to receive a letter: Letter from Roger Penn, July 25, 1967, Susan Stamberg papers, Box: 4, Folder: 12.0, University of Maryland, College Park, MD.

39 "smoke from angry fires": Susan Stamberg, *Talk: NPR's Susan Stamberg Considers All Things* (New York: Random House, 1993), 13.

39 Amid this backdrop: James Reston, "LBJ's Network of Knowledge," *New York Times*, November 9, 1967.

41 "undernourished and sickly enterprise": Robert K. Avery, "The Public Broadcasting Act of 1967: Radio's Real Second Chance," *Journal of Radio and Audio Media* 24, no. 2 (n.d.): 189–99.

42 Just as the words "and sex" had been slipped into: For a complete description of the twists and turns of inserting radio into the Public Broadcasting Act, see Michael McCauley, *The Trials and Triumphs of National Public Radio* (New York: Columbia University Press, 2005); and Jack Mitchell, *Listener Supported: The Culture and History of Public Radio* (New York: Praeger, 2005).

43 "That is the purpose of this act": Lyndon B. Johnson, "Radio and Television Remarks Upon Signing the Public Broadcasting Bill."

43 Several years later: McCauley, *The Trials and Triumphs of National Public Radio*, 23.

43 Associates described him as: Jack Mitchell, interview by Michael McCauley, August 28, 1995, Box 14, Michael P. McCauley papers, University of Maryland Special Collections, College Park, MD.

44 "but the whites, too, who had never heard": Marc Fisher, *Something in the Air: Radio, Rock, and the Revolution that Shaped a Generation* (New York: Penguin Random House, 2009), p. 173; also, Bill Siemering, conversations with author.

44 "The idea," Siemering said: Fisher, *Something in the Air*, 174.

45 "We need a more accurate barometer of": Bill Siemering, "Public Broadcasting: Some Essential Ingredients," *Educational/Instructional Magazine*, November 1969, 65–69.

46 "WAMU-FM provides an outlet": Tina Hope Laver, "Educational Radio: WAMU-FM Is Eight Years Old This Fall," *Washington Star Sunday*, November 16, 1969; clip in Susan Stamberg papers, Series 1, Box 1, Folder 6, University of Maryland Special Collections, College Park, MD.

46 "strict adherence of objectivity and balance": Scott Custin, "WAMU-FM Staffer Resigns, Charges Censorship, Poor Quality," (American University) *Eagle*, December 19, 1969, 10.

Chapter 4: Linda

50 "Girl Born to Cozbys": "Girl Born to Cozbys," *Carlsbad Current-Argus*, March 21, 1943, 6.

51 "I wish to continue serving the cash": "Miller Cozby Buys Grocery Store," *Carlsbad Current-Argus*, May 21, 1946, 1.

51 His younger daughter, Nancy, might cry: "No Matter the Menu, Wertheimer's New Mexico Family Comes to the Table," NPR, December 24, 2016, https://www.npr.org/2016/12/24/506721928/no-matter-the-menu-wertheimers-new-mexico-family-comes-to-the-table.

51 After these delicacies were removed: Linda Wertheimer, "Autumnal Calm in Turbulent Times," NPR, November 12, 2011, https://www.wbur.org/npr/142270027/autumnal-calm-in-turbulent-times.

51 "soft spot for overripe fruit": Linda Wertheimer, "The Basted Egg: A Foolproof Play on the Poach," NPR, August 9, 2015, https://www.npr.org/sections/thesalt/2015/08/06/430069996/the-basted-egg-a-foolproof-play-on-the-poach.

52 Concerned when she learned about unequal: Lisa A. Phillips, *Public Radio: Behind the Voices* (New York: Vanguard Press, 2006), 54.

52 "that beautiful park in the center": Ellen Harbaugh, "Libraries Change Lives," *Carlsbad Current-Argus*, April 17, 1994, D2.

52 As a kid growing up on a nearby ranch: "You Can't Keep a Good Librarian Down," *Carlsbad Current-Argus*, February 26, 1984, H4.

52 She routinely made the scholar's list: Rachel Prentice, "Whatever Happened to . . . ," *Carlsbad Current-Argus*, April 28, 1991.

53 sitting by an irrigation ditch that ran past: Sharon Nymeyer, "Local Girl Makes National News," *Carlsbad Current-Argus*, April 18, 1982, 17.

53 The drama of the vast corruption: Susan Sullivan and Lillian Stenfeldt, "Renowned Journalist Linda Wertheimer Discusses Her Career, Politics, and Women in the Workforce," *Sedgwick Newsletters*, December 1, 2014, https://casetext.com/analysis/renowned-journalist-linda-wertheimer-discusses-her-career-politics-and-women-in-the-workforce-1.

53 When it came to keeping up with: "Current-Argus Invites Public to Visit New Building Today," *Carlsbad Current-Argus*, September 16, 1951, 1.

53 Her dad liked to listen to Paul Harvey: Suzanne Perry, "All Things Considered, She's Glad She's in Radio," *Minneapolis Star*, February 10, 1979, 2.

54 "138 feet taller than the Empire State Building": "Tall Tower Proposed," *Ponca City News*, July 1, 1955, 1.

54 In newspaper ads for their products: Gamble's ad, *Carlsbad Current-Argus*, October 28, 1953, 5.

54 Two hundred locals stood in: Buck Lanier, "Water Pistol Hits Caverns," *Carlsbad Current-Argus*, November 28, 1955, 1.

55 This technological feat paled: Amita Parashar Kelly, "The Broadcast Pioneers," *Wellesley Magazine*, Winter 2020, https://magazine.wellesley .edu/winter-2020/the-broadcast-pioneers.

55 "To hell with being Edward R. Murrow's": Sullivan and Sienfeldt, "Renowned Journalist Linda Wertheimer Discusses Her Career."

55 "didn't know women could do that": Dreifus, "Cokie Roberts, Nina Totenberg, Linda Wertheimer."

56 "authoritative personality that men do": Joseph Cook, radio executive, in Graham, "Women Don't Like to Look at Women," *New York Times Sunday Magazine*, May 24, 1964, 48.

56 "At times, it was so discouraging": Judy Flander, "First Woman TV Reporter Pauline Frederick: From 'Women's News'" to UN Correspondent," *Washington Star*, 1976, reprinted February 9, 2019, https://judy flander.org/first-woman-tv-reporter-pauline-frederick-from-womens -news-to-un-correspondent-5c23cb0b6752.

57 The other story involved an important meeting: Pierre J. Huss, "Big 4 Stages Preliminary Discussions," (New Philadelphia, OH) *Daily Times*, November 4, 1946, 1.

58 "goddess with the right hairdo": Gloria Steinem, "Nylons in the Newsroom," *New York Times*, November 7, 1965, X23.

59 Her mother favored Mills: "Senior NPR Correspondent Linda Wertheimer at Mills College," YouTube, March 13, 2013, https://www.youtube .com/watch?v=bmvPofcm-M.

59 but Mrs. Charles Feezer, a neighbor: UPI, "Local Girl Has Summer Job Working in Washington," *Carlsbad Current-Argus*, July 14, 1963, 18.

60 "fixin' to," and her use of two syllables: "Broadcaster Linda Wertheimer on the Start of 'All Things Considered,'" interview, *Fresh Air with Terry Gross*, NPR, April 5, 1995, https://freshairarchive.org/search?keyword =Linda%20Wertheimer.

60   It was so clunky: "Linda Wertheimer's Commencement Address to the Wellesley College Class of 2003," My Wellesley, June 7, 2003, https://www .wellesley.edu/events/commencement/archives/2003commencement /commencementaddress.

60   Though she was not married herself: "Miss Margaret Clapp Resigns as Wellesley College President," *New York Times*, August 12, 1965, 14.

61   "You may have to work your ass off": Kelly, "The Broadcast Pioneers."

61   Midway through her sophomore year: "Sun Princess," *Carlsbad Current-Argus*, December 30, 1962, 1.

61   It was a family joke: Rachel Prentice, "Whatever Happened To: Wertheimer Has the Nation's Ear," *Carlsbad Current-Argus*, April 28, 1991, 18.

62   of around seven hundred dollars: Linda's salary in "Report of the Secretary of the Senate, from July 1, 1963 to June 30, 1964," https://books .google.com/books?id=_BA7AQAAMAAJ&pg=PA17&lpg=PA17&dq =Linda+Cozby+Senator+Anderson&source=bl&ots=CKUaeZdMHo&sig =ACfU3U3AZCnNCJ5l-_CFcMlgozhtwiE2UA&hl=en&sa=X&ved=2ah UKEwjE75_ahbjrAhUyKXoKHdhnDNYQ6AEwAH0ECAEQAQ#v=one page&q=Linda%20Cozby%20Senator%20Anderson&f=false.

62   "subtle facts of politics": "Local Girl Has Summer Job Working in Washington," *Carlsbad Current-Argus*, July 14, 1963, 18.

62   "I hope windows have been opened to you": George McKinnon, "Wellesley Grads Told to Join Poverty Fight," *Boston Globe*, June 8, 1965, 21.

62   To raise money for her plane ticket: Linda Wertheimer, WFAE Founding Mothers Event, Online via Zoom, August 29, 2020.

62   She was assigned to work at the BBC: "Community Concert Drive Hits Midway Point Today," *Carlsbad Current-Argus*, February 22, 1967, 1.

63   "It was in neon": Dreifus, "Cokie Roberts, Nina Totenberg, Linda Wertheimer."

63   Ads blanketed the city to trumpet: Martin Hardee, "WCBS Newsradio 88: A Historical Perspective from 1978," NY Radio News, http://www .nyradionews.com/wcbs/.

63   "flat-chested, brainy, dark": Mary Collins, *National Public Radio: The Cast of Characters* (Washington, DC: Seven Locks Press, 1993), 129–30.

64   "Loophole women": Caroline Bird, *Born Female* (New York: David McKay), 99–129; and Susan Brownmiller, *In Our Time: Memoir of a Revolution* (New York: Dial Press, 1999), 2.

64   She'd have been better off staying at the paper: Mary Pangalos, email to author, February 18, 2020.

Chapter Five: Purposes

66 "believed in playing by the rules": Barbara Slavin, "Major Rebel with a Common Cause Leaves Limelight," *Los Angeles Times*, November 20, 1994.

66 After Fred and Linda married: Interview with Fred Wertheimer, conducted by Susanne Abel, 2018, John W. Gardner Legacy Oral History Project (SC1355), Department of Special Collections and University Archives, Stanford Libraries, Stanford, CA.

66 The founders of National Public Radio: Joseph Brady Kirkish, "A Descriptive History of America's National Public Radio Network: National Public Radio, 1970–1974," PhD diss., University of Michigan, 1980, 12.

67 "Fertilizing the wastelands of the airwaves": Claudia Levy, "Broadcast Journalist Edward P. Morgan Dies," *Washington Post*, January 29, 1993.

68 Quayle and Siemering decided he had just: Kirkish, "A Descriptive History of America's National Public Radio Network: National Public Radio, 1970–1974," 35.

68 Foster turned down the chance to leave: Siemering, email to author, March 19, 2020.

68 "celebrate the human experience": "Bill Siemering Author of NPR's 1970 Mission Statement," *The Pub* (podcast), 2016, SoundCloud, https://soundcloud.com/currentpubmedia/bill-siemering-author-of-nprs-1970-mission-statement?in=currentpubmedia/sets/bill-siemering-author-of-nprs-1970-mission-statement.

69 "God, I'd love to do this": Bill Siemering, interview with Michael McCauley, August 8, 1995, Michael P. McCauley papers, Box 14, University of Maryland, College Park, MD.

70 She didn't have a preference: Linda K. Wertheimer, "A Tale of Two Lindas," *Lincoln* (NE) *Journal Star*, June 23, 1998, 19.

70 Siemering hired the best people he could: Bill Siemering, interview with Michael McCauley, August 8, 1995.

70 Suggestions included *Our Daily Bread*: Mitchell, *Listener Supported*, 67.

71 "The pieces were all the wrong": Kirkish, "A Descriptive History of America's National Public Radio Network: National Public Radio, 1970–1974," 82.

71 install a giant assignment whiteboard: Linda Wertheimer, interview with Michael McCauley, August 18, 1995, Michael P. McCauley Papers, Box 14, University of Maryland, College Park, MD.

72 "But, of course it's the war and stopping it": Associated Press, "Like Woodstock," *Indianapolis News*, May 1, 1971, 2.

72 "scented with spring flowers and tear gas": Linda Wertheimer, ed., *Listening to America: 25 Years in the Life of a Nation, as Heard on National Public Radio* (New York: Houghton Mifflin, 1995), xvii.

74 "A daily program was just like the dishes": In Cokie Roberts et al., *This Is NPR: The First Forty Years* (San Francisco: Chronicle Books, 2012), 15.

Chapter Six: Nina

75 "agreeable" and "efficient": *New York Herald Tribune*, November 20, 1936.

75 important women often proved: Elizabeth Clark, "Our Women 'Amazing' to Warsaw Musician," *New York Times*, November 20, 1935.

75 "You here are well put-together": Clark, "Our Women."

76 Mr. Totenberg, Mrs. Roosevelt reported in her syndicated: Eleanor Roosevelt, *My Day*, January 4, 1936, https://www2.gwu.edu/~erpapers/myday/displaydoc.cfm?_y=1936&_f=md054224.

78 They married eight months later: Roman Totenberg, *Old New York Stories* (blog), September 30, 2009, https://www.oldnewyorkstories.com/post/11666770971/roman-totenberg.

78 "I think everybody here is a big doody": Nina Totenberg, phone call with author, January 18, 2020.

79 "living vehicle of human expression": Bruce Weber, "Roman Totenberg, Violinist and Teacher, Dies at 101," *New York Times*, May 9, 2012, B19.

79 The lesson was made easier when: Brian Lamb, "Life and Career of Nina Totenberg," C-SPAN, January 7, 1992, https://www.c-span.org/video/?24046-1/life-career-nina-totenberg.

79 The most disruptive of antics: "Hurt by Firecrackers," *Scarsdale Inquirer*, November 9, 1956, 2.

80 But just as her mother had dropped piano: Nina Totenberg, telephone conversation with author, January 18, 2020.

80 Searching for a role model: Euna Kwon Brossman, "Not Nancy Drew but Close Enough," Princeton Info, May 10, 2006, https://princetoninfo.com/not-nancy-drew-but-close-enough-2/.

80 "so she didn't even have to compete": Chitra Ragavan interviews Nina Totenberg, *When It Mattered* (podcast), Good Story, August 27, 2019, https://goodstory.io/when-it-mattered/.

80 "[I]t is still hard to believe that high school": "Diary Cast Will Tour Israel: Poignant Drama Given Powerful Production," *Scarsdale Inquirer,* April 26, 1962, 1.

81 "I wouldn't be surprised": Marie Torre, "CBS Can't Get Judy to Make Up Her Mind on Spectacular Chore," *Philadelphia Inquirer,* January 11, 1957, 26.

82 "I have great hope": Edward Ranzal, "Marie Torre Starts 10-Day Sentence for Refusal to Tell News Source," *New York Times,* January 6, 1959, 22.

82 Her desire to have a "seat at the table": Nina said in a number of instances that reporting was just a fancy way of saying gossip, including in Raga-van interviews Nina Totenberg, August 27, 2019.

83 "Nina, we're both freshmen": Roman Totenberg, *Old New York Stories.*

83 cut classes "like mad": Gay Jervey, "Diva Nina," *The American Lawyer,* November 1993, 54.

83 "way too stupid": Noah Rubinton, "The Country's Reflection," *Brown Alumni Magazine,* November/December 2015, https://www.brownalumni magazine.com/articles/2015-11-13/the-countrys-reflection.

83 "lousy, lousy SAT scores": "CJS15 Graduation," Nina Totenberg's com-mencement speech at the Columbia Journalism School graduation, May 20, 2015, https://www.youtube.com/watch?v=Gzy1iM4fGbs.

83 "dream of a torn-off head": "Radio News Journalism," C-SPAN, Decem-ber 12, 1995, https://www.c-span.org/video/?68886-1/radio-news -journalism.

83 a "tough broad," Nina observed: Ellie Wymard, *Conversations with Uncom-mon Women: Insights from Women Who've Risen Above Life's Challenges to Achieve Extraordinary Success* (New York: AMACOM Books, 1999), 136.

84 "Nina, are you a virgin?": Ibid.

85 She was relieved when a priest: Nina Totenberg, WFAE Founding Moth-ers Event, online via Zoom, August 29, 2020.

86 To create a tabloid: Jack Limpert, "Becoming a Washington Journalist— and Editing Damon Runyon, Jr.," *About Writing and Editing* (blog), July 8, 2014, https://jacklimpert.com/2014/07/becoming-washington -journalist-editing-damon-runyon-jr/.

87 begging for someone to hire her: Jervey, "Diva Nina," 54.

87 Members continued to believe: "Women in National Press Club," C-SPAN, May 15, 1996, https://www.c-span.org/video/?72041-1/women -national-press-club.

87 "Start mixing the sexes and you know what you'll": Art Buchwald, "They

Have a Lady in Their Balcony," (Rochester, NY) *Democrat and Chronicle*, August 29, 1963, 28.

87 Swallowed her innate shyness and: David Michaelis, *Eleanor Roosevelt* (New York: Simon & Schuster, 2020).

88 One year, she declared it a costume: "Gridiron Widows Hold Own Show: With Mrs. Roosevelt as the Hostess, They Cavort in Stunts at White House," *New York Times*, December 22, 1936, 25.

88 Hundreds of counter-revelers: Karen Peterson, "Counter Gridiron on Way to Equaling '74 Success," *South Bend* (IN) *Tribune*, February 25, 1975, 27.

88 As a blue-jean clad bluegrass: "Boycott of Gridiron Fete Urged," *Los Angeles Times*, December 21, 1973, e22.

89 Loud and clear, she shouted out to arriving: Nina Totenberg, telephone conversation with author, February 2020.

Chapter Seven: *Ms.*

91 Had they called them: *NPR American Chronicles: Women's Equality*, audiobook read by Susan Stamberg, Highbridge Audio, March 2012.

92 she easily got the buy-in: "Griffiths, Martha Wright, 1912–2003," History, Art & Archives, United States House of Representatives, https://history. house.gov/People/Detail/14160.

93 To jab at the absurdity: "Leading Feminist Puts Hairdo Before Strike," *New York Times*, August 27, 1970, 30.

93 Never mind that the first Pulitzer: Nan Robertson, *The Girls in the Balcony: Women, Men and the New York Times* (New York: Random House, 1992), 20.

93 "Why don't you go home and get": Ibid., 139.

94 "Great legs, face only fair": Ibid., 183.

94 Joining their sisters at *Newsweek, Time*: "Harriet S. Rabb Oral History. Part 3: First Case" (video), The Rockefeller University, 2017, https://digital commons.rockefeller.edu/harriet-rabb/5.

96 "teaspoon to fill the Grand Canyon": Jeff Rosenberg, interviewed by Michael McCauley, August 14, 1995. Michael P. McCauley Papers, University of Maryland Special Collections and University Archives, College Park, MD.

96 hurled in there "like Frisbees": Cokie Roberts et al., *This Is NPR: The First Forty Years* (San Francisco: Chronicle Books, 2012), 15.

96 "Shape, form, style": Memo in Kirkish, "A Descriptive History of America's National Public Radio Network: National Public Radio, 1970–1974," 98.

97 As much as management might like the idea: Ibid., 146; Susan Stamberg, email to author, July 13, 2020.

97 One week, when the new cohost: "Susan Stamberg's 'Every Night at Five,'" *Fresh Air with Terry Gross*, NPR, May 3, 1982, https://freshair archive.org/segments/susan-stambergs-every-night-five.

97 "toilet bowl flush": Roberts et al., *This Is NPR*, 29.

97 "That's too many women": Susan Stamberg, *Talk: NPR's Susan Stamberg Considers All Things* (New York: Random House, 1993).

99 "I'm a feminist": Abigail Pogrebin, "How Do You Spell Ms.," *New York*, October 28, 2011.

Chapter Eight: Scoop

101 "It just seemed logical to": Jennifer Yachnin, "Sid Yudain, the Man Who Started It All," *Roll Call*, June 9, 2005.

101 Nixon wrote an obituary: *Roll Call* Staff, "Remembering the Little Paper that Could," *Roll Call*, June 10, 2005.

101 "Hill Pinup" . . . "the pixie 106-pounder": Bree Hocking, "'Pinups' Move on to Bigger Things," *Roll Call*, September 9, 2004, https://www.rollcall .com/2004/09/09/pinups-move-on-to-bigger-things/; Rachel Laura Pierce, "Capitol Feminism: Work, Politics and Gender in Congress, 1960–1980," PhD diss., University of Virginia, 2014.

102 "Oriental food gives me the trots": Adrienne LaFrance, "Nina Totenberg: What It Was Like to Be the Only Woman in the Newsroom," Medium .com, February 13, 2014, https://medium.com/the-only-woman-in-the -room/nina-totenberg-what-it-was-like-to-be-the-only-woman-in-the -newsroom-19fadba096c4.

103 "This was a very tall mountain to climb": Nina Totenberg at WFAE Founding Mothers Event, online via Zoom, August 29, 2020.

103 "sparkling, provocative and electric": Richard J. Tofel, *Restless Genius: Barney Kilgore, the Wall Street Journal, and the Invention of Modern Journalism* (New York: St. Martin's Press, 2009).

103 "didn't know anything from Shinola": Panel Discussion, "Reed v. Reed at 40: Equal Protection and Women's Rights," *Journal of Gender, Social Policy and the Law* 20, no. 2 (2011): Art. 1.

103 "too young and too stupid": Thomas Looker, *The Sound and the Story: NPR and the Art of Radio* (New York: Houghton Mifflin Harcourt, 1995), 386.

103 Nina flipped to the front: Nina has told this story many times, but I cite it here from Gretchen DeSutter, "Nina Totenberg: From the Fallopian Jungle to the Supreme Court Press Corps" (video), Legal Current, Thomson Reuters, November 21, 2014, http://www.legalcurrent.com /nina-totenberg-from-the-fallopian-jungle-to-the-supreme-court-press -corps/.

105 "This could be a very different country": Lamb, "Life and Career of Nina Totenberg."

105 "covering nine presidencies at the same time": Lisa Ryan, "Nina Totenberg: How I Get It Done," *The Cut*, June 11, 2019, https://www.thecut .com/2019/06/nina-totenberg-npr-supreme-court-how-i-get-it-done .html.

105 "It's about time women grew up": Nina Totenberg, "Women Out to Be Life of the Parties: Activists Train Female Pols to Grab Power in the Conventions," *National Observer*, February 12, 1972, 24.

105 Mother Blackmun revealed that: Bob Woodward, *The Brethren: Inside the Supreme Court* (New York: Simon & Schuster, 2005), 87; also, in Jervey, "Diva Nina," 54.

106 "an extra pair of hands to help wash dishes": Letter from Nina Totenberg to Judge Harry and Mrs. Blackmun, April 27, 1970, "April 1970 General Correspondence" Folder, Box 1360, Harry Blackmun Papers, Library of Congress, Washington, DC.

106 "Like blackmail or heroin": Letter from Warren Burger to Harry Blackmun, "April 1970 General Correspondence" Folder, Box 1360, Harry Blackmun Papers, Library of Congress, Washington, DC.

106 "rips hard right down the middle": Henry Gemmill, "Postscript from the Editor," *National Observer*, February 12, 1972, 25.

106 "It was awful": Howard Kurtz, "The Legal Reporter's Full Court Press," *Washington Post*, October 10, 1991.

106 A woman lucky enough to land a job: Diane K. Shah, *A Farewell to Arms, Legs and Jockstraps: A Sportswriter's Memoir* (Bloomington, IN: Red Lightning Books, 2020), 13.

107 "master of political influence": Nina Totenberg, "Hoover: The Life and Times of a 76-Year-Old Cop," *National Observer*, April 12, 1971.

107 "I dare say I am the only": Gemmill, "Postscript from the Editor," 25.

107 a profile of Tip O'Neill: Nina Totenberg, "Tip O'Neill: An Old Pol Spots the New Issues," *National Observer,* January 13, 1973.

108 "scared the holy beejezus": Albert Hunt, "Tales of Ignominy: Beyond Thomas and Hill," *Wall Street Journal,* October 17, 1991.

108 No branch of government, she said: Nina Totenberg, "Beneath the Marble, Beneath the Robes," *New York Times Magazine,* March 16, 1975, SM14.

108 "classically segregated work force": Nina Totenberg, "The Supreme Court: The Last Plantation," *New Times,* July 26, 1974, 26.

109 another memorable sensation: Nina Totenberg, "The Ten Dumbest Congressmen," *New Times,* July 1974, 14.

109 "I wouldn't dignify that prostitute": Frederick L. Berns, "Erie Congressman Steams over 'Dumbest' Labeling," *Simpson's Leader-Times* (Kittanning, PA), June 6, 1974, 1.

109 The man whom she'd crowned: Harry Stein, "How I Accidentally Joined the Vast Right-wing Conspiracy," *Booknotes,* C-SPAN, http://booknotes.org /FullPage.aspx?SID=158396-1.

110 Being able to tap into a reporter: Bob Zelnick, interview with Michael McCauley, August 11, 1995. Michael P. McCauley Oral History Collection, University of Maryland, College Park, MD.

110 For a while, she'd enjoyed her time: Marilyn S. Greenwald, *Pauline Frederick Reporting* (Lincoln, NE: Potomac Books/University of Nebraska Press, 2015), 244.

111 Frederick loved being back on the radio: Frederick, in internal "NPR Report," 26, undated, Pauline Frederick papers, Box 18, Folder 13, Sophia Smith Collection, Smith College, Northampton, MA.

111 "I'm much prettier": Michael H. Hodges, "The Divine Ms. N," *Detroit News,* January 18, 1992, C1.

112 "There's no stopping her": Jervey, "Diva Nina," 54.

Chapter Nine: Cokie

113 Eleven years later: Lindy Boggs, *Washington Through a Purple Veil: Memoirs of a Southern Woman* (New York: Harcourt, Brace and Company, 1994), 89–90.

113 "After the sun goes down": Ibid., 78.

115 "refined, educated, intelligent": Burt Solomon, *The Washington Century: Three Families and the Shaping of the Nation's Capital* (New York: Harper Perennial, 2005), 271; and Boggs, *Washington Through a Purple Veil,* 101.

115 "I decided if I could get sick": Boggs, *Washington Through a Purple Veil*, 19.

115 Lindy might have had a silver spoon: Myra MacPherson, "Lindy Boggs Running for Hale's Old Seat," (Rochester, NY) *Democrat and Chronicle*, March 8, 1973, C1.

115 "because everybody loved me": Kenneth A. Weiss, "Lindy Boggs a Contradiction," *Atlanta Constitution*, July 17, 1976, 12B.

116 She was doing others a favor: Boggs, *Washington Through a Purple Veil*, 106, 42.

116 The other gift the sisters imparted: Bess Carrick, prod., *Lindy Boggs: Steel and Velvet*, documentary, Louisiana Public Broadcasting, 2006, http://ladigitalmedia.org/video_v2/asset-detail/LLBSV, http://ladigital media.org/video_v2/asset-detail/LLBSV.

117 Working as part of Hale's staff: Bruce Collins, "Life and Career of Lindy Boggs" (video), C-SPAN, August 2, 1990. https://www.c-span.org /video/?13795-1/life-career-lindy-boggs.

118 "learning about different cultures": Boggs, *Washington Through a Purple Veil*, 59.

119 Mondays meant paying: Ibid., 102.

119 He recognized the asset he had: Hon. Mary Rose Oakar, "The Boggs Legacy," Extensions of Remarks, January 23, 1984, https://www.govinfo .gov/content/pkg/GPO-CRECB-1984-pt1/pdf/GPO-CRECB-1984-pt1-1-3 .pdf.

120 "He honored me by": Garry Boulard, *The Big Lie: Hale Boggs, Lucille May Grace, and Leander Perez* (Gretna, LA: Pelican Publishing Company, 2001), 79.

120 Eventually, he put her on the: "Alexandria, La. Congressmen Put Kin on Payroll," *Town Talk*, February 24, 1959, p. 2; and William McGaffin, "Congressman and Family Net $40,000," *Charlotte NC News*, March 14, 1963, 1.

120 Still, when she traveled back to the constituents: Sarah Booth Conroy, "Lindy Is a Lady in Louisiana, Talks Politics from a Rocking Chair," *Washington Post*, May 25, 1958, F11.

120 pushed her man into a more progressive: Boggs, *Washington Through a Purple Veil*, 174.

120 "In cooperating with his tendency": Ibid., 175.

121 "constitutional miracle": Ibid., 268.

121 "pink as a wedding cake": Ibid., 74.

121   The very beauty of: Carol Saline and Sharon J. Wohlmuth, *Mothers and Daughters* (New York: Doubleday, 1997), 114.

121   "Hale Boggs ain't no Communist": Boulard, *The Big Lie*, 184.

122   You might think someone was wrong: "Cokie Roberts," Oral History, History, Art & Archives, U.S. House of Representatives, August 28, 2007, https://history.house.gov/Oral-History/People/Cokie-Roberts/.

122   After all, she was considered capable: Ibid.

123   That the girl had been baptized "Rebecca": Ibid. and Solomon, *The Washington Century*, 80.

123   "Some people have antiques and jewelry:" Carl Bernstein, "King of the Hill," *Vanity Fair*, March 1998, 174.

123   Distressed to see little Cokie: Boggs, *Washington Through a Purple Veil*, 140–41.

124   Since age five, she'd been indoctrinated: "Cokie Boggs Roberts '60" (video), Cor Unum/One Heart, https://www.stoneridgeschool.org/campaign/join-us/make-a-gift/pillars/cokie-roberts.

124   Though as reverent an admirer: Paul Hendrickson, "Roberts Rules," *Washington Post*, June 20, 1993.

125   "We've left our baby in a Yankee": "Cokie Roberts' Address to Wellesley's Graduating Class of 1994," My Wellesley, https://www.wellesley.edu/events/commencement/archives/1994commencement/commencementaddress.

125   "Oh, she's the daughter of the House": Dreifus, "Cokie Roberts, Nina Totenberg, Linda Wertheimer."

125   "You're so efficient": Cokie Roberts and Steven V. Roberts, *From This Day Forward* (New York: William Morrow, 2000), 3.

126   "white, racist, imperialist": Cook, "One Smart Cokie," 55.

126   "someone of Irish and Italian extraction": Mary Ann Walsh, "Cokie Roberts, Catholic Woman in a Public Square," *America*, November 18, 2014.

126   "supposed" to go out with: Steven V. Roberts, *My Fathers' Houses: Memoir of a Family* (New York: William Morrow, 2005), 201.

127   "thinking WASPs were a minority group": Steven V. Roberts, *From Every End of This Earth: 13 Families and the New Lives They Made in America* (New York: Harper, 2009), 3.

129   Later, Steve began to suspect that might: Nancy L. Segal, *Entwined Lives: Twins and What They Tell Us About Human Behavior* (New York: Dutton, 1999), 262.

129   drag strips for teenagers: "Bayonne Boy Elected Next N.J. 'Governor,'"
      (Camden, NJ) *Courier-Post*, July 27, 1959, 3.

129   whom he'd first encountered: Steven V. Roberts, "Bayonne, Pop-Culture
      Titan (Sort-of)," *New York Times*, June 12, 2005, NJ14.

130   he even wrote a story about taking a girl: Steven V. Roberts, "My Date:
      Rain and a Gung-Ho Girl," *Harvard Crimson*, November 5, 1962. https://
      www.thecrimson.com/article/1962/11/5/my-date-rain-and-a-gung-ho/.

130   The first story he filed: Steven V. Roberts, interviewed on *Charlie Rose*
      (video), May 18, 2005, https://charlierose.com/videos/9809.

131   tinged, a bit, by envy: Roberts and Roberts, *From This Day Forward*, 232.

131   "six to twelve children": Richard K. Rein, "Hale and Lindy Boggs' Daugh-
      ter Is Following in Their Campaign Trails," *People*, May 24, 1982, 107.

132   "a little restorative toddy": Boggs, *Washington Through a Purple Veil*, 201.

134   By the time of Harvard's own grand: John H. Fenton, "Harvard Cites 17
      in Commencement," *New York Times*, June 12, 1964, 40.

136   "With all respects," said the novice: Cokie Boggs (moderator), "Sena-
      tor McCarthy Quizzed on CIA Control," *Meeting of the Minds*, May 26,
      1966. https://www.cia.gov/library/readingroom/docs/CIA-RDP75
      -00149R000500020024-2.pdf.

137   "There's nothing better than working in Washington": Steven V. Roberts,
      "Another First for Nancy," *New York Times*, January 3, 1965, x16.

138   women were trained to give: Roberts and Roberts, *From This Day For-
      ward*, 17.

138   "demonic intensity": William H. Chafe, *Never Stop Running: Allard Low-
      enstein and the Struggle to Save American Liberalism* (New York: Basic
      Books, 1993), 110.

139   "but for the sword, the dear old sword there": Ibid., 153.

139   At the wedding of his sister: Ibid., 154.

139   "fundamental differences": Ibid., 496.

140   "We don't do things in a": Solomon, *Washington Century*, 140.

140   "Yes, I do think you'll have problems": Roberts and Roberts, *From This
      Day Forward*, 19.

140   "That's a party": Ibid., 25; and Boggs, *Washington Through a Purple
      Veil*, 205.

141   "like looking for an abortionist": Solomon, *Washington Century*, 176.

142   "Some gals might have caved in": Associated Press, "Bride-to-be Sur-
      mounts a Ghastly Situation," September 10, 1966.

Chapter Ten: "Not even slightly a feminist"

144 The ugly interior was made worse: Roberts and Roberts, *From This Day Forward*, 86.

145 "I knew an 'Our servants are so close'": Cokie Roberts, *We Are Our Mothers' Daughters* (New York: William Morrow, 1998), 176.

145 she began to feel like a "basket case": Roberts and Roberts, *From This Day Forward*, 38.

146 "happily ever after" feeling: Ibid., 90.

146 Over a bottle of Asti Spumante: Ibid., 92.

147 "lunch at the fancy Pump Room: WFAE Editor, "50 Years Later: Cokie Roberts on the 1968 Democratic Convention," WFAE, August 30, 2018, https://www.wfae.org/post/50-years-later-cokie-roberts-1968-democratic-convention#stream/0.

147 "kid following the high school band": Steven V. Roberts, "*We* Had a Baby," *Good Housekeeping*, May 1969, 102.

148 "advanced case of Eastern myopia": Steven V. Roberts, *Eureka!: Earthquakes, Chicanos, Celebrities, Smog, Feds, Outdoor Living, Charles Manson's Legacy, Berkeley Rebels, San Francisco Scenes, Southern California Style, Ronald Reagan, and Other Discoveries in the Golden State of California* (New York: Quadrangle Books/New York Times Book Company, 1974), XI.

149 It was worth the hassle for the chance: Roberts, *Eureka!*, 73, 259.

149 While researching a story on the rise of pornography: Ibid., 113.

149 "just" a wife and mother: Roberts and Roberts, *From This Day Forward*, 120.

150 "You won't recognize nine-tenths of them": Roberts and Roberts, "What's Doing in Los Angeles," *New York Times*, October 21, 1973, 560.

150 Then it would occur to her: Roberts and Roberts, *From This Day Forward*, 148.

Chapter Eleven: Woman, Ascendant

151 The last years had been tough: Roger Davidson, *Masters of the House* (Transforming American Politics series) (Abingdon, UK: Taylor and Francis, 2018), 240; and Boggs, *Washington Through a Purple Veil*, 187.

151 "We would go to a party and": Clare Crawford, "Lindy Boggs Makes History with a Gavel," *People*, July 12, 1976.

151 "As liberal as any deep southerner could be": Associated Press, "Louisiana's Boggs Praised for Directions," *Greenville* (SC) *News*, August 28, 1968, 9.

152 didn't like to take the lithium: Solomon, *The Washington Century*, 226.

152 "slim as hell": "The FBI: What's Bugging Boggs," *Newsweek*, April 19, 1971, 35.

152 At the Gridiron Club Dinner: Solomon, *The Washington Century*, 226.

152 At another official dinner: Clark Hoyt, "Boggs Went Wild, Say Jaycees," *Detroit Free Press*, May 21, 1971, 4.

152 As reports of her husband's drinking: "Smarty-pants Lindy Boggs Seems House Shoo-in," *Albany Democrat-Herald*, March 10, 1973, 5.

153 The ringing phone startled her alert: Boggs, *Washington Through a Purple Veil*, 321.

154 This deeply unsettling reality didn't help: "In Depth: Cokie Roberts" (video), C-SPAN, December 6, 2015, https://www.c-span.org/video/?326445-1/depth-cokie-roberts.

154 "I know it's an oversimplification to say": "Lindy Boggs Knows Congress Well," *Courier-Journal*, March 25, 1973, G14.

154 Nineteen seventy-three. Women, ascendant: Eve Sharbutt, "Women of the World Who Made News in 1973," *Philadelphia Inquirer*, December 16, 1973, 126.

156 "maddening," but for their ability: Cokie and Steven V. Roberts, "What's Doing in Athens," *New York Times*, July 18, 1976, 246.

156 As they roamed the Continent: Cokie Roberts, "Traveling with Children: How to Set the Pace," *New York Times*, August 10, 1977, 50.

157 "Late this evening": *CBS Evening News with Walter Cronkite*, July 23, 1974.

158 left her feeling as if she were being buried alive: Roberts and Roberts, *From This Day Forward*, 169.

159 "ridiculous" ostracism of not having an answer: Cokie Roberts, *We Are Our Mothers' Daughters* (New York: William Morrow, 1998), 150.

159 "first-class witch": Ibid., 98.

Chapter Twelve: Transition

161 Mercifully for all, this remained: David Corn, "Did Nixon Try to Assassinate a Reporter," *Mother Jones*, September 30, 2010, https://

www.motherjones.com/politics/2010/09/nixon-jack-anderson-mark
-feldstein/.

161 The "unelected elite": Richard Harris, "The Presidency and the Press,"
the *New Yorker*, October 1, 1973, accessed online, https://www.new
yorker.com/magazine/1973/10/01/the-presidency-and-the-press.

162 "Get the left-wing commentators who are": Les Brown, "Files of Nixon
White House Show Bid to Control Public Broadcasting," *New York Times*,
February 24, 1979, 1.

163 "The President is capable of anything": Cecil Smith, "Nixon Reaching for
'Off' Switch," *Los Angeles Times*, January 17, 1973, D12.

163 "direction and stability that's difficult to shake": "NPR's Frischknecht:
Don't Look Back," *Broadcasting*, January 17, 1977, 65.

164 "Let me see if I can get this straight": Jim Russell, interview by Michael
McCauley, April 3, 1995, Michael P. McCauley Papers, University of
Maryland, College Park, MD.

164 "pimple on the ass": Steve Symonds, interview by Michael McCauley,
September 24, 1995, Michael P. McCauley Papers, University of Maryland, College Park, MD.

165 Member stations, the story said: Edward Cowan, "National Public Radio
Network Downplays News," *New York Times*, May 10, 1976, 43.

165 "didn't know dog shit about news": Bob Zelnick, interview by Michael
McCauley, August 11, 1995, Michael McCauley Papers, University of
Maryland, College Park, MD.

166 "make her a star": Steve Chapman, "We're Going to Make You a Flop,"
Harvard Crimson, August 15, 1975, accessed online, https://dev.the
crimson.com/article/1975/8/15/were-gonna-make-you-a-flop/.

168 Afterward, when two women reporters asked him: Bob Edwards, email
to author, July 1, 2020; Isabel Shelton, "Tale of Two Thomases: Helen a
Hit, Danny a Flop," *High Point* (NC) *Enterprise*, May 15, 1975, p. 8; Donald
Kaul, "Over the Coffee," *Des Moines Register*, May 19, 1975, 20.

168 "trivializing and demeaning": Germaine Greer, National Press Club,
May 18, 1971, Pacifica Radio Archives, https://archive.org/details
/pacifica_radio_archives-BC0051.

168 "Well, that should be pretty useful": Elaine Shannon, "Twisting the Knife
at the Club," (Nashville) *Tennesseean*, May 24, 1971, 6.

169 "just what's up front; it doesn't do the job": Ellie Grossman, "She Brings
Humanity to Airwaves," *Evening Sun*, March 18, 1980, A7.

170 "Mrs. Kennedy, how does it feel": Dick Cowen, "Nothing like own

book for thrills, author says," (Allentown, PA) *Morning Call*, August 8, 1982, F11.

170   someone else's pain: Susan Stamberg, interviewed by Terry Gross, "Susan Stamberg's 'Every Night at Five,'" *Fresh Air*, May 3, 1982, https://freshairarchive.org/segments/susan-stambergs-every-night-five.

171   "eternally on gender watch": Susan Stamberg, *Talk: NPR's Susan Stamberg Considers All Things* (New York: Random House, 1993), 27.

171   "I'd like to believe that the reason": Michael Weiss, "Hamberg, Steinborg . . . Who Is Susan Stamberg," *Iowa City Press-Citizen*, February 1, 1977, 5.

171   "magazine format brimming with light and serious": Dwight Newton, "Peabody for 'All Things,'" *San Francisco Examiner*, March 27, 1973, 23.

172   "kind of informality that one might expect": Richard Harrington, "All Things Considered," *Washington Post*, May 3, 1981, D1.

172   "Hamberg, Steinborg . . . Who Is Susan Stamberg?": Weiss, "Hamberg, Steinborg . . . Who Is Susan Stamberg."

172   "I know your voice": Gary Clifford, "Name the First Network Anchorwoman," *People*, August 6, 1979, accessed online, https://people.com/archive/name-the-first-network-anchorwoman-wrong-it-was-public-radios-susan-stamberg-vol-12-no-6/.

172   *Iowa Press-Citizen* published a love letter: William A. Mueller, "A Love Letter to Susan Stamberg," *Iowa Press-Citizen*, February 9, 1980, 4.

173   When revered CBS newsman: Karl E. Meyer, "Radio's Born-Again Serenity," *Next*, January February 1981, 47.

174   "It's Only a Radio Program": Susan Stamberg, "Personal Glimpses of Washington," *Washington Post*, October 1979, 21.

174   "An Elvis fan seeing The King": Stamberg, *Talk*, 162.

175   "Big deal," the magazine's editors wrote: "Editorials: A Little Bit Commercial," *Broadcasting*, October 18, 1976, 74.

175   Lofty salaries commensurate with her notoriety: Randy Sue Cohen, "On the Airwaves with Susan Stamberg," *New Age*, 35.

175   Why must she have to work: Susan Stamberg papers, 0009-MMC-NPBA. Special Collections and University Archives, Correspondence and Memos 1971–2000, Memo to Rick Lewis, November 13, 1978.

176   The justices, she reported: New York News, "Ex-Nixon Aides Plead Story Could Hurt Top-Court Appeal," *Charlotte Observer*, April 28, 1977, 2.

176   "there's no profit in it except self-glorification": T. R. Reid, "High Court

Dilemma Over Leak," *Washington Post*, April 27, 1977, https://www
.washingtonpost.com/archive/politics/1977/04/27/high-court-dilemma
-over-leak/4c9e924f-d8bd-4993-a348-428c3b0d94b8/.

177 "I just wanted you to know that I am terribly sorry": Nina Totenberg to
Potter Stewart, April 28, 1977, Folder 322, Box 598, Stewart MSS, Yale
University, New Haven, CT.

Chapter Thirteen: Frank

178 building a battleship: Bill Kling, interview with Michael McCauley,
July 26, 1995, Michael P. McCauley papers, University of Maryland Special Collections and University Archives, College Park, MD.

178 "stinkhole": James Ledbetter, *Made Possible By . . . : The Death of Public
Broadcasting in the United States* (London, New York: Crown, 2009), 122.

179 "desegregated Georgia": Tauber interview with Ambassador Edward E.
Elson, Association for Diplomatic Studies and Training Foreign Affairs,
April 18, 2012, accessed online, https://adst.org/wp-content/uploads
/2013/12/Elson-Edward-E-1.pdf.

179 "The only color that the city of Atlanta": Emma Edmonds, "Ed Elson: All
the News and More," *Atlanta Constitution*, September 20, 1970, B1.

180 "a significant role": "A New Magna Carta: The Pornography Report, Both
Sides," *Chicago Tribune*, October 4, 1970.

180 "My god," Elson said to himself: Edward Elson, interview with Michael
McCauley, November 2, 1995, Michael P. McCauley Papers, Univer-
sity of Maryland Special Collections and University Archives, College
Park, MD.

181 A keen sense of showmanship: Frank Mankiewicz, "John Houseman,
with Honors: Producer, Actor, Joyous Spirit: A Friend's Fond Look Back,"
Washington Post, November 6, 1988, G1.

181 "If I stayed with the firm": Margie Bonnett, "Frank Mankiewicz," *People*, May 24, 1982, https://people.com/archive/frank-mankiewicz-vol-17
-no-20/.

181 The experience of leading part of this: Larry J. Hackman, Frank Mankiewicz Oral History Interview, RFK #1, June 26, 1969, John F. Kennedy Presidential Library and Museum, Boston, MA, https://www.jfk
library.org/asset-viewer/archives/RFKOH/Mankiewicz%2C%20Frank
/RFKOH-FM-01/RFKOH-FM-01.

182   "Who gets hurt if I don't go to": Ibid.

184   The television special that finally resulted: Les Brown, "Shunned by TV, Maker of Rare Castro Film Will Close," *New York Times*, October 1974, 83.

184   "Everybody said, 'Don't be silly' ": "Q&A: Frank Mankiewicz" (video), C-SPAN, August 19, 2009, https://www.c-span.org/video/?288472-1 /qa-frank-mankiewicz.

186   "smooshed like a boxer": Nicholas von Hoffman, "Mank and the One-of-a-Kind Network," *Channels*, June/July 1981, 62.

186   Picking up the rights to air: Brian Richardson, "WFMU Has Come a Long Way," *Tallahassee Democrat*, May 1, 1979, 12.

186   A $70,000 grant from the government: "WFSU-FM to Increase Power," *Tallahassee Democrat*, July 22, 1974, 3.

187   "plethora of slick, bourgeois": Lucius Gantt, "Letter to Editor: Reports Misrepresent," *Tallahassee Democrat*, August 10, 1979, 4.

188   "I'm like the guy selling shoes": James Brown, "NPR: A View from the Top," *Los Angeles Times*, August 21, 1977, 85.

188   "make waves—to raise less corn and more hell": Joseph McLellan and Michael Kernan, "New Job, Same People: Mankiewicz Still Deals with Politicians," *Austin American-Statesman*, March 19, 1979, C8.

188   "Appointment of Mankiewicz Questioned": Magee Adams, "Appointment of Mankiewicz Questioned," *Cincinnati Enquirer*, July 31, 1977, F11.

188   "sharpen the watch for political footprints": Brown, "NPR: A View from the Top," 85.

188   "not called for . . . Let's hope": E. M. Beard, "Thoughts While Strolling," *Greater* (Albany) *Oregon*, September 9, 1977, 2.

188   "half of them owed him something": Margie Bonnett, "Frank Mankiewicz," *People*, May 24, 1982, https://people.com/archive/frank-mankiewicz-vol-17-no-20/.

189   "That's why we hired him": Noah Adams, in Cokie Roberts et al., *This Is NPR: The First Forty Years* (San Francisco: Chronicle Books, 2012), 48.

190   "Hi. I'm shop steward": Quoted in Bob Edwards, *A Voice in the Box: My Life in Radio* (Lexington: University Press of Kentucky, 2011), 56.

191   "Today is the first time": Robert Siegel on "Revisiting the Debate over the 'Big Ditch,' " NPR, March 24, 2008, https://www.npr.org/templates /story/story.php?storyId=88984796.

192   "That of course will depend": Associated Press, "Gavel to Gavel Coverage Offered," *Odessa American*, February 8, 1978, 16.

192 "This is a sexist town": Phyllis Theroux, "Great Washington Charmers," *Washington Post Sunday Magazine*, June 20, 1982, SM8.

193 "lowest form of life at the BBC": Perry, "All Things Considered, She's Glad She's in Radio," 2.

193 During the Watergate hearings: McCauley, *NPR: The Trials and Triumphs of National Public Radio*, 22.

193 "When you turn thirty,": William Gildea, "Broadcaster Thrives on Reporting Canal Debate," *Californian*, April 16, 1978, 6.

193 "top-flight" . . . "not because of her beauty": Charles Downie, "Wertheimer Proves Radio Isn't Dead," *San Francisco Examiner*, May 27, 1979, 41.

194 "If NPR ever had any listeners": "Radio Is Pro Tem in the Senate for Canal Debates," *Broadcasting*, February 13, 1978, 27.

194 "It was just by the grace of God": Linda Wertheimer on "Revisiting the Debate over the "Big Ditch,'" NPR, March 24, 2008, https://www.npr.org/templates/story/story.php?storyId=88984796.

194 For the next thirty-seven days: Andrew Mollison, "Historic Debate on Treaties Begins in Senate," *Miami News*, February 8, 1978, 8.

195 Yet, those who were typically: William Gildea, "Broadcaster Thrives on Reporting Canal Debate," *Californian*, April 16, 1978, 6.

195 "That sounds like my sister": Ibid.

195 Later, Linda learned: Linda Wertheimer at WFAE (Charlotte, NC) Founding Mothers Event, online via Zoom, August 29, 2020.

196 convince the Supreme Court: Karen Cox, "Radio Head Wants Live Coverage of High Court," *Daily Press*, November 10, 1978, 35.

Chapter Fourteen: *Star Wars*

197 including one career public media man: Bill Kling, interview with Michael McCauley, July 26, 1995, Michael P. McCauley Papers, University of Maryland, College Park, MD.

198 "ornament" for the network: "Frank Mankiewicz Roast," C-SPAN, December 9, 2004, https://www.c-span.org/video/?184755-1/frank-mankiewicz-roast.

199 Lindy agreed to sell her daughter: Solomon, *The Washington Century*, 281.

199 "I'm sorry I couldn't make": Mankiewicz, letter to Lindy Boggs, February 24, 1978, Frank Mankiewicz papers, Series 2, Box 3, University of Maryland, College Park, MD.

199 Time was always working against: "Susan Stamberg Proves that Women Can Do News," interview, *Fresh Air with Terry Gross*, NPR, May 26, 1993, https://freshairarchive.org/guests/susan-stamberg.

200 "You have to give up something": Lorrie Lynch, "The Prime of Cokie Roberts," *USA Weekend*, June 20, 1993, 4–5.

200 "And Steven couldn't walk in the door": Cokie Roberts, "More than a Wife and Mother," *Working Woman*, July/August 1998, 53.

200 "It's that business of being able to tell": Nicholas von Hoffman, "Mank and the One-of-a-Kind Network," *Channels*, June/July 1981, 62.

200 When the Pope came to town: Roberts, *We Are Our Mothers' Daughters*, 232.

201 "born in the boiler room": Dreifus, "Cokie Roberts, Nina Totenberg, Linda Wertheimer."

201 clerk in the congressional takeout joint: "Cokie Roberts, Journalist" (video), interview with Jenni Matz, *The Interviews*, Television Academy Foundation, October 2, 2018, https://interviews.televisionacademy.com /interviews/cokie-roberts.

202 It seemed silly for her to continue: Roberts and Roberts, *From This Day Forward*, 226.

202 There was enough of Capitol Hill: Linda Wertheimer in "Remembering Cokie Roberts, 1943–2019," NPR, aired September 25, 2019, https://www.npr.org/series/764249402/remembering-cokie-roberts -1943-2019.

203 "Your children will be called bastards": *Primetime Live* with Diane Sawyer, ABC, November 7, 1991.

204 "you get more bang for the buck": WFAE Founding Mothers Event, online via Zoom, August 29, 2020.

204 "Nobody reported on the widespread": *Primetime Live*, November 7, 1991.

204 Cokie's annual (and growing) "shiksa seder": Cokie Roberts and Steven V. Roberts, *Our Haggadah: Uniting Traditions for Interfaith Families* (New York: Harper, 2011), xlvii.

204 When someone in the press corps: Cokie Roberts, at the "Frank Mankiewicz Roast," C-SPAN, December 9, 2004, https://www.c-span.org /video/?184755-1/frank-mankiewicz-roast.

205 Linda had been chased around: Linda Wertheimer on *Primetime Live*, ABC, November 7, 1991.

205 "You knew who was a bottom pincher": Dreifus, "Cokie Roberts, Nina Totenberg, Linda Wertheimer."

205 When the producers of the Miss America pageant: Bob Edwards, email to author, September 10, 2020.

207 He was unerringly conscientious, the man reported: Linda Wertheimer, ed., *Listening to America: 25 Years in the Life of a Nation, as Heard on National Public Radio* (New York: Houghton Mifflin, 1995), 90.

207 first "television president": Richard Reeves, "Maestro of the Media," *New York Times Magazine*, May 15, 1977, 203.

207 For Cronkite, this presented a problem: Susan Stamberg, email to author, September 11, 2020.

208 "There were shrieks of delight": Associated Press, "Radio Host Thinks Oval Office Swell Studio," *White Plains Journal-News*, October 14, 1979, 3A.

208 Susan admired the bookcases: Susan Stamberg, "Personal Glimpses of Washington," *Washington Post*, October 21, 1979, https://www.washington post.com/archive/opinions/1979/10/21/personal-glimpses-of -washington/ee7c4380-653b-4ef0-b17c-f3425c5f6da9/.

209 "We're kind of strolling around the country by phone": Jimmy Carter, Public Papers of the Presidents of the United States: Jimmy Carter, 1979, 1885 (accessible via Google Books).

212 "newsy Catholic male": Edwards, *A Voice in the Box*, 50.

212 "Mr. Prig" attitude: Ibid., 52.

213 An aborted attempt to rescue: Roger Worthington, " 'Morning Edition' Wakes Up America," *Chicago Tribune*, September 17, 1980, 29.

214 "one of the great achievements": Anthony Lewis, "Jonestown NPR Program Is a Historic Achievement," *Baltimore Evening Sun*, April 24, 1981, A11.

214 Excited over his successful: Letter from Barrett McGurn, Supreme Court Public Information Office, to Frank Mankiewicz, April 5, 1978, Frank Mankiewicz papers, Series 2, Box 3, University of Maryland Special Collections, College Park, MD.

214 *Laverne and Shirley* of public radio: Frank Mankiewicz Oral History, August 14, 1995, Michael P. McCauley papers, University of Maryland Special Collections, College Park, MD.

215 "depends on the goddamn post office": "Satellites: Tomorrow Is Here Today,"*Broadcasting*, March 27, 1978, 57.

216 "Create a scandal": Richard Toscan, former head, USC Theater Department, telephone conversation with author, May 11, 2020.

217 "You may think you've seen": Brian J. Robb, *A Brief Guide to Star Wars* (New York: Little, Brown, 2012).

217 "a flashy smorgasbord": James Brown, "Star Wars Debut," *Los Angeles Times*, Calendar, March 8, 1981, 82.

217 "like the lungs of someone": David Bianculli, "NPR President Mankiewicz Puts in a Plug for Public Radio," *Fort Lauderdale News*, December 5, 1979, 56.

Chapter Fifteen: The Drive to Survive

219 "You didn't need office parties in those days": Bob Edwards, in Lisa A. Phillips, *Public Radio: Behind the Voices* (New York: Vanguard Press, 2006), 30.

221 "Television tends to wear out formats and": NPR board member Bill Kling, memo to Mankiewicz, July 28, 1981, Frank Mankiewicz papers, Series 2, Box 3, Folder 5, University of Maryland Special Collections, College Park, MD.

222 "There is supposed to be an element": John J. O'Connor, "TV: Sharks and 'All Things' on PBS," *New York Times*, January 13, 1982, C24.

222 "A lone tape recorder placed": David Bianculli, "Cable Cameras Capture Radio News Programs," *Arizona Republic*, January 11, 1983, 21.

222 "extremely cumbersome": Leslie Berger, "Down on Main Street," *Washington Post*, January 13, 1982, B1.

223 "I know you're frightened": Kristin Hohenadel, "Please Won't You Be My Inspiration?," *New York Times*, March 16, 2012, AR14.

223 her idea of "hell on earth": "Cokie Roberts Congressional Oral History Interview," Office of the Historian, U.S. House of Representatives, May 25, 2017, https://history.house.gov/OralHistory/Detail?id=15032450401.

223 "just another Hill story": Arthur Unger, "An 'Unglamorous' Beat?: 'The Lawmakers'—Public TV's Eye on Congress," *Christian Science Monitor*, September 11, 1981, https://www.csmonitor.com/1981/0911/091100 .html.

223 "know how to handle the nuance": Marilynn Preston, " 'The Lawmakers' Give TV News Some Insights from Radio," *Chicago Tribune*, January 16, 1981, 13.

224 If "you were polka-dotted with three heads": "Cokie Roberts," Oral History Interview, U.S. House of Representatives.

225 once described as "mellow-roast": Louise Betts, "Public Radio Outgrowing Growing Pains," UPI, December 18, 1979.

225 His was the St. Louis Cardinals: Joe Holleman, "Democratic Giant Frank Mankiewicz Was Proud Cards Fan," *St. Louis Post-Dispatch*, October 27, 2014, A7.

225 Rumors had even been circulating: Barbara Cohen on "National Public Radio" (video), C-SPAN, January 11, 1983, https://www.c-span.org/video/?200617-1/national-public-radio.

226 This required a two-bus schlep: Jay Kernis, interview with Michael McCauley, September 8, 2003, Michael P. McCauley Papers, University of Maryland Special Collections and University Archives, College Park, MD.

229 "Computers were rolling in here": Jeff Rosenberg, interview with Michael McCauley, August 14, 1995, Michael P. McCauley papers, University of Maryland Special Collections and University Archives.

229 Notoriously short on reporters: Cohen on "National Public Radio" (video), C-SPAN.

232 "There is no deficit": "What Happened to Mankiewicz?" *Broadcasting*, April 25, 1983, 28.

233 a kid's lemonade stand: Steve Symonds, interview by Michael McCauley, September 24, 1995, Michael P. McCauley papers, University of Maryland Special Collections and University Archives.

234 "new pride in our work": Cokie Roberts et al., *This Is NPR: The First Forty Years* (San Francisco: Chronicle Books, 2012), 115.

234 "My job is not to affix blame:" "NPR's Bad News Gets Worse," *Broadcasting*, July 27, 1983, 37.

234 "Anywhere you turned, there was trouble": Ronald O. Bornstein, interview with Michael McCauley, July 3, 1995, Michael P. McCauley Papers, University of Maryland Special Collections and University Archives, College Park, M.D.

235 "I don't think so": "Ronald Bornstein" (video), Hall of Fame, Wisconsin Broadcasting Museum, https://www.wisconsinbroadcastingmuseum.org/hall-of-fame/ronald-bornstein/.

235 "No amount of cutting": Mitchell, *Listener Supported*, 105.

236 "See, to some people, the question arises": Collins, *National Public Radio: The Cast of Characters*, 74.

237 There wasn't much in the way of a prize: McCauley, *NPR: The Trials and Triumphs of National Public Radio*, 62.

238 "My responsibility was not to spend all day": Irvin Molotsky, "National

Public Radio's Saddest Story Is Its Own," *New York Times*, May 27, 1983, 14.

238 "Warner Communications had a twenty-million": Jack Thomas, "Frank Mankiewicz," *Boston Globe*, May 3, 1983.

240 "the damage to NPR's": UPI, "NPR News Staff Fights Funding Cuts," *Brattleboro Reformer*, May 17, 1983, 3.

240 She also hedged her bets, taping: Randy Sue Cohen, "On the Airwaves with Susan Stamberg," *New Age*, December 1983, 87.

240 "sizeable checks in the form of loans": Susan Stamberg to Ronald Bornstein, letter, May 15, 1983, Susan Stamberg Papers, Correspondence, 1980–1989, Box: 5, Folder: 19.0, University of Maryland Special Collections and University Archives, College Park, MD.

241 "It's not bad publicity, it's bad *news*": Susan Stamberg on C-SPAN, June 7, 1983, https://www.c-span.org/video/?123668-1/national-public -radio.

243 With a half-million-dollar check in hand: Mitchell, *Listener Supported*, p. 111, and email from Ron Bornstein to author, July 28, 2020.

244 "Well, what about the millions": John Price, "NPR Fund-raiser Needed Explanation," *Eau Claire* (WI) *Leader-Telegram*, August 6, 1983, 31.

244 Forevermore, he'd be the man who brought: Ronald Bornstein Oral History, July 3, 1995, Michael P. McCauley Papers, University of Maryland Special Collections, College Park, MD.

Epilogue: Hollywood Walk of Fame

245 "mom and pop store": Stamberg on *Fresh Air*, "Susan Stamberg Proves That Women Can Do News," May 26, 1993, https://freshairarchive.org /segments/susan-stamberg-proves-women-can-do-news.

246 "legitimizing the sound of women in serious": Ibid.

247 Linda relayed that she and Cokie: Susan Stamberg, *Talk: NPR's Susan Stamberg Considers All Things* (New York: Random House, 1993), 199.

248 After loans were repaid several years: "Ambassador Edward E. Elson," The Association for Diplomatic Studies and Training, Foreign Affairs Oral History Project, interviewed by Charles Stuart Kennedy, April 18, 2012, https://adst.org/wp-content/uploads/2013/12/Elson-Edward -E-1.pdf.

250 "It's a joke": Coburn, "On the Airwaves with Susan Stamberg."

250 What are the rules: Stamberg, *Talk*, 41.

250 To the famous director: Ibid., 374.

251 "It's a goodbye to being the one": "On Radio, Hello Again," *Broadcasting*, September 15, 1986, 96.

251 "'You know, it's amazing'": Dennis McDougal, "All Things Considered, She Would Rather Not," September 13, 1986, D1.

251 "cheer people up or make them feel better": "Susan Stamberg Proves that Women Can Do News."

252 "They know how to talk into microphones": Ibid.

253 "nerve synapse": Coburn, "On the Airwaves with Susan Stamberg."

254 "I'm forty-two and not ready yet": Jeffrey Yorke, "Susan Stamberg Leaving 'All Things Considered'?" *Washington Post*, September 5, 1986, B7.

254 "mundane and dull, very traditional": Marc Fisher, "Soul of a News Machine," *Washington Post*, June 6, 1989.

254 "I did not go to Woodstock": Ibid.

254 "I'm not nostalgic for those days": Bruce Porter, "Has Success Spoiled NPR?," *Columbia Journalism Review* (September/October 1990): 26.

255 After Neary returned from her honeymoon: Jeffrey Yorke, "On the Dial: Pat Robertson's Priorities," *Washington Post*, June 6, 1989, B7.

255 A lawsuit filed in the late seventies: "Hiring Policy Re-Examined," *Washington Post*, February 8, 1978, A3.

256 "If I talked to Bennet about it": Fisher, "Soul of a News Machine."

256 "elitist enterprise": Thomas B. Edsall, "Defunding Public Broadcasting," *Washington Post*, April 15, 1995, A4.

256 "sensitive cultural or scientific reporting": Bill Buzenberg, in Linda Wertheimer, ed., *Listening to America: 25 Years in the Life of a Nation, as Heard on National Public Radio* (New York: Houghton Mifflin, 1995), N15.

256 "a conservative sell-out with no principles": John Hockenberry, *Moving Violations: A Memoir* (New York: Hyperion, 1995), 162.

257 And, at the bottom of the top: Ellen Edwards, "The $92,000 Questions: CPB's Voluminous Reply to Sen. Pressler's Query," *Washington Post*, February 14, 1995, B2.

257 In fact, Nina's salary of: Howard Kurtz, "The Legal Reporter's Full Court Press: NPR's Nina Totenberg and Her Anita Hill Scoop," *Washington Post*, October 10, 1991, D1.

257 a vexing series of lawsuits: Steven A. Holmes, "Sex Bias Lawsuit Filed Against N.P.R.," *New York Times*, May 24, 1995, A16.

257 After she charged NPR with: Clara Jeffery, "NPR Not P.C.? Veteran Reporter Sues Network for Sexual Discrimination," *Washington City*

Paper, May 12, 1995, https://washingtoncitypaper.com/article/295087 /npr-not-pc/.

258 *Vanity Fair* reported several years: Ann Louise Bardach, "Nina Totenberg: Queen of the Leaks," *Vanity Fair*, January 1992, 46, http://www.bardach reports.com/articles/v_19920100.html.

258 "Douglas Ginsburg . . . was breaking": Dennis McDougal, "Media Moralism Sparks Cries of Outrage," *Los Angeles Times*, November 14, 1987, 23.

259 "Here is a person who": "Transcript of Nina Totenberg's NPR Report on Anita Hill's Charges of Sexual Harassment by Clarence Thomas," National Public Radio, October 6, 1991, Jewish Women's Archive, https:// jwa.org/media/transcript-of-nina-totenbergs-npr-report-on-anita-hills -charges-of-sexual-harassment-by-o.

260 "the most riveting television drama": Joe Logan, "Totenberg: My Lips are Sealed—Sort Of," *Philadelphia Inquirer*, November 3, 1991, pH1.

260 "It was as if a river of raw": Mary McGrory, "For All, a Time of Revulsion," *Pittsburgh Post*, October 13, 1991, B2.

262 "Purposeful plagiarism": Albert Hunt, "Tales of Ignominy, Beyond Thomas and Hill," *Wall Street Journal*, October 17, 1991.

262 "three women who inspire respect and their": Diane Sawyer, on *Primetime Live*, November 7, 1991.

263 "I find myself a bit embarrassed": Statement of Nina Totenberg, Legal Affairs Correspondent, National Public Radio, Before Senate Special Independent Counsel Peter E. Fleming Jr., Monday, February 24, 1992, Senate Hart Office Building, Washington, DC.

263 "[T]here would have been no leaks": "A Fruitless Investigation Winds Up," *Hartford Courant*, May 11, 1992, 73.

263 "like a press release for me": "NPR Objectivity at Work," editorial, *Wall Street Journal*, May 11, 1992, A10.

263 "In the future, if someone has important": Ibid.

264 "I asked Anita Hill to stand up": Associated Press, "Stand Up for Your Rights," *Miami Herald*, May 23, 1994, 20.

265 "You can't do what you do on NPR anyplace else": Mark Lorando, "TV Focus," (New Orleans) *Times-Picayune*, April 11, 1993, 7.

265 "an evolutionary adaptation": John F. Kennedy Jr., "Cokie Is It," *George*, January 1997, 51.

266 who slept with a photo of the Pope: Former NPR executive Jay Kernis, telephone conversation with author, August 2020.

266   "She thinks it's funny": Colleen O'Connor, "Lady on the Hill," *Detroit Free Press*, November 27, 1994, 77.

266   In fact, she was *inside*: Ellen Edwards, "ABC News' Live Volcano," *Washington Post*, April 12, 1994, E1.

267   One year, this ballooned: Ken Auletta, "Fee Speech," the *New Yorker*, September 5, 1994, 40.

267   trade associations, corporate annual meetings: Kurtz, *Hot Air*, 213.

267   "Our interests are different": Cokie Roberts, Theodore White Lecture, Harvard University, November 17, 1994, https://shorensteincenter.org/wp-content/uploads/2012/03/th_white_1994_roberts.pdf.

267   "They have come like children to be": Billy Warden, "Politics Is All in the Family," *News and Observer*, April 10, 1990, 27.

268   "Those who collect fees are increasingly": Alicia C. Shepard, "Talk Is Expensive," *American Journalism Review* (May 1994), https://ajrarchive.org/Article.asp?id=1607&id=1607.

268   stoked her generosity: Her nephew Stephen discusses this in an elegy for Cokie on the first anniversary of her death. Stephen Sigmund, "Missing Cokie Roberts," NJ.com, September 17, 2020, https://www.nj.com/opinion/2020/09/missing-cokie-roberts-opinion.html.

268   "It's a classic free market": Howard Kurtz, "Money Talks," *Washington Post*, January 21, 1996, N32.

268   "Reprehensible": Ibid.

269   "more than zero": Mike Royko, "Who's Unhappy Now? Media Stars," *Beatrice* (NE) *Daily Sun*, July 25, 1995, 4.

269   tripped and broke a toe: Cook, "One Smart Cookie," 94.

269   "Is this situation totally free": Paul Hendrickson, "Roberts Rules," *Washington Post*, June 20, 1993, N8.

270   "have played many roles": Pam Wyne, "College Club of Ridgewood Spotlights Cokie Roberts," *Ridgewood* (NJ) *News*, January 7, 2001, B8.

270   Because she knew of: Michel Martin, "The Cokie Roberts I Knew," NPR, September 21, 2019, https://www.npr.org/2019/09/21/763073699/the-cokie-roberts-i-knew.

270   Cokie seemed to see herself in: Mary Louise Kelly on "Remembering Cokie Roberts," *Brian Lehrer Show*, WNYC, September 18, 2019, https://www.wnyc.org/story/cokie-roberts-remembered/.

271   wrangling of several dozen guests for Sunday supper: Kitty Eisele, "Cokie Roberts Loved Being in the Know and Not Just Because It Was Her Job,"

Washington Post, September 20, 2019, https://www.washingtonpost.com
/outlook/cokie-roberts-loved-being-in-the-know-and-not-just-because
-it-was-her-job/2019/09/20/791190d2-db23-11e9-bfb1-849887369476
_story.html#comments-wrapper.

272 painstakingly inserted his proposal: Linda Matchan, "At Home with Nina
Totenberg and David Reines," *Boston Globe*, March 15, 2001, 118.

272 Belgian-born chef Frederik De Pue: Nina Totenberg, "How to Hack Béar-
naise, a Mother of a French Sauce," New Orleans Public Radio, July 18,
2015, https://www.wwno.org/post/how-hack-b-arnaise-mother-french
-sauce.

272 a fact Nina lorded over the graduating: Nina Totenberg at Columbia
Journalism School graduation, May 20, 2015, https://www.youtube.com
/watch?v=Gzy1iM4fGbs.

273 On the last Saturday night: Remarks made by the Founding Mothers at
WFAE Founding Mothers Event, online via Zoom, August 29, 2020.

Methodology and Bibliography

A biography is written using a compendium of sources, including many tucked away in far-flung locations. Because memory is fallible, a more accurate picture of a time or event can be had by studying source material from that time. Where possible and when needed, I've asked individuals for clarification.

Since this book was researched during the course of the pandemic of 2020, libraries and archives shuttered, sending researchers like me into paroxysms of fear. (Contrary to what some believe, not everything is available on the internet.) Fortunately, I had spent a week in December 2019 mining the superlative collection of materials at the University of Maryland Special Collections, home to the National Public Broadcasting Archives. Additionally, I had requisitioned materials from other locations before they closed down.

Libraries, archives, and librarians are repositories of our history, and as such, they perform an essential service. Even if you have no occasion to use them, please be aware of their importance in preserving our history and advancing our understanding of our past. History matters. I offer particular thanks to these institutions:

American Archive of Public Broadcasting
Archive.org
Cal State Fullerton Library
Carlsbad Public Library, Carlsbad, New Mexico

Library of American Broadcasting, University of Maryland Libraries
Library of Congress
Los Angeles Public Library
Louisiana Research Collection at Tulane University (for Lindy Boggs papers)
NewspaperArchive.com
Newspapers.com
Scarsdale (NY) High School
Smith College Special Collections (for Pauline Frederick papers)
Stanford University Special Collections
Television Academy Foundation / The Interviews (https://interviews.television
    academy.com)
Vanderbilt Television News Archives
Wellesley College Special Collections
Wisconsin Center for Film and Theater Research
Women's National Press Club Oral Histories (http://beta.wpcf.org/oralhistory
    /intvwees.html)
United States House of Representatives, Office of the Historian
United States National Student Association International Commission records,
    Hoover Institution Archives
University of Maryland Special Collections

Books

Altman, Sophie. *From A to Z: The "It's Academic" Quiz Book: More Than 70 Quizzes to Challenge Your Knowledge: Be a TV Contestant Right in Your Own Home.* New York: Acropolis Books, 1989.

Auletta, Ken. *Backstory: Inside the Business of News.* New York: Penguin Books, 2004.

Beasley, Maurine H. *The Women's National Press Club: Case Study of Professional Aspirations.* Association for Education in Journalism and Mass Communication, 1986.

Benedict, Elizabeth, ed. *What My Mother Gave Me: Thirty-One Women on the Gifts That Mattered Most.* New York: Algonquin, 2013.

Bird, Caroline. *Born Female: The High Cost of Keeping Women Down.* New York: David McKay Company, Inc., 1968.

Boggs, Lindy. *Washington Through a Purple Veil: Memoirs of a Southern Woman.* New York: Harcourt, Brace and Company, 1994.

Boulard, Gary. *The Big Lie: Hale Boggs, Lucille May Grace, and Leander Perez in 1951*. Gretna, LA: Pelican Publishing Company, 2001.

Brinkley, David. *Washington Goes to War: The Extraordinary Story of the Transformation of a City and a Nation*. New York: Alfred A. Knopf, 1988.

Brownmiller, Susan. *In Our Time: Memoir of a Revolution*. New York: The Dial Press, 1999.

Chafe, William. *Never Stop Running: Allard Lowenstein and the Struggle to Save American Liberalism*. Princeton: Princeton University Press, 1995.

Collins, Gail. *When Everything Changed: The Amazing Journey of American Women from 1960 to the Present*. New York: Little, Brown & Company, 2009.

Collins, Mary. *National Public Radio: The Cast of Characters*. Washington, DC: Seven Locks Press, 1993.

Crouse, Timothy. *The Boys on the Bus*. New York: Random House, 1973.

Dickerson, John. *On Her Trail: My Mother, Nancy Dickerson, TV News' First Woman Star*. New York: Simon & Schuster, 2006.

Dickerson, Nancy. *Among Those Present: A Reporter's View of 25 Years in Washington*. New York: Random House, 1976.

Edwards, Bob. *A Voice in the Box: My Life in Radio*. Lexington: University Press of Kentucky, 2011.

Engleman, Ralph. *Public Radio and Television in America: A Political History*. Thousand Oaks, CA: SAGE Publications, 1996.

Friedan, Betty. *The Feminine Mystique*. New York: W. W. Norton, 1963.

Gelfman, Judith S. *Women in Television News*. New York: Columbia University Press, 1976.

Goodman, Ellen. *I Know Just What You Mean: The Power of Friendship in Women's Lives*. New York: Simon & Schuster, 2000.

Greenwald, Marilyn S. *Pauline Frederick Reporting: A Pioneering Broadcaster Covers the Cold War*. Lincoln, NE: Potomac Books, 2014.

Halper, Donna L. *Invisible Stars: A Social History of Women in American Broadcasting*. Armonk, NY: M. E. Sharpe, 2014.

Harris, David. *Dreams Die Hard: Three Men's Journey Through the Sixties*. San Francisco: Mercury House, 1993.

Hershey, Lenore. *Between the Covers: The Lady's Own Journal*. New York: Coward-McCann, 1983.

Hockenberry, John. *Moving Violations: War Zones, Wheelchairs and Declarations of Independence*. New York: Hyperion, 1995.

Isber, Caroline, and Muriel Cantor, *Report of the Task Force on Women in Public Broadcasting*, Corporation for Public Broadcasting, 1975.

Kennedy, Kerry. *Being Catholic Now: Prominent Americans Talk About Change in the Church and the Quest for Meaning.* New York: Crown, 2009.

Ledbetter, James. *Made Possible By . . . : The Death of Public Broadcasting in the United States.* London, New York: Verso, 1997.

Kaptur, Marcy. *Women of Congress: A Twentieth Century Odyssey.* Washington, DC: Congressional Quarterly Press, 1996.

Kurtz, Howard. *Hot Air: All Talk All the Time—How the Talk Show Culture Has Changed America.* New York: Basic Books, 1996.

Lewis, Tom. *Empire of the Air: The Men Who Made Radio.* New York: Harper-Collins, 1991.

Looker, Thomas. *The Sound and the Story: NPR and the Art of Radio.* Wilmington, MA: Houghton Mifflin, 1995.

Mankiewicz, Frank. *So as I Was Saying . . . : My Somewhat Eventful Life.* New York: Thomas Dunne Books/St. Martin's Press, 2016.

McCauley, Michael. *NPR: The Trials and Triumphs of National Public Radio.* New York: Columbia University Press, 2005.

McLendon, Winola, and Scottie Smith. *Don't Quote Me!: Washington Newswomen and the Power Society.* New York: E. P. Dutton, 1970.

Miller, William "Fishbait." *Fishbait: The Memoirs of the Congressional Doorkeeper.* Englewood Cliffs, NJ: Prentice-Hall, 1977.

Mills, Kay. *A Place in the News: From the Women's Pages to the Front Pages.* New York: Dodd, Mead and Co., 1988.

Mitchell, Jack W. *Listener Supported: The Culture and History of Public Radio.* New York: Praeger, 2005.

Phelps, Timothy. *Capitol Games: Clarence Thomas, Anita Hill, and the Story of a Supreme Court Nomination.* New York: Hyperion, 1992.

Pierce, Paul. *Take an Alternate Route.* Los Angeles: Sherbourne Press, 1968.

Povich, Lynn. *The Good Girls Revolt: How the Women of Newsweek Sued Their Bosses and Changed the Workplace.* New York: Public Affairs, 2012.

Purdum, Todd S. *An Idea Whose Time Has Come: Two Presidents, Two Parties, and the Battle for the Civil Rights Act of 1964.* New York: Henry Holt, 2014.

Quinn, Sally. *We're Going to Make You a Star.* New York: Simon & Schuster, 1975.

Roberts, Cokie, et al. *This Is NPR: The First Forty Years.* San Francisco: Chronicle Books, 2012.

Roberts, Cokie. *Founding Mothers: The Woman Who Raised Our Nation.* New York: William Morrow, 2004.

———. *We Are Our Mothers' Daughters.* New York: William Morrow and Company, 1998.

Roberts, Rebecca. *Suffragists in Washington, D.C.: The 1913 Parade and the Fight for the Vote.* Charleston, SC: The History Press, 2017.

Roberts, Cokie, and Steven V. Roberts. *From This Day Forward.* New York: William Morrow, 2000.

———. *Our Haggadah: Uniting Traditions for Interfaith Families.* New York: Harper, 2011.

Roberts, Steven V. *Eureka! Earthquakes, Chicanos, Celebrities, Smog, Feds, Outdoor Living, Charles Manson's Legacy, Berkeley Rebels, San Francisco Scenes, Southern California Style, Ronald Reagan, and Other Discoveries in the Golden State of California.* New York: Quadrangle/New York Times Book Company, 1974.

———. *My Fathers' Houses: Memoir of a Family.* New York: William Morrow, 2005.

Robertson, Nan. *The Girls in the Balcony: Women, Men, and the New York Times.* New York: Random House, 1992.

Sanders, Marlene, and Marcia Rock. *Waiting for Prime Time: The Women of Television News.* Champaign: University of Illinois Press, 1994.

Sigmund, Barbara. *An Unfinished Life.* Princeton, NJ: Arts Council of Princeton, 1990.

Stahl, Lesley. *Reporting Live.* New York: Simon & Schuster, 2000.

Solomon, Burt. *The Washington Century: Three Families and the Shaping of the Nation's Capital.* New York: William Morrow, 2004.

Stamberg, Susan. *Every Night at Five: Susan Stamberg's "All Things Considered" Book.* New York: Pantheon, 1982.

———. *Talk: NPR's Susan Stamberg Considers All Things.* New York: Random House, 1993.

———. *The Wedding Cake in the Middle of the Road: 23 Variations on a Theme.* New York: W. W. Norton, 1992.

Thomas, Helen. *Front Row at the White House: My Life and Times.* New York: Lisa Drew/Scribner, 1999.

Torre, Marie. *Don't Quote Me.* Garden City, NY: Doubleday, 1965.

Walton, William, and Evelyn Hofer. *The Evidence of Washington.* New York: Harper and Row, 1966.

Weisberg, Stuart E. *Barney Frank: The Story of America's Only Left-Handed, Gay, Jewish Congressman.* Amherst: University of Massachusetts Press, 2009.

Wertheimer, Linda, ed. *Listening to America: 25 Years in the Life of a Nation, as Heard on National Public Radio.* Boston: Houghton Mifflin, 1995.

White, Theodore. *The Making of the President: 1968.* New York: Atheneum Publishers, 1968.

———. *The Making of the President: 1972.* New York: Atheneum Publishers, 1973.

Wymard, Ellie. *Conversations with Uncommon Women: Insights from Women Who've Risen Above Life's Challenges to Achieve,* New York: Amacon, 1999.

Media

Burns, Ken, dir. *Empire of the Air: The Men Who Made Radio.* Ken Burns American Stories. Florentine Films in association with WETA. Washington, DC. DVD. 1991.

Mock, Freida Lee, dir. *Anita: Speaking Truth to Power.* First Run Features, DVD, 2014.

National Public Radio. *NPR American Chronicles: Women's Equality.* Read by Susan Stamberg. Highbridge Audio, 2012.

National Public Radio. *NPR: Twenty Years with NPR.* National Public Radio, 1990.

National Public Radio. *NPR: The First 40 Years.* HighBridge Audio, CD, 2010.

Index

ABC News, 1–2, 4
acting, 79–80
activism
　for Black Americans, 90–91
　for civil rights, 60–61
　media, 92
　news and, 72–73, 131–32
　politics and, 93
　against Vietnam War, 72
　for women, 91, 154–55
　Women's Caucus for, 94
　for work, 42, 283
Adams, Abigail, 271
Adams, John, 194, 236, 271
Adams, Magee, 188
Adams, Noah, 214, 254, 257
Adler, Margot, 255
advertising, 46, 54, 168
age discrimination, 122
Agnew, Spiro, 161–62
Albert, Carl, 153
Ali, Muhammad, 64
Allen, Fred, 247
Allen, James, 193–95
All India Radio and TV, 38
All Things Considered (radio show)
　All Things Considered . . . on Main Street,
　　221–22
　audiences of, 189, 213
　history of, 70–71, 163–65, 251, 273,
　　284–85
　leadership for, 95–99, 206

for NPR, 70–74
popularity of, 100, 109–10, 172–73, 175,
　236, 242
for women, 169–73, 210–11
Altman, Norman, 135
Altman, Robert, 169
Altman, Sophie B., 135–36
American Journalism (magazine), 268
American University, 22, 55–56
Amos, Deborah, 214
Anderson, Clinton, 61–62
Anderson, Jack, 161
Anderson, Thomas, 141
Andretti, Mario, 7
anti-Semitism, 98, 179
Arnaz, Desi, 82
Associated Press, 86
AT&T, 167
audiences, 6–9, 46, 68, 101–2, 194–96
　of *All Things Considered*, 189, 213
　fundraising by, 239–42
　of news, 4, 175–76
　NPR for, 210–13, 274–75
　of radio, 36, 160, 166, 171–72, 186–87,
　　217
Auletta, Ken, 267

Back of the Book (PBS), 240n
"Balcony Rock" (Brubeck), 18
Banks and the Poor (documentary), 162
Barber, Red, 225
Barnard College, 17–18

Barnett, John, 53–54
Barnouw, Erik, 43
Barry, Bill, 183
Bates, Katherine Lee, 59
Baukhage, H. R., 56–57
BBC. *See* British Broadcasting Company
Begich, Nick, 152–53
Bening, Annette, 249, 249n
Bennet, Doug, 253–54, 253n, 256
The Beverly Hillbillies (TV show), 219
Bianculli, David, 222
Biden, Joe, 259
Bigelow, John, 60
Bird, Caroline, 64
Black Americans, 44, 52, 64, 68, 255
    activism for, 90–91
    civil rights for, 26–27, 34–35
    Jews and, 179
    women and, 27, 31, 33n, 60–61
    work for, 108, 115
Blackmun, Harry, 105–6
Boardman, Jim, 236
Boggs, Barbara, 7, 118–19, 143
    Lowenstein and, 138–39
    as role model, 123, 125, 131
Boggs, Cokie. *See* Roberts, Mary
Boggs, Hale, 4–5, 92, 107–8, 113–21, 142–43
    feminism for, 140
    in politics, 125, 134n, 151–54, 284
Boggs, Lindy, 5, 113–21, 123–25, 270
    in politics, 151–55, 198, 202, 247n, 284
    religion for, 140–41, 266
Boggs, Tommy, 122–23, 198
Bolton, Frances, 31–32
Bond, Julian, 7
Bono, Sonny, 147
Bornstein, Ronald, 234–37, 239, 243
Bowles, Chester, 39
Bradley, Bill, 180
Brandeis University, 19
breast cancer, 6–8
Brinkley, David, 2–3, 4
British Broadcasting Company (BBC),
    62–63, 71, 216–17
broadcasting. *See also specific topics*
    analysis in, 69
    BBC, 62–63, 71
    competition in, 235–36, 254
    economics of, 96, 210, 216–17, 238
    education for, 55–56
    Evening News with Walter Cronkite, 157
    feminism in, 70
    for Johnson, Lyndon, 40–44, 40n,
        162–63

lobbying for, 66–67
media and, 191
news, 71–72
Public Broadcasting Laboratory, 67–68
on radio, 209–10
status quo, 67–68
Supreme Court and, 196
on television, 42, 53–54, 57–58, 135–36
towers for, 53–54
for Wertheimer, L., 74, 254–55
women and, 23–25, 46, 57–58, 64–65,
    83–84, 97–98, 165–71, 174–77, 192–93
Brokaw, Tom, 240
Brown, Helen Gurley, 261
Brown, James, 217
Brubeck, Dave, 15, 18, 174
Bundy, McGeorge, 130
Burger, Warren, 105–6, 214
Byrd, Robert, 191–92, 195–96

Cabrini, Frances, 8
California, 148–50
Camelot (musical), 237
Campanella, Roy, 179
Campbell's Soup Cans (Warhol), 37
Camus, Albert, 194
cancer, 6–8
The Canterbury Tales, 18
Capital Cloakroom (TV show), 137
Carpien, Cindy, 225
Carter, Jimmy, 111n, 180, 206–10, 273, 284
Castro, Cuba and the USA (TV special), 184
Castro, Fidel, 183, 184n
The Catcher in the Rye (Salinger), 16
CBS World News Roundup, 220
celebrity journalism, 267–69
Celler, Emanuel, 31
Central Intelligence Agency (CIA), 136
Chalk, O. Roy, 86
Chancellor, John, 240
Chaney, Renee, 70
chauvinism, 56, 63–64, 83–84, 88–89
    in culture, 85–86, 205–6, 257–61
    against Stamberg, S., 192, 212–13
Cheney, Dick, 257n
Church of Jesus Christ of Latter-day Saints,
    163
CIA. *See* Central Intelligence Agency
Citizen Kane (Welles), 181, 215
civil rights, 26–28, 34–35, 179
    activism for, 60–61
    Civil Rights Act, 29–31, 33, 63, 90, 94,
        151–52, 167, 258, 283
    Equal Rights Amendment, 33–34, 284

Clapp, Margaret, 60
Clinton, Bill, 265–66
Cohen, Barbara, 211–12, 231, 236
Cokie. *See* Roberts, Mary
Collins, Bruce, 231
Coltrane, John, 15
Columbia University, 17–18
commercial media, 67–68
commercials, 46
communications, 83
communism, 76–77
Conley, Robert, 43, 68, 71–74, 96, 284
Conte, Silvio, 66–67
Corporation for Public Broadcasting (CPB),
    47, 180, 255
  economics of, 43, 190, 210, 232, 235
  NPR and, 67, 242–43, 283
  politics of, 162–63, 256–57
Cosmopolitan (magazine), 261
Cotton, Norris, 102
counterculture, 149
Cozby, June, 50–53, 55
Cozby, Linda, 50–55, 59–65, 125, 283. *See
    also* Wertheimer, Linda
Cozby, Vernon, 50–53
CPB. *See* Corporation for Public
    Broadcasting
Craft, Christine, 6
Cranston, Alan, 192
Cronkite, Walter, 43, 182, 184, 207n, 240–41
C-SPAN, 220–21, 224, 226–27, 230–31
Cuban Missile Crisis, 24, 61
culture, 7
  of California, 148–50
  chauvinism in, 85–86, 205–6, 257–61
  Civil Rights Act for, 90
  counterculture, 149
  diversity in, 126–27
  of Europe, 75
  feminism and, 87–88, 166, 168–70, 270,
    272
  during Great Depression, 116–17
  of Hollywood, 245
  journalism and, 118
  marriage for, 32–33
  of New Mexico, 48–50
  of NPR, 237–38
  radio for, 22–23, 35–36, 45
  television for, 13–14, 40, 134, 223–24
  of United States, 15, 39–40, 60, 73–74,
    114–15, 141–42, 147, 209
  Vietnam War for, 35, 44, 182
  of Washington, DC, 2–3, 75–76, 101–2,
    113–14, 131, 188–89, 203–5, 266–69

women in, 2–3, 27–28, 31–32, 56–57, 62,
    81–82, 95, 145–46
  after World War II, 26–27
Current-Argus (newspaper), 48–50
Cyprian, Emma, 115

Daley, Brian, 216
Daniels, Anthony, 216
Davis, Miles, 15
debates, 53–54, 194
Dee, Sandra, 129
De Pue, Frederik, 272
Designing Women (TV show), 261
d'Harnoncourt, René, 78
Dickerson, Nancy, 137–38
The Dick Van Dyke Show (TV show), 166
Didion, Joan, 174
discrimination, 7, 122, 257–61, 266, 283
  against women, 30–31, 94, 103–4, 167
  at work, 159–60
diversity, 94, 98, 126–27, 246, 275, 285
Dr. Zhivago (Pasternak), 82
Donaldson, Sam, 4, 262
Downey, Thomas, 239
Dows, Alice, 75–76
Drummond, Bill, 238
Duchesne, Rose Philippine, 8, 124
Duke, Paul, 223, 240

Eagleton, Thomas, 184
Earplay (radio show), 215
Eastern Radio Network, 226
economics
  of broadcasting, 96, 210, 216–17, 238
  of CPB, 43, 190, 210, 232, 235
  discrimination and, 266
  equality in, 256–57
  fundraising, 239–42, 254
  of inflation, 208
  of journalism, 176–77
  of marriage, 20–21
  for NPR, 110–11, 210–11, 229–32
  of oil, 53–54
  politics and, 244
  of radio, 56, 190–91, 232–33, 235, 237–38,
    248
  of speeches, 267–69
  for women, 32–33
Eddy, Charles B., 49
education, 8, 52, 59–61, 67–68, 130. *See
    also specific topics*
  for broadcasting, 55–56
  communications, 83
  FBI in, 107

education (cont.)
  NSA, 125, 139
  politics and, 121
  private, 78–79
  public school, 14–15, 19
  radio and, 35, 44, 62–63, 184
  segregation in, 122–23
  television and, 41, 43
Edwards, Bob, 167–68, 205, 212–13, 217, 257
  on *Morning Edition*, 222, 225–27, 236–37
  Wertheimer, L., and, 218–19
Ehrlichman, John, 176
elections, 6, 9, 118–19, 151–53
Eliot, T. S., 18
Elson, Edward E., 179–80, 185, 210, 234
Emancipation Proclamation, 26
Emmanuel, Victor, III, 75
The Empire Strikes Back (film), 216–17, 229, 240
Engle, Clair, 34
entertainment, 67–68
Epstein, Diane, 70
Equal Credit Opportunity Act, 167
Equal Employment Opportunity
  Commission, 34, 108
equality, 166–67, 255n, 256–57, 283
  feminism and, 5, 58–59
  marriage and, 104, 119–20
Equal Rights Amendment, 33–34, 284
Ermolov, Alexei, 76
Ervin, Sam, 90
ethics, of journalism, 81–82
Europe, 75, 77, 157
Evers, Medgar, 27
Every Night at Five (Stamberg, S.), 251

Fair Employment Commission, 27
family, 156, 172–73, 199–203
Fancher, Edwin, 43
fashion, 14–15
Father Cares (documentary), 214
FBI. *See* Federal Bureau of Investigation
Fear and Loathing on the Campaign Trail '72
  (Thompson), 187
Federal Bureau of Investigation (FBI), 107
Feezer, Charles, 59
The Feminine Mystique (Friedan), 93
feminism
  for Boggs, H., 140
  in broadcasting, 70
  civil rights and, 27–28
  culture and, 87–88, 166, 168–70, 270, 272

equality and, 5, 58–59
Equal Rights Amendment for, 33–34, 284
family and, 172–73, 199–203
fashion and, 14–15
founding mothers for, 247, 249, 273–75
Frederick for, 55–56
gender imbalance for, 30–31
higher education and, 20–21
history of, 2–3, 9–10, 92–93, 246–47, 276–77
ideology of, 145
in journalism, 3, 63–65
media after, 252–53
Order of the Rainbow for Girls, 52–53
politics of, 102–3
for radio, 24–25
reputation of, 90–91
sociology and, 17
Stamberg, S., for, 35, 174–75
status quo for, 87–88
suffrage and, 31–32
Totenberg, N., for, 175–77
Walters for, 174–75
Women in the Modern World, 17
work and, 28, 50–51, 93–94, 203–4
Ferraro, Geraldine, 246–47
Florida, 186–87
Fogg, Sam, 168
Fonda, Jane, 260
Ford, Betty, 121–22
Ford, Gerald, 111n, 121–22, 169
foreign news, 111n
Foster, George, 68
founding mothers
  after Cokie, 276–77
  discrimination for, 257–61
  for feminism, 247, 249, 273–75
  history of, 271–72, 283–85
  for NPR, 203–6, 255–56
Frank, Barney, 128, 128n
Frankenthaler, Helen, 174
Frederick, Pauline, 55–59, 110–12, 111n, 137, 196
freelance journalism, 155–58, 159
Friedan, Betty, 93
Friendly, Fred, 173
Frischknecht, Lee, 163–65, 179
From the Terrace (O'Hara), 82
From This Day Forward (Cokie), 271
fundraising, 239–42, 254

Gandhi, Indira, 97
Garland, Judy, 81, 263
Garner, Jack, 76

Geesey, George, 29, 70
Gemmill, Henry, 106–7
gender imbalance, 30–31, 283
George (magazine), 265
Ginsberg, Allen, 74
Ginsburg, Douglas, 258, 261
Ginsburg, Ruth Bader, 103–4, 272
glamour laws, 58
glass ceiling, 166–67
Gleason, Jackie, 82
Glinton, Sonari, 247
Goldberg, Arthur, 141
Goldfarb, Jo-Ann, 165
Goldman, Connie, 97
Gomez, Jennifer, 208
Good Evening (radio show), 254
Gordimer, Nadine, 206
Gore, Pauline, 119
Graham, Katherine, 91
Grand Central Station (radio show), 11
The Great American Dream Machine (TV
    show), 162
Great Depression, 32, 116–17
great society movement, 39–40
Greece, 155–58
Green, Edith, 33n
Greer, Germaine, 168
Gridiron Club, 87–89, 152, 168
Griffiths, Hicks, 32
Griffiths, Martha Wright, 32–33, 92
Gross, Terry, 166, 251n, 257n, 275
Gumbel, Bryant, 222

Hamill, Mark, 216
Hammarskjöld, Dag, 58
Hancock, Herbie, 7
hard news, 68–69
Harrison, Gilbert, 21
Harvard University, 124–26, 129–35
Harvey, Paul, 53
Haskell, Floyd, 103n, 104, 204
Hayes, Helen, 174
Hayes, Wayne, 193
Hearst, William Randolph, 181
Henderson, Gary, 192
Hill, Anita, 258–61, 263–64, 285
Hill Street Blues (TV show), 219
Hoctor, Barbara, 212–13, 284
Holland, Eddie, 84
Hollywood, 64, 217, 245
Hoover, Herbert, 23
Hoover, J. Edgar, 107, 152
HouseBreak (radio show), 97
Houseman, John, 215–16, 215n

Howdy Doody (TV show), 57n
Hruska, Roman, 109
Hudley, Gwen, 70, 74
Hulsen, Al, 47
Humphrey, Hubert, 97
Hunt, Al, 262

ideology, 145
immigration, 13–14, 77
India, 37–39, 97
intimacy, 83–84
Israel, 158
Italy, 75
It's Academic (radio show), 199

Javits, Jacob, 78
Jazz Goes to College (Brubeck), 18
Jensen, Georg, 145
jobs. See work
Johnson, Lady Bird, 40n, 119, 154
Johnson, Lyndon B., 34, 134n, 137
    Boggs, H., and, 141–42
    broadcasting for, 40–44, 40n, 162–63
    great society movement, 39–40
Jones, Jim, 213–14
journalism
    American Journalism, 268
    celebrity, 267–69
    chauvinism in, 56, 83–84
    culture and, 118
    diversity in, 94
    economics of, 176–77
    education for, 130
    ethics of, 81–82
    feminism in, 3, 63–65
    freelance, 155–58, 159
    at Harvard, 130–31
    history of, 55–56, 268n
    news and, 117, 128
    on NPR, 234
    plagiarism in, 107–8, 262
    politics and, 48–49, 109, 161–63,
        197–98, 269
    professionalism in, 104–5, 112
    in public school, 15
    radio and, 47, 53, 273
    Stamberg, S., in, 28, 45–46
    Supreme Court for, 108, 274
    tabloid, 86
    Totenberg, N., in, 82–83, 106–8
    United Nations for, 110–11
    in Washington, DC, 86–87
    women in, 21, 28, 57, 137, 167–68,
        205–6

Joyce, James, 18
Judaism, 13, 98, 126–27, 140–42, 179

Kadushin, Carol, 70
Kael, Pauline, 181, 181n
Kaleidoscope, 35–36, 45–46, 173
Kassell, Carl, 220n, 257
Kazan, Elia, 250
Keller, George, 115
Kelly, Mary Louise, 270–71
Kennedy, Ethel, 183
Kennedy, John F., 20, 22n, 26–27, 30, 82
    assassination of, 133, 147
    as senator, 129, 137
    television for, 162
Kennedy, Robert, 62, 181–82, 184, 187, 244
Kennedy, Ted, 182
Kernis, Jay, 226–27, 238
Khrushchev, Nikita, 28
King, Martin Luther, Jr., 29–30, 34, 39,
    107, 147
Kissinger, Henry, 184n
Kleban, Ed, 15–16
Klemp, Jack, 267
Kling, Bill, 221
Komarovsky, Mirra, 17
Kondolf, Claire, 124
Koppel, Ted, 238, 240, 265
Kroc, Joan, 248, 248n, 285
Krulwich, Robert, 198n
Kuhn, Bowie, 225
Kuralt, Charles, 173
Kurtz, Howard, 261–62

La Guardia, Fiorello, 14
Lamb, Brian, 220, 230–31, 241
Lance, Burt, 180
Landgrebe, Earl, 109
Lautier, Louis, 27
Laver, Tina Hope, 46
The Lawmakers (TV show), 223, 284
Led Zeppelin, 264
Lee, Robert E., 155
Lehrer, Jim, 240
Levitt, Anne, 12–13
Levitt, Robert, 12–13, 16
Levitt, Susan, 11–19, 283. *See also* Stamberg,
    Susan
Litinsky, Ruby, 86
Little, Walter, 122–23
live events, 29–30
live production, 74
lobbying, 66–67, 239–40
Longworth, Nicholas, 76

Louisiana, 115–19
Lowenstein, Allard, 138–39, 139n
Lucas, George, 216, 240
Lugosi, Bela, 58

MacArthur, Douglas, 53
MacNeil, Robert, 162
MacPherson, Myra, 108
Madonna, 264
The Making of the President: 1960 (White,
    T.), 82, 187
Mankiewicz, Frank, 198–99, 221, 230n, 253
    leadership of, 206, 209–17, 228–29,
        233–34, 236, 275, 284
    for NPR, 185–94, 196, 202–3, 232, 233,
        238, 244, 284
    in politics, 180–84, 184n
Mankiewicz, Herman, 181
Mankiewicz, Holly, 181
marriage, 20–21, 32–33, 66–67, 167, 271
    for Cokie, 140–46, 148–50
    equality and, 104, 119–20
    religion and, 138, 140–42
    for Roberts, S., 204–5, 276
    as social issues, 134–35
Marshall, Thurgood, 89
Martin, Michael, 270
Mason, Bobbie Ann, 227
McCarthy, Eugene, 136
McCormick, Anne O'Hare, 93
McCullough, David, 7
McGovern, George, 151, 184, 188
McGrory, Mary, 260
McIntosh, Millicent Carey, 17–18
Meeting of the Minds (TV show), 136
Meet the Press (TV show), 5, 135–36, 135n
Melton, Helen, 52
Michaelis, Diana, 22
Midler, Bette, 111
Miller, Bill, 122
Miller, Helen Hill, 20–21
Miller, Judith, 159–60, 197
Mills College, 59
Minnelli, Liza, 80–81
Minow, Newton, 40
Mister Rogers' Neighborhood (TV show), 43,
    162
Mitchell, Jack, 73, 98–99, 169, 233n, 235
Mitchell, John, 176
Mondale, Walter, 247
Montagne, Renee, 254–55
Moore, Mary Tyler, 166
Moore, Maurice T., 62
Morgan, Edward P., 67–68

Morning Edition (radio show), 213, 222,
  225–27, 236–37, 275, 284
Morse, Samuel, 41
Mortensen, Kris, 70
Moyers, Bill, 223, 240
Ms. (magazine), 99–100
Mudd, Roger, 109
Mueller, William, 172
Murphy Brown (TV show), 261
Murrow, Edward R., 53, 55–56, 179, 219n
Murrow, Janet, 196
music, 75–80, 124–25
Mutual Radio Network, 230

Nancy Drew stories, 80
Nashville (film), 169
National Observer, 262
National Organization for Women
  (NOW), 93
National Press Club, 87–88, 168, 283
National Public Radio (NPR), 3–4
  All Things Considered for, 70–74
  for audiences, 210–13, 274–75
  Bornstein for, 234–37
  Cokie for, 265
  CPB and, 67, 242–43, 283
  culture of, 237–38
  economics for, 110–11, 210–11, 229–32
  founding mothers for, 203–6, 255–56
  fundraising for, 239–42, 254
  hard news for, 68–69
  history of, 43–44, 71–72, 184–88, 213–17,
    242–44, 284–85
  Kroc for, 248, 285
  leadership at, 98–99, 169, 178–79,
    188–96, 202–3
  Mankiewicz, F., for, 185–94, 196, 202–3,
    232, 233, 238, 244, 284
  news on, 10, 207–8, 218–19, 227–28
  popularity of, 256–57
  programming on, 66–67, 163–65,
    206–7, 229
  "Project Independence" for, 229–30
  reputation of, 224, 233–34, 245–47,
    252–53
  on television, 221
  for Totenberg, N., 112, 165
  for women, 47, 160, 197–99, 250–51
National Student Association (NSA), 125,
  139
National Women's Museum, 277
Neary, Lynn, 255
Newman, Barbara, 70, 97
New Mexico, 48–53, 59

The New Republic (magazine), 21
news. *See also specific topics*
  ABC News, 1–2, 4
  activism and, 72–73, 131–32
  audiences of, 4, 175–76
  broadcasting, 71–72
  CBS World News Roundup, 220
  Evening News with Walter Cronkite, 157
  foreign, 111n
  hard, 68–69
  history of, 2–3
  journalism and, 117, 128
  local, 1–2
  Meet the Press, 5
  newsrooms, 218–22
  on NPR, 10, 207–8, 218–19, 227–28
  politics and, 191–92, 194–96, 223
  press conferences for, 28–29, 96
  professionalism in, 254
  on radio, 95, 110–11, 157–58, 194–96,
    200–201
  social issues as, 74
  for Stamberg, S., 96–99
  on television, 146, 183–84
  This Week, 2
  for Totenberg, N., 85–89
New Yorker, 15–16, 181n
New York Times, 134, 148–49, 236
Nightline with Ted Koppel, 238, 265
9 to 5 (film), 260
Nixon, Richard, 97, 101, 152, 183
  impeachment of, 193
  Watergate scandal, 161–63, 169–70, 176
NOW. *See* National Organization for
  Women
NPR. *See* National Public Radio
NSA. *See* National Student Association

O'Brien, Tom, 123
obscenity, 180
Occidental College, 59
O'Connor, John J., 222
O'Hara, John, 82
oil, 53–54
Oklahoma, 48–49
Olmsted, Frederick Law, Jr., 59
Olson, Wayne, 74
O'Neill, Tip, 107–8, 202, 262
Order of the Rainbow for Girls, 52–53
Oswald, Lee Harvey, 176

Panama Canal Treaty, 194–96, 284
Pangalos, Mary, 64–65
Parton, Dolly, 260

Pasternak, Boris, 82
Pauley, Jane, 222
Peabody Times, 85, 85n
Peace Corps, 181–82
Pelosi, Nancy, 276
Petinaud, Ernest, 122
Phelps, Timothy, 259, 263
Pickel, Margaret, 18
Pierce, Paul "Panther," 160
plagiarism, 107–8, 262
podcasting, 221n
polio, 127–28
politics
    activism and, 93
    audiences of, 101–2
    Boggs, H., in, 125, 134n, 151–54, 284
    Boggs, L., in, 151–55, 198, 202, 247n, 284
    of Civil Rights Act, 30–31
    Cokie and, 6, 230–31, 254
    communism, 76–77
    of CPB, 162–63, 256–57
    of Cronkite, 182, 184
    debates in, 53
    economics and, 244
    education and, 121
    elections in, 6, 9, 118–19, 151–53
    in Europe, 157
    of Fair Employment Commission, 27
    of feminism, 102–3
    journalism and, 48–49, 109, 161–63, 197–98, 269
    lobbying in, 239–40
    in Louisiana, 118
    Mankiewicz, F., in, 180–84, 184n
    news and, 191–92, 194–96, 223
    of newsrooms, 218–22
    professionalism in, 120
    sexism and, 106–7
    of Supreme Court, 33, 258–61
    Totenberg, N., in, 108–9, 258–62
    for United Nations, 58
    in United States, 120–21
    of Vietnam War, 146–47
    in Washington, DC, 22, 28, 61–62, 66–67, 69, 121–23
    Watergate scandal, 161–63, 169–70, 176
    women in, 4–5, 31–32, 87, 87n, 119, 123, 144, 274
    of workplace injustice, 257–61
Pons, Lily, 76
pornography, 180
A Portrait of the Artist as a Young Man (Joyce), 18

Powell, Lewis, 107
power, 203–4
Powers, Ron, 264
A Prairie Home Companion (radio show), 214, 214n
premarital sex, 133
press conferences, 28–29, 96
Preston, Marilynn, 223
Price, John, 244
private education, 78–79
professionalism, 67, 102–5, 112, 120, 125–26, 254
programming
    on NPR, 66–67, 163–65, 206–7, 229
    for radio, 73–74, 179, 212–13, 215–16
    by Siemering, 219–20, 227
    television, 136
"Project Independence," 229–30
Prospects of Mankind (TV show), 22
protests, 29
Public Broadcasting Act, 41–43, 66–67, 162–63, 214, 283
Public Broadcasting Laboratory, 67–68
public media, 179
public school, 14–15, 19

Quayle, Donald, 43–45, 68, 98, 163
Quinn, Sally, 166

racism, 151–52
Raddatz, Martha, 5–6
radio, 2–4, 11–12. *See also specific topics*
    All India Radio and TV, 38
    audiences of, 36, 160, 166, 171–72, 186–87, 217
    Black Americans on, 68
    broadcasting on, 209–10
    chauvinism in, 63–64
    for culture, 22–23, 35–36, 45
    Eastern Radio Network, 226
    economics of, 56, 190–91, 232–33, 235, 237–38, 248
    education and, 35, 44, 62–63, 184
    feminism for, 24–25
    in higher education, 22
    history of, 160, 215–16
    Hollywood and, 217
    journalism and, 47, 53, 273
    live events on, 29–30
    live production for, 74
    Mutual Radio Network, 230
    news on, 95, 110–11, 157–58, 194–96, 200–201
    professionalism on, 67

programming for, 73–74, 179, 212–13, 215–16
Public Broadcasting Act for, 42–43, 66–67, 283
satellites for, 214–15
Stamberg, S., in, 23–24, 29–30, 169–73
television and, 43, 160n, 170, 178–79, 191, 210, 220–22, 252–53
women and, 69–70, 192–93, 226–27
Randolph, Asa Philip, 26–27
Rankin, Jeanette, 87, 87n
Rather, Dan, 89, 183
Rayburn, Sam, 123, 151
Reagan, Ronald, 214, 230–31
Reddy, Helen, 91
refugees, 88
Reid, T. R., 176–77
Reiner, Carl, 240
Reines, David, 272
religion, 138, 156, 163, 266
    for Cokie, 1, 6, 8
    Judaism, 13, 98, 126–27, 140–42, 179
    in United States, 116, 124, 126–27
Remote Control (Mankiewicz, F.), 184
Reston, James, 93, 213–14
Reuss, Henry, 109
Rigdon, Floyd B., 48
Roberts, Marc, 125–29, 140
Roberts, Marcus, 127
Roberts, Mary (Cokie), 122n, 151, 197–98, 283. See also founding mothers
    for audiences, 6–7
    breast cancer for, 6–8
    celebrity-status for, 1–4, 232, 264–72
    childhood for, 113–15, 121–24
    in culture, 276–77
    death of, 9–10
    family for, 153–54
    in Greece, 155–58
    in higher education, 124–26
    marriage for, 140–46, 148–50
    politics and, 6, 230–31, 254
    pregnancy for, 146–48
    romance for, 132–35
    Washington, DC for, 158–60
    Wertheimer, L., and, 223–24, 239, 262
    work for, 135–38, 199–203
Roberts, Rebecca, 150
Roberts, Steve, 9, 197, 199–200, 268–69, 271–72
    career for, 139–40, 144–50, 158–59
    childhood for, 125–31
    in Greece, 155–58

in higher education, 131–35
marriage for, 204–5, 276
Roberts, Will, 127, 129–31
Robinson, Sophie, 135–36
Rockefeller, Nelson, 145
Rogers, Fred, 223
Roll Call (newspaper), 101–3
Roosevelt, Eleanor, 22n, 76, 87–88
Roosevelt, Franklin, 26–27, 76
Rose, Axl, 264
Rountree, Martha, 135n
Royko, Mike, 269
Rubenstein, Helena, 77–78
Russell, Jim, 96

St. George, Katherine, 33–34
Salinger, J. D., 16, 36
satellites, 214–15
Saturday Night Live (TV show), 261
Sawyer, Diane, 262
Scheuer, James, 224
School of the Air (radio show), 44
Schorr, Daniel, 97, 161, 161n, 256
Scott, William, 109
segregation, 108, 122–23, 179
Sesame Street (TV show), 43, 162
Seton, Elizabeth, 8
Sevareid, Eric, 43
sexism, 88–89, 106–7, 224
sexual harassment, 258–64, 285
Shepard, Alicia, 268
Shirer, William, 219n
Shroder, Melanie, 78, 81, 83
Siegel, Robert, 198n, 254, 256–57, 257n
Siemering, Bill, 44–45, 96, 163, 169
    diversity for, 98, 246, 275, 285
    programming by, 219–20, 227
    Wertheimer, L., and, 69–73
Sigmund, Paul, 139–40, 139n
Simon, Scott, 236–37
Simpson, Alan, 261
singing, 79–80, 124–25
16 (magazine), 19
Skinner, Cornelia Otis, 76
Smith, Cecil, 163
Smith, Ed, 44
social issues, 74, 134–35
socialization, 120–21
sociology, 17
Southern Manifesto, 151–52
Spanish Flu, 115
speeches, 267–69
Spivak, Lawrence, 135n
sports, 225

Sports Illustrated (magazine), 179
Spy (magazine), 264
Stamberg, Josh, 172, 249–50, 249n
Stamberg, Louis, 19–20, 24, 37–39, 206, 249
Stamberg, Susan (née Levitt), 3, 11–19, 283.
  See also founding mothers
  celebrity status for, 245–54, 285
  chauvinism against, 192, 212–13
  for feminism, 35, 174–75
  in India, 37–39
  in journalism, 28, 45–46
  Kaleidoscope for, 35–36, 45–46
  news for, 96–99
  Quayle and, 43
  in radio, 23–24, 29–30, 169–73
  reputation of, 202–3, 206–10, 217, 236, 240–41
  television for, 222–23
  traditional roles for, 60
  Wertheimer, L., and, 99–100
Star Wars, 216–17, 229, 254, 284
Stavers, Gloria, 19
Steele, Alison, 166
Steinem, Gloria, 99–100
Stevenson, Adlai, 53
Stewart, Potter, 176–77
Stratovision, 41
streaming television, 221n
Sue's Blues (radio show), 35
suffrage, 31–32, 105, 116
Supreme Court, 119, 151–52, 272
  broadcasting and, 196
  for journalism, 108, 274
  politics of, 33, 258–61
  Watergate scandal for, 176
  for women, 103–5
Susskind, David, 133

tabloid journalism, 86
Talmadge, Herman, 179–80
technology, 219n
telegraph, 41
television
  advertising for, 54
  All India Radio and TV, 38
  broadcasting on, 42, 53–54, 57–58, 135–36
  in California, 149–50
  for culture, 13–14, 40, 134, 223–24
  debates on, 53–54
  education and, 41, 43
  glamour laws, 58

for Kennedy, J., 162
  for media, 220–21
  Meet the Press, 5
  news on, 146, 183–84
  NPR on, 221
  programming, 136
  Prospects of Mankind, 22
  Public Broadcasting Act for, 41–43
  radio and, 43, 160n, 170, 178–79, 191, 210, 220–22, 252–53
  streaming, 221n
  This Week, 2, 8–9
  tubes, 49
  women on, 55
Thailand, 158
This Week (TV show), 2, 8–9, 266
Thomas, Clarence, 258–61, 264, 285
Thomas, Danny, 168
Thomas, Helen, 168
Thompson, Hunter S., 186–87
Thoreau, Henry David, 41n
Thurmond, Strom, 151–52, 267
Tillotson, Mary, 212n
Time (magazine), 53
Tomlin, Lily, 260
Torre, Marie, 81–82, 82n, 263
Toscan, Richard, 216
Totenberg, Nina, 3, 85n, 103n, 254. *See also* founding mothers
  childhood for, 78–81, 283
  Cokie and, 160
  for feminism, 175–77
  in journalism, 82–83, 106–8
  news for, 85–89
  NPR for, 112, 165
  in politics, 108–9, 258–62
  reputation of, 167–68, 262–64
  Wertheimer, L., and, 197–99, 201–2
  work for, 83–84, 101–6
Totenberg, Roman, 75–79, 83, 272
towers, 53–54
Trotta, Liz, 64
Truman, Harry, 53
Trump, Donald, 6
Tubman, Harriet, 208
Tulane, 116–17
Turner, Ted, 220
Two Decades of American Painting (art exhibition), 37

Ungar, Sanford, 222
United Nations, 57–58, 110–11
United Press, 86

United States
anti-Semitism in, 179
Castro, Cuba and the USA, 184
Civil Rights Act in, 29–31, 33, 63, 90, 94, 151–52, 167, 258, 283
culture of, 15, 39–40, 60, 73–74, 114–15, 141–42, 147, 209
education in, 8
Emancipation Proclamation for, 26
Equal Employment Opportunity Commission, 34
government, 124
Great Depression for, 32, 116–17
immigration in, 13–14, 77
Peace Corps, 181–82
politics in, 120–21
racism in, 151–52
refugees for, 88
religion in, 116, 124, 126–27
segregation in, 108
sexism in, 88–89
women in, 9–10
World War II for, 2, 23

Vanocur, Sander, 162
Victor, Jeffrey, 127
Vietnam War, 35, 44, 61, 72, 146–47, 182, 194
Vietor, Dean, 173
Viewpoint: Washington (radio show), 24, 42
Vigorito, Joe, 109
Voegeli, Don, 72–73
Voegeli, Tom, 216
Voting Rights Act, 151

Walters, Barbara, 174–75, 240
Warhol, Andy, 37
The War of the Worlds (radio show), 215–16
Warren, Jim, 268–69
Warren Commission, 134n
Washington, DC, 1–2, 86–87, 158–60
culture of, 2–3, 75–76, 101–2, 113–14, 131, 188–89, 203–5, 266–69
politics in, 22, 28, 61–62, 66–67, 69, 121–23
Viewpoint: Washington about, 24
Washington Week in Review (TV show), 223
The Waste Land (Eliot), 18
Watergate scandal, 161–63, 169–70, 176
Waters, Mike, 96
We Are Our Mothers' Daughters (Cokie), 270
Welch, Carolyn, 70
Welles, Orson, 181, 181n, 215n

Wellesley (college), 59, 124–26, 132–35
Wertheimer, Fred, 66–67, 240
Wertheimer, Linda (née Cozby), 3, 8, 283. *See also* founding mothers
for audiences, 194–96
broadcasting for, 74, 254–55
Cokie and, 223–24, 239, 262
Edwards and, 218–19
marriage for, 66–67
reputation of, 192–93, 220, 246–47
Siemering and, 69–73
Stamberg, S., and, 99–100
Totenberg, N., and, 197–99, 201–2
Wetzel, Kati, 70, 97
White, Margaret Bourke, 118
White, Theodore H., 82, 187
Whitman, Walt, 16
Wide Wide World (TV show), 54
Will, George, 240
Williams, Kim, 252
Williams, Pete, 212n
Winchell, Walter, 86
Wirth, Tim, 243
Wisdom, John Minor, 103, 103n, 204
The Wizard of Oz (film), 80
women. *See also* feminism
activism for, 91, 154–55
All Things Considered for, 169–73, 210–11
Black Americans and, 27, 31, 33n, 60–61
broadcasting and, 23–25, 46, 57–58, 64–65, 83–84, 97–98, 165–71, 174–77, 192–93
in culture, 2–3, 27–28, 31–32, 56–57, 62, 81–82, 95, 145–46
discrimination against, 30–31, 94, 103–4, 167
economics for, 32–33
in education, 60
equality for, 255n
higher education for, 16–18, 59, 128
intimacy for, 83–84
in journalism, 21, 28, 57, 137, 167–68, 205–6
marriage for, 271
in media, 267–68
Ms. for, 99–100
Nancy Drew stories for, 80
National Press Club for, 87–88
National Women's Museum, 277
NPR for, 47, 160, 197–99, 250–51
Order of the Rainbow for Girls, 52–53

women (cont.)
  in politics, 4–5, 31–32, 87, 87n, 119, 123,
    144, 274
  power for, 203–4
  premarital sex for, 133
  professionalism for, 102–3, 125–26
  public school for, 14–15
  radio and, 69–70, 192–93, 226–27
  sexual harassment for, 258–64
  suffrage for, 116
  Supreme Court for, 103–5
  on television, 55
  traditional roles of, 51–52
  in United States, 9–10
  Women's Caucus, 94
  women's liberation movement, 91–92,
    100, 107, 149, 165–66
  Women's National Press Club, 283
  Women's Strike for Equality, 283
  work for, 20–21, 63, 90, 118, 120–21,
    136–37, 144–45, 158–59, 246–47
  World War II for, 50–51
  writing about, 6–7

Women in the Modern World
  (Komarovsky), 17
Woodruff, Judy, 240
work
  activism for, 42, 283
  for Black Americans, 108, 115
  for Cokie, 135–38, 199–203
  discrimination at, 159–60
  feminism and, 28, 50–51, 93–94, 203–4
  for Totenberg, N., 83–84, 101–6
  for women, 20–21, 63, 90, 118, 120–21,
    136–37, 144–45, 158–59, 246–47
  workplace injustice, 257–61
World War II, 2, 23, 26–27, 50–51, 77,
  219n
writing, 6–7

Yarrow, Peter, 15
Yudain, Sid, 101–2

Zelnick, Robert, 109–12, 165
Zorinsky, Edward, 180
Zuck, Alexandra, 129